AUTOMATA THEORY AND LOGIC

Automata Theory and Logic

Edited by:
Gerard Prudhomme

ARCLER
PRESS

www.arclerpress.com

Automata Theory and Logic

Gerard Prudhomme

Arcler Press
2010 Winston Park Drive,
2nd Floor
Oakville, ON L6H 5R7
Canada
www.arclerpress.com
Tel: 001-289-291-7705
001-905-616-2116
Fax: 001-289-291-7601
Email: orders@arclereducation.com

ISBN: 978-1-77361-271-3 (Hardcover)

Declaration

Some content or chapters in this book are open access copyright free published research work, which is published under Creative Commons License and are indicated with the citation. We are thankful to the publishers and authors of the content and chapters as without them this book wouldn't have been possible.

About the Editor

Gerard I. Prudhomme has a graduate degree (M.S.) for Computer Science from University College London (UCL). He has also worked as a software programmer and tech writer for different Fortune 500 companies, and studied at UCL, Harvard, and Oxford.

Contents

List of Contributors

Gerard I. Prudhomme

Karan Mangla

Department of Computer Science, Stanford University, Stanford, California, United States of America

David L. Dill

Department of Computer Science, Stanford University, Stanford, California, United States of America

Mark A. Horowitz

Department of Electrical Engineering, Stanford University, Stanford, California, United States of America

Ovidiu Pârvu

Department of Computer Science, College of Engineering, Design and Physical Sciences, Brunel University London, London, United Kingdom

David Gilbert

Department of Computer Science, College of Engineering, Design and Physical Sciences, Brunel University London, London, United Kingdom

Haiyang Xu

School of Science and Information, Qingdao Agricultural University, Qingdao, Shandong, China

School of Computer Science and Technology, Nanjing University of Aeronautics and Astronautics, Nanjing, Jiangsu, China

Ping Wang

School of Science and Information, Qingdao Agricultural University, Qingdao, Shandong, China

Ezio Bartocci

Faculty of Informatics, Technische Universität Wien, Vienna, Austria

Pietro Lió

Computer Laboratory, University of Cambridge, Cambridge, United Kingdom

Misbah Razzaq

Department of Computational Sciences, Research Center for Modeling & Simulation (RCMS), National University of Sciences and Technology (NUST), Islamabad, Pakistan

Jamil Ahmad

Department of Computational Sciences, Research Center for Modeling & Simulation (RCMS), National University of Sciences and Technology (NUST), Islamabad, Pakistan

Giovanni Minervini

Dept. of Biomedical Sciences, University of Padua, Padua, Italy

Elisabetta Panizzoni

Dept. of Biomedical Sciences, University of Padua, Padua, Italy

Manuel Giollo

Dept. of Biomedical Sciences, University of Padua, Padua, Italy

Dept. of Information Engineering, University of Padua, Padua, Italy

Alessandro Masiero

Dept. of Biomedical Sciences, University of Padua, Padua, Italy

Carlo Ferrari

Dept. of Information Engineering, University of Padua, Padua, Italy

Silvio C. E. Tosatto

Dept. of Biomedical Sciences, University of Padua, Padua, Italy

Annika Jacobsen

Centre for Integrative Bioinformatics (IBIVU), VU University Amsterdam, Amsterdam, The Netherlands

Department of Computer Science, VU University Amsterdam, Amsterdam, The Netherlands

Amsterdam Institute for Molecules, Medicines and Systems, VU University Amsterdam, Amsterdam, The Netherlands

Nika Heijmans

Section of Molecular Cytology and Van Leeuwenhoek Centre for Advanced Microscopy, Swammerdam Institute for Life Sciences, University of Amsterdam, Amsterdam, The Netherlands

Folkert Verkaar

Amsterdam Institute for Molecules, Medicines and Systems, VU University Amsterdam, Amsterdam, The Netherlands

Division of Medicinal Chemistry, VU University Amsterdam, Amsterdam, The Netherlands

Martine J. Smit

Amsterdam Institute for Molecules, Medicines and Systems, VU University Amsterdam, Amsterdam, The Netherlands

Division of Medicinal Chemistry, VU University Amsterdam, Amsterdam, The Netherlands

Jaap Heringa

Centre for Integrative Bioinformatics (IBIVU), VU University Amsterdam, Amsterdam, The Netherlands

Department of Computer Science, VU University Amsterdam, Amsterdam, The Netherlands

Amsterdam Institute for Molecules, Medicines and Systems, VU University Amsterdam, Amsterdam, The Netherlands

Renée van Amerongen

Section of Molecular Cytology and Van Leeuwenhoek Centre for Advanced Microscopy, Swammerdam Institute for Life Sciences, University of Amsterdam, Amsterdam, The Netherlands

K. Anton Feenstra

Centre for Integrative Bioinformatics (IBIVU), VU University Amsterdam, Amsterdam, The Netherlands

Department of Computer Science, VU University Amsterdam, Amsterdam, The Netherlands

Amsterdam Institute for Molecules, Medicines and Systems, VU University Amsterdam, Amsterdam, The Netherlands

Luca Albergante

Department of Computer Science and Department of Electronics, University of York, York, United Kingdom

Jon Timmis

Department of Computer Science and Department of Electronics, University of York, York, United Kingdom

Lynette Beattie

Center for Immunology and Infection, Department of Biology and Hull York Medical School, University of York, York, United Kingdom

Paul M. Kaye

Center for Immunology and Infection, Department of Biology and Hull York Medical School, University of York, York, United Kingdom

Naeem Akhtar Khan

Faculty of Information Technology, University of Central Punjab, Lahore, Pakistan

Farooq Ahmad

Department of Computer Science, COMSATS Institute of information Technology, Lahore, Pakistan

Sher Afzal Khan

Department of Computer Sciences, Abdul Wali Khan University, Mardan, Pakistan

Faculty of Computing and Information Technology in Rabigh, King Abdul Aziz University, Jeddah, KSA

Preface

The automata theory and logic in theoretical computer science is critical for the development of theoretical computer science. The objective of the theory of automata theory and logic is to propose models of mathematical mechanisms that formalize calculation methods. This theory is the foundation of several important branches of theoretical computing.

The first chapter refers to automota theory. Chapter 2 shows that the durability of organic designs seems to have come about in the form of a significant basic principle in solutions biology. Chapter 3 looks at how ideas acquired from multi-level computational varieties of organic models could very well be converted into actual functions only as long as the strategy accurateness appears to have been confirmed to start with.

Chapter 4 offers a model-based incorporation way of thinking for redesigning coupled with confirmation of the time aspect. Chapter 5 exchanges views about the most widely read, not to mention thrilling, computational techniques, and also equipment, on the market today for systems biologists, antagonizing design patterns as well as a partnership between all of them. Chapter 6 proves that Web malware are comparable to organic infections.

Chapter 7 shows that Von Hippel-Lindau (VHL) disorder is a genetic problem predisposing to the growth and development of various cancer malignancy types. Chapter 8 showcases how the Wnt/β-catenin alerting path is essential for several developing procedures and also cells upkeep. Chapter 9 describes how visceral leishmaniasis, brought on by contamination of mice with the protozoan parasite Leishmania donovani, is identified by central amassing.

Chapter 10 looks at how Wifi broadband seems to have obtained exceptional consideration from the analysis environment.

Editor

1 AUTOMATA THEORY AND LOGIC

Gerard I. Prudhomme M.Sc.

Automata theory and logic is the foundation of important branches of computing like calculability, by the model of Turing machines. This principle is also the basis of a number of crucial divisions of theoretical understanding, along the lines of those which are used in natural language analysis, finite automata, or automatic verification of logic circuits, various text manipulation algorithms such as search algorithms, and their variants, and much more.

A few more of the crucial divisions of automata theory and logic theoretical understanding are as alternatively automated confirmation, translation of applications by compilers, and an assortment of textual content treatment calculations along the lines of substring lookup calculations, not to mention their variations, which also happen to be utilized in natural verbal communication evaluation.

The algorithmic complexity theory is also a valuable component of automata theory and logic, which aims to categorize the formulae in accordance with the temporal as well as memory space assets required for their performance. The model checking used to prove program correction also falls under the rubric of automata theory and logic.

- Truly, the Automata Theory and Logic is essential for theoretical computer research. The goal of the principle of automata theory and logic would be to suggest types of arithmetical systems that formalize computation techniques.
- The item dealt with by an automaton is an expression of a dialect. To get the most wanted generality, one changes a "problem" into a dialect, together with dealing with the situation, in the research of a component of this dialect. The philosophy of automata is, therefore, the research of abstract pieces of equipment which ensure it is likely that you can formalize the strategies for computation.
- Each and every case of a "problem" is described by a phrase. To be aware of what is required in the event that the example of the issue possesses an answer is dependent on verifying if this type of phrase is a member of the vocabulary of the phrases which represents the situations this challenge was designed for. As well as if it is one of those who have a remedy.
- Complementary integers are symbolized by binary series, composing in a base two system. An automaton that handles the situation needs in the form of suggestions a phrase as well as chooses whether it be recognized or otherwise not. As an illustration, the issue of understanding whether or not an integer I is prime, primarily evaluation, could be interpreted provided below.
- An appropriate automaton requires in the form of contribution a binary series and, as a consequence, is in receipt of it distinctly in the event that it corresponds to a prime number. The issue of the primarily evaluation, after that, is made up in being aware that whether or not the binary string which represents a range N is a member of this group or otherwise not. Within this vocabulary, phrases which represents prime numbers create a group.
- The subsequent region questions the alteration of terms. The composition of difficulties as well as their conclusion, or maybe

even their computability, when it comes to elegant vocabulary is at the basis of intricate hierarchies, and, as a consequence, hierarchies of formal linguistics. In this particular area of specialization, the key phrase "machine" or, perhaps just, transducer, is utilized as an alternative.

- Linguistics, but at the same time compilation, take advantage of these kinds of transducers for the evaluation as well as alteration of tomes in addition to software applications. There are simply too many different types of automata to list them all. The features typical to multiple automata are provided below, and, as you can imagine, there are lots of fluctuations.
- An automaton normally requires different computer data in the form of contribution. That is despite the fact that a number of automata, generally known as timed automata, currently have limitations which are often real figures. These types of items are likely to be limited terms on a limited alphabet.
- Nevertheless, they have also been unlimited trees, terms, graphs, if not even more difficult to understand systems. An automaton provides you with a limited variety of interior styles, generally known as states. If you read further, at the same time, we are able to give some thought to automata with the help of an unlimited wide variety of situations.
- Good examples are, in the commonplace philosophy of automata, just about every formalized traditional grammar that is equipped with an original of a bare minimum of automaton. And, that happens to be limited only as long as the traditional grammar is logical. Transformation devices utilized in version analyzing do not have a restriction on the massive number of situations.
- An automaton could also have a superficial additional memory space, organized in a particular method in accordance with the kind of automaton. A finite automaton does not have any additional memory space, and a stack controller provides you with a stack memory space. There is certainly memory space automata in queue frameworks, multi-stack controllers, stack-based automatons, or anything else like that.

- Turing pieces of equipment currently have a supplementary memory space in the shape of an unlimited ring about which they are able to shift, scan, and also publish. An automaton develops in accordance with guidelines. These types of guidelines are limited in amount.
- Each and every guideline gives information about the advancement of the controller in accordance with the contribution figures, the standing, as well as details about the additional memory space. This advancement could possibly be deterministic or otherwise not. It happens to be deterministic in the event that an individual guideline is relevant in a particular arrangement, it happens to be non-deterministic if they are not.
- An automaton provides you with an assortment of recognition designs. In the event they provide a controller that is more or less in these types of a arrangements, the scan information and facts are well received. In a finite automaton, these types of modifications are recognized situations.
- In a stack automaton, that it is possible to say yes to the argument in the event that the stack is drained. In a Turing apparatus, we get to grips with it in the event that the situation is able to submit an application for an update.
- It is an abstract machine stated in a different way. A finite automaton every once in while goes by the name of a clumsy literal translation of the finite state machine as an alternative for an apparatus with a finite variety of states. In English they are known as finite state automaton or finite state machines.
- Most of them are associated with control and program verification, in the research of formalized languages and in published compilation, telecommunications specifications, Process modeling, and computability theory. They are utilized in seeking forms in a textual content. Whatever you call them, they are a highly important piece of equipment in discrete arithmetic and as a consequence computer science. Finite automata are familiar with, by all means, rational languages.
- In addition to being the most straightforward apparatus in the Chomsky hierarchy, they are definitely substantially less highly

effective. That is, if you were to compare them to the ones like battery controlled automata, as well as, needless to say, a Turing apparatus. Truly, the aforementioned automata are the most straightforward apparatus in the Chomsky hierarchy.

- The automata moves around from situations to situations, following the changes, on reading through each and every phrase of the contribution. Its very own behavior patterns is instructed by a phrase provided in the form of contribution. An automaton is comprised of situations as well as changes. In the illustration above, for the contribution, in the event that the controller begins in, it goes on successively by means of the states, the associated computation is then done.
- The automaton is considered as "finite" because the device provides you with a limited variety of situations. It is also, due to this fact that it provides you with merely a confined memory space. You possibly can very well indeed give some thought to automata without restriction on the wide variety of situations.
- A limited automaton may be seen in the form of a categorized focused chart. The situations are the vertices as well as the changes are the categorized sides. The resultant philosophy can be quite comparable to the normal philosophy.
- The introductory situations is specially formulated with an inbound arrow. Your final situation is, in accordance with the writers decision, a choice between a circle drawn two times, or labeled with an outgoing arrow.

TURING MACHINES

- Launched by Turing in 1937, Turing Machines understand specifically the recursively enumerable linguistics. These types of linguistics, as well as the Turing pieces of equipment, are widely-used in the form of a analytical description of what on earth is determinable. Near the top of the automaton pecking order are the Turing apparatus.
- The Church-Turing thesis, and that may not be a mathematical announcement, nevertheless it still deserves recognition, states

that that an analytical explanation accurately echoes what "common sense" can think of as comprehensible by a human beings brain. A number of other similar characterizations are often known. The pecking order of the Chomsky hierarchy possesses a number of varieties of grammars together with linguistics.

- The pecking order of the Chomsky hierarchy is as follows: level zero = recursively enumerable, level one = contextual, level two = algebraic, and level three = logical. Turing equipment and also their versions present an increase to a hierarchical pecking order of programs of abundant, as well as intricate, complication. These programs aim to identify algorithmic difficulties in accordance with their complexity.

PROBABILISTIC AUTOMATA AND QUANTUM AUTOMATA

- Probabilistic automata were launched extremely early on, during 1963, by Michael O. Rabin. Each and every one change bears a possibility. The possibilities increase in numbers on the pathways. And, as a consequence, for a phrase to be recognized, the degree of the possibilities on the pathways really should try to approach a particular minimum threshold. Each one of these automata seem to have gone on to, as well as modified, a completely different point of view, by quantum automata.

LINEAR BOUNDED AUTOMATON

- These types of automata realize just the related linguistics. They allow it to be likely that you can keep track of guaranteed limits on the negotiation environment in different languages. Nevertheless, with these linguistics they make the automata much more limited. That is because grammars of adjoining trees have proven workable.

TIMED AUTOMATONS

- The timed automata currently have restrictions on the changes that happen to be stated by circumstances related to the remaining length of time on a timer.

PUSHDOWN AUTOMATON (PDA)

- Pushdown automaton identify precisely the algebraic linguistics. The reasoning behind pushdown automaton was formalized when dealing with these automata. They provide you with a range in a great many places of work, syntactic evaluation, as with encoding with recursion, in the form of a highly important computer data framework. If you read further at the same time, deterministic stack automata are generally more bounded when compared with pushdown automata.

TREE AUTOMATON

- We are able to distinguish fundamentally growing automata, which understand trees, from the leaves, as well as up wards when it comes to the source. That functions as well as for the abating automata which run in the contrary course. Finite automata were extremely early on prolonged to utilize trees. It is just a little like the analysis of mathematical words and phrases. A couple of principles are equal in the non-deterministic circumstance.

TREE WALKING AUTOMATON (TWA)

- The self-regulating walkways were released in 1971. They may be small automata which wander a tree in a preset time.

PETRI NET

- A Petri net is a graphical piece of equipment for the portrayal and, as a consequence, research of simultaneous techniques which come forth in devices with many different accessories or components. These types of automata know the possibility of performing operations in almost any manner. They are utilized in procedure models.

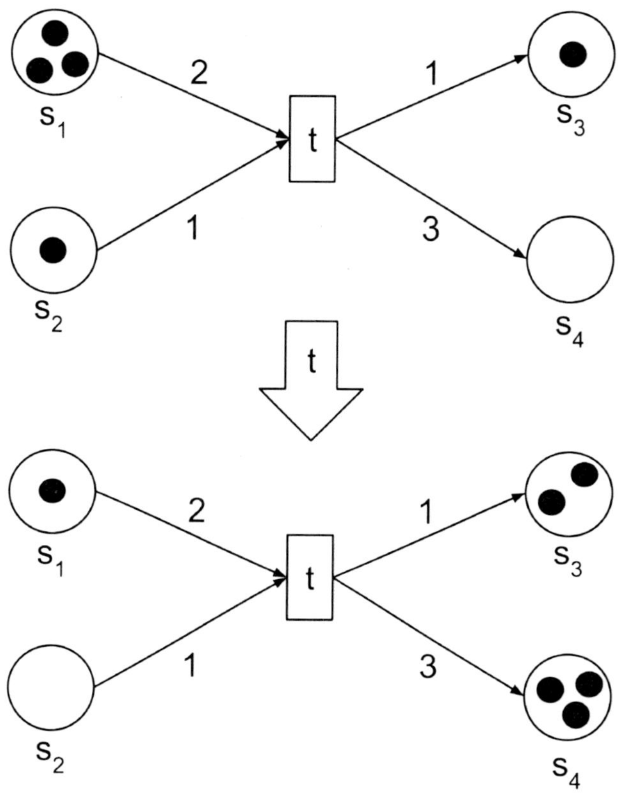

Figure 1: Petrinet Transition Example.

STATE TRANSITION SYSTEMS AND KRIPKE STRUCTURE

- Condition change devices are an expansion of finite automata to most certainly unlimited models, as well as it does not matter the circumstances. In their vast majority of elementary incarnations, these are generally basically binary interactions.

In an infinitely more extravagant model, the above-mentioned details are automata without preliminary situations as well as without critical situations.

- The majority of the complicated variations are the Kripke structures. Kripke structures have available rational formulations connected with situations.

BIBLIOGRAPHY

1. Boolos, G. and Jeffrey, R., Computability and Logic, 2nd ed., Cambridge: Cambridge University Press, 1980.
2. Baier, Christel. Polynomial time algorithms for testing probabilistic bisimulation and simulation. In C V '96: Proceedings of the 8th International Conference on Computer ided Verification, pages 50–61, London, UK, 1996. Springer-Verlag.
3. Collins, George, E., Quantifier elimination for real closed fields by cylindrical algebraic decompostion. utomata Theory and Formal Languages 2nd GI Conference Kaiserslautern, May 20-23, 1975, 1975.
4. Jones, N., D., Space bounded reducibility among combinatorial problems. J. Computer and System Sci., pages 68–75, 1975.
5. Putnam, H., "The Nature of Mental States", in Mind, Language and Reality: Philosophical Papers II, Cambridge: Cambridge University Press, 1975.
6. Rabin, Michael, O., (1963). "Probabilistic Automata". Information and Control. 6 (3): 230–245. doi:10.1016/s0019-9958(63)90290-0. Retrieved 27 March 2015.
7. Salomaa, Arto, Theory of Automata (1969) Pergamon Press, Oxford.
8. Turing, A., "On Computable Numbers, With an Application to the Entscheidungsproblem", Proceedings of the London Mathematical Soceity, Series 2, Volume 42, 1936; reprinted in M. David (ed.), The Undecidable, Hewlett, NY: Raven Press, 1965.

2 TIMING ROBUSTNESS IN THE BUDDING AND FISSION YEAST CELL CYCLES

Karan Mangla[1], David L. Dill[1], Mark A. Horowitz[2]

[1] Department of Computer Science, Stanford University, Stanford, California, United States of America
[2] Department of Electrical Engineering, Stanford University, Stanford, California, United States of America

ABSTRACT

Robustness of biological models has emerged as an important principle in systems biology. Many past analyses of Boolean models update all pending changes in signals simultaneously (i.e., synchronously), making it impossible to consider robustness to variations in timing that result from noise and different environmental conditions. We checked previously published mathematical models of the cell cycles of budding and fission yeast for robustness to timing variations by constructing Boolean models and analyzing them using model-checking software for the property of speed independence. Surprisingly, the models are nearly, but not totally, speed-independent. In some cases, examination of timing problems discovered in the analysis exposes apparent inaccuracies in the model. Biologically justified revisions to the model eliminate the timing problems. Furthermore, in silico random mutations in the regulatory interactions of a speed-independent Boolean model are shown to be unlikely to preserve speed independence, even in models that are otherwise functional, providing evidence for selection pressure to maintain timing robustness. Multiple cell cycle models exhibit strong robustness to timing variation, apparently due to evolutionary pressure. Thus, timing robustness can be a basis for generating testable hypotheses and can focus attention on aspects of a model that may need refinement.

INTRODUCTION

Since reaction rates vary widely both because of the stochastic nature of interactions at low copy numbers and from diverse and dynamically changing environmental conditions, cells that grow and divide robustly in the face of these variations can be expected to have a competitive advantage over less robust cells. The principle of robustness to variation in reaction rates can be exploited to check the accuracy of models, and to narrow the range of possibilities when incomplete biological knowledge gives rise to multiple plausible models.

There are a variety of approaches available to define and evaluate robustness to noise, variation of parameters, and environmental conditions. One approach is to model the dynamics of the system with differential equations, and numerically integrate many times for various values of parameters to compute trajectories of the various signals in the system. However, this approach is problematic because there is a lack of detailed knowledge of quantitative reaction kinetics for most of the reactions in a cell, and because only a small fraction of the space of possible parameters can be examined.

Given the lack of quantitative information about reaction kinetics, a reasonable approach is to use Boolean models, which represent concentrations of proteins with a few discrete qualitative levels (strictly interpreted, the term "Boolean" implies variables can only take two values, but we use it in the more general sense that allows more than two discrete levels variables). Variations in reaction rates are reflected in Boolean models as variations in the *timing* of transitions between qualitative levels of reactants and products. The ability of a cell to maintain its function in the presence of timing perturbations is called *timing robustness*.

Since the 1960's [1], the dynamics of Boolean models of biological control have been based on the *synchronous update rule*: At each point in time, all variables that are logically able to change are updated simultaneously at the next time step. This approach has yielded many interesting results, but it allows no variation in timing, and consequently makes examination of timing robustness impossible. There are many ways to introduce varying amounts of freedom in the timing of reactions. A model that makes weaker assumptions about timing is more conservative, in that it is more likely to violate a given specification than a model with stronger timing assumptions. For example, the model could allow variables to change in one or two steps after they are enabled [2], [3], or variables could change within a continuous but bounded window, as can be specified with timed automata [4], or reactions could be classified as "fast" and "slow" reactions, with "fast" reactions occurring (effectively) infinitely faster than slow reactions [5], [6]. One of the most conservative models, which we call *fully asynchronous*, assumes nothing about the timing of reactions. The delay of a transition could be any finite time. A system that has a desired property in a fully asynchronous model is *speed-independent*. Speed independence implies timing robustness in most other plausible models. In particular, if the cell cycle works correctly in the fully asynchronous model, it also works in a synchronous model.

This paper explores the timing robustness of several Boolean models of the cell cycles of budding yeast (*S. Cerevisiae*) and fission yeast (*S. Pombe*). The Boolean model of budding yeast was published previously, and we derived the fission yeast models from published differential equations models. To test for timing robustness, our approach was to begin with a fully asynchronous model in each case, examine the cases where the models fail to be robust, and either change the model or introduce additional constraints on timing (making the model less-than-fully asynchronous) as necessary. Surprisingly, it was not necessary to weaken the assumption of full asynchrony. With changes that are either justified from the literature or at least as plausible as the original model, the cell cycle models could be made fully speed-independent. These results indicate that (1) the cell cycle is highly timing-robust, and (2) analyzing models for timing robustness can generate testable predictions about the details of cell cycle control.

To check for speed independence, we analyze the behavior of cell cycle models using the *asynchronous update rule* [7], which allows at most one variable to change at a time. When multiple variables are enabled to change, one of them is chosen arbitrarily. The asynchronous update rule models a system in which the delays are assumed to be arbitrary – nothing is known about the delays except that they are finite. In such a model, the system behavior depends only on the order in which variables change values. The situation where two signals may transition in the "wrong order," leading to a disruption of the normal function of the cell, is called a *hazard*. If there are no hazards (i.e., if the model satisfies the specified property for all possible orders of variable transitions, corresponding to all possible delays), the model is speed-independent.

The property that a cell successfully completes cell division for all possible delays was checked using the NuSMV model checker [8], which systematically explores all of the possible orders in which variables can change. When this property failed, the cause of the hazard was diagnosed and the biological literature re-examined to determine whether revisions to the model could be justified from biological evidence. In all cases, hazards could be eliminated by biologically plausible revisions, and in some cases, these revisions could be considered corrections to the biology in the model.

Previous work has noted that the synchronous update rules is unrealistic, and explored the effects of introducing random variation in the update times [9]–[11]. Unlike that work, our speed-independent model has no concept of probability; it answers whether *every* possible timing of reactions results in a successful cell cycle.

Others have used model checking and similar techniques to explore the state space of biological systems [3], [5], [12], [13]. In particular, we found previously that *Caulobacter Crescentus* was almost speed-independent [6] (in that work, it was necessary to add a small number of timing constraints to the Caulobacter model to eliminate all hazards). However, in previous work, timing robustness appears not to have been used to critique and improve Boolean models, nor has selection pressure for speed independence been demonstrated *in silico*.

RESULTS AND DISCUSSION

Hazards can be detected by the use of software tools, called *model checkers*, that check a specified logical property on every possible state of a Boolean model. Model checking can be used with a synchronous or asynchronous update rule. Model checking with asynchronous updating effectively checks the property for *all possible* delays by systematically exploring every possible order in which enabled signals can occur. The inputs to a model checker consist of a boolean model, described as a set of variables and rules that modify their values, an initial state, and a logical property to check.

Timing Robustness of the Budding Yeast Cell Cycle

A simplified Boolean model of the budding yeast cell cycle of (Figure 1A) was proposed and evaluated with a synchronous update rule by Li, et al. in 2004 [14]. In this model, nodes are labeled with protein names. At any given time, each node has a *level* representing a qualitative degree of activation of the protein. The activation state of a protein may represent that it is modified, forms a complex with other proteins, or is simply present so as to have an effect on other nodes in the system.

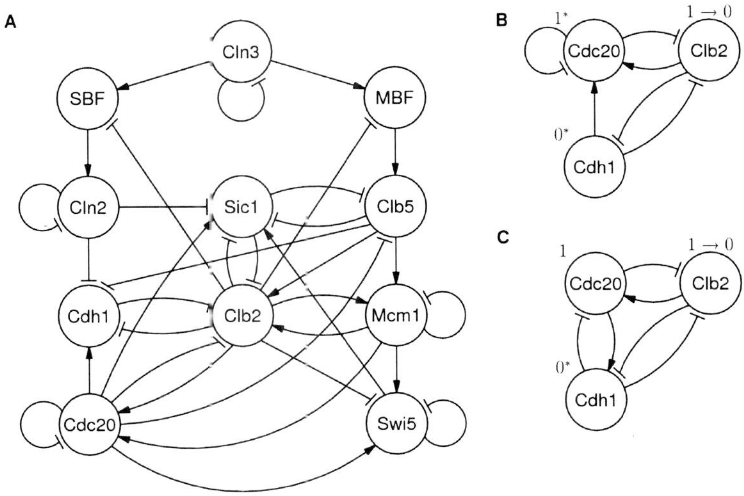

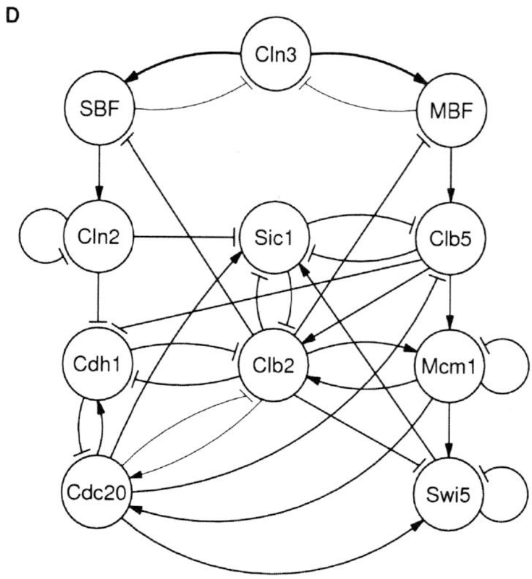

Figure 1: Budding yeast models.

Nodes in the graph represent molecules, complexes, etc. Arrows with pointed heads represent activation, and arrows with bars indicate inhibition. Thin arrows represent a weight of 1/3, normal arrows represent a weight of 1 and thick arrows represent weight 3. (A) The model from Li, et al. [14]. (B) A subset of the model that highlights the first timing hazard. Nodes with values marked with * are enabled to change. If Cdc20 transitions from 1 to 0 before Cdh1 transitions from 0 to 1, Cdh1 will stay at 0, causing the cell cycle to arrest before it has returned to G1. (C) The hazard can be eliminated by replacing Cdc20 self-degradation with inhibition of Cdc20 by Cdh1, ensuring that Cdh1 transitions to 1 before Cdc20 transitions to 0. (D) The final speed-independent model for budding yeast.

The originally published model had a node, Start, representing the conditions that initiate transition from the G1 to S phase of the cell cycle. We removed this node because it does not represent a real molecule. Instead, the initial state of our model is the same as G1, except that Cln3 is 1, representing that the cell cycle has just entered S. NuSMV was used to check the property that, from this state, the model inevitably leads back to G1, where it halts.

The first hazard is shown in Figure 1B. Cell cycle progression can reach a state where Cdh1 is enabled to change from 0 to 1 and Cdc20 is ready to change from 1 to 0. If Cdh1 changes first, the cell cycle proceeds normally and reaches G1, but, if Cdc20 changes first, Cdh1 stops trying to change, causing the cell cycle to halt before reaching G1.

The model can be revised to eliminate this hazard by replacing the self-inhibition of Cdc20 with inhibition of Cdc20 by Cdh1, as shown in Figure 1C, ensuring that Cdh1 transitions to 1 before Cdc20 transitions to 0. This change is supported by Huang, et al. [15], who show that APC-Cdh1 accelerates the degradation of APC-Cdc20 *in vivo*.

Continuing to analyze and revise successive models reveals a series of hazards, each of which can be resolved by small revisions until a fully hazard-free model is finally obtained. The second hazard occurs after a transition in Clb5 causes Clb2 to transition to 1, after which Cdc20 and Mcm1 are both enabled to transition to 1. If Cdc20 transitions first, Mcm1 can be disabled causing the cell to exit mitosis without Mcm1 ever going high, causing the cell cycle potentially to fail to enter G1.

According to the literature [16], [17], activation of Clb5 first causes Clb2 to be transcribed at a low level, which is sufficient to activate Clb2's own transcription factors, Mcm1/SFF (represented as Mcm1 in the model), which then cause Clb2 to be transcribed at a higher level.

To capture this understanding, the model was revised so that Clb2 has one of three possible values: 0, representing a negligible concentration of Clb2; 1, representing a low concentration; and 2, representing a high concentration. The modeling formalism of Li, et al. [14] was extended to permit three-valued signals (more details in Methods). The model was additionally modified so that Clb2 must be 2 before Cdc20 transitions to 1, eliminating the hazard by ensuring that Mcm1 transitions to 1 before Clb2 transitions to 2.

The revised model has one more hazard. When Cln3 becomes 1, it enables both MBF and SBF to transition from 0 to 1. But Cln3 inhibits itself, so it can return to 0 before either SBF or MBF changes, causing the cell cycle to arrest. The hazard can be eliminated by replacing self-degradation of Cln3 with inhibition by SBF and MBF, so that SBF and MBF both must change before Cln3 returns to 0. As observed in Orlando, et al. [18], MBF and SBF indirectly inhibit Cln3 by activating Yox1 and Yhp1.

With this revision, there are no more hazards. Upon entering the cell cycle from G1, the cell inevitably returns to G1 for every possible combination of delays at each of the nodes.

Another Boolean model of budding yeast by Irons appeared recently [19] that is more complete and introduces more molecular components. Interestingly this model includes most of the revisions discussed above, except for the inhibition of Cdc20 by Cdh1. Analysis of this model using NuSMV with the asynchronous update rule shows that it suffers from the same hazard involving Cdc20 and Cdh1 as the model of Li, et al. shown in Figure 1D. The Irons model has additional hazards involving the new components that were added beyond the Li *et al.* model, and it is unclear how to resolve them because they have not been extensively discussed in the biological literature. While a deeper study of hazards in the Irons model would be merited in the future, the fact that the model has the same issues as the simpler and more tractable models discussed above indicates that a simple model can reveal insights into issues that also occur in more complex models.

Timing Robustness of the Fission Yeast Cell Cycle

The biology of fission yeast is less well documented than that of budding yeast, making it difficult to provide biological justifications for revisions based on hazards in the cell cycle. However, timing robustness can be used to compare models and suggest possible revisions.

We constructed three Boolean models based on previously published ODE models. In each case, we started with the "wiring diagram" presented in the ODE paper, adjusted the edge weights and made minor changes until the cell cycle worked properly under the synchronous update rule. The first model was based on a paper by Sveiczer, et al. in 2000 [20]. Analysis with NuSMV revealed many hazards involving a hypothetical protein, PP, that appeared in the model. Revisions to eliminate these hazards seemed pointless, since there is no biology to refer to. A Boolean model of fission yeast was published recently [21], also based on Sveiczer, et al., 2000 but that was similar to the model we constructed.

We created two other Boolean models based on more recent papers, published in 2001 and 2004 [22], [23], shown in Figure 2. The 2004 paper has more hazards than the 2001 paper, and fixing the hazards in the 2004 paper results in a model that is very similar to that from the 2001 paper. The first hazard from the 2004 model is that SK can degrade before Cdc2 is produced. This allows Ste9 and Rum1 to reactivate and prevent production of Cdc2, halting the cell cycle. This hazard can be eliminated by replacing SK self-inhibition with inhibition of SK by Cdc2, as hypothesized in in the 2001 paper.

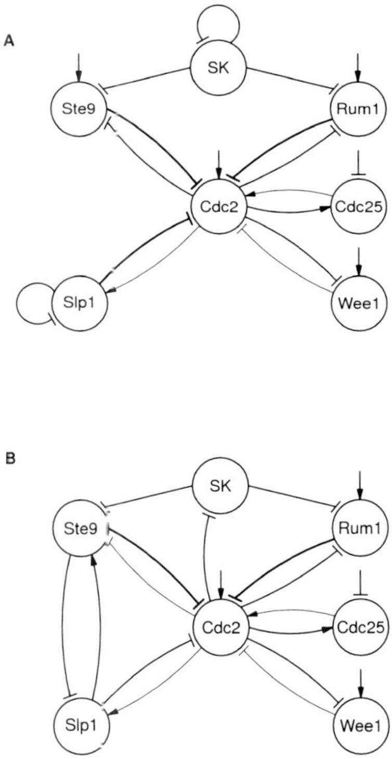

Figure 2: Fission yeast models.

(A) Fission yeast model derived from Sveiczer, et al, 2004 [23]. (B) Revised speed-independent model.

Another hazard occurs when Slp1 is 1 and Cdc2 is 1. Then either Cdc2 can transition to 0 or Cdc2 can degrade SK to 0. If Cdc2 changes first, SK remains at 1 and the cell cycle arrests. The hazard can be removed be reducing the weight of the inhibitory edge from Slp1 to Cdc2 and replacing constitutive Ste9 production with an activating edge from Slp1 to Ste9 [22].

Finally, one hazard occurs in both models. When Slp1 inhibits Cdc2, causing it to decrease from 2 to 1, Cdc2 is ready to decrease again to 0. However, Slp1 is also enabled to return to 0 because of self-inhibition. If Slp1 transitions first, Cdc2 can again transition to 2, leading to a deviation from the cell cycle. Interestingly, Slp1 and Ste9 are homologous with Cdh1 and Cdc20 in budding yeast, so this is essentially the same hazard that was detected in several budding yeast models above. We could fix the hazard by making the same change that was made in the budding yeast model: replace the self-inhibition of Slp1 by inhibition of Slp1 by Ste9. In budding yeast, there was some evidence in the literature for interaction. Furthermore, similar interaction has been noted in the Xenopus cell cycle, but no evidence of such an interaction has been noted in fission yeast [24]. In general, this hazard can be resolved by ensuring that Slp1 does not return to 0 until Ste9 has transitioned to 1. An alternative revision with this effect would be to replace self-inhibition of Slp1 with inhibition from Wee1 or Rum1. We could find no evidence for or against this possibility in the literature.

Evolutionary Pressure for Timing Robustness

We tested *in silico* the hypothesis that timing robustness is not an accidental property, but results from natural selection, by introducing random mutations. The models were mutated by deleting, adding, or re-weighting inputs. The mutant networks were checked under the *synchronous* update rule using NuSMV, and those whose cell cycles failed were discarded. The remaining mutants (called "viable mutants") were further checked for speed independence using NuSMV under the *asynchronous* update rule.

The fraction of viable mutants that are speed-independent declines rapidly as mutations accumulate, as shown in Table 1. From this experiment, it appears that speed-independence is a fragile property that is easily destroyed by random mutations even in cells that are otherwise viable. It is therefore reasonable to conclude that the property is maintained by selection pressure.

Table 1. In silico mutation results

Mutation distance from model	Fraction of viable mutants that are speed-independent in budding yeast	Fraction of viable mutants that are speed-independent in fission yeast
1	0.304	0.202
2	0.216	0.102
3	0.174	0.084
4	0.094	0.056
5	0.062	0.066
6	0.058	0.044

From one to six random mutations were simulated in each model 500 times. Mutants were considered viable if they correctly completed their cell cycles when analyzed with a synchronous update rule. However, mutations tended to reduce timing robustness even in the viable mutants, indicating that timing robustness is maintained by selection.

doi:10.1371/journal.pone.0008906.t001

Other Notions of Robustness

Robustness, the ability of a system to maintain a function in the presence of perturbations, has been an important theme in systems biology for many years [25]. Different classes of perturbations yield different notions of robustness.

One perturbation is a change of the system state. This leads to one of the notions of robustness explored by the paper by Li, et al. [14]. In that paper, robustness is measured by the size of the "basin of attraction" of G1 (i.e., the set of states which, if the system is started in them, cause it to progress to G1). This notion of robustness is unrelated to timing robustness, and difficult to transfer to asynchronous systems. The definition of the basin of attraction in Boolean systems depends on a state determining a trajectory to a unique attractor. In an asynchronous system, there are usually many trajectories out of any state that visit various attractors.

Another type of robustness is robustness to mutations. One question that has been examined is the relationship between robustness to mutations and evolvability [25]–[27]. Interestingly, our simulation of mutations produces the seemingly opposing result that *timing robustness* is not itself robust to mutations – from which we conclude that it is a property that must be actively maintained by evolution. However, this observation does not necessarily imply that speed independent systems are not robust to mutations. First, timing robustness probably should not be considered a "function," since a reduction in timing robustness may only change the phenotype of the organism with a small probability. More importantly, timing robustness may also imply mutation robustness because timing robustness depends only on the "wiring diagram" and the logical combinations of input signals at each node. So, a timing-robust organism may freely vary reaction rates without compromising function, allowing evolution to fine-tune and optimize functions smoothly. For example, reaction rates could be freely varied to maximize the speed of the cell cycle or to maximize energy efficiency while preserving the correct function of the cell cycle.

Are Real Cells Speed-Independent?

There are reasons to suspect that real cells are not quite as timing-robust as the models here seem to suggest. Speed independence may have a cost in time and energy, making it disadvantageous when reactions operate on such different time scales that hazards are unlikely. We conjecture that the observed speed-independence results in part from the simplified representations of the cell cycle models analyzed here, and that more detailed cell cycle models would probably exhibit strong timing robustness while not being completely speed-independent. A reasonable less conservative model would allow for qualitatively different delays [5], [6], [9]. A less conservative model would also allow the possibility that the cell cycle would be fully or partially intact when genes are knocked out, a property of actual cells [18]. It will be possible to answer more of the many open questions about timing robustness as additional details about the regulation of the cell cycle and other cellular processes are discovered.

METHODS

Many of the Boolean networks from the literature are *threshold networks* [11]. Each node can have a 0 or 1 value, and the value of a node when it is next updated is one if the sum of positive inputs minus the of negative inputs exceeds a constant threshold for that node. In analyzing and modifying these models, we found it to be necessary to extend threshold networks to handle more than two values.

Nodes have k+1 levels of activation, 0...k, where 0 represents a functionally inactive level and k represents maximum activity. Three levels were sufficient for all of the networks appearing here. Each node has a specified threshold between each successive activation level, and each node input has an associated real-valued weight representing the strength of the reaction on the node.

Formally, a Boolean network is defined to have a set of *N* nodes associated with proteins. Each node has a set of inputs, which are other nodes. Each input also has an *input weight*, w_{ij}. In the networks here, only three magnitudes of weights are required: $\pm\frac{1}{3}$, ± 1, and ± 3. Inputs with positive weights are *activating* and inputs with negative weights are *inhibiting*. Each node *i* has thresholds $\theta_{i1} < \theta_{i2} < \ldots < \theta_{ik}$. The weighted sum of the inputs to a node are compared with these thresholds to determine whether the node level is enabled to increase or decrease. In the networks here, $\theta_{i1} = .5$ and $\theta_{i2} = 1.5$ for all nodes.

The network can be depicted as a directed graph. Nodes are labeled circles, and lines with arrowheads (for activating inputs) or flat ends (for inhibiting inputs) represent the inputs to nodes. The thickness of the line represents the weight on that input.

The dynamics of a network are represented as a *Kripke structure*, which is a directed graph of *states*, where each state consists of an assignment of a value of 0 to k to each node in the network. The Kripke structure has edges from each state to one or more *successor states*; these edges represent possible ways that the states can change over time. The Kripke structure is *deterministic* if each state has exactly one successor. If one or more states have multiple successors, the Kripke structure is *nondeterministic*. The Kripke structure also has a designated *initial state*, which represents a state in which the network can start. The Kripke structure is completely defined by the network and an initial state.

Every possible assignment of values to nodes is a state in the Kripke structure. To define the successors of a state S, we first define the *next value*, S'_i, for a node i (intuitively the next value is a value that the node will have when next updated, if nothing else changes). S'_i depends on how the weighted sum of inputs to a node compares with thresholds for the node.

Then, the next value can be defined for each node, given a state S, as:

$$S'_i = \begin{cases} S_i - 1 & \text{if } \Sigma_{1 \le j \le N}\, w_{ij}\, S_j < \theta_{i,S_i} \\ S_i + 1 & \text{if } \Sigma_{1 \le j \le N}\, w_{ij}\, S_j \ge \theta_{i,S_i+1} \\ S_i & \text{otherwise.} \end{cases}$$

Once the next value of each node is defined, the set of successor states depends on what *update rule* is used. The *synchronous update rule* that was used in much past work defines a single successor of each state S in which each node is given its next value. Intuitively, every node is updated as soon as it can be, and all such nodes are updated simultaneously. Using the synchronous update rule results in a deterministic Kripke structure.

The *asynchronous update rule* specifies that each successor state to S has at most one node updated to its next value (it is always possible that no nodes are updated, in other words, S is always a successor of itself). Intuitively, a particular node is chosen arbitrarily for updating. This represents a model with no timing constraints. When , node i is said to be *enabled*. Using the asynchronous update rule, any node that is enabled may change after an arbitrary delay (but only one such node may change at a time). Any state that has at least one enabled node has multiple successor states, so the Kripke structure is nondeterministic.

NuSMV

Network behavior (under the synchronous and asynchronous update rules) was analyzed using a symbolic model checking tool, NuSMV, to test the robustness of the cell cycle model [8]. NuSMV explores the paths of states starting from the initial state to check a specific property of interest.

The theory and algorithms in NuSMV are the results of several decades of research published in many books and papers, so we cannot explain them in depth. In brief, NuSMV is able to check dynamic properties of finite-state systems for infinitely many possible variations in inputs or internal non-deterministic choices by exhaustively searching the finite states of the system for individual states or loops that violate the property. NuSMV has several alternative implementations for searching the state of states. We used the implementation based on Boolean decision diagrams (BDDs), a data structure that can be used to explore large state sets relatively quickly (however, the models of the cell cycle only have a few thousand states, so any reasonable implementation of model checking should work well on them).

NuSMV has an input language, similar to a programming language, for describing the system to be checked. Descriptions in the language consist of a set of state variables ranging over discrete sets of values, along with rules that update those variables based on the previous state. These rules can be non-deterministic, meaning that state variables can be updated to several alternative values, in which case NuSMV will check the property for all of those possibilities. The NuSMV input language is naturally synchronous: time is divided into steps, and all variables are updated on each step. However, asynchronous updating can be encoded in NuSMV by exploiting non-determinism. Each reaction in SMV was coded as a separate rule updating its reactants and products. To implement the asynchronous update rule, an additional control variable was added to the rule, along with logic that only allows the rule to update if the control variable is set to a particular value that triggers that rule. At each time step, a value is non-deterministically chosen for the control variable, so at most one rule can fire at a time. To implement the synchronous update rule, the control variables are omitted from the rules so that all of them update simultaneously.

The property is written in NuSMV's logical specification language, CTL. It requires that the cell *inevitably* reach G1 for all of the sequences of states that occur with the chosen update rule. This property is violated if the cell cycle halts in some other state or continues without reaching G1. For the budding yeast models, G1 is considered to be the state where Sic1 and Cdh1 are 1 and all other variables are 0, and the initial state is the same except Cln3 is also 1. For fission yeast, G1 is taken to be the state where Wee1, Ste9 and Rum1 are 1 and all other variables are 0, and the initial state is the same except SK is also 1. We have also checked the more stringent (and complex) properties that the cell progresses through the correct sequence of stages as it progresses to G1. The models are not detailed enough to specify many intermediate states, but, in budding yeast, Clb5 is associated with DNA replication and Clb2 is associated with mitosis. In the final budding yeast model, as expected, a property requiring that the Clb5 go to 1 before Clb2 goes to 1, before finally returning to G1, holds for all possibly reaction delays. The final fission yeast model is even smaller than the budding yeast model, but we can check that Cdc2, the main driver protein causes both replication and mitosis, reaches its highest level.

The source descriptions of the models and a translator to generate NuSMV descriptions from them are available at http://verify.stanford.edu/TimingRobustnessInYeast.html. NuSMV is a widely-used open source system that can easily found by searching the Web.

Mutation Simulation

To test whether there is selection pressure on the cells to be speed-independent, the speed-independent models for both budding yeast and fission yeast were mutated *in silico*. The mutations were chosen by first choosing, with probability $\frac{1}{3}$, whether to add an input, delete an input, or re-weight an input. If the decision was to add an input, nodes i and j were chosen with equal probability and node i was added as an input to j with a non-zero weight chosen with equal probability from $\{\pm\frac{1}{3}, \pm 1, \pm 3\}$. If the decision was to delete in input, a pair of nodes i and j were chosen with equal probability, where i was an input to j, and i was deleted from the set of inputs of j. If re-weighting was chosen, an input was selected at random and the weight was changed with equal probability from $\{\pm\frac{1}{3}, \pm 1, \pm 3\}$, excluding the current input weight.

Mutations were performed in a series of steps. At each step, mutants were checked with NuSMV, using the CTL properties above, but with a *synchronous* update rule. Mutants that failed this test were considered "non-viable" and discarded. The viable mutants were further checked using NuSMV and the *asynchronous* update rule to discover the proportion that were speed-independent. 500 viable mutants were generated at each mutation step, from 1 to 6 steps.

AUTHOR CONTRIBUTIONS

Conceived and designed the experiments: KM DLD MAH. Performed the experiments: KM. Analyzed the data: KM. Wrote the paper: KM DLD MAH.

REFERENCES

1. Kauffman S (1969) Metabolic stability and epigenesis in randomly constructed genetic nets. J Theor Biol 22: 437–67.S. Kauffman1969Metabolic stability and epigenesis in randomly constructed genetic nets.J Theor Biol2243767
2. Fisher J, Piterman N, Hajnal A, Henzinger T (2007) Predictive modeling of signaling crosstalk during C. elegans vulval development. PLoS Computational Biology 3: e92.J. FisherN. PitermanA. HajnalT. Henzinger2007Predictive modeling of signaling crosstalk during C. elegans vulval development.PLoS Computational Biology3e92
3. Fisher J, Henzinger T, Mateescu M, Piterman N (2008) Bounded Asynchrony: Concurrency for Modeling Cell-Cell Interactions. Lecture Notes in Computer Science 5054: 17.J. FisherT. HenzingerM. MateescuN. Piterman2008Bounded Asynchrony: Concurrency for Modeling Cell-Cell Interactions.Lecture Notes in Computer Science505417
4. Alur R, Dill D (1994) A theory of timed automata. Theoretical Computer Science 126: 183–235.R. AlurD. Dill1994A theory of timed automata.Theoretical Computer Science126183235
5. Faure A, Naldi A, Chaouiya C, Thieffry D (2006) Dynamical analysis of a generic Boolean model for the control of the mammalian cell cycle. Bioinformatics 22: A. FaureA. NaldiC. ChaouiyaD. Thieffry2006Dynamical analysis of a generic Boolean model for the control of the mammalian cell cycle.Bioinformatics22
6. Shen X, Collier J, Dill D, Shapiro L, Horowitz M, et al. (2008) Architecture and inherent robustness of a bacterial cell-cycle control system. Proc Natl Acad Sci U S A 105: 11340.X. ShenJ. CollierD. DillL. ShapiroM. Horowitz2008Architecture and inherent robustness of a bacterial cell-cycle control system.Proc Natl Acad Sci U S A10511340
7. Thomas R (1973) Boolean formalization of genetic control circuits. J Theor Biol 42: 563–85.R. Thomas1973Boolean formalization of genetic control circuits.J Theor Biol4256385
8. Cimatti A, Clarke E, Giunchiglia E, Giunchiglia F, Pistore M, et al. (2002) NuSMV Version 2: An OpenSource Tool for Symbolic

Model Checking. In: Goos G, Hartmanis J, van Leeuwen J, editors. Computer-Aided Verification. Copenhagen: Springer. pp. 359–364.A. CimattiE. ClarkeE. GiunchigliaF. GiunchigliaM. Pistore2002NuSMV Version 2: An OpenSource Tool for Symbolic Model Checking.G. GoosJ. HartmanisJ. van LeeuwenComputer-Aided VerificationCopenhagenSpringer359364

9. Chaves M, Albert R, Sontag E (2005) Robustness and fragility of Boolean models for genetic regulatory networks. J Theor Biol 235: 431–449.M. ChavesR. AlbertE. Sontag2005Robustness and fragility of Boolean models for genetic regulatory networks.J Theor Biol235431449
10. Braunewell S, Bornholdt S (2007) Superstability of the yeast cell-cycle dynamics: Ensuring causality in the presence of biochemical stochasticity. J Theor Biol 245: 638–643.S. BraunewellS. Bornholdt2007Superstability of the yeast cell-cycle dynamics: Ensuring causality in the presence of biochemical stochasticity.J Theor Biol245638643
11. Bornholdt S (2008) Boolean network models of cellular regulation: prospects and limitations. J R Soc Interface 5: 85–94.S. Bornholdt2008Boolean network models of cellular regulation: prospects and limitations.J R Soc Interface58594
12. Fages F, Soliman S, Chabrier-Rivier N (2004) Modelling and querying interaction networks in the biochemical abstract machine BIOCHAM. J Biol Physics Chem 4: 64–73.F. FagesS. SolimanN. Chabrier-Rivier2004Modelling and querying interaction networks in the biochemical abstract machine BIOCHAM.J Biol Physics Chem46473
13. Garg A, Di Cara A, Xenarios I, Mendoza L, De Micheli G (2008) Synchronous versus asynchronous modeling of gene regulatory networks. Bioinformatics 24: 1917.A. GargA. Di CaraI. XenariosL. MendozaG. De Micheli2008Synchronous versus asynchronous modeling of gene regulatory networks.Bioinformatics241917
14. Li F, Long T, Lu Y, Ouyang Q, Tang C (2004) The yeast cell-cycle network is robustly designed. Proc Natl Acad Sci U S A 101: 4781–4786.F. LiT. LongY. LuQ. OuyangC. Tang2004The yeast cell-cycle network is robustly designed.Proc Natl Acad Sci U S A10147814786

15. Huang JN, Park I, Ellingson E, Littlepage LE, Pellman D (2001) Activity of the APCCdh1 form of the anaphase-promoting complex persists until S phase and prevents the premature expression of Cdc20p. J Cell Biol 154: 85–94.JN HuangI. ParkE. EllingsonLE LittlepageD. Pellman2001Activity of the APCCdh1 form of the anaphase-promoting complex persists until S phase and prevents the premature expression of Cdc20p.J Cell Biol1548594
16. Amon A, Tyers M, Futcher B, Nasmyth K (1993) Mechanisms that help the yeast cell cycle clock tick: G2 cyclins transcriptionally activate G2 cyclins and repress G1 cyclins. Cell 74: 993–1007.A. AmonM. TyersB. FutcherK. Nasmyth1993Mechanisms that help the yeast cell cycle clock tick: G2 cyclins transcriptionally activate G2 cyclins and repress G1 cyclins.Cell749931007
17. Maher M, Cong F, Kindelberger D, Nasmyth K, Dalton S (1995) Cell cycle-regulated transcription of the CLB2 gene is dependent on Mcm1 and a ternary complex factor. Mol Cell Biol 15: 3129–3137.M. MaherF. CongD. KindelbergerK. NasmythS. Dalton1995Cell cycle-regulated transcription of the CLB2 gene is dependent on Mcm1 and a ternary complex factor.Mol Cell Biol1531293137
18. Orlando DA, Lin CY, Bernard A, Wang JY, Socolar JES, et al. (2008) Global control of cell-cycle transcription by coupled cdk and network oscillators. Nature 453: 944–947.DA OrlandoCY LinA. BernardJY WangJES Socolar2008Global control of cell-cycle transcription by coupled cdk and network oscillators.Nature453944947
19. Irons D (2009) Logical analysis of the budding yeast cell cycle. J Theor Biol 257: 543–559.D. Irons2009Logical analysis of the budding yeast cell cycle.J Theor Biol257543559
20. Sveiczer A, Csikasz-Nagy A, Gyorffy B, Tyson JJ, Novak B (2000) Modeling the fission yeast cell cycle: Quantized cycle times in wee1-cdc25Δ mutant cells. Proc Natl Acad Sci U S A 97: 7865–7870.A. SveiczerA. Csikasz-NagyB. GyorffyJJ TysonB. Novak2000Modeling the fission yeast cell cycle: Quantized cycle times in wee1-cdc25Δ mutant cells.Proc Natl Acad Sci U S A9778657870
21. Davidich MI, Bornholdt S (2008) Boolean network model predicts cell cycle sequence of fission yeast. PLoS ONE 3: e1672.MI

DavidichS. Bornholdt2008Boolean network model predicts cell cycle sequence of fission yeast.PLoS ONE3e1672

22. Novak B, Pataki Z, Ciliberto A, Tyson JJ (2001) Mathematical model of the cell division cycle of fission yeast. Chaos 11: 277–286.B. NovakZ. PatakiA. CilibertoJJ Tyson2001Mathematical model of the cell division cycle of fission yeast.Chaos11277286
23. Sveiczer A, Tyson JJ, Novak B (2004) Modeling the fission yeast cell cycle. Brief Funct Genomic Proteomic 2: 298–307.A. SveiczerJJ TysonB. Novak2004Modeling the fission yeast cell cycle.Brief Funct Genomic Proteomic2298307
24. Pfleger CM, Kirschner MW (2000) The KEN box: an APC recognition signal distinct from the D box targeted by Cdh1. Genes Dev 14: 655–665.CM PflegerMW Kirschner2000The KEN box: an APC recognition signal distinct from the D box targeted by Cdh1. Genes Dev14655665
25. Kitano H (2004) Biological robustness. Nature Reviews Genetics 5: 826–837.H. Kitano2004Biological robustness.Nature Reviews Genetics5826837
26. Wagner A (2005) Robustness, evolvability, and neutrality. FEBS letters 579: 1772–1778.A. Wagner2005Robustness, evolvability, and neutrality.FEBS letters57917721778
27. Lenski R, Barrick J, Ofria C (2006) Balancing robustness and evolvability. PLoS Biol 4: e428.R. LenskiJ. BarrickC. Ofria2006Balancing robustness and evolvability.PLoS Biol4e428

3 A NOVEL METHOD TO VERIFY MULTILEVEL COMPUTATIONAL MODELS OF BIOLOGICAL SYSTEMS USING MULTISCALE SPATIO-TEMPORAL META MODEL CHECKING

Ovidiu Pârvu, David Gilbert

Department of Computer Science, College of Engineering, Design and Physical Sciences, Brunel University London, London, United Kingdom

ABSTRACT

Insights gained from multilevel computational models of biological systems can be translated into real-life applications only if the model correctness has been verified first. One of the most frequently employed in silico techniques for computational model verification is model checking. Traditional model checking approaches only consider the evolution of numeric values, such as concentrations, over time and are appropriate for computational models of small scale systems (e.g. intracellular networks). However for gaining a systems level understanding of how biological organisms function it is essential to consider more complex large scale biological systems (e.g. organs). Verifying computational models of such systems requires capturing both how numeric values and properties of (emergent) spatial structures (e.g. area of multicellular population) change over time and across multiple levels of organization, which are not considered by existing model checking approaches. To address this limitation we have developed a novel approximate probabilistic multiscale spatio-temporal meta model checking methodology for verifying multilevel computational models relative to specifications describing the desired/expected system behaviour. The methodology is generic and supports computational models encoded using various high-level modelling formalisms because it is defined relative to time series data and not the models used to generate it. In addition, the methodology can be automatically adapted to case study specific types of spatial structures and properties using the spatio-temporal meta model checking concept. To automate the computational model verification process we have implemented the model checking approach in the software tool Mule (http://mule.modelchecking.org). Its applicability is illustrated against four systems biology computational models previously published in the literature encoding the rat cardiovascular system dynamics, the uterine contractions of labour, the Xenopus laevis cell cycle and the acute inflammation of the gut and lung. Our methodology and software will enable computational biologists to efficiently develop reliable multilevel computational models of biological systems.

INTRODUCTION

Multilevel computational models of complex biological systems are abstract representations of living systems that span multiple levels of organization. They encode the hierarchical organization of biological systems explicitly, and therefore enable reasoning about how events initiated at one level of organization reflect across multiple levels of organization. In systems biology [1, 2] multilevel, also commonly referred to as multiscale [3] computational models can be employed for gaining a better understanding of the underlying mechanisms of living systems, and to generate new hypotheses for driving experimental studies. Conversely in systems medicine it is argued [4] that multilevel computational models could potentially facilitate delivering personalized treatments by providing a patient specific understanding of how diseases and their treatment reflect across multiple levels of organization [5].

However any insights gained from model simulation results can be successfully translated into real-life applications only if the correctness of the models has been verified first. Computational models of biological systems can be validated either in the in vitro environment by checking if the model simulation results can be reproduced experimentally, or in the in silico environment by verifying if the model simulation results conform to a formal specification describing the desired/expected system behaviour. An in silico approach that automates the process of verifying models relative to formal specifications is called model checking [6, 7]. Due to the complex, stochastic nature of biological systems only approximate probabilistic model checking approaches are considered throughout this paper.

Validating multilevel computational models in the in vitro environment is challenging because there is a need for experimental data from all levels of organization and the interactions between different levels, which is often not available. Moreover in vitro validation procedures need to account for the variability inherent in biological systems [8, 9] which can be of different orders of magnitude at different levels. Conversely, verifying multilevel computational models in the in silico environment is challenging because there is a lack of model checking approaches that can explicitly distinguish between different levels of organization. Existing model checking approaches can be employed to verify submodels corresponding to each level of organization individually without the possibility of referring to interactions between different levels.

In this paper we address this issue by developing a novel multiscale model checking methodology for automatically verifying multilevel computational models relative to given specifications. Our approach is generic and supports computational models encoded using various high-level modelling formalisms because it is defined relative to time series data representing the model simulation results and not the models themselves. Moreover our methodology could be potentially employed for analysing time series data recorded in the wet-lab as well. This could enable checking if a computational model correctly describes a physical system, or that a physical system correctly implements an in silico design, but this is beyond the scope of this paper.

Both spatial and non-spatial computational models can be verified using our approach. The specifications against which the computational models are verified can describe both how numeric values (e.g. concentration of protein X) and properties of (emergent) spatial structures, called spatial entities, (e.g. area of multicellular population) are expected to change over time and across multiple levels of organization. For instance, assuming we would like to verify a computational model describing tumour growth, the specification could state that if the concentration of protein X in a cancerous cell rises above a certain threshold level (e.g. 0.8 M), then the cell will divide and the cellular density or area of the tumour (structure) will increase.

Assuming that the computational model considered is spatial, the type of spatial entities and their properties, called spatial measures, can differ between case studies. For instance given a tumour growth computational model one could be potentially interested in how the area of the tumour structure changes over time, whereas in case of a migrating multicellular population tracking the position of the population over time could be of interest.

We defined an abstraction of our approach, called multiscale spatio-temporal meta model checking that enables the automatic reconfiguration of the model checking methodology according to case study specific spatial entity types and measures. The spatio-temporal metamodel checking approach resembles the meta-programming [10] concept from computer science where an abstract type is defined that acts as a template for creating specific type instances tailored to particular applications. Our spatio-temporal meta model checking approach is not restricted to biologically relevant spatial entity types and properties, and therefore could be employed to adapt the methodology to case studies from other fields of science. However we do not illustrate this in this paper. Due to the intended general applicability of the approach, and the fact that hierarchical systems in multiple domains of science (e.g. astrophysics, energy, engineering, environmental science and materials science [11]) are commonly referred to as multiscale, our approach is called multiscale rather than multilevel spatio-temporal meta model checking.

To enable the automatic verification of multilevel computational models of biological systems relative to formal specifications we have implemented the model checking method in the software tool Mule which is made freely available online (http://mule.modelchecking.org) in binary and source code format. Moreover a Docker [12] image has been created that provides a self-contained environment for running Mule without additional setup on all major operating systems.

We illustrate the applicability of Mule by verifying the correctness of four multilevel computational models previously published in the literature. The models considered are of different complexity, have been encoded using different modelling formalisms and software, are deterministic, stochastic or hybrid, and encode space explicitly or not. The case studies corresponding to the four multilevel computational models are the rat cardiovascular system dynamics [13], the uterine contractions of labour [14], the Xenopus laevis cell cycle [15], and the acute inflammation of the gut and lung [16]. The formal specifications against which the models are verified were derived from the original papers introducing the models. The main reason for this is that in the following we focus on describing the model verification methodology and not on presenting novel biologically relevant results.

In brief, the main contributions of our paper are:

- Definition of a multiscale spatio-temporal model checking methodology for verifying multilevel computational models of biological systems relative to formal specifications describing the desired/expected system behaviour.
- Definition of the spatio-temporal meta model checking concept which enables automatically reconfiguring the methodology according to case study specific spatial entity types and measures.
- Implementation of the multiscale spatio-temporal meta model checking approach in the freely available software Mule. Both Bayesian and frequentist model checking algorithms can be employed to verify multilevel computational models (considering user-defined error bounds).
- Illustrative examples of how to verify multilevel computational models of biological systems using multiscale spatio-temporal meta model checking.

Related Work

In computational (systems) biology, model checking approaches have been employed for model verification [17–32], parameter estimation/synthesis [33–42], model construction (i.e. both model parameters and structure/topology) [43, 44], and robustness computation (considering various perturbations) [39, 44–47]; see recent review papers [48–50] for a more detailed description.

One common characteristic of these model checking approaches is that they only consider how numeric values (e.g. concentrations) change over time. They are appropriate for small scale systems where the spatial domain is usually not represented explicitly (e.g. cell cycle [23, 27, 32, 36, 44, 46, 51], gene expression/regulatory networks [20, 35, 39, 52, 53], signalling pathways [17, 22, 25, 28–30, 38, 46, 54–56]). These model checking approaches cannot be directly employed to verify either spatial computational models because they do not consider how spatial properties change over time, or multilevel computational models because they do not distinguish between different levels of organization.

In previous work [57] we have defined a model checking methodology which enables verifying computational models of biological systems with respect to both how numeric values and spatial properties change over time. However the main limitation of this approach is that it cannot explicitly distinguish between different levels of organization and therefore cannot be employed to verify multilevel computational models of biological systems. Moreover the types of spatial entities and measures are hardcoded in the methodology and cannot be reconfigured according to the model verification requirements of different case studies.

METHODS

Using the novel model checking approach introduced in this paper multilevel computational models of biological systems can be verified relative to formal specifications as described by the workflow depicted in Fig 1, which comprises four steps:

- **Model construction:** Using biological observations and/or relevant references from the literature to construct the computational model.
- **Multiscale spatio-temporal analysis:** Each time the model is simulated time series data are generated in which spatial entities from multiple scales are automatically detected and analysed.
- **Formal specification:** The specification of the system is

mapped from natural language into formal logic.

- **Model checking:** The model checker takes as input the processed time series data (representing the behaviour of the modelled system) and the formal specification, and verifies if the model is correct relative to the specification using the model checking algorithm chosen by the user (e.g. frequentist statistical model checking). In the case that the model is incorrect it is updated and verified again.

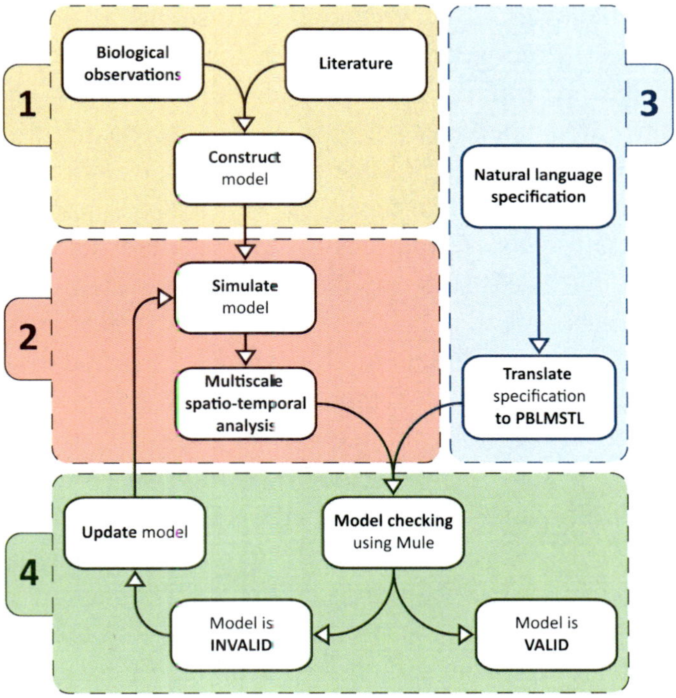

Figure 1: Multiscale spatio-temporal model checking workflow.

The first step (1) in the workflow is using biological observations and/or information from the literature to construct the multilevel computational model of the biological system considered. Next (2) the model is simulated to produce time series data in which spatial entities from multiple scales are automatically detected and analysed using a multiscale spatio-temporal analysis module. Then (3) the specification against which the model is verified is translated from natural language to a formal multiscale spatio-temporal language called PBLMSTL. Finally (4) using the model checker Mule the model is automatically verified relative to the given PBLMSTL specification considering the processed time series data representing the modelled system behavior. If the model is declared incorrect relative to the given specification then it is updated and the steps (2) and (4) are repeated.

Model Construction

The biological systems considered here are assumed to be inherently complex, stochastic, and to span multiple levels of organization [58], where different levels of organization correspond to different spatio-temporal scales. Moreover we assume in the following that biological systems which are multilevel (i.e. span multiple levels of biological organization) are inherently multiscale (i.e. span multiple spatio-temporal scales). Therefore the terms multiscale and multilevel are used interchangeably in this paper. However, since our methodology is "multiscale" instead of "multilevel" we will refer to "scales" rather than "levels" when describing it. The multiscale system representation is assumed to be hierarchical, with the most coarse-grained scales represented at the top of the hierarchy and the most fine-grained scales at the bottom. Time can be represented either in a discrete (using non-negative integer values) or continuous (using non-negative real values) manner. Whenever space is represented explicitly, we assume throughout, similarly to our previous work [57], that it is discretised and represented in pseudo-3D i.e. 2D space in which pile up is allowed, where the degree of pile up for each spatial position is computed using a density measure (e.g. representing cellular density). However adapting the methodology to other numbers of spatial dimensions requires minor changes which are described later. Furthermore we consider that the behaviour of such systems can be represented as sequences of discrete states where the system probabilistically transitions between states only when an event (e.g. a biochemical reaction) occurs.

Such systems are usually represented using high-level modelling languages (e.g. agent based models, cellular automata etc.), examples of which are given in the Results section. However, for model checking purposes, the behaviour of the computational models is usually described using an equivalent low level representation (e.g. a state transition system). The main reason for this is to enable defining the model checking algorithms relative to a single common rather than multiple different model representations.

Low level modelling formalisms often employed to encode systems that have the above mentioned properties are stochastic discrete-event systems (SDES) [59] when no constraint is imposed on the representation of time, respectively discrete-time/continuous-time Markov chains (DTMC/CTMC) when time is assumed to be discrete/continuous. One limitation of SDESs (and DTMCs/CTMCs) is that they do not explicitly distinguish between how numeric and spatial properties of the system change over time and across multiple scales. An extension of SDESs called stochastic spatial discrete-event systems (SSpDES) was defined in [57] to enable explicitly differentiating between numeric and spatial properties. However, similarly to SDESs, SSpDESs do not enable distinguishing between different scales.

In order to address this issue a multiscale extension of SSpDESs called Multiscale Stochastic Spatial Discrete Event Systems, or MSSpDES for short, is defined next. Formally an MSSpDES m is a 9-tuple ⟨S, T, μ, NSV, SpSV, NV, CSpV, MA, SVSS⟩ where:

- $S = \{s_0, s_1, \ldots, s_k\}$ is the set containing all possible states of the system.
- T is the set representing time and it is typically equal to the set of non-negative integer numbers in case of a discrete-time representation (i.e. $T = \mathbb{Z}_+$), respectively the set of non-negative real numbers in case of a continuous-time representation (i.e. $T = \mathbb{R}_+$).
- μ is a probability measure employed to compute the probability of the system to transition along the sequences of states described by a collection of model simulation traces. In case of biological systems it is often assumed that the Markov (memoryless) property holds i.e. the probability of the systems to transition between states depends only on the current and not on previous states. Considering this assumption, if a discrete-time representation is employed then μ is defined similarly as for DTMCs [60] relative to a transition probability function **P**: $S \times S \rightarrow [0, 1]$ which records the probability of transitioning between any two states $s_i, s_j \in S$. Conversely, if a continuous-time representation is employed then μ is defined similarly as for CTMCs [61] considering a transition rate matrix **Q**: $S \times S \rightarrow$

$\mathbb{R}$ which records the rate at which a system transitions between any two states s_i, $s_j \in S$ and from which the corresponding state transition probabilities can be derived.

- $NSV = \{nsv_1, nsv_2, \ldots, nsv_l\}$ is the set of numeric state variables describing the state of the system.
- $SpSV = \{spsv_1, spsv_2, \ldots, spsv_m\}$ is the set of spatial state variables describing the state of the system.
- $NV: S \times NSV \rightarrow \mathbb{R}$ is the numeric value assignment function employed to compute for a given state of the system $s \in S$ the value $val_{NSV} \in \mathbb{R}$ of the numeric state variable $nsv \in NSV$, where $val_{NSV} = NV(s, nsv)$.
- $CSpV = \{SpV_1, SpV_2, \ldots, SpV_n\}$ is the collection of spatial value assignment functions, where each spatial value assignment function $SpV_i \in CSpV$, $SpV_i : S \times SpSV \rightarrow \mathbb{R}^{m_i \times n_i}$, is employed to compute for a given state of the system $s \in S$ the value $val_{SpSV} \in \mathbb{R}^{m_i \times n_i}$ of spatial state variable $spsv \in SpSV$ that corresponds to a discretised spatial domain of size $m_i \times n_i$, where $val_{SpSV} = SpV_i(s, spsv)$.
- $MA = (V_{MA}, E_{MA})$ is the multiscale architecture graph encoding the hierarchical multiscale structure of the system under consideration.
- $SVSS: NSV \cup SpSV \rightarrow V_{MA}$ is the state variable scale and subsystem assignment function which associates each state variable $sv \in NSV \cup SpSV$ with a vertex $v_{scsubsys} \in V_{MA}$ encoding a particular scale and subsystem, where $v_{scsubsys} = SVSS(sv)$.

The multiscale architecture graph $MA = (V_{MA}, E_{MA})$ is employed to formally encode the hierarchical top-down structure of multiscale systems and is represented as a rooted (directed) tree, where V_{MA} represents the set of vertices and E_{MA} the set of directed edges. The main reason for choosing the rooted directed tree representation is that its structure is inherently hierarchical and therefore similar to the organization of biological organisms. We assume throughout that vertices higher in the tree correspond to coarse-grained scales, and vertices lower in the tree correspond to fine-grained scales. Each vertex $v \in V_{MA}$ is encoded as a tuple (sc, subsys) where subsys represents a particular biological subsystem (e.g. heart) and sc its corresponding scale (e.g. organ). Both scales and subsystems are recorded by the MA graph to enable distinguishing between different scales (e.g. organ and cellular), and/or different subsystems (e.g. heart and liver) corresponding to the same scale (e.g. organ). Directed edges $(v, v_i) \in E_{MA}$, $i = \overline{1, m}$, link the biological subsystem represented by vertex v to all its m constituent subsystems from finer-grained scales represented by vertices v_i.

The assumption made here is that biological systems can be decomposed in a top-down manner from coarse-grained (e.g. population/organism) to fine-grained (e.g. intracellular/molecular) scales. Moreover at each scale (e.g. organ) one or multiple biological subsystems (e.g. heart and kidney) could be explicitly considered. The number and type of biological subsystems and/or scales considered differs depending on the biological question addressed.

Considering that the MA graph is represented as a rooted directed tree, a strict partial order < can be defined over the set of vertices V_{MA}, where $v_1 < v_2$, for all $v_1, v_2 \in V_{MA}$, if the unique path from the root to v_1 passes through v_2. Similarly a non-strict partial order $\leq$ can be defined over V_{MA}, where $v_1 \leq v_2$ if the unique path from the root to v_1 passes through v_2, or $v_1 = v_2$. One of the main practical benefits of defining these partial orders is that they enable writing expressions for referring to all subsystems v_i of a system v_j ($v_i \leq v_j$), and all ancestor/parent systems v_k of a subsystem v_l ($v_l < v_k$) in a concise manner. Therefore such expressions could be employed to write shorter formal specifications against which the computational models are verified.

A simple illustrative example of how to construct a (discrete-time) MSSpDES model for a biological system spanning multiple levels of organization is given below.

Example 1 Simple illustrative example of how to construct an MSSpDES model.

Let us assume that we would like to model the movement (considering the von Neumann neighbourhood relation) of a unicellular microorganism in a fixed size environment (here a discretised rectangular grid of size 2 × 2). In order to move, the cell requires energy which it can chemically convert from an abstractly denoted nutrient A; the chemical reaction for converting A to energy is A → Energy. If nutrient A is available intracellularly then it can be converted directly to energy. Otherwise it has to be assimilated from the environment first; the cell can only assimilate nutrients from the position of the discretised space which it currently occupies. The probability of the cell to move is 20%, respectively 30% to convert A to energy and 50% to assimilate A from the environment.

Although the system considered in this example is much simpler than a real-life one, it suffices to illustrate the principles of abstractly representing a multiscale stochastic spatial discrete-event system. Throughout this example a discrete time representation is employed.

The spatial state variables employed to describe the behaviour of the system are Cell—encoding the position of the cell in the discretised space, and A_extracellular—representing the distribution of nutrient A in the environment. Conversely the employed numeric state variables are A_intracellular—encoding the intracellular availability of nutrient A, and Energy—representing the cell's energy supply. The considered subsystems and corresponding scales are energy production reaction network at the intracellular scale, microorganism at the cellular scale, and growth media at the environment scale. State variables associated with the energy production reaction network (intracellular scale) are A_intracellular and Energy, respectively Cell with the microorganism (cellular scale), and A_extracellular with the growth media (environment scale). In the initial state (S_0) of the system, depicted in Fig 2, the cell is positioned in the lower right part of the environment, A_extracellular is uniformly distributed across the entire environment (A_extracellular[i, j] = 1, for all $i, j = \overline{1,2}$), and the initial levels of A_intracellular and Energy are zero.

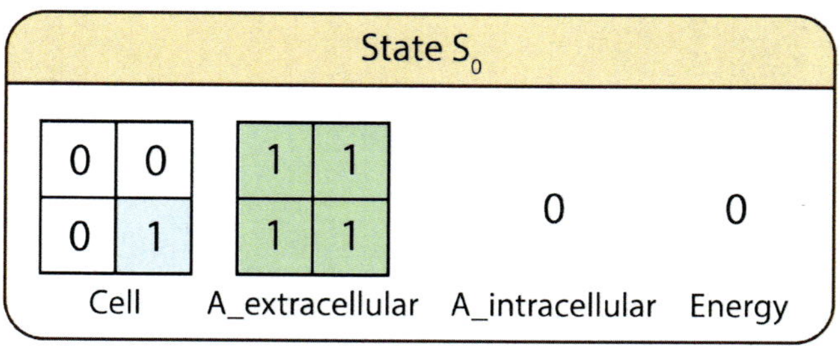

Figure 2: Initial state of the system.

Cell and A_extracellular are the spatial state variables representing the position of the cell, respectively distribution of nutrient A in the environment. A_intracellular and Energyrepresent the intracellular availability of nutrient A, respectively energy.

Starting from the initial state S_0 the system can (in)directly transition to any of the states depicted in Fig 3.

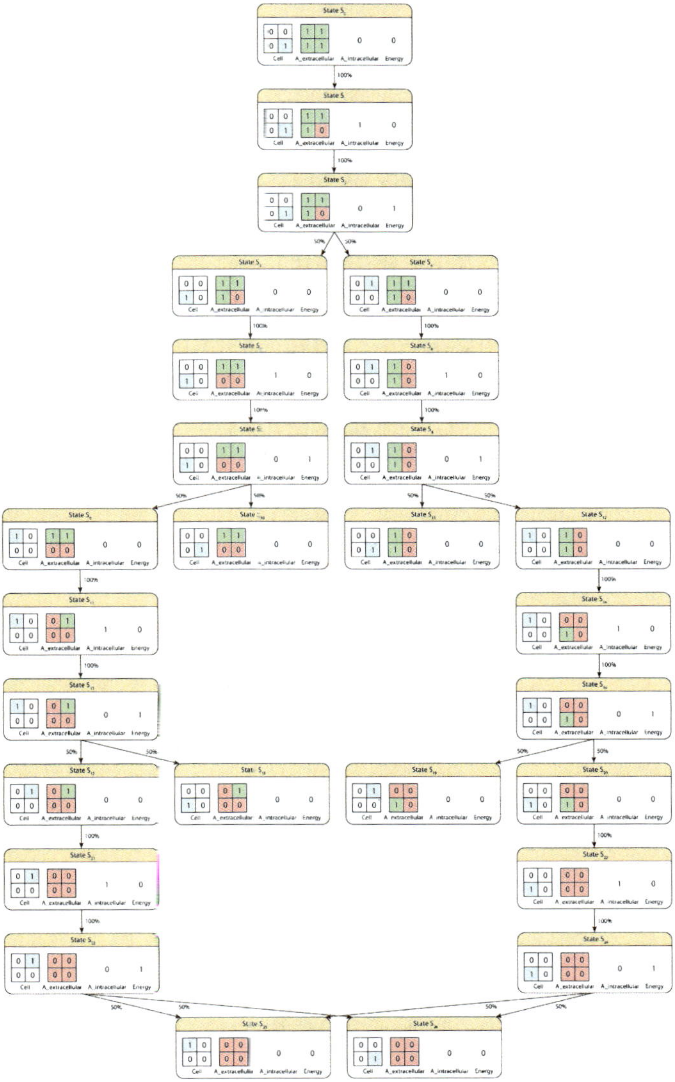

Figure 3: The state space of the system i.e. all possible states which can be reached from the initial state S_0.

Cell and A_extracellular are the spatial state variables representing the position of the cell, respectively distribution of nutrient A in the environment. A_intracellular and Energyrepresent the intracellular availability of nutrient A, respectively energy. The percentage associated with the arrows connecting each pair of states represents the probability of transitioning from one state to the other.

Given that in S_0 the cell has no supplies of intracellular nutrient A or energy, the only possible action is for it to assimilate A from its environment ($S_0 \rightarrow S_1$, probability 100%). Since only one supply of nutrient A is available the only possible next action is to convert the newly gained intracellular A supply to energy ($S_1 \rightarrow S_2$, probability 100%). Once a supply of energy is available the cell can move either above ($S_2 \rightarrow S_4$) or to its left ($S_2 \rightarrow S_3$). The probability of moving to either of the neighbouring positions is therefore equal to 100% / 2 = 50%. Continuing from either state S_3 or S_4 the cell will try to assimilate new A nutrient supplies, which can be converted to energy and then used to move in the environment. This process is repeated multiple times until the cell reaches a state in which it has no A nutrients available extracellularly/intracellularly, respectively no supplies of energy (i.e. S_{10}, S_{11}, S_{18}, S_{19}, S_{25}, S_{26}). In such cases the cell becomes dormant and the system reaches its final state.

Using the notations above we formally define the corresponding MSSpDES model M and (state) transition probability function **P** as follows:

- M = ⟨S, T, μ, NSV, SpSV, NV, CSpV, MA, SVSS⟩, where:
  - $S = \{S_0, S_1, S_2, S_3, S_4, S_5, S_6, S_7, S_8, S_9, S_{10}, S_{11}, S_{12}, S_{13}, S_{14}, S_{15}, S_{16}, S_{17}, S_{18}, S_{19}, S_{20}, S_{21}, S_{22}, S_{23}, S_{24}, S_{25}, S_{26}\}$.
  - $T = \mathbb{Z}_+$ is the set representing time.
  - μ is the function used to compute the probability associated with a set of paths Paths(S_0) starting from S_0 having a common finite prefix $\sigma_{finite} = \{s_0, s_1, \ldots, s_n\}$, which means that for all σ ∈ Paths(S_0), $\sigma[i] = \sigma_{finite}[i] = s_i, i = \overline{0, n}$, where σ[i] denotes the i-th state in σ. The probability value corresponding to Paths(S_0) is computed by multiplying the probabilities of the state transitions associated with the common finite path prefix σ_{finite}. For instance given the finite state sequence $\sigma_{finite} = \{S_0, S_1, S_2, S_3, S_5, S_7, S_{10}\}$, $\mu(\{\sigma \in Paths(S_0) \mid \sigma[i] = \sigma_{finite}[i], 0 \leq i \leq 6\}) = \mathbf{P}(S_0, S_1) \cdot \mathbf{P}(S_1,$

S_2) · **P**(S_2, S_3) · **P**(S_3, S_5) · **P**(S_5, S_7) · **P**(S_7, S_{10}), where the probability values **P**(S_i, S_j) with S_i, S_j ∈ S are recorded by the transition probability function **P** provided below.

- NSV = {A_intracellular,Energy}, and NV is the function used to compute the value of A_intracellular and Energy in a given state of a computation path. The values of the numeric state variables for each state (e.g. NV(S_0, Energy) = 0) are depicted in Fig 3 and therefore will not be explicitly restated here.
- SpSV = {Cell, A_extracellular}, and CSpV = {SpV} is the collection containing the spatial value assignment function SpV used to evaluate Cell and A_extracellularin a given state of a computation path. The values of the spatial state variables for each state (e.g. SpV(S_0,Cell) = [0, 0;0, 1]) are depicted in Fig 3 and therefore will not be explicitly restated here.
- MA is the multiscale architecture graph depicted in Fig 4 encoding the hierarchical organization of the considered subsystems, namely the growth media (environment scale), the microorganism (cellular scale) and the energy production reaction network (intracellular scale).
- SVSS is the state variable scale and subsystem assignment function which associates state variables to particular subsystems encoded as vertices in the MA graph. The values returned by SVSS for the considered state variables are: SVSS(A_intracellular) = (Intracellular, EnergyProductionReactionNetwork), SVSS(Energy) = (Intracellular, EnergyProductionReactionNetwork), SVSS(Cell) = (Cellular, Microorganism), and SVSS(A_extracellular) = (Environment. GrowthMedia).

- **P** is the transition probability function which records the probability of transitioning between any two states of the system s_i, s_j ∈ S. Due to page size constraints it is not possible to represent **P** explicitly. Instead only its non-zero entries are given below: **P**(S_0, S_1) = 100%, **P**(S_1, S_2) = 100%, **P**(S_2, S_3) = 50%, **P**(S_2, S_4) = 50%, **P**(S_3, S_5) = 100%, **P**(S_4, S_6) = 100%, **P**(S_5, S_7) = 100%, **P**(S_6, S_8) = 100%, **P**(S_7, S_9) = 50%, **P**(S_7, S_{10}) = 50%, **P**(S_8, S_{11}) = 50%, **P**(S_8, S_{12}) = 50%, **P**(S_9, S_{13}) = 100%, **P**(S_{12}, S_{14}) =

100%, **P**(S_{13}, S_{15}) = 100%, **P**(S_{14}, S_{16}) = 100%, **P**(S_{15}, S_{17}) = 50%, **P**(S_{15}, S_{18}) = 50%, **P**(S_{16}, S_{19}) = 50%, **P**(S_{16}, S_{20}) = 50%, **P**(S_{17}, S_{21}) = 100%, **P**(S_{20}, S_{22}) = 100%, **P**(S_{21}, S_{23}) = 100%, **P**(S_{22}, S_{24}) = 100%, **P**(S_{23}, S_{25}) = 50%, **P**(S_{23}, S_{26}) = 50%, **P**(S_{24}, S_{25}) = 50%, **P**(S_{24}, S_{26}) = 50%.

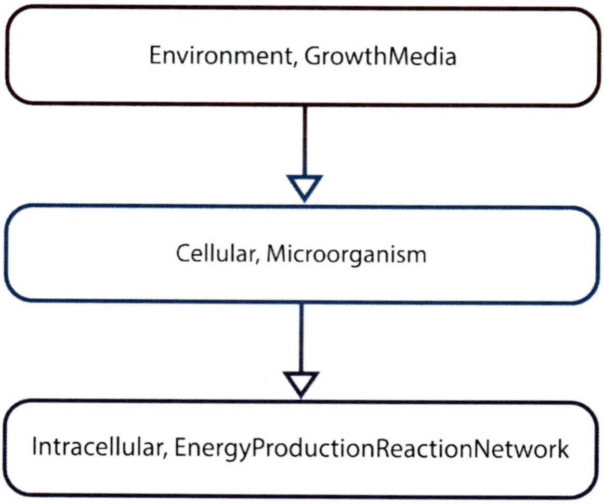

Figure 4: The multiscale architecture graph corresponding to the simple illustrative MSSpDES example.

Each vertex in the graph (e.g. (Environment, GrowthMedia)) corresponds to a subsystem (e.g. growth media) and its associated scale (e.g. environment). Directed edges between vertices (e.g. ((Environment, GrowthMedia), (Cellular, Microorganism))) indicate how one subsystem from a coarse-grained scale (e.g. (Environment, GrowthMedia)) can be decomposed in one or multiple subsystems from more fine-grained scales (e.g. (Cellular, Microorganism)).

In spite of the simplicity of the scenario described above the same model development principles apply to more complex multiscale real-life systems. However due to the inherent complexity of such systems the size of the state space is expected to be larger.

The main reason for encoding multiscale stochastic biological systems using a low-level modelling formalism such as MSSpDES is to enable our model checking approach to be employed for the general class of SDESs, which MSSpDESs extend, instead of restricting it to a particular high-level modelling formalism.

Although MSSpDES models are restricted to a two-dimensional spatial representation (see codomain of spatial value assignment functions $SpV_i \in CSpV$), extending the models from a two- to, for instance three-dimensional spatial representation, requires only replacing the codomain $\mathbb{R}^{m_i \times n_i}$ of each $SpV_i \in CSpV$ with $\mathbb{R}^{m_i \times n_i \times p_i}$.

MSSpDESs are multiscale extensions of SSpDESs ⟨S, Tr, μ, NSV, SpSV, NV, SpV⟩, where the semantics of S, μ, NSV, SpSV and NV is preserved, the transition rates matrix Tr was replaced by the set T representing time and the state transition probabilities are defined by a transition probability function **P** for discrete-time systems, respectively are derived from a transition rates matrix **Q** for continuous-time systems. The single spatial value assignment function SpV in an SSpDES is replaced by CSpV, the MA graph is defined to explicitly encode the hierarchical representation of the systems under consideration, and SVSS is introduced to associate state variables with particular scales and subsystems encoded as vertices in the MA graph. The main advantage of defining MSSpDESs as extensions of SSpDESs is backwards compatibility. SSpDESs can be encoded as MSSpDESs where the set T and probability measure μ are defined accordingly, CSpV contains a single element SpV, and the MA graph contains only one vertex to which all state variables are assigned using SVSS. Due to this, multiple SSpDESs employing the same representation of time can be easily integrated into a single MSSpDES by defining the set T and probability measure μ accordingly, gathering all spatial value assignment functions SpV into a single collection, constructing a corresponding MA graph, mapping state variables to appropriate vertices in the graph and adding interactions between submodels.

Multiscale Spatio-temporal Analysis

Detection and analysis of spatial entities.

Let us denote execution traces (or time series data) generated by MSSpDES models as $\sigma = \{(s_0, t_0), (s_1, t_1), \ldots\}$, where $s_0, s_1, \ldots$ represent the states of the execution trace and $t_0, t_1, \ldots$ the time durations spent in each corresponding state. Typically in case of a continuous-time representation the time durations are represented by non-negative real values $t_0, t_1, \ldots \in \mathbb{R}_+$, whereas in case of a discrete-time representation by non-negative integer values $t_0, t_1, \ldots \in \mathbb{Z}_+$.

Given an execution trace $\sigma = \{(s_0, t_0), (s_1, t_1), \ldots\}$, a numeric state variable nsv and a spatial state variable spsv, it is possible to reason about how the values of nsv and spsv change over time by evaluating them for each state in σ using $NV(s_0, nsv)$, $NV(s_1, nsv)$, ..., respectively $SpV(s_0, spsv)$, $SpV(s_1, spsv)$, ... Although the sequence $SpV(s_0, spsv)$, $SpV(s_1, spsv)$, ... describes how the entire discretised spatial domain $DSD = \mathbb{R}^{m_{spsv} \times n_{spsv}}$ corresponding to spsvchanges over time, we are interested in reasoning about how emergent spatial structures, called spatial entities, identified by subsets of positions in DSD change over time. For instance assuming that spsv records the cellular density in a 2D environment DSD and that we would like to reason about spatial entities denoting multicellular populations, then only the subsets comprising at least x (e.g. x = 20) neighbouring positions in DSD having the cellular density value greater than 0 would be considered. To reason about such spatial entities there is a need for an additional processing step which automatically detects and analyses how the spatial entities change over time.

This processing step is denoted as the multiscale spatio-temporal analysis and its associated workflow is depicted in Fig 5. The first step in the workflow is to split up the time series data corresponding to all spatial state variables such that each resulting time subseries corresponds to a single subsystem and scale. Next each time subseries is passed to a uniscale spatio-temporal analysis module which automatically detects, analyses and annotates spatial entities with their corresponding scale and subsystem. Finally, during the last step the collections of detected spatial entities are merged such that spatial entities corresponding to the same time point are grouped together.

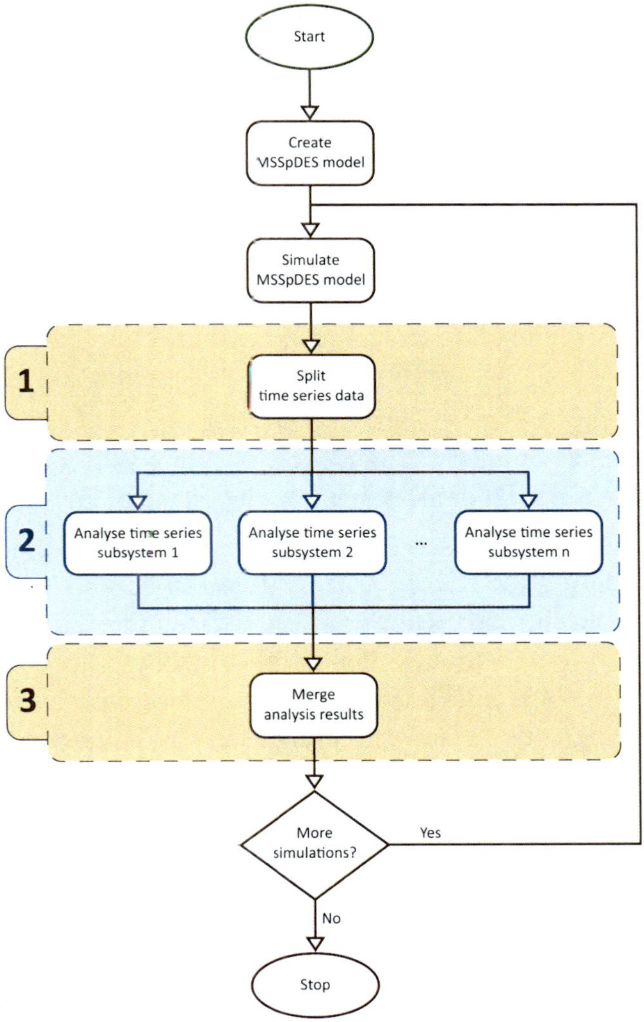

Figure 5: The multiscale spatio-temporal analysis workflow.

An MSSpDES model of the system under consideration is constructed and simulated to generate time series data. This time series data is split up into subsets (1) such that each subset corresponds to a single subsystem and scale. The time series data subsets are passed to a uniscale spatio-temporal analysis module (2) which automatically detects, analyses and annotates spatial entities with their corresponding scale and subsystem. The results of the uniscale spatio-temporal analysis are then merged

(3) such that spatial entities corresponding to the same time point are grouped together. If more simulations are required, a new time series dataset is generated, for which steps (1)–(3) are repeated.

The uniscale spatio-temporal analysis module assumes that the problem of detecting and analysing spatial entities at a given time point is transformed into an image processing problem. This transformation is possible because the spatial domain is assumed to be discretised and (the value of) each position in the discretised space can be mapped to (the intensity of) a pixel in an image. One of the main advantages of this is that existing image processing approaches for detecting and analysing objects in images can be directly reused.

We define parameterized detection and analysis modules for two generic types of spatial entities, namely regions and clusters [57].

Regions represent subsets of neighbouring positions in the discretised space (considering the Moore neighbourhood relation) with associated values (e.g. concentrations) above a user-defined threshold. For instance considering a computational model that encodes the evolution of a population of cells in a 2D environment, regions could represent patches of neighbouring cells where the cellular density is greater than a user-defined value. More formally a region R is defined with respect to a state s and spatial state variable spsv as a subset $\{0, 1\}^{m_{spsv} \times n_{spsv}}$ (i.e. positions of the discretised space included in R are marked with 1, all others with 0) of neighbouring positions in Sp V(s,spsv) such that for all positions of the discretised space (i, j) ∈ R marked with 1, the corresponding value Sp V(s, spsv)[i, j] ≥ THRESHOLD, and the number of positions included in R is greater than ϵ_{size}, where THRESHOLD ∈ $\mathbb{R}$, ϵ_{size} ∈ $\mathbb{N}$ are user-defined parameters. The module for detecting and analysing regions is an implementation of Algorithm 1 in [57] using image processing functions from the open source Computer Vision library OpenCV [62].

Conversely clusters represent subsets of neighbouring regions in the discretised space where the maximum distance between two neighbouring regions is bounded above by a user-defined threshold. For instance considering again the computational model encoding the evolution of a population of cells, clusters could represent groups of patches of cells where the distance between neighbouring patches is less or equal to a user-defined threshold value. Clusters are computed using an improved version of the DBSCAN algorithm [63]. The output of this algorithm depends on the given set of regions REG, the pseudometric d used to compute the distance between any two regions in REG, the maximum distance $\epsilon_{distance}$ between two neighbouring regions, and the minimum number of regions ϵ_{size} neighbouring a core region, where a region is denoted as core if its number of neighbouring regions is greater or equal to ϵ_{size}. The pseudometric d considered here is defined with respect to a set of regions REG, d: REG × REG → $\mathbb{R}_+$, $d(A,B) = \sqrt{(x_B - x_A)^2 + (y_B - y_A)^2}$, where (x_A, y_A) and (x_B, y_B) are the centroids of regions A, respectively B. Moreover two regions REG_1, $REG_n \in REG$ are called density-reachable if there exists a sequence of regions $REG_1, REG_2, \ldots, REG_n \in REG$, where $i \geq 1$ and $n \geq 2$ such that for all $i < n$, REG_i is a core region, and REG_{i+1} is a neighbour of REG_i. Using the notations above a cluster C is defined as a maximal subset $\{0,1\}^{m_1 \times n_1} \times \{0,1\}^{m_2 \times n_2} \times \ldots \times \{0,1\}^{m_p \times n_p}$ (i.e. regions' positions included in C are marked with 1, all others with 0) of the given set of regions $REG = \{REG_1, REG_2, \ldots, REG_p\}$ such that all regions in C are density-reachable from an arbitrary core region of C [63].

Each detected region/cluster is characterized by a set of general quantitative spatial measures that enable describing how the spatial entity changes over time. A description of the set of spatial measures considered is given in Table 1.

Table 1: Description of the spatial measures considered

Name	Values	Description
clusteredness	[0, 1]	Indicates if regions contain holes (clusteredness <1) or not (clusteredness = 1), respectively measures if the average distance between all positions considered in a cluster is small (clusteredness →1) or large (clusteredness →0).
density	[0, 1]	Computes the average value associated with the discretised spatial positions defining a region/cluster.
area	$\mathbb{R}_+$	Represents the number of positions in the discretised space associated with a region/cluster.
perimeter	$\mathbb{R}_+$	Represents the length of the outer contour of a region, respectively the convex hull of a cluster.
distance from the origin	$\mathbb{R}_+$	Computes the minimum distance between the outer contour of a region, respectively the convex hull of a cluster, and the centre point of the discretised spatial domain.
angle	[0, 360] (degrees)	Determined by the lines that pass through the discretised spatial domain's centre point and are tangent to a region's outer contour, respectively cluster's convex hull.
triangle/rectangle/circle measure	[0, 1]	Indicates if the shape of the region's outer contour, respectively cluster's convex hull, is similar to a triangle/rectangle/circle (triangle/rectangle/circle measure →1) or not (triangle/rectangle/circle measure →0).
centroid Ox/Oy coordinate	$\mathbb{R}_+$	Represents the Ox/Oy coordinate of the geometric centre of the region's outer contour, respectively cluster's convex hull.

Each spatial measure considered has a name (column "Name"), an associated range of valid values (column "Values") and a corresponding description (column "Description"). In case of spatial measures which have similar semantics the table rows have been merged and the spatial measure names are separated by the "/" symbol (see last two table rows).

doi:10.1371/journal.pone.0154847.t001

The spatial entity types and measures were chosen relative to the case studies considered here. Therefore depending on case study specific requirements different sets of spatial entity types and/or measures may need to be employed. For instance, extending the spatial representation from two to three dimensions requires employing appropriate types of spatial entities (e.g. 3D structure) and measures (e.g. volume), and updating the multiscale spatio-temporal analysis module (implementation) accordingly. Moreover (the value corresponding to) each position in the discretised space is mapped to (the intensity of) a voxel, rather than a pixel in an image. The model checking approach is adapted automatically to different spatial entity types and/or measures using the spatio-temporal meta model checking concept described later.

The output of the multiscale spatio-temporal analysis is time series data describing how the values of the spatial measures considered change over time for each detected spatial entity, scale and subsystem.

Multiscale Spatial Temporal Markup Language.

The MSSpDES model simulation results are represented by time series data produced by the multiscale spatio-temporal analysis and time series data describing the evolution over time of numeric state variables values.

To represent these model simulation results in a uniform manner which facilitates exchange of data sets and integration of software tools a corresponding standard data representation format is required. To the best of our knowledge such a standard data representation format does not exist.

One of the main requirements for the data representation format is that it supports recording different numbers of values at different time points because the collection of (emergent) spatial entities considered could potentially change over time. Traditional tabular (e.g. csv) representation formats are not suitable because they assume that the number of recorded values (or columns) is constant throughout the entire time series. Moreover defining a representation format similar to csv that does not annotate numeric values with their meaning could be potentially difficult to interpret.

For portability, structuring and readability purposes an eXtensible Markup Language (XML) based standard representation format is defined called Multiscale Spatial Temporal Markup Language (MSTML). The rules and constraints for the structure of MSTML files are formalised in XML Schema Definition (xsd) files. The latest version of the MSTML format is made available at http://mule.modelchecking.org/standards, and an example of an MSTML formatted file is depicted in Listing 1.

Listing 1. An example MSTML file recording multiscale spatio-temporal time series data.

```
<?xml version="1.0" encoding="utf -8"?>
<experiment>
  <timepoint value="1">
    <spatialEntity spatialType="cluster" scaleAndSubsystem="Organ.Liver">
      <clusteredness>0.01</clusteredness>
      <density>0.4</density>
      <area>15</area>
      <perimeter>28</perimeter>
      <distanceFromOrigin>81</distanceFromOrigin>
       <angle>10.5</angle>
       <triangleMeasure>0.5</triangleMeasure>
       <rectangleMeasure>1.0</rectangleMeasure>
       <circleMeasure>0.1</circleMeasure>
       <centroidX>703.4999</centroidX>
       <centroidY>118.087</centroidY>
    </spatialEntity>
    <numericStateVariable scaleAndSubsystem="Cellular.Hepatocyte">
       <name>dysfunction</name>
       <value>0.1</value>
    </numericStateVariable>
  </timepoint>
  ...
</experiment>
```

For model checking purposes the number of MSTML files #MSTML generated for an MSSpDES model assuming fixed parameter values varies depending if the model is deterministic (#MSTML = 1) or stochastic (#MSTML $\geq$ 1), and if the required level of confidence for the model checking result is high (e.g. 99%) or low (e.g. 70%).

To determine the correctness of a model the model checker verifies if its behavior captured by a corresponding set of MSTML files conforms to a given formal specification.

Formal Specification

The temporal logic employed to write the formal specification needs to enable reasoning about how values of numeric state variables and/or spatial measures, which are the state variables considered, are expected to change over time and multiple scales.

To the best of our knowledge the only formal language for reasoning about numeric and spatial properties corresponding to computational models of biological systems is called Bounded Linear Spatial Temporal Logic (BLSTL), which we have previously introduced in [57]. One of the main limitations of BLSTL is that it does not enable different scales to be explicitly distinguished. Therefore it is not possible to relate how changes at one scale reflect at another scale and vice versa.

Bounded Linear Multiscale Spatial Temporal Logic.

To address the issue of relating changes between scales we define the Bounded Linear Multiscale Spatial Temporal Logic (BLMSTL) which enables explicitly distinguishing between state variables corresponding to different scales and subsystems. Throughout it is assumed that the scales and subsystems considered are the same as the ones defined in the MA graph of the corresponding MSSpDES model. Although MSSpDESs can be employed to represent both discrete- and continuous-time stochastic discrete-event systems, the semantics of a temporal logic usually varies with the considered representation of time. Therefore in this paper we restrict the semantics of BLMSTL to a continuous-time representation (similarly to CSL [64] and in contrast to BLSTL). However adapting BLMSTL to a discrete-time representation requires changing only the semantics of the time dependent operators, whereas the definition of all other atomic propositions (related to different scales and subsystems, numeric state variables, and spatial entities) is preserved.

BLMSTL enables reasoning about how collections, or more formally bags, of spatial measures values from one time point, and collections of numeric state variables and spatial measures values corresponding to multiple time points change over time using statistical functions. Transfer relations between state variables from the same and/or different scales are encoded using standard arithmetic functions. An informal natural language description of the most relevant BLMSTL features is given below.

Similarly to BLSTL, BLMSTL employs temporal and Boolean operators for describing how a system changes over time, respectively for composing simple logic statements into more complex ones. BLMSTL atomic propositions enable describing relations between numeric state variables and/or spatial measures associated to subsets of spatial entities.

Numeric state variables are specified by their name (e.g. heartBeat) and their associated scale and subsystem (e.g. (organ, heart)); the corresponding BLMSTL notation for specifying scales and subsystems is scale.subsystem (e.g. organ.heart). Conversely spatial measures associated with subsets of spatial entities are specified by their spatial measure type (e.g. area), associated spatial entity type (e.g. regions) and their corresponding scale and subsystem. Similarly to MSTML the sets of spatial entity types and spatial measures considered are $SET_{considered}$ = {clusters, regions}, respectively $SM_{considered}$ = {clusteredness, density, area, perimeter, distanceFromOrigin, angle, triangleMeasure, rectangleMeasure, circleMeasure, centroidX, centroidY}.

Instead of considering all spatial entities of a given type it is possible to select only a subset of spatial entities by imposing constraints over the spatial measure values (e.g. spatial entities with area > 10), by using subset operators \ (difference), ∩ (intersection) and ∪ (union), or specifying one or multiple scales and subsystems using the partial orders $<$ and $\leq$ defined over the set of vertices V_{MA} (e.g. spatial entities whose corresponding scale and subsystem < (organ, heart)).

The resulting collection of spatial measures values corresponding to multiple spatial entities (e.g. value of the area for all detected spatial entities) can be described using unary (e.g. mean), binary (e.g. covariance) or binary quantile (e.g. percentile) statistical functions. These statistical functions can be additionally employed to reason about collections of numeric state variables and spatial measures values corresponding to multiple time points (e.g. the value of numeric state variable X for all time points in the time interval [0, 100]). By considering different numbers of time points for different state variables it is possible, for instance, to describe how values corresponding to one time point (and a coarse-grained scale) relate to other values corresponding to multiple time points (and a fine-grained scale), or vice versa.

Transfer functions defined over state variables from different scales can be encoded using unary (e.g. square root) and binary (e.g. add) arithmetic functions. For instance if the value of a state variable sv_{cg} from a coarse-grained scale is equal to the arithmetic mean of four state variables sv_{fg1}, sv_{fg2}, sv_{fg3}, sv_{fg4} from a more fine-grained scale, this can be written as $sv_{cg} = (sv_{fg1}+sv_{fg2}+sv_{fg3}+sv_{fg4})/4$; in BLMSTL "+" and "/" would be replaced by the arithmetic functions add, respectively div.

Illustrative examples of statements written both in natural language and BLMSTL are given below. For simplicity the number of scales and subsystems explicitly specified is two in all examples.

- **Natural language:** Always during the time interval [0, 95] if the concentration of EGFR (corresponding to scale and subsystem (Intracellular, RasERKPathway)) increases over 20 M, then the cancerous cell (corresponding to scale and subsystem (Cellular, Cancerous)) will divide i.e. the cell count will increase.
  BLMSTL: G[0, 95] (({EGFR}(scaleAndSubsystem = Intracellular.RasERKPathway) > 20) ⇒
  (d(count(density(filter(regions, scaleAndSubsystem = Cellular.Cancerous)))) > 0)).
- **Natural language:** If the concentration of drug X (corresponding to scale and subsystem (Organism, Human)) eventually increases during time interval [5, 10], then the area of the aorta cross section (corresponding to scale and subsystem (OrganSystem, Aorta)) will be larger during time interval [10, 30] than [0, 10].
  BLMSTL: (F [5, 10] d({X}(scaleAndSubsystem = Organism.Human)) >0) ⇒
  (min([10, 30] min(area(filter(regions, scaleAndSubsystem = OrganSystem.Aorta)))) >
  max([0, 10] max(area(filter(regions, scaleAndSubsystem = OrganSystem.Aorta))))).
- **Natural language:** Always during the time interval [0, 100] the liver dysfunction measure (corresponding to scale and subsystem (Organ, Liver)) is equal to the average density of damaged liver tissues (corresponding to scales and subsystems ≤ (Tissue, DamagedLiverTissue)). The assumption made here is that the density value represents the degree of damage suffered by the liver tissue.
  BLMSTL:G [0, 100] ({LiverDysfunction} (scaleAndSubsystem =

Organ.Liver) = avg(density(filter(regions, scaleAndSubsystem ≤ Tissue.DamagedLiverTissue)))).

To enable the explicit encoding of the probability with which a BLMSTL statement is expected to hold, a probabilistic extension of BLMSTL called Probabilistic Bounded Linear Multiscale Spatial Temporal Logic is defined.

Probabilistic Bounded Linear Multiscale Spatial Temporal Logic.

A Probabilistic Bounded Linear Multiscale Spatial Temporal Logic (PBLMSTL) property φ is a logic property of the form $P_{\bowtie\theta}[\psi]$ where $\bowtie \in \{<, <=, >=, >\}$, $\theta \in (0, 1)$ and ψ is a BLMSTL property.

An illustrative example of a natural language probabilistic statement mapped into PBLMSTL is given below:

1. **Natural language:** The probability is greater than 0.99 that always during the time interval [0, 95] if the concentration of EGFR (corresponding to scale and subsystem (Intracellular, RasERKPathway)) increases over 20 M, then the cancerous cell (corresponding to scale and subsystem (Cellular, Cancerous)) will divide i.e. the cell count will increase.
   PBLMSTL: P > 0.99 [G[0, 95] (({EGFR}(scaleAndSubsystem = Intracellular.RasERKPathway) > 20) ⇒ (d(count(density(filter(regions, scaleAndSubsystem = Cellular.Cancerous)))) > 0))].

A PBLMSTL property $\varphi \equiv P_{\bowtie\theta}[\psi]$ holds for an MSSpDES $\mathcal{M}$ if and only if the probability of ψ to hold for a model simulation is $\bowtie\theta$. Therefore in order to determine the truth value of a PBLMSTL property φ the likelihood of ψ being true needs to be computed.

Model Checking

The multiscale spatio-temporal model checking problem is to automatically verify if an MSSpDES $\mathcal{M}$ satisfies a PBLMSTL property φ.

In order to solve the model checking problem only approximate probabilistic model checking approaches are considered throughout. As illustrated in Table 2 the approaches considered are either Bayesian or frequentist, and estimate or hypothesis testing based; a brief description of each approach was given in our previous work [57] and will not be restated here.

Table 2: Considered approximate probabilistic model checking approaches

Name	Type	Input	Description	Sample size	Ref.
Chernoff-Hoeffding bounds based	FE	ϵ, δ	The absolute difference between the estimated p and true p' probability of ψ to hold is greater than ϵ with probability less than δ (i.e. $P[\lvert p - p' \rvert > \epsilon] < \delta$).	$n = \frac{4}{\epsilon^2} \log\left(\frac{2}{\delta}\right)$	[65]
Improved frequentist statistical hypothesis testing	FH	α, β	Wald's sequential probability ratio test [66] is employed to decide if the null hypothesis H_0 is rejected in favour of the alternative hypothesis H_1 considering the upper bounds on the probability of type I and type II errors α, respectively β.	The value of n is determined during the execution of the model checking approach considering α, β and the number and order of MSTML files against which ψ evaluates true; see ([67] [p. 21]) for an approach on how to compute an upper bound for n.	[59, 68]
Probabilistic black-box	FH	-	The p-value associated with the null and alternative hypotheses H_0, respectively H_1 is computed after evaluating the n MSTML files against ψ. The hypothesis with the lowest corresponding p-value holds.	$n > 0$	[69, 70]
Bayesian mean and variance based	BE	α, β, T	The probability p and variance v of ψ to hold are estimated considering the given MSTML files and the Beta prior parameters α and β. New MSTML files are evaluated against ψ until the condition $v < T$ holds.	The value of n is determined during the execution of the model checking approach considering α, β, T and the number and order of MSTML files against which ψ evaluates true.	[71]
Bayesian statistical hypothesis testing	BH	α, β, T	A measure $\mathcal{B}$ of confidence in the null hypothesis H_0 relative to the alternative hypothesis H_1 is computed considering the Beta prior parameters α and β. New MSTML files are evaluated against ψ until either $\mathcal{B} > T$ or $\mathcal{B} < 1/T$.	The value of n is determined during the execution of the model checking approach considering α, β, T and the number and order of MSTML files against which ψ evaluates true.	[72, 73]

Each table body row corresponds to a different approximate probabilistic model checking approach. The columns from left to right record the name, type (i.e. F—Frequentist, B—Bayesian, E—Estimate, H—Hypothesis testing), input parameters (excluding ϕ and MSTML files), description, sample size (i.e. n) and reference corresponding to a model checking approach. The null (i.e. H_0) and alternative (i.e. H_1) hypotheses represent ϕ (e.g. $P_{>\theta}[\psi]$), respectively the opposite of ϕ (e.g. $P_{\leq\theta}[\psi]$). Bayesian methods consider prior knowledge when deciding if a logic property holds. Conversely frequentist approaches assume that no prior knowledge is available. All methods except probabilistic black-box take as input a user-defined upper bound on the approximation error. They request additional model simulations until the result is sufficiently accurate. Conversely probabilistic black-box model checking takes a fixed number of model simulations as input and computes a p-value as the confidence measure of the result.

doi:10.1371/journal.pone.0154847.t002

By means of approximate probabilistic model checking approaches the verification of a PBLMSTL specification against an MSSpDES model is guaranteed to terminate. Therefore the corresponding multiscale spatio-temporal model checking problem is well-defined. Intuitively the main idea behind the proof is to show that in order to verify an MSSpDES model the number of required model simulations is finite, and that the number of time points considered for each model simulation is bounded. Therefore the PBLMSTL specification is evaluated against a finite number of time points and model simulations, which can be done in a finite number of steps.

Spatio-temporal Meta Model Checking

One of the main limitations of our methodology, as described up to this point, is that the evolution over time of spatial properties can be described only with respect to the predefined collections of spatial entity types $SET_{considered}$ = {clusters, regions} and spatial measures $SM_{considered}$

= {clusteredness, density, area, perimeter, distanceFromOrigin, angle, triangleMeasure, rectangleMeasure, circleMeasure, centroidX, centroidY}.

In order to overcome this limitation and enable automatically reconfiguring the methodology according to case study specific spatial entity types and measures, we define a generalized version of the multiscale spatio-temporal model checking methodology called multiscale spatio-temporal meta model checking in which $SET_{considered}$ and $SM_{considered}$ are replaced with meta collections of spatial entity types SET, and spatial measures SM, defined as follows:

- $SET = \{sety \mid sety$ is a spatial entity type for which there exists a corresponding spatial detection mechanism f_{sety}, $f_{sety} : SpSV^p \rightarrow \{0,1\}^{m_1 \times n_1} \times \{0,1\}^{m_2 \times n_2} \times \ldots \times \{0,1\}^{m_p \times n_p}$, which detects sets of spatial entities SE of type $sety$ in the discretised spatial domain$\}$.

  Considering the spatial state variable tuples spsvt ∈ $SpSV^p$, f_{sety} computes which positions of the discretised space are occupied (1) by spatial entities or not (0); see [57] for examples of spatial detection mechanisms corresponding to the spatial entity types clusters and regions.
- SM = {sm | sm is a spatial measure, sm: SE → SMV ⊆ ℝ, where SE is a set of spatial entities and SMV is the corresponding domain of valid spatial measure values}; similarly see [57] for examples of spatial measures corresponding to the spatial entity types clusters and regions.

These collections are called meta because they provide only a description of the conditions which should hold for each spatial entity type and spatial measure but do not explicitly define instances thereof.

The multiscale spatio-temporal meta model checking methodology enables the creation of different multiscale spatio-temporal model checking methodology instances by replacing SETand SM with case study specific collections of spatial entity types and spatial measures. These instances can then be used to verify corresponding MSSpDES models. For instance, in order to verify computational models considering a 3D representation of space a corresponding model checking methodology instance could be created that replaces SET and SM with SET_{3D} =

{cuboid, cylinder, sphere} and SM_{3D} = {volume, centroidX, centroidY, centroidZ}.

A graphical description of the workflow employed to create multiscale spatio-temporal model checking methodology instances is given in Fig 6. For simplicity a single multiscale model checking methodology instance is considered throughout this paper corresponding to the collections of spatial entity types and measures $SET_{considered}$, respectively $SM_{considered}$.

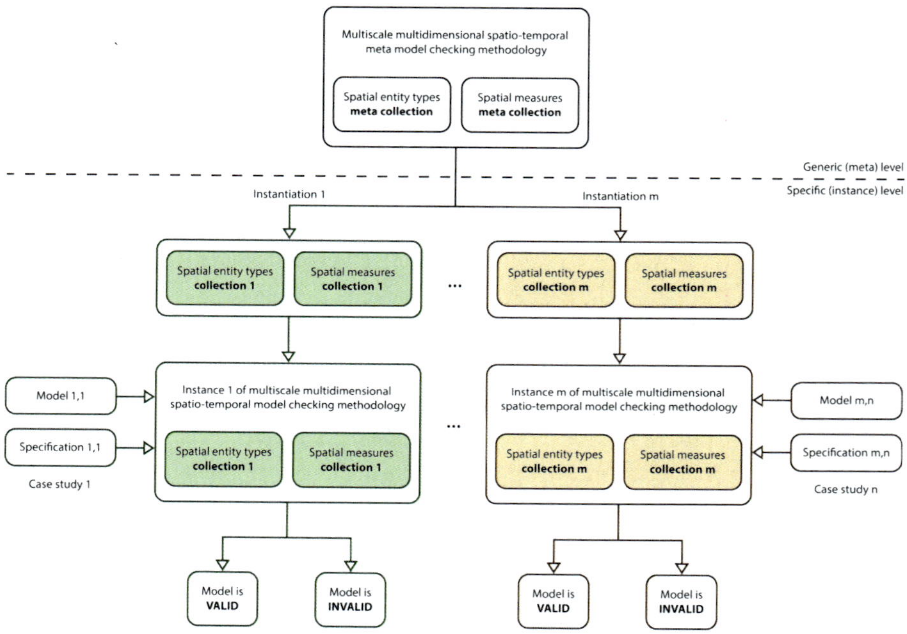

Figure 6: Workflow for creating multiscale spatio-temporal model checking methodology instances.

The workflow comprises two levels, the upper generic (meta) level, and the lower specific (instance) level. The upper level comprises the multiscale spatio-temporal meta model checking methodology. Conversely the lower level consists of the specific collections of spatial entity types and measures employed to create multiscale spatio-temporal model checking methodology instances. For each considered pair (e.g. m) of spatial entity types and spatial measures collections a corresponding multiscale model checking methodology instance is created. The resulting methodology instances (e.g. m) can then be employed for various case studies (e.g. n) to decide if computational models (e.g. m,n) are correct relative to corresponding formal specifications (e.g. m,n) or not. Rounded rectangles and arrows having the same border/line colour correspond to the same collections of spatial entity types and spatial measures.

Whenever creating new multiscale model checking methodology instances there is an additional need to define corresponding image processing functions for automatically detecting and analysing spatial entities in time series data. However such functions can often be defined based on existing approaches from the image processing literature.

When verifying an MSSpDES model relative to a formal PBLMSTL specification, the number of required model simulations and the number of required state transitions for each model simulation do not depend directly on the considered collections of spatial entity types and spatial measures. Therefore regardless of the considered instances of SET and SM the multiscale spatio-temporal model checking problem is well-defined.

Implementation

The multiscale spatio-temporal meta model checking approach was implemented in the model checking software Mule which enables automatically verifying multilevel computational models of biological systems relative to formal specifications; the model checker name is a concatenation of the first and last two letters in the word "Multiscale". For efficiency purposes Mule was implemented in C++ and supports all approximate probabilistic model checking approaches described in Table 2.

Depending on the approximate probabilistic model checking approach employed the number of MSTML files required to verify if the computational model is valid relative to a PBLMSTL specification is computed differently. In case of Chernoff-Hoeffding bounds based and probabilistic black-box model checking approaches the number of required MSTML files can be computed before running Mule (i.e.

statically). Conversely in case of the improved frequentist and Bayesian statistical hypothesis testing, and Bayesian mean and variance based model checking approaches the number of required MSTML files is determined only during the execution of Mule (i.e. dynamically). To support generating MSTML files on-demand Mule can take as input the path to a script (in our case Bash script) that simulates a computational model and stores the resulting output in MSTML files; run Mule with the command line argument —help for more execution details.

The workflow for generating multiscale spatio-temporal model checker instances was implemented as described in Fig 7. The main idea behind the implementation is to use two instead of one compilation (or translation) steps. The first compilation step takes a description of the spatial entity types and measures as input and produces C++ source code as output. The second compilation step translates the generated C++ source code in binary (i.e. executable) format. Conceptually this approach is called "meta" because Mule is an abstract multiscale spatio-temporal (meta) model checker that can be instantiated according to case study specific spatial entity types and measures. From a practical point of view the user modifies only the description of the spatial entity types and measures, while the source code and the corresponding executables are automatically generated for him/her.

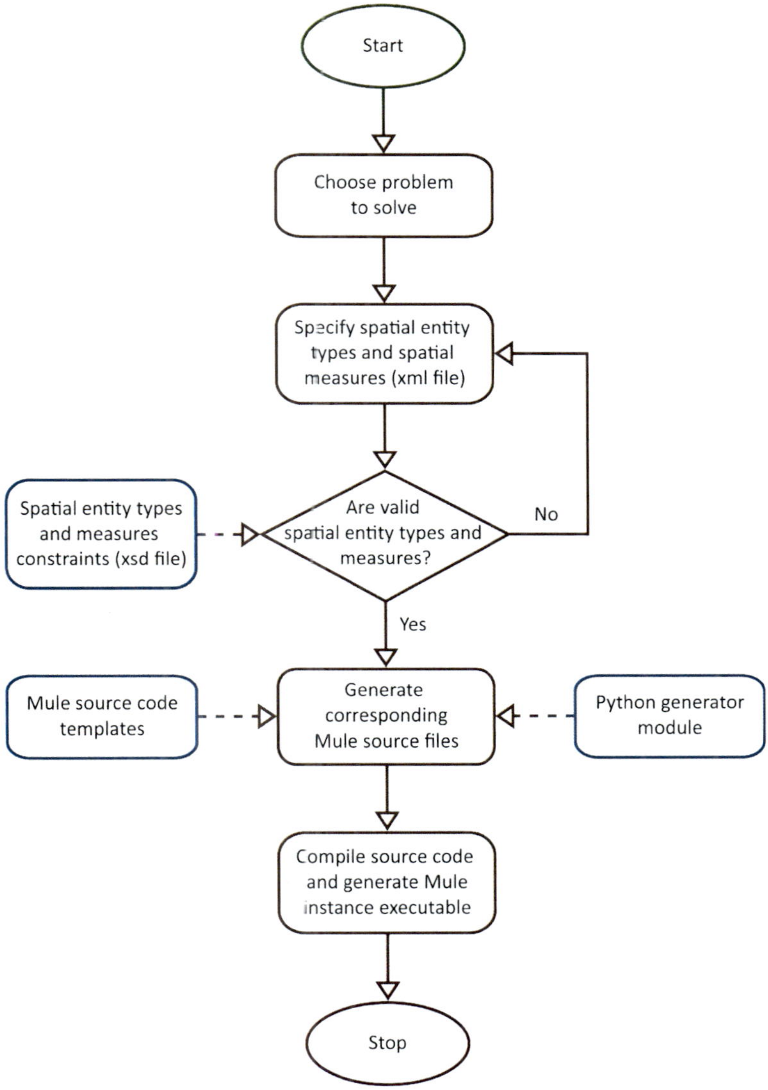

Figure 7: Implementation of workflow for generating multiscale spatio-temporal model checker instances according to user-defined spatial entity types and spatial measures.

Starting from the problem one tries to solve, an xml file is created describing the collections of spatial entity types and spatial measures of interest. These collections are then verified with respect to relevant constraints captured by an xsd file; see http://mule.modelchecking.org/

standards for the latest version of the xsd file. If the xml file verification fails then the specification of the spatial entity types and measures needs to be updated accordingly. Otherwise the xml file is employed by a C++ source code generator/translator written in Python to generate the corresponding Mule source files based on a set of predefined templates. The source files are compiled to produce an executable version of the corresponding Mule instance. This instance can then be employed to verify corresponding computational models.

The main advantage of the workflow depicted in Fig 7 is that it enables the considered spatial entity types and measures to be compiled into the model checking executable instead of being (dynamically) loaded at runtime, which could negatively impact the model checker performance.

Mule was implemented as an offline model checker and takes as input model simulation traces rather than the computational models used to generate them. Using trace analysis each model simulation trace is evaluated against the PBLMSTL specification. The trace analysis results corresponding to multiple model simulation traces are used by the employed model checking approach to determine if the PBLMSTL specification holds for the model.

The main advantage of implementing Mule as an offline model checker is that it is decoupled from the specific modelling formalisms employed to encode the computational models. Consequently Mule can be employed to verify computational models encoded using various modelling formalisms provided that the corresponding computational models satisfy the constraints of an MSSpDES model without requiring the explicit translation of the computational models to MSSpDES. In addition given that Mule takes simulation traces (i.e. time series data) as input it can be employed to evaluate PBLMSTL specifications both against time series data generated in silico or recorded in vitro. Conversely the main disadvantages of Mule are that the computational models need to be constructed and simulated using external tools, and the model simulation output needs to be stored in or translated to csv format. To generate model simulations on demand Mule needs to be able to execute the model simulator from the command line.

In contrast to Mule inline approximate probabilistic model checkers (e.g. COSMOS [74], PLASMA [75], PRISM [76], UPPAAL-SMC [77], Ymer [78]) are integrated modelling and verification environments that can be employed not only to verify, but also to construct and simulate computational models. In addition inline model checkers are usually more efficient than their offline counterparts, because model simulations can be generated on-demand, in-memory and potentially stopped early (i.e. as soon as the considered logic statement is accepted/rejected). However inline model checkers typically require explicitly encoding computational models in the model checker specific modelling formalism, and they can not be employed to evaluate formal specifications against time series data recorded in vitro.

Both the source code and the executable corresponding to the Mule instance employed throughout this paper are made freely available online at http://mule.modelchecking.org; this Mule instance is defined with respect to the collection of spatial entity types $SET_{considered}$ and spatial measures $SM_{considered}$. Moreover a corresponding Docker image has been created providing a self-contained environment for executing/updating model checker instances which can be run on all major operating systems without additional setup (except installing the freely available software Docker).

RESULTS

We illustrate the applicability of the model checker based on four multiscale systems biology case studies published in the literature. The case studies were chosen such that the corresponding computational models are of different types (i.e. deterministic/hybrid/stochastic), span different levels of organization (e.g. cellular/organ) and are encoded using different modelling formalisms (e.g. ordinary differential equations/ cellular automata) and software (e.g. Morpheus/NetLogo); see Table 3 for a brief comparison of the multilevel computational models considered.

Table 3: Considered multilevel systems biology computational models against which the proposed model checking methodology and implementation were validated

	M1	M2	M3	M4
Description	Rat cardiovascular system dynamics	Uterine contractions of labour	*Xenopus laevis* cell cycle	Acute inflammation of the gut and lung
Model type	Deterministic	Deterministic	Hybrid	Stochastic
Modelling formalism(s)	Ordinary differential equations (ODE)	Cellular automata (CA)	ODEs + Cellular Potts model (CPM)	Agent based modelling (ABM)
Modelling software	JSim	Mathematica	Morpheus	NetLogo
Explicit spatial representation	N	Y	Y	Y
Levels of organization	Cellular + Organ system	Cellular + Tissue	Intracellular + Cellular	Cellular + Tissue + Organ
Case study reference	[13]	[14]	[15]	[16]
Model download link	http://virtualrat.org/sites/default/files/downloads/Workflow_Model_Files_12April2012.zip	http://s3-eu-west-1.amazonaws.com/files.figshare.com/1720626/Supporting_Information_S1	http://imc.zih.tu-dresden.de/wiki/morpheus/doku.php?id=examples:multiscale#odes_in_cpm_cellscell_cycle_and_proliferation	http://bionetgen.org/SCAI-wiki/images/7/7d/GutLungAxis2.1.nlogo

Each model (M1–M4) has an associated description and type (i.e. deterministic, stochastic or hybrid), was encoded using specific modelling formalisms and software, represents space explicitly or not (Y—Yes, N—No), spans different levels of organization, and has a corresponding reference paper and download link.

doi:10.1371/journal.pone.0154847.t003

Since Mule is implemented as an offline model checker and all approximate probabilistic model checking algorithms employed here (see Table 2) are defined relative to simulation traces, the computational models M1–M4 were not explicitly translated to an MSSpDES representation. Instead the computational models encoded using high-level modelling formalisms were simulated and the simulation output was stored in MSTML files. These MSTML files were then provided as input to the model checker Mule. There are two main reasons for employing the computational models encoded in high-level modelling formalisms (as developed by their original authors) instead of MSSpDES. First of all simulating an MSSpDES computational model on a computer requires defining an MSSpDES operational semantics, which was not given here. Secondly approximations inherent to the translation of computational models between different modelling formalisms could potentially impact the outcome of the model checker execution.

In case of the deterministic continuous-state computational model M1 an alternative approach, which is not considered here, would have been to translate M1 into a stochastic discrete-state computational model. Using the approach described by Wilkinson [79] and under the assumption that the volume of the media containing the species in the model is known, concentrations can be converted into discrete numbers of molecules, and deterministic into stochastic kinetic rate constants. The main reason for not translating M1 into a stochastic model is that we want to illustrate that Mule can be employed to verify existing deterministic continuous-state computational models relative to PBLMSTL specifications without the need to initially alter the models. The probability of a PBLMSTL specification to hold for the deterministic continuous-state model M1 is either 1 (i.e. true) or 0 (i.e. false).

The natural language and corresponding formal specifications, against which the models were verified, have been derived from the original papers introducing the case studies. Quotes from the original papers have been employed to create initial natural language statements describing the expected system behaviour. The initial natural language statements were then rephrased to match the constructs and structure typical to formal PBLMSTL statements; the resulting statements are called rephrased natural language statements. Finally the rephrased natural language statements were manually mapped into corresponding PBLMSTL statements. Where insufficient information was available (e.g. probabilities) the numeric values employed in the formal specification are quantitative approximations of the corresponding natural language descriptions (e.g. with high probability ⇒ 0.9). The main purpose of the PBLMSTL statements considered is to illustrate the expressivity of the methodology and not to predict previously unknown biologically relevant properties. For reproducibility purposes the mapping between quotes from the original papers, derived natural language statements and corresponding PBLMSTL specifications is documented in the supplementary materials.

The model checking approach employed to verify the deterministic computational models (M1 and M2) was probabilistic black-box because it does not place a lower bound on the required number of model simulations and therefore is suitable for computational models which are simulated only once. Conversely for the verification of the hybrid (M3) and stochastic (M4) computational models improved frequentist statistical hypothesis testing was employed setting the values of both input parameters α (i.e. probability of type I errors) and β (i.e. probability of type II errors) to 5%. Therefore the number of model simulations considered for the verification of computational models M3 and M4 was variable and computed relative to the values of the input parameters α and β, respectively fixed and was equal to one for computational models M1 and M2.

All approximate probabilistic model checking approaches supported by Mule (see Table 2) were previously introduced by other authors and are not directly dependent on PBLMSTL. Therefore a comparison between the different model checking approaches, although interesting, goes beyond the scope of this paper.

The computational models have been simulated, analysed and verified using the same regular desktop computer (Linux x64, Intel Core i5-2500 CPU @1.6 GHz, 16 GB DDR3 RAM memory). To assess the performance of the approach execution times have been recorded for all relevant steps of the model checking workflow.

Finally, for comparison purposes, the case studies and the corresponding computational models will not be described individually but in parallel considering the steps of the model checking workflow (i.e. model construction, multiscale spatio-temporal analysis, formal specification, model checking).

Model Construction

Rat cardiovascular system dynamics.

The cardiovascular system comprises the heart, blood and blood vessels, and is the organ system responsible for delivering oxygen and nutrients to, and removing waste products from the entire organism. Its dynamics changes in case of a transient increase of the thoracic pressure (e.g. by performing the Valsalva manoeuvre) which leads to reduced blood flow in the right atrium, reduced cardiac output and decreased aortic pressure [13].

In order to describe the behavioural changes of the cardiovascular system during the Valsalva manoeuvre Beard et al. built a multiscale non-spatial ODE model [13] by integrating two previously existing models. The first model is an abstract representation of the cardiovascular system [80]. Conversely the second model encodes the baroreflex mechanism [81] which is employed to maintain the blood pressure of an organism at approximately constant levels. One of the main advantages of the integrated multiscale model is that it enables relating changes at the entire cardiovascular system level with changes at the baroreflex mechanism level and vice versa, which was not possible when employing the constituent models separately. The hierarchical organization of the resulting model is encoded by the MA graph depicted in Fig 8.

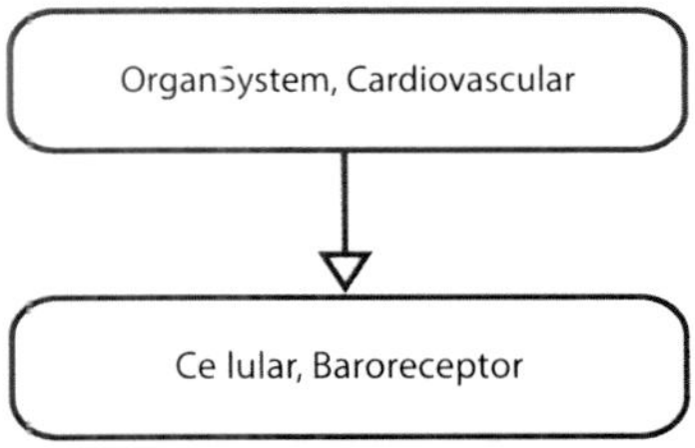

Figure 8: MA **graph representing the** multiscale organization of the rat cardiovascular system dynamics computational model.

For verification purposes the numeric state variables considered at the organ system scale are the thoracic pressure and the heart rate, and the aortic pressure at the cellular scale.

Uterine contractions of labour.

Although it is known that usually during human labour regions across the entire uterus contract in a coordinated fashion the underlying mechanisms by which an initial local contraction propagates to the entire organ level are not fully understood [14].

One hypothesis is that a positive feedback loop is created between the tissue level contractions and the intrauterine pressure as follows: An initial tissue level contraction increases the intrauterine pressure and adds tension to the neighbouring regions, which in response start to contract, thus increasing the intrauterine pressure even further and adding tension to their corresponding neighbouring regions which also start to contract, and the entire process is repeated until all contractible regions across the entire organ are recruited.

In order to test this hypothesis Young and Barendse developed a corresponding predictive deterministic computational model [14]. The model was encoded as a cellular automaton in Mathematica and spans two levels of organization, the organ level for the uterus, and the tissue level for the uterine regions; see Fig 9 for the corresponding MA graph.

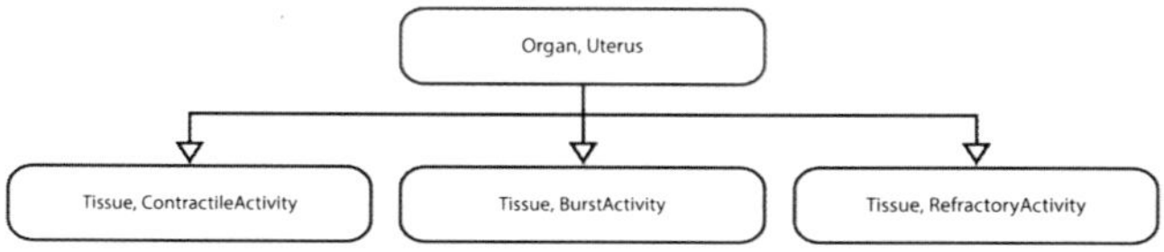

Figure 9: MA **graph representing the** multiscale organization of the uterine contractions of labour computational model.

At the organ (i.e. uterus) scale the numeric state variable considered is the intrauterine pressure and space is encoded explicitly as a 4×4 grid, where each grid position represents a tissue (i.e. uterine region). Conversely at the tissue level there is no explicit representation of space and the recorded numeric state variables are the contractile, burst and refractory activities of the uterine regions.

Xenopus laevis cell cycle.

The cell cycle is a fundamental biological process which is responsible for the replication/division of cells and is involved in the development and partial renewal of organisms. Its complexity is usually proportional to the complexity of the considered organism. Therefore it is studied in lower and less complex organisms such as the Xenopus laevis frog.

To gain a better understanding of the Xenopus laevis embryonic cell cycle and how it affects cellular population growth the developers of the modelling software Morpheus [82] built a corresponding multiscale computational model [83]. The computational model describes how three proteins CDK1, Plk1 and APC regulate the cell cycle at the intracellular level using ODEs [15], and how cells divide and are displaced in 2D space at the cellular level using a CPM. The corresponding MA graph is depicted in Fig 10.

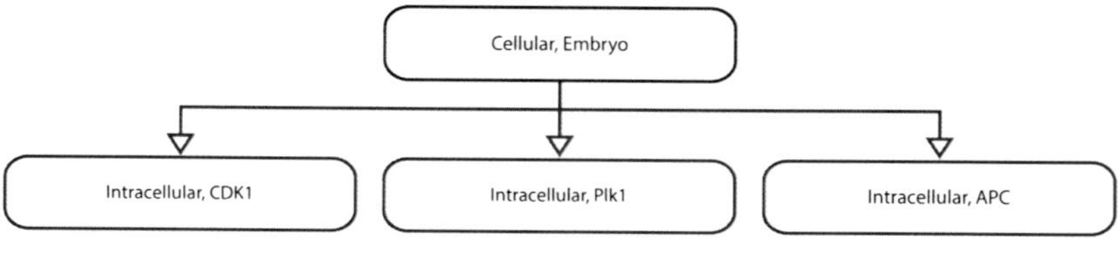

Figure 10: MA **graph representing the** multiscale organization of the Xenopus laeviscell cycle computational model.

At the cellular level space is represented explicitly as a 52 × 52 grid recording the spatial distribution of the population of cells. Conversely at the intracellular level there is no explicit representation of space and the numeric state variables considered are the concentrations of CDK1, Plk1 and APC.

Acute inflammation of the gut and lung.

There is no single definition of inflammation in the literature [84] but here we will interpret it as the response of a biological system to bodily damaging stimuli. Depending on the intensity of the stimulus an inflammatory response initiated in one organ can propagate to other organs and eventually lead to multiple organ failure [16].

To gain a better understanding of the relation between inflammatory responses and multiple organ failure, G. An [16] built a multiscale agent-based computational model using the software NetLogo which describes how the inflammation of either the gut (i.e. gut ischemia) or lung (i.e. pneumonia) could potentially lead to the failure of both organs. The levels of organization considered in the computational model are cellular (for representing endothelial and epithelial cells), tissue (for representing the organ luminal space, the blood vessel luminal space, and the endothelial and epithelial layers), and organ (for representing the gut and lung); see Fig 11 for the corresponding MA graph.

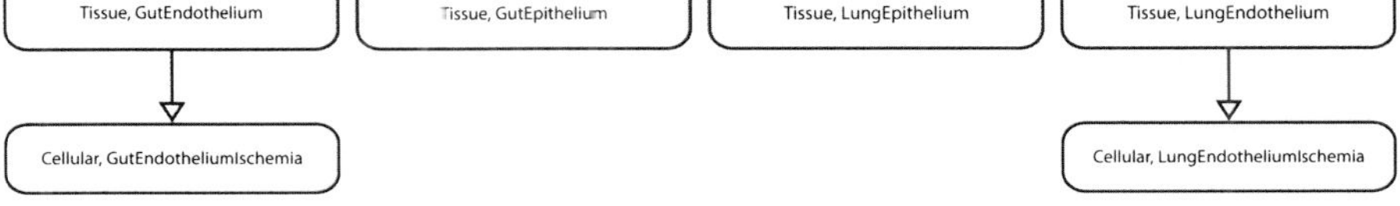

Figure 11: MA **graph representing the** multiscale organization of the acute inflammation of the gut and lung computational model.

The organism level is not modelled explicitly and the corresponding vertex (Organism, Human) was added to the MA graph in Fig 11 only to ensure that its structure is tree-like. At the organ level space is not represented explicitly and the numeric state variables considered represent the amount of solute which leaked into the gut and lung. Conversely at the tissue level space is represented explicitly as a 31×31 grid where each grid position represents a cell. The tissue level numeric state variables considered for both gut and lung are the total concentration of cytoplasm and cell wall occludin, and the total cell damage by-product. At the cellular level the numeric state variables considered encode the level of ischemia for both gut and lung endothelial cells.

Multiscale Spatio-temporal Analysis

The computational models M1–M4 were simulated and the simulation results were translated to MSTML. The computational model simulation end time was computed as per Definition 1.

The translation of the simulation results to MSTML comprises multiple steps. First of all the model simulation output is converted to csv format in order to ensure that the time series data provided as input to the multiscale spatio-temporal analysis module is represented in a uniform manner. Secondly an MSTML subfile is generated for each considered time point, numeric state variable and spatial region comprising one or multiple grid positions. In the end all subfiles are merged into a single MSTML file. The main difference between the csv and corresponding MSTML file is that for each time point the former records the values associated to entire discretised spatial domains, whereas the latter only captures the properties of the detected spatial entities. The main advantage of storing to disk the results of the csv to MSTML translation, and providing MSTML instead of csv files as input to the model checker is reusability. MSTML files can be employed for the evaluation of different PBLMSTL specifications in separate executions of the model checker without the need to run the csv to MSTML translation each time.

Execution times for the model simulation and subsequent translation steps corresponding to all computational models are given in Table 4.

Table 4: Model simulation and analysis execution times for the rat cardiovascular system dynamics, the uterine contractions of labour, the Xenopus laevis **cell cycle, and the acute inflammation of** the gut and lung case studies

	Execution time (seconds)			
	M1	M2	M3	M4
Model simulation	37.22	1.13	1.79	329.6
Convert simulation output to csv format	0.33	0.02	1.31	2.62
Generate MSTML subfiles	25.52	25.15	12.06	64.82
Merge subfiles into single MSTML file	31.21	0.44	1.66	2.88

The steps considered are model simulation, conversion of the simulation output to csv format, generating an MSTML subfile for each considered time point, numeric state variable and spatial region comprising one or multiple grid positions, and merging subfiles into a single MSTML file. Depending on the computational model type (i.e. deterministic/stochastic/hybrid) and the formal specification against which it was verified, the number of considered model simulations and time points per model simulation differed. Computational models are distinguished by their model id (i.e. M1–M4). The execution time of the deterministic computational models M1 and M2 was computed by simulating the models and analysing the resulting model simulation output one time. Conversely the execution time of the hybrid (M3) and stochastic (M4) computational models was computed as the average execution time of 1500, respectively 500 repeated runs of the model simulation and model simulation output analysis steps. The number of time points recorded for each model simulation was 30001 for computational model M1, 330 for M2, 103 for M3, and 1000 for M4. The number of time points was fixed due to two reasons. First of all the model simulation time interval considered was bounded. Secondly the model simulators recorded state changes considering a fixed user-defined simulation time step size (chosen by the original model authors).

doi:10.1371/journal.pone.0154847.t004

The most time consuming step for the rat cardiovascular system dynamics (i.e. 37.22s) and the acute inflammation of the gut and lung (i.e. 329.6s) case studies was the model simulation due to the large number of time points considered (i.e. 30001), and the stochastic nature and high complexity associated with the model. Conversely the most time consuming step for the uterine contractions of labour (i.e. 25.15s) and Xenopus laevis cell cycle (i.e. 12.06s) case studies was generating the MSTML subfiles due to the spatial regions which have been automatically detected and analysed for each spatial state variable considered.

The least time consuming step for all case studies was converting the model simulation output to csv format.

Formal Specification

The generated MSTML files representing the behaviour of the computational models and the corresponding MA graphs are employed during the evaluation of the formal specifications described in natural language in Table 5. The equivalent PBLMSTL specifications for the rat cardiovascular system dynamics, the uterine contractions of labour.

Table 5: Natural language descriptions of the formal specifications employed for the rat cardiovascular system dynamics, the uterine contractions of labour, the Xenopus laevis **cell cycle, and the acute inflammation of** the gut and lung case studies

MId	SId	Description
1	1	The probability is greater than 0.9 that after initiating the Valsava manoeuvre (time = 5000 ms) the thoracic pressure increases from the baseline value -4 to 16 for 10 seconds (time interval [5001 ms, 14999 ms]), and then drops back to the baseline value -4.
	2	The probability is greater than 0.9 that during the initial phase of the response (time interval [5001 ms, 6500 ms]) the aortic pressure increases and the heart rate decreases.
	3	The probability is less than 0.1 that after the initial response phase (time interval [5001 ms, 6500 ms]) the aortic pressure continues to increase or stay constant, respectively the heart rate continues to decrease or stay constant throughout the remainder of the Valsava interval (time interval [6501 ms, 14999 ms]).
2	4	The probability is greater than 0.9 that the intrauterine pressure increases/decreases with the contractile activity of uterine regions.
	5	The probability is less than 0.1 that the intrauterine pressure decreases when the entire uterus experiences an action potential burst.
	6	The probability is greater than 0.9 that the intrauterine pressure decreases when the entire uterus is in the refractory period.
3	7	The probability is greater than 0.9 that whenever the concentration of CDK1 reaches very high levels (in our case >96% of its maximum value) all cells will divide.
	8	The probability is greater than 0.9 that whenever the average concentration of APC increases and reaches its local maximum value no cell will divide.
	9	The probability is greater than 0.9 that the average concentrations of CDK1, Plk1 and APC increase and then decrease (i.e. oscillate) over time at least three times.
4	10	The probability is greater than 0.9 that if the level of cytoplasm occludin in the lung decreases then eventually the number of ischemic endothelial lung cells will increase.
	11	The probability is greater than 0.9 that always an increase of the cell damage by-product in the gut will lead to an increase of the cell damage by-product in the lung.
	12	The probability is greater than 0.9 that if the level of cell wall occludin in the gut decreases then eventually the amount of solute leaking in the gut lumen will increase.

Each model is identified by an id (column "MId") and has an associated set of natural language statements. Conversely each natural language statement has a corresponding id (column "SId") and description (column "Description").

doi:10.1371/journal.pone.0154847.t005

Throughout natural language specifications are translated to PBLMSTL such that the i-th natural language statement corresponds to the i-th PBLMSTL statement.

Model Checking

Each computational model has been verified against the relevant PBLMSTL statements 500 times, where each PBLMSTL statement was stored in a separate file. The main reason for repeating the model verification procedure 500 times for each computational model and PBLMSTL statement is to compute the variation of the model checker execution time between runs, and the variation of the number of MSTML files considered for the hybrid (M3) and stochastic (M4) computational models. Results obtained for each of the 500 model checker executions and PBLMSTL statements corresponding to the computational models M1, M2, M3 and M4 are given. The output of the statistical analysis of the model checking results is summarized in Table 6.

Table 6: Statistical analysis of the model checking results for the rat cardiovascular system dynamics, the uterine contractions of labour, the Xenopus laevis **cell cycle, and the acute inflammation** of the gut and lung case studies

MId	SId	% true PBLMSTL	#total MSTML		#true MSTML		#false MSTML		Execution time	
			μ	σ	μ	σ	μ	σ	μ	σ
1	1	100	1	0	1	0	0	0	17.67	0.12
	2	100	1	0	1	0	0	0	17.61	0.13
	3	100	1	0	0	0	1	0	17.8	0.36
2	4	100	1	0	1	0	0	0	0.55	0.01
	5	100	1	0	0	0	1	0	0.54	0.01
	6	100	1	0	1	0	0	0	0.54	0.01
3	7	100	28.79	2.04	28.61	1.62	0.19	0.44	35.35	2.44
	8	100	28	0	28	0	0	0	34.29	0.09
	9	100	28	0	28	0	0	0	35.36	0.99
4	10	100	28	0	28	0	0	0	87.39	0.72
	11	100	28	0	28	0	0	0	90.27	2.23
	12	100	28	0	28	0	0	0	87.03	0.65

Entries in the "MId" and "SId" columns represent the numeric identifiers associated with each computational model and its corresponding PBLMSTL statements. The "% true PBLMSTL" column describes what percentage of the 500 model checker executions concluded that the PBLMSTL statement is true. "#total MSTML" represents the total number of MSTML files evaluated for the PBLMSTL statement during a single model checker execution; columns "#true MSTML" and "#false MSTML" represent the number of MSTML files for which the PBLMSTL statement was evaluated true, respectively false, during a single model checker execution. "Execution time" records the average runtime in seconds for each model checker execution. "μ" and "σ" represent the mean and standard deviation. Due to the deterministic nature of computational models M1 and M2 only one simulation trace was employed for their verification (see table rows corresponding to MId 1 and MId 2, table column 4). Conversely the number of simulation traces considered for the verification of computational models M3 and M4 was equal to ≈28 (see table rows corresponding to MId 3 and MId 4, table column 4), and was computed as a function of the input parameters α and β of the improved statistical hypothesis testing model checking approach. The model simulation traces employed for the verification of computational models M3 and M4 were chosen randomly from the collection of 1500, respectively 500 simulation traces generated to compute the average execution times given in Table 4.

doi:10.1371/journal.pone.0154847.t006

Empirical evidence shows that all computational models are correct relative to the formal specifications derived from the original papers introducing the models.

Due to the deterministic nature of computational models M1 and M2, the corresponding model checking results were obtained by considering a single MSTML file, and therefore were identical across all 500 model checker executions. The main difference between the PBLMSTL statements considered is that in case of statements 1, 2, 4 and 6 the estimated probability p for them to hold, computed as #true MSTML divided by #total MSTML, was p = (1 / 1) = 1, whereas for the PBLMSTL statements 3 and 5 it was $p = (0 / 1) = 0$. However since the associated probabilistic specification for the PBLMSTL statements 1, 2, 4 and 6 was $p > 0.9$ (i.e. $1 > 0.9$), and $p < 0.1$ (i.e. $0 < 0.1$) for the PBLMSTL statements 3 and 5, all PBLMSTL statements hold.

Conversely in case of the hybrid (M3) and stochastic (M4) computational models the model checking results were obtained by considering multiple MSTML files. Moreover the number of MSTML files against which the corresponding PBLMSTL statements evaluated true varied between model checker executions (e.g. see Table 6, row corresponding to SId 7). However the result of the model verification procedure was always the same (see Table 6, column 3).

The average model checker execution times corresponding to the verification of the deterministic computational models M1 and M2 were smaller than for the hybrid, respectively stochastic computational models M3 and M4. This is due to the difference in the number of MSTML files considered which was one for computational models M1 and M2, and ≊28 for computational models M3 and M4. Moreover the variation in the average model checker execution times between the computational models M1 and M2, respectively M3 and M4 is due to the difference in the number of time points considered per model simulation which was 30001 for M1 and 330 for M2, respectively 103 for M3 and 1000 for M4. Average model checker execution times corresponding to the same computational model but different PBLMSTL statements were approximately equal throughout because most of the execution time is spent on reading the MSTML file(s) from disk and not the evaluation of the PBLMSTL statements.

By storing the PBLMSTL statements corresponding to a computational model in separate files each MSTML file read by the model checker from disk is evaluated against only one rather than all PBLMSTL statements. Therefore in order to reduce the average model checker execution time all PBLMSTL statements corresponding to the same computational model could be written into a single file. A comparison between average execution times obtained for 500 model checker executions considering all PBLMSTL statements written into single, respectively multiple separate files are given in Table 7. Regardless of the computational model considered the average model checker execution time was approximately three times smaller when storing PBLMSTL statements in single rather than multiple separate files. The main reason for this is that the total number of MSTML files read from disk, which takes up most of the model checker execution time, was reduced by a factor equal to the number of PBLMSTL statements considered (i.e. 3).

Table 7: Comparison of average model checker execution times when PBLMSTL statements corresponding to a computational model are stored in a single, respectively multiple separate files

MId	Execution time (seconds)	
	Single file	Separate files
1	17.9	53.07
2	0.56	1.63
3	36.3	105
4	87.51	264.68

The "MId" column records the numeric identifiers associated with each computational model. Average model checker execution times corresponding to PBLMSTL statements stored in a single, respectively multiple separate files are given in columns "Single file" and "Separate files".

doi:10.1371/journal.pone.0154847.t007

The model checker execution times given in Tables 6 and 7 were measured when providing pre-generated MSTML files as input to Mule. However Mule can be additionally employed to verify computational models by generating MSTML files on demand. In order to measure the model checker execution time when all MSTML files are generated on-demand the computational model M3 was verified 500 times relative to the corresponding PBLMSTL statements stored in a single file, without providing any pre-generated MSTML files as input. The average execution time of the 500 runs was 317.7s i.e. ≈9 times more than when providing pre-generated MSTML files as input (i.e. 36.3s). The large difference in execution time is due to the fact that when generating MSTML files on-demand Mule needs to wait for the MSTML files to be generated (i.e. for the computational model to be simulated and the model simulation output to be translated to MSTML) before evaluating the PBLMSTL specification against them. Therefore there is a model checker execution time overhead when verifying computational models using on-demand generated MSTML files. The magnitude of the execution time overhead depends on the number of MSTML files against which the PBLMSTL specification is evaluated, and the time required to generate a new model simulation and translate the model simulation output to MSTML.

A comparison between the average execution times recorded for simulating the model, translating the output to MSTML and verifying it using model checking is given in Fig 12.

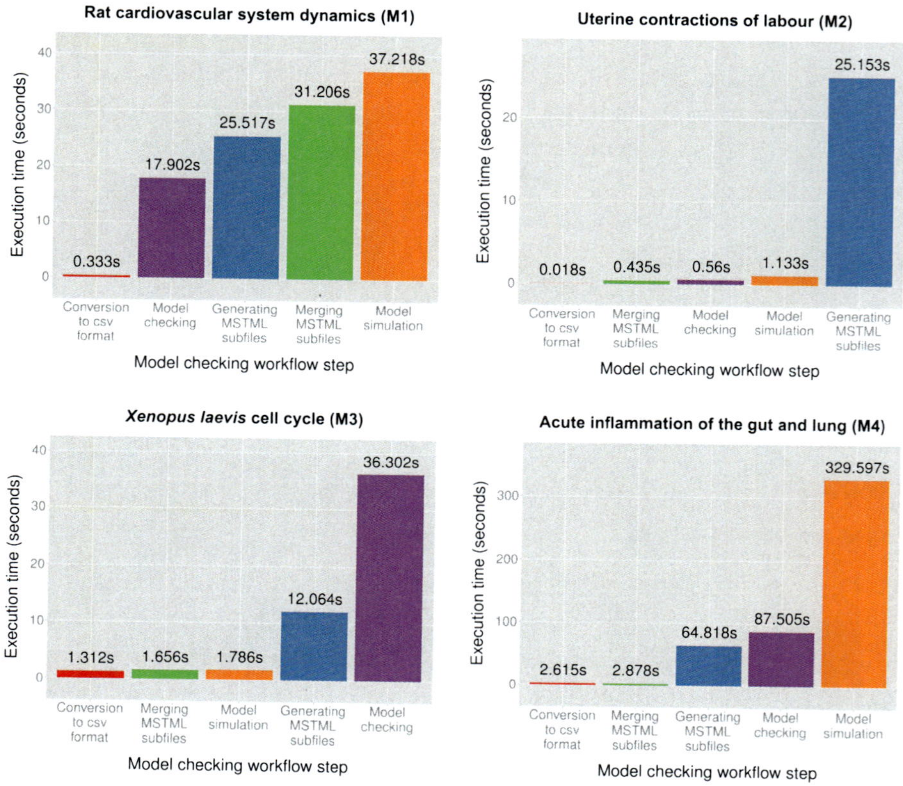

Figure 12: Average execution times (measured in seconds) corresponding to the verification of the rat cardiovascular system dynamics, the uterine contractions of labour, the Xenopus laevis **cell cycle, and the acute inflammation of the gut and lung computational models.**

Execution times were recorded for the computational model simulation, converting the output to csv format, generating MSTML subfiles for each considered time point, numeric state variable and spatial entity, merging the subfiles into a single MSTML file, and model checking.

The most time consuming step in the model checking workflow for both the cardiovascular system dynamics and acute inflammation of the gut and lung case studies is the model simulation. This is due to the large number of time points considered in case of the former, and the high complexity associated with the stochastic computational model in case of the latter. Conversely for the uterine contractions of labour case study the most time consuming step in the model checking workflow is generating the MSTML subfiles due to the additional need to automatically detect and analyse spatial regions of three types (i.e. corresponding to the contractile, burst and refractory activities) for each simulation time point. In contrast, the most time consuming step in the model checking workflow for the Xenopus laevis cell cycle case study is model checking due to the need to evaluate each PBLMSTL statement against multiple MSTML files. The least time consuming step in the model checking workflow for all case studies is converting the simulation output to csv format.

For reproducibility purposes the MA graph, the pre-generated MSTML file(s), the formal PBLMSTL specification, and the excerpts from the referenced papers used to write the formal specification for each case study are made available as supplementary materials; see Table 8for details. Due to file size constraints only a subset of the total number of generated MSTML files was made available for the Xenopus laevis cell cycle and the acute inflammation of the gut and lung case studies; the complete datasets are made freely available online at http://mule.modelchecking.org/case-studies.

Table 8: Availability of the MA **graph, the generated MSTML file(s), the formal PBLMSTL specification, and the excerpts from the referenced papers used to write the formal specificat**ion for each case study

MId	*MA* graph	MSTML file(s)	PBLMSTL specification	Excerpts from referenced papers
1	S5 File	S1 Dataset	S1 File	S10 Text
2	S6 File	S2 Dataset	S2 File	S11 Text
3	S7 File	S3 Dataset	S3 File	S12 Text
4	S8 File	S4 Dataset	S4 File	S13 Text

The "MId" column records the numeric identifiers associated with each computational model.

doi:10.1371/journal.pone.0154847.t008

DISCUSSION

The need for reasoning about how systems evolve over multiple temporal and spatial scales has been previously emphasized in the literature. For instance Van de Weghe et al. [85] have defined a theoretical framework which enables describing and analysing how geographical phenomena observed at higher scales are reflected at lower scales and vice versa.

However there is a lack of corresponding model checking approaches for computational models of such systems.

To the best of our knowledge the only related multiscale model checking approach which explicitly distinguishes between multiple spatial scales without (initially) accounting for time was introduced by Grosu et al. [86] for detecting patterns in images. The multiscale representation of space was created by recursively splitting a spatial domain in quadrants (a finite number of times) and representing the resulting hierarchy as a quadtree. A formal logic called Linear Spatial Superposition Logic (LSSL) and a corresponding model checking algorithm were introduced in order to encode specifications relative to spatial subdomains along a linear path through the quadtree. More recently both the formal logic and corresponding model checking algorithm were extended by Gol et al. [87] to account for branching paths through quadtrees (Tree Spatial Superposition Logic), and by Haghighi et al. [88] to account for the evolution of the quadtrees over time (SpaTel). Although efficient for pattern detection (and generation) these approaches could be potentially too restrictive for reasoning about general multiscale systems since only one spatial domain is considered and the relationship between consecutive levels/scales is fixed. Moreover it is not possible to describe how spatial entities potentially spanning multiple quadrants of the spatial domain, and their properties change over time.

In this paper we have introduced a novel multiscale spatio-temporal meta model checking methodology which enables automatically verifying multilevel computational models of biological systems relative to specifications describing the desired/expected system behaviour.

Our approach is generic and supports multilevel computational models of biological systems encoded using various high-level modelling formalisms (e.g. CPMs, ABMs) because it is defined relative to time series data and not the models used to produce them. This is illustrated by the four case studies which were formally encoded using ODEs (rat cardiovascular system dynamics), CAs (uterine contractions of labour), CPMs (Xenopus laevis cell cycle), ABMs (acute inflammation of the gut and lung) or combinations thereof.

Although the model checker is flexible regarding the modelling formalism employed to encode the computational models it requires that the model simulation output is translated to the standard MSTML format. During the translation process non-spatial state variables (e.g. concentrations) are mapped directly from their native format to MSTML. Conversely in case of spatial state variables the multiscale spatio-temporal analysis module is additionally executed for automatically detecting emergent spatial entities (e.g. clusters) and computing their properties (e.g. area).

The model checker can be adapted automatically to case study specific spatial entity types (e.g. 3D spatial structure) and/or properties (e.g. minimum distance to a fixed point) not covered by our multiscale spatio-temporal analysis module. External analysis tools can be employed to automatically detect and analyse these case study specific spatial entities, and to convert the output to the MSTML format. The corresponding instance of the multiscale spatio-temporal meta model checker can be generated automatically based on a configuration file without the need to modify the implementation by hand.

The set of MSTML files representing the model behaviour can be generated either before or during the evaluation of a PBLMSTL specification. In case of the latter the model checker must be executed with an additional parameter representing the path to an external program which runs model simulations on demand, translates the output to MSTML and stores the resulting files in a predefined location. The overhead of generating MSTML files during (i.e. on demand) rather than before the evaluation of the PBLMSTL specification depends on the number of required MSTML files and the time required to simulate the computational model and translate the output to MSTML.

We have illustrated the applicability and flexibility of the model checker Mule by verifying four systems biology computational models previously published in the literature relative to formal specifications derived from the original papers introducing the models. Although only the probabilistic black box (see rat cardiovascular system dynamics and uterine contractions of labour case studies) and frequentist statistical model checking algorithms (see Xenopus laeviscell cycle and acute inflammation of gut and lung case studies) were employed here, additional frequentist (i.e. based on Chernoff-Hoeffding bounds) and Bayesian (i.e. hypothesis testing, mean and variance estimate based) model checking algorithms are supported.

The scalability of the entire model verification workflow depends on the scalability of the model simulation, multiscale spatio-temporal analysis and model checking steps. The execution time of the model simulation depends on the complexity of the system under consideration. Conversely the execution times of both the multiscale spatio-temporal analysis and the model checker depend on the size of the simulation output. In addition, the model checker execution time also depends on the formal specification. Our expectation is that scaling up to more complex systems will lead to an increase of the computational model complexity but not necessarily the size of the simulation output and/or formal specification. Therefore the expected scalability bottleneck of the entire model checking workflow is the model simulation and not the model verification step. This is supported by empirical evidence obtained from the case studies; the ratio between the maximum and minimum execution times for the model simulation step was ≊290, ≊5 for the multiscale spatio-temporal analysis, and ≊156 for model checking. In addition it would be possible to speed up the model checking step by evaluating MSTML files against the formal specification in parallel rather than sequentially as it is done now.

To enable computational modellers to easily adopt our approach for the verification of multilevel computational models of biological systems the model checker Mule (source code, binary, Docker image) and relevant supplementary materials are made freely available online via the official web page http://mule.modelchecking.org.

Building on our model checking methodology we could consider the following extensions in the future. First of all it is assumed throughout that computational models are translatable to an MSSpDES representation which means that any computational model encoded using a potentially incompatible high-level modelling formalism will be translated to a corresponding MSSpDES representation subject to potential approximation errors (e.g. consider continuous computational models). Alternative representations could be employed instead. Secondly, although our methodology is automatically reconfigurable according to case study specific spatial entity types and measures, there is a need for the corresponding spatio-temporal analysis tools to be developed. The spatio-temporal analysis modules described here are currently restricted to pseudo-3D spatial entity types and measures, but could be extended in the future for other numbers of dimensions. Thirdly the efficiency of Mule could be improved by supporting on-the-fly model checking. However this means that all computational models considered would need to be explicitly translated to a common (e.g. MSSpDES) representation before being verified. Fourthly the efficacy of the methodology was tested only against in silicogenerated time series data, but our expectation is that it could be employed for analysing experimental time series data as well. Moreover since the methodology is not restricted to biological case studies, non-biological case studies could be additionally considered in order to test the limitations of the approach and potentially identify new features which could be included in forthcoming versions. Finally the efficacy of the multiscale model checking approach could be assessed in the future in the context of robustness analysis, parameter estimation/ synthesis, and model construction problems.

CONCLUSIONS

In this paper we have defined a multiscale spatio-temporal meta model checking methodology which enables the automatic verification of multilevel computational models with respect to how both numeric (e.g. concentrations) and spatial (e.g. area) properties change over time considering multiple levels of organization.

The approach was implemented in our model checking software Mule which is made freely available online. To encourage potential contributions (e.g. extensions) the source code is hosted in a public GitHub repository. For flexibility purposes Mule supports both frequentist and Bayesian, estimate and statistical hypothesis testing based model checking approaches.

We have illustrated the applicability of the model verification approach using four representative systems biology case studies published in the literature, namely the rat cardiovascular system dynamics, the uterine contractions of labour, the Xenopus laevis cell cycle and the acute inflammation of the gut and lung.

Our approach enables computational modellers to construct reliable multilevel computational models of biological systems in a faster manner than it is done currently. These computational models could then be potentially translated into systems medicine to provide patient specific predictions on the evolution of diseases and their treatment across multiple levels of organization.

ACKNOWLEDGMENTS

We would like to thank the anonymous reviewers, Monika Heiner, Alessandro Pandini and Allan Tucker for their insightful comments which helped improve the quality of the paper.

AUTHOR CONTRIBUTIONS

Conceived and designed the experiments: OP DG. Performed the experiments: OP. Analyzed the data: OP. Contributed reagents/materials/analysis tools: OP. Wrote the paper: OP DG. Developed and implemented the meta model checking methodology: OP. Proved that the multiscale model checking problem is well-defined: OP.

REFERENCES

1. Ideker T, Galitski T, Hood L. A NEW APPROACH TO DECODING LIFE: Systems Biology. Annual Review of Genomics and Human Genetics. 2001;2(1):343–372. Available from: http://www.annualreviews.org/doi/abs/10.1146/annurev.genom.2.1.343. pmid:11701654
2. Kitano H. Systems Biology: A Brief Overview. Science. 2002 Jan;295(5560):1662–1664. Available from: http://www.sciencemag.org/content/295/5560/1662. pmid:11872829
3. Dada JO, Mendes P. Multi-scale modelling and simulation in systems biology. Integrative biology: quantitative biosciences from nano to macro. 2011 Feb;3(2):86–96.
4. Boissel JP, Auffray C, Noble D, Hood L, Boissel FH. Bridging Systems Medicine and Patient Needs. CPT: Pharmacometrics & Systems Pharmacology. 2015 Mar;4(3):135–145. Available from: http://onlinelibrary.wiley.com/doi/10.1002/psp4.26/abstract.
5. Wolkenhauer O, Auffray C, Brass O, Clairambault J, Deutsch A, Drasdo D, et al. Enabling multiscale modeling in systems medicine. Genome Medicine. 2014 Mar;6(3):21. Available from: http://

genomemedicine.com/content/6/3/21. pmid:25031615

6. Clarke EM, Emerson EA. Design and synthesis of synchronization skeletons using branching time temporal logic. In: Kozen D, editor. Logics of Programs. No. 131 in Lecture Notes in Computer Science. Springer Berlin Heidelberg; 1982. p. 52–71. Available from: http://link.springer.com/chapter/10.1007/BFb0025774.
7. Queille JP, Sifakis J. Specification and verification of concurrent systems in CESAR. In: Dezani-Ciancaglini M, Montanari U, editors. International Symposium on Programming. No. 137 in Lecture Notes in Computer Science. Springer Berlin Heidelberg; 1982. p. 337–351. Available from: http://link.springer.com.v-ezproxy.brunel.ac.uk:2048/chapter/10.1007/3-540-11494-7_22.
8. Carusi A, Burrage K, Rodríguez B. Bridging experiments, models and simulations: an integrative approach to validation in computational cardiac electrophysiology. American Journal of Physiology—Heart and Circulatory Physiology. 2012 Jul;303(2):H144–H155. Available from: http://ajpheart.physiology.org/content/303/2/H144. pmid:22582088
9. Carusi A. Validation and variability: Dual challenges on the path from systems biology to systems medicine. Studies in History and Philosophy of Science Part C: Studies in History and Philosophy of Biological and Biomedical Sciences. 2014 Dec;48, Part A:28–37. Available from: http://www.sciencedirect.com/science/article/pii/S1369848614001265.
10. Sheard T. Accomplishments and Research Challenges in Meta-programming. In Taha W, editor. Semantics, Applications, and Implementation of Program Generation. No. 2196 in Lecture Notes in Computer Science. Springer Berlin Heidelberg; 2001. p. 2–44. Available from: http://link.springer.com/chapter/10.1007/3-540-44806-3_2.
11. Groen D, Zasada SJ, Coveney PV. Survey of Multiscale and Multiphysics Applications and Communities. Computing in Science Engineering. 2014 Mar;16(2):34–43.
12. Docker. Docker—Build, Ship, and Run Any App, Anywhere;. Available from: https://www.docker.com/ [cited 2015-05-20].

13. Beard DA, Neal ML, Tabesh-Saleki N, Thompson CT, Bassingtwaighte JB, Shimoyama M, et al. Multiscale Modeling and Data Integration in the Virtual Physiological Rat Project. Annals of Biomedical Engineering. 2012 Nov;40(11):2365–2378. Available from: http://www.ncbi.nlm.nih.gov/pmc/articles/PMC3463790/. pmid:22805979
14. Young RC, Barendse P. Linking Myometrial Physiology to Intrauterine Pressure; How Tissue-Level Contractions Create Uterine Contractions of Labor. PLoS Comput Biol. 2014 Oct;10(10):e1003850. pmid:25330227
15. Ferrell JE Jr, Tsai TYC, Yang Q. Modeling the Cell Cycle: Why Do Certain Circuits Oscillate? Cell. 2011 Mar;144(6):874–885. Available from: http://www.sciencedirect.com/science/article/pii/S0092867411002431. pmid:21414480
16. An G. Introduction of an agent-based multi-scale modular architecture for dynamic knowledge representation of acute inflammation. Theoretical Biology and Medical Modelling. 2008 May;5(1):11. Available from: http://www.tbiomed.com/content/5/1/11/abstract. pmid:18505587
17. Ballarini P, Gallet E, Gall PL, Manceny M. Formal Analysis of the Wnt/β-catenin through Statistical Model Checking. In: Margaria T, Steffen B, editors. Leveraging Applications of Formal Methods, Verification and Validation. Specialized Techniques and Applications. No. 8803 in Lecture Notes in Computer Science. Springer Berlin Heidelberg; 2014. p. 193–207. Available from: http://link.springer.com/chapter/10.1007/978-3-662-45231-8_14.
18. Barbuti R, Levi F, Milazzo P, Scatena G. Probabilistic model checking of biological systems with uncertain kinetic rates. Theoretical Computer Science. 2012 Feb;419:2–16. Available from: http://www.sciencedirect.com/science/article/pii/S0304397511008929.
19. Barnat J, Brim L, Černá I, Dražan S, Fabriková J, Láník J, et al.: A Framework for Parallel Analysis of Biological Models. Electronic Proceedings in Theoretical Computer Science. 2009 Oct;6:31–45. ArXiv: 0910.0928. Available from: http://arxiv.org/abs/0910.0928.
20. Batt G, Ropers D, Jong Hd, Geiselmann J, Mateescu R, Page M, et al. Validation of qualitative models of genetic regulatory networks

by model checking: analysis of the nutritional stress response in Escherichia coli. Bioinformatics. 2005 Jun;21(suppl 1):i19–i28. Available from: http://bioinformatics.oxfordjournals.org/content/21/suppl_1/i19. pmid:15961457

21. Bernot G, Comet JP, Richard A, Guespin J. Application of formal methods to biological regulatory networks: extending Thomas' asynchronous logical approach with temporal logic. Journal of Thecretical Biology. 2004 Aug;229(3):339–347. Available from: http://www.sciencedirect.com/science/article/pii/S0022519304001444. pmid:15234201

22. Calder M, Vyshemirsky V, Gilbert D, Orton R. Analysis of Signalling Pathways Using Continuous Time Markov Chains. In: Priami C, Plotkin G, editors. Transactions on Computational Systems Biology VI. No. 4220 in Lecture Notes in Computer Science. Springer Berlin Heidelberg; 2006. p. 44–67. Available from: http://link.springer.com/chapter/10.1007/11880646_3.

23. Chabrier N, Fages F. Symbolic Model Checking of Biochemical Networks. In: Priami C, editor. Computational Methods in Systems Biology. No. 2602 in Lecture Notes in Computer Science. Rovereto, Italy: Springer Berlin Heidelberg; 2003. p. 149–162. Available from: http://link.springer.com/chapter/10.1007/3-540-36481-1_13.

24. Chabrier-Rivier N, Chiaverini M, Danos V, Fages F, Schächter V. Modeling and querying biomolecular interaction networks. Theoretical Computer Science. 2004 Sep;325(1):25–44. Available from: http://www.sciencedirect.com/science/article/pii/S030439750400218X.

25. Clarke EM, Faeder JR, Langmead CJ, Harris LA, Jha SK, Legay A. Statistical Model Checking in BioLab: Applications to the Automated Analysis of T-Cell Receptor Signaling Pathway. In: Heiner M, Uhrmacher AM, editors. Computational Methods in Systems Biology. No. 5307 in Lecture Notes in Computer Science. Springer Berlin Heidelberg; 2008. p. 231–250. Available from: http://link.springer.com/chapter/10.1007/978-3-540-88562-7_18.

26. David A, Larsen KG, Legay A, Mikučionis M, Poulsen DB, Sedwards S. Runtime Verification of Biological Systems. In: Margaria T, Steffen B, editors. Leveraging Applications of Formal

Methods, Verification and Validation. Technologies for Mastering Change. No. 7609 in Lecture Notes in Computer Science. Springer Berlin Heidelberg; 2012. p. 388–404. Available from: http://link.springer.com/chapter/10.1007/978-3-642-34026-0_29.

27. Gong H, Feng L. Computational analysis of the roles of ER-Golgi network in the cell cycle. BMC Systems Biology. 2014 Dec;8(Suppl 4):S3. Available from: http://www.biomedcentral.com/1752-0509/8/S4/S3/comments.
28. Heath J, Kwiatkowska M, Norman G, Parker D, Tymchyshyn O. Probabilistic model checking of complex biological pathways. Theoretical Computer Science. 2008 Feb;391(3):239–257. Available from: http://www.sciencedirect.com/science/article/pii/S0304397507008572.
29. Heiner M, Gilbert D, Donaldson R. Petri Nets for Systems and Synthetic Biology. In: Bernardo M, Degano P, Zavattaro G, editors. Formal Methods for Computational Systems Biology. No. 5016 in Lecture Notes in Computer Science. Springer Berlin Heidelberg; 2008. p. 215–264. Available from: http://link.springer.com/chapter/10.1007/978-3-540-68894-5_7.
30. Kwiatkowska M, Norman G, Parker D. Stochastic Model Checking. In: Bernardo M, Hillston J, editors. Formal Methods for Performance Evaluation. No. 4486 in Lecture Notes in Computer Science. Springer Berlin Heidelberg; 2007. p. 220–270. Available from: http://link.springer.com/chapter/10.1007/978-3-540-72522-0_6.
31. Monteiro PT, Wassim AJ, Thieffry D, Chaouiya C. Model Checking Logical Regulatory Networks. In: Discrete Event Systems. vol. 12. Ecole Normale Supérieure de Cachan, Cachan, France: International Federation of Automatic Control; 2014. p. 170–175. Available from: http://www.ifac-papersonline.net/Detailed/65093.html.
32. Van Goethem S, Jacquet JM, Brim L, Šafránek D. Timed Modelling of Gene Networks with Arbitrarily Precise Expression Discretization. Electronic Notes in Theoretical Computer Science. 2013 Mar;293:67–81. Available from: http://www.sciencedirect.com/science/article/pii/S1571066113000212.
33. Barnat J, Brim L, Šafránek D, Vejnár M. Parameter Scanning by Parallel Model Checking with Applications in Systems Biology. In:

Second International Workshop on Parallel and Distributed Methods in Verification, 2010 Ninth International Workshop on, and High Performance Computational Systems Biology; 2010. p. 95–104.

34. Batt G, Belta C, Weiss R. Model Checking Genetic Regulatory Networks with Parameter Uncertainty. In: Bemporad A, Bicchi A, Buttazzo G, editors. Hybrid Systems: Computation and Control. No. 4416 in Lecture Notes in Computer Science. Springer Berlin Heidelberg; 2007. p. 61–75. Available from: http://link.springer.com/chapter/10.1007/978-3-540-71493-4_8.

35. Batt G, Belta C, Weiss R. Temporal Logic Analysis of Gene Networks Under Parameter Uncertainty. IEEE Transactions on Automatic Control. 2008 Jan;53(Special Issue):215–229.

36. Brim L, Češka M, Dražan S, Šafránek D. Exploring Parameter Space of Stochastic Biochemical Systems Using Quantitative Model Checking. In: Sharygina N, Veith H, editors. Computer Aided Verification. No. 8044 in Lecture Notes in Computer Science. Springer Berlin Heidelberg; 2013. p. 107–123. Available from: http://link.springer.com/chapter/10.1007/978-3-642-39799-8_7.

37. Češka M, Dannenberg F, Kwiatkowska M, Paoletti N. Precise Parameter Synthesis for Stochastic Biochemical Systems. In: Mendes P, Dada JO, Smallbone K, editors. Computational Methods in Systems Biology. No. 8859 in Lecture Notes in Computer Science. Springer International Publishing; 2014. p. 86–98. Available from: http://link.springer.com/chapter/10.1007/978-3-319-12982-2_7.

38. Donaldson R, Gilbert D. A Model Checking Approach to the Parameter Estimation of Biochemical Pathways. In: Heiner M, Uhrmacher AM, editors. Computational Methods in Systems Biology. No. 5307 in Lecture Notes in Computer Science. Springer Berlin Heidelberg; 2008. p. 269–287. Available from: http://link.springer.com/chapter/10.1007/978-3-540-88562-7_20.

39. Giacobbe M, Guet CC, Gupta A, Henzinger TA, Paixao T, Petrov T. Model Checking Gene Regulatory Networks. arXiv:14107704 [cs, q-bio]. 2015 Oct;ArXiv: 1410.7704. Available from: http://arxiv.org/abs/1410.7704.

40. Jha SK, Langmead CJ. Synthesis and infeasibility analysis for stochastic models of biochemical systems using statistical model

checking and abstraction refinement. Theoretical Computer Science. 2011 May;412(21):2162–2187. Available from: http://www.sciencedirect.com/science/article/pii/S0304397511000387.

41. Liu B, Kong S, Gao S, Zuliani P, Clarke EM. Parameter Synthesis for Cardiac Cell Hybrid Models Using δ-Decisions. In: Mendes P, Dada JO, Smallbone K, editors. Computational Methods in Systems Biology. No. 8859 in Lecture Notes in Computer Science. Springer International Publishing; 2014. p. 99–113. Available from: http://link.springer.com/chapter/10.1007/978-3-319-12982-2_8.
42. Palaniappan SK, Gyori BM, Liu B, Hsu D, Thiagarajan PS. Statistical Model Checking Based Calibration and Analysis of Bio-pathway Models. In: Gupta A, Henzinger TA, editors. Computational Methods in Systems Biology. No. 8130 in Lecture Notes in Computer Science. Springer Berlin Heidelberg; 2013. p. 120–134. Available from: http://link.springer.com/chapter/10.1007/978-3-642-40708-6_10.
43. Calzone L, Chabrier-Rivier N, Fages F, Soliman S. Machine Learning Biochemical Networks from Temporal Logic Properties. In: Priami C, Plotkin G, editors. Transactions on Computational Systems Biology VI. No. 4220 in Lecture Notes in Computer Science. Springer Berlin Heidelberg; 2006. p. 68–94. Available from: http://link.springer.com/chapter/10.1007/11880646_4.
44. Fages F, Rizk A. From Model-Checking to Temporal Logic Constraint Solving. In: Gent IP, editor. Principles and Practice of Constraint Programming—CP 2009. No. 5732 in Lecture Notes in Computer Science. Springer Berlin Heidelberg; 2009. p. 319–334. Available from: http://link.springer.com/chapter/10.1007/978-3-642-04244-7_26.
45. Česka M, Šafránek D, Dražan S, Brim L. Robustness Analysis of Stochastic Biochemical Systems. PLoS ONE. 2014 Apr;9(4):e94553. pmid:24751941
46. Rizk A, Batt G, Fages F, Soliman S. On a Continuous Degree of Satisfaction of Temporal Logic Formulae with Applications to Systems Biology. In: Heiner M, Uhrmacher AM, editors. Computational Methods in Systems Biology. No. 5307 in Lecture Notes in Computer Science. Springer Berlin Heidelberg; 2008. p. 251–268. Available from: http://link.springer.com/

chapter/10.1007/978-3-540-88562-7_19.

47. Rizk A, Batt G, Fages F, Soliman S. A general computational method for robustness analysis with applications to synthetic gene networks. Bioinformatics. 2009 Jun;25(12):i169–i178. Available from: http://bioinformatics.oxfordjournals.org/content/25/12/i169. pmid:19477984
48. Brim L, Češka M, Šafránek D. Model Checking of Biological Systems. In: Bernardo M, Vink Ed, Pierro AD, Wiklicky H, editors. Formal Methods for Dynamical Systems. No. 7938 in Lecture Notes in Computer Science. Springer Berlin Heidelberg; 2013. p. 63–112. Available from: http://link.springer.com/chapter/10.1007/978-3-642-38874-3_3.
49. Fisher J, Piterman N. Model Checking in Biology. In: Kulkarni VV, Stan GB, Raman K, editors. A Systems Theoretic Approach to Systems and Synthetic Biology I: Models and System Characterizations. Springer Netherlands; 2014. p. 255–279. Available from: http://link.springer.com/chapter/10.1007/978-94-017-9041-3_10.
50. Zuliani P. Statistical model checking for biological applications. International Journal on Software Tools for Technology Transfer. 2014 Aug;p. 1–10. Available from: http://link.springer.com/article/10.1007/s10009-014-0343-0.
51. Maria ED, Fages F, Soliman S. On Coupling Models Using Model-Checking: Effects of Irinotecan Injections on the Mammalian Cell Cycle. In: Degano P, Gorrieri R, editors. Computational Methods in Systems Biology. No. 5688 in Lecture Notes in Computer Science. Springer Berlin Heidelberg; 2009. p. 142–157. Available from: http://link.springer.com/chapter/10.1007/978-3-642-03845-7_10.
52. Ciocchetta F, Gilmore S, Guerriero ML, Hillston J. Integrated Simulation and Model-Checking for the Analysis of Biochemical Systems. Electronic Notes in Theoretical Computer Science. 2009 Mar;232:17–38. Available from: http://www.sciencedirect.com/science/article/pii/S157106610900053X.
53. Yordanov B, Belta C. A formal verification approach to the design of synthetic gene networks. In: 2011 50th IEEE Conference on Decision and Control and European Control Conference (CDC-ECC); 2011. p. 4873–4878.

54. Gilbert D, Heiner M, Lehrack S. A Unifying Framework for Modelling and Analysing Biochemical Pathways Using Petri Nets. In: Calder M, Gilmore S, editors. Computational Methods in Systems Biology. No. 4695 in Lecture Notes in Computer Science. Springer Berlin Heidelberg; 2007. p. 200–216. Available from: http://link.springer.com/chapter/10.1007/978-3-540-75140-3_14.
55. Gong H, Zuliani P, Komuravelli A, Faeder JR, Clarke EM. Computational Modeling and Verification of Signaling Pathways in Cancer. In: Horimoto K, Nakatsui M, Popov N, editors. Algebraic and Numeric Biology. No. 6479 in Lecture Notes in Computer Science. Springer Berlin Heidelberg; 2012. p. 117–135. Available from: http://link.springer.com/chapter/10.1007/978-3-642-28067-2_7.
56. Guerriero ML. Qualitative and Quantitative Analysis of a Bio-PEPA Model of the Gp130/JAK/STAT Signalling Pathway. In: Priami C, Back RJ, Petre I, editors. Transactions on Computational Systems Biology XI. No. 5750 in Lecture Notes in Computer Science. Springer Berlin Heidelberg; 2009. p. 90–115. Available from: http://link.springer.com/chapter/10.1007/978-3-642-04186-0_5.
57. Pârvu O, Gilbert D. Automatic validation of computational models using pseudo-3D spatio-temporal model checking. BMC Systems Biology. 2014 Dec;8(1):124. Available from: http://www.biomedcentral.com/1752-0509/8/124/abstract. pmid:25440773
58. Southern J, Pitt-Francis J, Whiteley J, Stokeley D, Kobashi H, Nobes R, et al. Multi-scale computational modelling in biology and physiology. Progress in Biophysics and Molecular Biology. 2008 Jan;96(1–3):60–89. Available from: http://www.sciencedirect.com/science/article/pii/S0079610707000673. pmid:17888502
59. Younes HL, Simmons RG. Statistical probabilistic model checking with a focus on time-bounded properties. Information and Computation. 2006 Sep;204(9):1368–1409. Available from: http://www.sciencedirect.com/science/article/pii/S0890540106000678.
60. Hansson H, Jonsson B. A logic for reasoning about time and reliability. Formal Aspects of Computing. 1994 Sep;6(5):512–535. Available from: http://link.springer.com/article/10.1007/BF01211866.
61. Baier C, Katoen JP, Hermanns H. Approximative Symbolic Model Checking of Continuous-Time Markov Chains. In: Baeten JCM,

Mauw S, editors. CONCUR'99 Concurrency Theory. No. 1664 in Lecture Notes in Computer Science. Springer Berlin Heidelberg; 1999. p. 146–161. Available from: http://link.springer.com/chapter/10.1007/3-540-48320-9_12.

62. Bradski G, Kaehler A. Learning OpenCV: Computer Vision with the OpenCV Library. Cambridge, MA: O'Reilly; 2008.

63. Tran TN, Drab K, Daszykowski M. Revised DBSCAN algorithm to cluster data with dense adjacent clusters. Chemometrics and Intelligent Laboratory Systems. 2013 Jan;120:92–96. Available from: http://www.sciencedirect.com/science/article/pii/S0169743912002249.

64. Aziz A, Sanwal K, Singhal V, Brayton R. Verifying Continuous Time Markov Chains. In: CAV. vol. 1102 of Lecture Notes in Computer Science. Springer; 1996. p. 269–276.

65. Hérault T, Lassaigne R, Magniette F, Peyronnet S. Approximate Probabilistic Model Checking. In: Steffen B, Levi G, editors. Verification, Model Checking, and Abstract Interpretation. No. 2937 in Lecture Notes in Computer Science. Springer Berlin Heidelberg; 2004. p. 73–84. Available from: http://link.springer.com/chapter/10.1007/978-3-540-24622-0_8.

66. Wald A. Sequential Tests of Statistical Hypotheses. The Annals of Mathematical Statistics. 1945 Jun;16(2):117–186. Available from: http://projecteuclid.org/DPubS?service=UI&version=1.0&verb=Display&handle=euclid.aoms/1177731118.

67. Younes HLS. Verification and Planning for Stochastic Processes with Asynchronous Events [Doctor of Philosophy]. Carnegie Mellon. Pittsburgh; 2005.

68. Koh CH, Palaniappan SK, Thiagarajan PS, Wong L. Improved statistical model checking methods for pathway analysis. BMC Bioinformatics. 2012 Dec;13(Suppl 17):S15. Available from: http://www.biomedcentral.com/1471-2105/13/S17/S15/abstract. pmid:23282174

69. Sen K, Viswanathan M, Agha G. Statistical Model Checking of Black-Box Probabilistic Systems. In: Alur R, Peled DA, editors. Computer Aided Verification. No. 3114 in Lecture Notes in Computer Science. Springer Berlin Heidelberg; 2004. p. 202–215. Available from:

http://link.springer.com/chapter/10.1007/978-3-540-27813-9_16.

70. Younes HLS. Probabilistic Verification for "Black-Box" Systems. In: Etessami K, Rajamani SK, editors. Computer Aided Verification. No. 3576 in Lecture Notes in Computer Science. Springer Berlin Heidelberg; 2005. p. 253–265. Available from: http://link.springer.com/chapter/10.1007/11513988_25.
71. Langmead CJ. Generalized Queries and Bayesian Statistical Model Checking in Dynamic Bayesian Networks: Application to Personalized Medicine. In: Proc. of the 8th International Conference on Computational Systems Bioinformatics (CSB). California: Life Sciences Society; 2009. p. 201–212.
72. Jha SK, Clarke EM, Langmead CJ, Legay A, Platzer A, Zuliani P. A Bayesian Approach to Model Checking Biological Systems. In: Degano P, Gorrieri R, editors. Computational Methods in Systems Biology. No. 5688 in Lecture Notes in Computer Science. Springer Berlin Heidelberg; 2009. p. 218–234. Available from: http://link.springer.com/chapter/10.1007/978-3-642-03845-7_15.
73. Jha SK, Clarke EM, Langmead CJ, Legay A, Platzer A, Zuliani P. Statistical Model Checking for Complex Stochastic Models in Systems Biology. Carnegie Mellon University; 2009. Available from: http://repository.cmu.edu/cgi/viewcontent.cgi?article=2244&context=compsci.
74. Ballarini P, Djafri H, Duflot M, Haddad S, Pekergin N. COSMOS: A Statistical Model Checker for the Hybrid Automata Stochastic Logic. In: 2011 Eighth International Conference on Quantitative Evaluation of Systems (QEST); 2011. p. 143–144.
75. Jegourel C, Legay A, Sedwards S. A Platform for High Performance Statistical Model Checking—PLASMA. In: Flanagan C, König B, editors. Tools and Algorithms for the Construction and Analysis of Systems. No. 7214 in Lecture Notes in Computer Science. Springer Berlin Heidelberg; 2012. p. 498–503. Available from: http://link.springer.com/chapter/10.1007/978-3-642-28756-5_37.
76. Kwiatkowska M, Norman G, Parker D. 4.0: Verification of Probabilistic Real-Time Systems. In: Gopalakrishnan G, Qadeer S, editors. Computer Aided Verification. No. 6806 in Lecture Notes in Computer Science. Snowbird, UT, USA: Springer Berlin

Heidelberg; 2011. p. 585–591. Available from: http://link.springer.com/chapter/10.1007/978-3-642-22110-1_47.

77. Bulychev PE, David A, Larsen KG, Mikucionis M, Poulsen DB, Legay A, et al. UPPAAL-SMC: Statistical Model Checking for Priced Timed Automata. In: Proceedings 10th Workshop on Quantitative Aspects of Programming Languages and Systems, QAPL 2012, Tallinn, Estonia, 31 March and 1 April 2012.; 2012. p. 1–16. Available from: http://dx.doi.org/10.4204/EPTCS.85.1.
78. Younes HLS. Ymer: A Statistical Model Checker. In: Etessami K, Rajamani SK, editors. Computer Aided Verification. No. 3576 in Lecture Notes in Computer Science. Springer Berlin Heidelberg; 2005. p. 429–433. Available from: http://link.springer.com/chapter/10.1007/11513988_43.
79. Wilkinson DJ. Stochastic Modelling for Systems Biology, Second Edition. 2nd ed. Boca Raton: CRC Press; 2011.
80. Smith BW, Chase JG, Nokes RI, Shaw GM, Wake G. Minimal haemodynamic system model including ventricular interaction and valve dynamics. Medical Engineering & Physics. 2004 Mar;26(2):131–139.
81. Bugenhagen SM, Cowley AW, Beard DA. Identifying physiological origins of baroreflex dysfunction in salt-sensitive hypertension in the Dahl SS rat. Physiological Genomics. 2010 Jun;42(1):23–41. pmid:20354102
82. Starruß J, Back Wd, Brusch L, Deutsch A. Morpheus: a user-friendly modeling environment for multiscale and multicellular systems biology. Bioinformatics. 2014 May;30(9):1331–1332. Available from: http://bioinformatics.oxfordjournals.org/content/30/9/1331. pmid:24443380
83. Starruß, J, Back Wd. Morpheus examples;. Available from: http://imc.zih.tu-dresden.de/wiki/morpheus/doku.php?id=examples:examples [cited 2015-05-20].
84. Scott A, Khan KM, Cook JL, Duronio V. What is “inflammation”? Are we ready to move beyond Celsus? British Journal of Sports Medicine. 2004 Jun;38(3):248–249. Available from: http://bjsm.bmj.com/content/38/3/248. pmid:15155418

85. Van de Weghe N, de Roo B, Qiang Y, Versichele M, Neutens T, de Maeyer P. The continuous spatio-temporal model (CSTM) as an exhaustive framework for multi-scale spatio-temporal analysis. International Journal of Geographical Information Science. 2014;28(5):1047–1060.

86. Grosu R, Smolka SA, Corradini F, Wasilewska A, Entcheva E, Bartocci E. Learning and Detecting Emergent Behavior in Networks of Cardiac Myocytes. Commun ACM. 2009 Mar;52(3):97–105. Available from: http://doi.acm.org/10.1145/1467247.1467271.

87. Gol EA, Bartocci E, Belta C. A Formal Methods Approach to Pattern Synthesis in Reaction Diffusion Systems. arXiv:14095671 [cs]. 2014 Sep;arXiv: 1409.5671. Available from: http://arxiv.org/abs/1409.5671.

88. Haghighi I, Jones A, Kong Z, Bartocci E, Gros R, Belta C. SpaTeL: A Novel Spatial-temporal Logic and Its Applications to Networked Systems. In: Proceedings of the 18th International Conference on Hybrid Systems: Computation and Control. HSCC '15. New York, NY, USA: ACM; 2015. p. 189–198. Available from: http://doi.acm.org/10.1145/2728606.2728633.

4 REAL-TIME RELIABILITY VERIFICATION FOR UAV FLIGHT CONTROL SYSTEM SUPPORTING AIRWORTHINESS CERTIFICATION

Haiyang Xu[1,2], Ping Wang[1]

[1] School of Science and Information, Qingdao Agricultural University, Qingdao, Shandong, China
[2] School of Computer Science and Technology, Nanjing University of Aeronautics and Astronautics, Nanjing, Jiangsu, China

ABSTRACT

In order to verify the real-time reliability of unmanned aerial vehicle (UAV) flight control system and comply with the airworthiness certification standard, we proposed a model-based integration framework for modeling and verification of time property. Combining with the advantages of MARTE, this framework uses class diagram to create the static model of software system, and utilizes state chart to create the dynamic model. In term of the defined transformation rules, the MARTE model could be transformed to formal integrated model, and the different part of the model could also be verified by using existing formal tools. For the real-time specifications of software system, we also proposed a generating algorithm for temporal logic formula, which could automatically extract real-time property from time-sensitive live sequence chart (TLSC). Finally, we modeled the simplified flight control system of UAV to check its real-time property. The results showed that the framework could be used to create the system model, as well as precisely analyze and verify the real-time reliability of UAV flight control system.

INTRODUCTION

UAV has been used in a vast range of civil and military applications, and also brought accidents caused by airborne software failure[1–3], we expect to develop a high reliable UAV flight control system. The traditional approach used for manned aircrafts takes robust time and resources, which is not practical to analyze and validate UAV flight control system. For shortening the development cycle and improve the reliability and performance of flight control system, developing an integrated framework for the design process of flight control system is in need[4]. This framework could integrate the existing design methods and verification tools, and use iterative development cycle to implement and quickly validate UAV flight control system design. Therefore, it is important to enhance the reliability and robustness of UAV flight control system by improving the method of modeling, testing and verifying.

Federal Aviation Administration (FAA) requires that the airborne software system must be conducted by airworthiness certification[5]. Thus, we should model and verify the UAV flight control system in term of corresponding airworthiness certification standards.

In airworthiness certification, we considered the DO-178B standard, which is the current software certification standard that released by Radio Technical Commission for Aeronautics (RTCA). DO-178B prescribes the objectives for each important step during the development process of airborne software[6]. With the development of the software verification technology, RTCA and European Organization for Civil Aviation Equipment (EUROCAE) revised the DO-178B and published the DO-178C/ED-12C standard in 2011. DO-178C/ED-12C proposed several technical supplements such as software tool qualification considerations, model-based development and verification, object-oriented technology and formalizing methods [7–9].

Development and verification based on executable models can optimize the process of airborne software. During the stage of requirement and design, we should find out the software fault as early as possible in order to eliminate the errors of design and enhance the robustness of software. According to DO-178C/ED-12C, source code should be generated from design model directly, and they all should pass the validation.

In the development of airborne software, object-oriented technology benefits the generation of source code for test and certification via model driven architecture (MDA) or MARTE tool. It can improve the reusability and validity of software. DO-178C/ED-12C therefore requires adopting object-oriented technology.

DO-l78C officially indicated the effectiveness of formal methods during airborne software development process. Formal method is consisted of formal model and formal analysis. Formal model is used for defining unambiguous abstract model of system based on mathematic syntax and semantic. Formal analysis proved the consistency between system property and software requirement by theorem proving or model checking.

The design and verification of airborne software should comply with the guidance of DO-178C to obtain certification approval[10]. Recently, in order to improve the development method of airborne software and meet airworthiness certification, researchers have proposed several integrated development frameworks. Most of these methods focus on the model-based development environment to make different tools and techniques adopted an applied. The main challenge of model-based development approach is that we should generate precision appropriate dynamic models of airborne software at different development stages[1]. Mathematical model can only be used to describe simplified real flight control, and is just an approximation of the airborne software, because sensors of UAV are inaccurate and aerodynamic data are not understandable enough. Therefore, mathematical model is not be able to be used for predicting the real-time reliability responses.

To study the feasibility of applying model checking to avionic embedded software, Sreemani et al. took advantage of software cost reduction to describe software requirement specification of military aircraft A-7E, and then translated specification to symbolic model verifier

(SMV)[11]. They pointed out that model checking was of help to provide a safe and reliable software, but it could not be extended to large-scale software.

To verify the requirement specification of large-scale software, Chan et al. proposed an interactive design process based on the progressive refinement of the models. This process can specify the set of properties, and adopt SMV to check the requirements specification of TCAS II. The limitation is that model checkers cannot be integrated with other CASE tools.

Pingree et al. applied model checking to the development of flight software for NASA's Deep Space 1 mission[12]. They used State flow to create software model and translated it into SPIN. The approach can automatically generate software code from State chart model, but they cannot assure that all design errors could be showed in the model.

For rapidly synthesize, analyze and validate a candidate UAV software design, Yew Chai Paw et al. proposed a model-based framework, which integrates a set of design tools to realize software model synthesis, off-line and real-time simulation[1]. They pointed out that simulation based on tests is important for saving cost and time. However, Seveg et al. compared simulation with formal verification in SoCs design process[13]. They indicated that formal verification requires more time and memory, but it can identify failed properties and get the highest credibility of the verified system.

Cofer et al. inserted formal analysis tools into a model-based development process to improve quality of avionics software[14]. They used State flow to generate model-based specification, and used Lustre as an intermediate representation for the models, and then translated specification into NuSMV model checker. They applied the method to the FCS 5000 flight control system and an adaptive flight control system for UAV[15].By analyzing the causes of 156 failures on 129 space crafts, Tafazoli pointed out that 6% of these failures are due to software failure[16].

In this study, our purpose is to verify real-time reliability for UAV flight control system. Combining model-based method with formal analysis tool, we can reduce the cost of building separate analysis models, and keep the model consistent with the software design.

Combining with the requirements of DO-178C, we utilized MARTE class diagrams to set up a time-related static model of flight control system based on MDA. We also employed dynamic models triggered by time to describe system state changes. As MARTE is a graphical model, we proposed a formal PTA-OZ model and constructed its model transformation rules. Using these rules, we can translate both static models and dynamic models into corresponding Object-Z model and PTA models, which are fit for system real-time reliability verification and code automatic generation. In order to get the real-time specification of design model, we presented a method to extract real-time property from TLSC.

This paper proceeds as follows. Section 2 outlines the logic structure of flight control system. Section 3 describes the PTA-OZ model based on MDA. Section 4 gives the real-time property extract method from scenario-based language. Section 5 reports a case study of real-time reliability verification. Finally, Section 6 concludes the paper.

THE LOGIC STRUCTURE OF FLIGHT CONTROL SYSTEM

The software architecture of UAV flight control system mainly consists of communication link (CL) module, sensor signal processing module, flight guidance (FG) module, servo control (SC) module, mode supervise (MS) module and PWM steering output modules.

- CL module is used for receiving telecommand (TC) from the ground control station (GCS), down-transporting telemetry (TM) to GCS and for data communication among the airborne modules.
- The function of FG module includes control law computing, TC verification and response, route planning, operator scheduling and sending control command.
- SC module is applied to response control command and send servo control.
- MS module is mainly used for conflict detection and conflict resolution.

The flight control system uses embedded system design which is based on PC104 bus. It includes five main components: processor module, serial port module, A/D, D/A card module and power module. The communication among modules uses PC104 bus. Processor module communicates with FG module and SC module by adopting TCP/UDP protocol. Serial port module uses RS232 protocol to communicate with sensor module in serial communication. The system uses A/D of AVR to collect signals, such as six degree of freedom information and supply voltage, and uses D/A card to output PWM signal. Fig 1 shows part of hardware and software architecture of the flight control system.

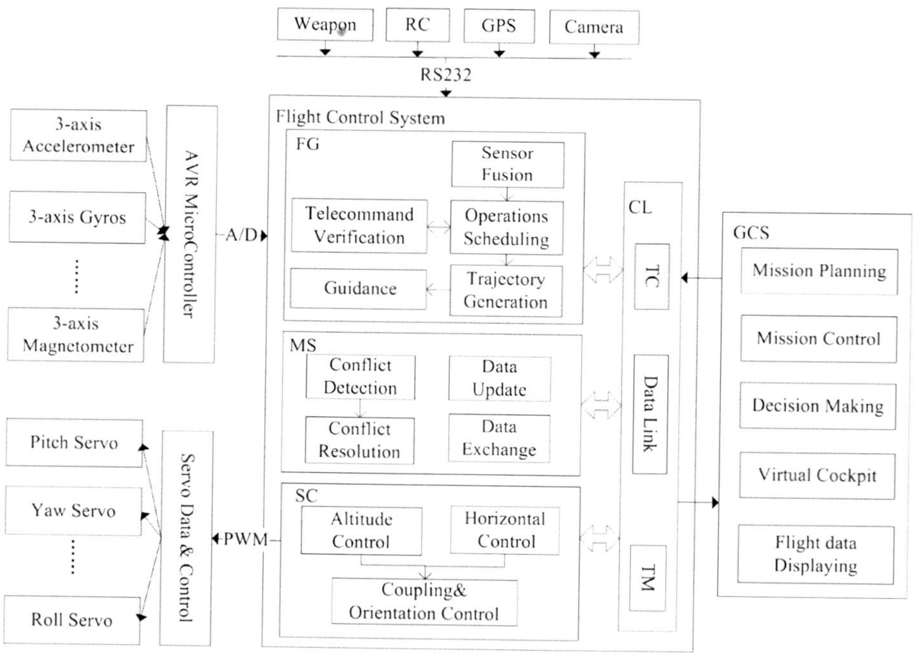

Figure 1: Part of hardware and software architecture of the flight control system.

The figure shows parts of the organizational structure of a flight control system, and describes the data interaction among module.

We focused on the commands and data processing structure among GCS and FG module, SC module, and MS module. We not only require the UAV flight control software to satisfy the DO-178C airworthiness certification requirements, but also fully reference ECSS-E-70-41A standard to standardize the service offered by each module. So we employed telecomm and verification service and onboard operations scheduling service which adopt ECSS-E-70-41A standard in FG module of flight control software.

MODELING AND DESCRIPTION OF TIME PROPERTY

The advantages of development method based on MDA in the design process of embedded software are as follows. Firstly, the execution platform of embedded software is usually heterogeneous and reconfigurable. Secondly, applications often need to react with an external environment, and embedded software design focuses on handling data or control flow. Finally, software design is often subject to real-time requirements and resources availability[17]. Above all, in the early stage of embedded software design, the development method based on MDA could detect if resources and services meet the requirements specification under the given constraints.

Time Static Model based on MARTE

Although model-based development tool such as SCADE suite has been used to formal verify critical avionics software[15], it is difficult to generate code from time synchronism system. SCADE employs a reference or master clock to define all clocks as a functional sample of the master clock[18]. It can provide a solution for generating code in uniprocessor system. However, it is difficult to generate distributed system code. For parallel implementation, MARTE can generate the multi-threaded code from concurrent specification[19].

MARTE, which could be used to establish formal model of real-time and embedded system (RTES), is a new UML extension profile. MARTE defines a mathematically expressive model of time to annotate UML diagrams with formal timing interpretation. MARTE also defines the necessary concepts to build software model of HW/SW embedded system, and its performance depends on the interaction among the different components.

Although UML2 introduces *SimpleTime* package to create time model, it is too simple for RTES. The time models based on MARTE are more suitable for software design. They may be physical, logical, or user-defined. MARTE uses a collection of clocks to represent time, and each clock specifies a totally ordered set of instant.

In MARTE, «*ClockType*» and «*Clock*» stereotypes can be used to represent the concept of clock. «*ClockType*», which is the type of «*Clock*», specifies common features shared by a family of clocks. «*Clock*» includes more detailed information. We adopted above stereotypes to define a «*ClockType*» and several clock instants (Fig 2).

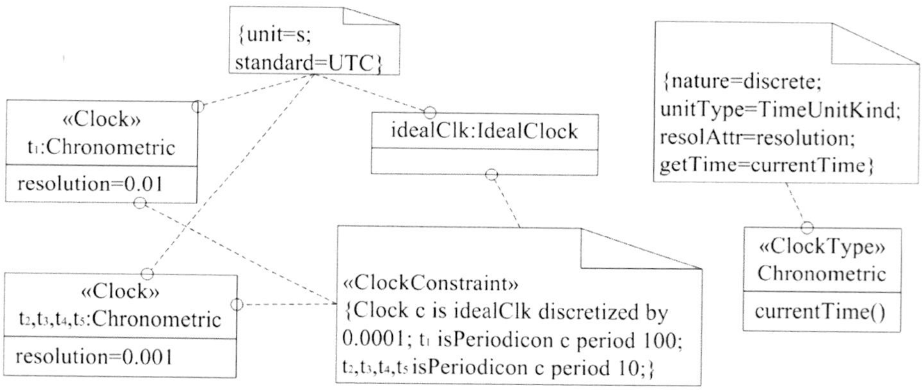

Figure 2: ClockType and its clock.

We can use MARTE time stereotypes to define and describe clock class.

Firstly, we use «*ClockType*» stereotype to define a new clock type, and specify the feature of clock type with tagged value. The new discrete «*ClockType*» *Chronometric,* whose supportive unite is *s*, uses a readable *resolution* to determine the resolution of the associated clock, and uses *currentTime* operation to get the current time.

Secondly, we introduced a predefine clock *idealClk* in MARTE library, which is an instance of *IdealClock*. It represents the continuous clock of physical time, and uses *s* as its unit of time. t_1, t_2, t_3, t_4, t_5, which are instances of *Chronometric,* use clock constraint to specify their deviations with respect to the ideal one. In «ClockConstraint» stereotype, we adopted clock constraint specification language(CCSL) to express the clock constraints. The *c* is defined as an ideal discrete clock whose resolution is 0.001 *s*. For idealClk, we declare a clock t_1 with a period of 10 *ms* and resolution of 0.01 *s*. The t_2, t_3, t_4, t_5, whose resolution is 0.001 *s*, can be sampled every 10 periods.

As MARTE can support system-level design, we adopted RtUnited and PpUnit for the active object of UML to create model of flight control system. Fig 3 showed the class diagrams in software logic structure of flight control system. The structure consists of GCS and airborne system. The logic entities of airborne system include CL module, FG module, SC module and MS module. GCS interacts with airborne system through TC and TM signal. RtUnit is used to represent the entities, which can encapsulate object and behavior in a single entity. Any real-time unit can invoke services of other real-time units to send/receive data flow. In class diagrams, we defined attributes, operations and associations, and offered the interface definitions with entity. FG module can dynamically create schedulable resources to execute its services, and MS module has a pool of 10 schedulable resources.

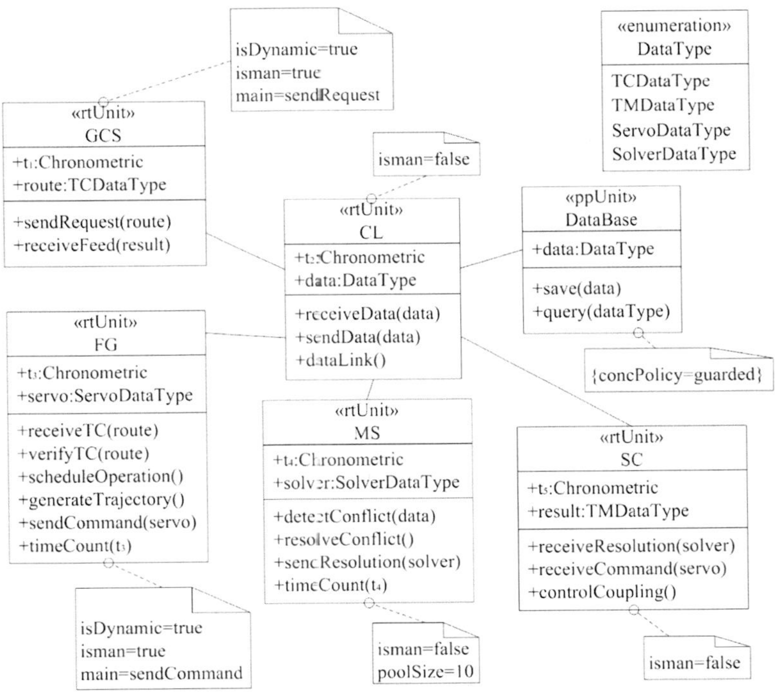

Figure 3: The software logic structure of flight control system.

Using RtUnited and PpUnit, we build part of the software logic modle of flight control system.

All real-time units share data that is represented by the class *DataBase*. As the concurrent execution of real-time units, we need to protect the data access encapsulated in the class *DataBase*. In order to do this, we tagged the class *DataBase* by «*PpUnit*» stereotype, whose concPolicy property of *DataBase* is set to guarded, which means that real-time unit should access the *DataBase* property one after another.

DYNAMIC MODEL SUPPORTING TIME-TRIGGERED

State chart can describe the dynamic behaviors of object through creating object model about its life cycle, and focuses on the object behavior changes caused by events. In state chart, an event is an occurrence of motivation, which can trigger state transition. As a special event,Time event represents the state transition triggered by time related factors.

According to the clocks defined in 3.1, we described all kinds of time-triggered mechanisms to create UML dynamic model. So we need to extend UML state chart with time model to support events and behaviors triggered by time.

To reference time-related concept for state chart, we use «*TimedProcessing*» stereotype of MARTE to specify duration for a behavior and improve the use of UML behavior. Through reference defined clocks, we specified behavior of state chart with user-defined clocks to support time-triggered dynamic mechanism, and described RTES software to offer support for multi-clock mechanism of distributed environment.

In MARTE, we use «*TimedEvent*» stereotype to represent time event, which extends from the meta-class *SimpleTime::TimeEvent* of UML. Time event is used to specify the state transition triggered by time in state chart.

Flight control system is forced to obey the following operation rules:

- GCS_request: GCS requests a flight command.
- FG_command: FG sends a flight command to SC.

- MS_command: If a flight conflict is detected, MS would send a specific flight command to SC to resolve the flight conflict. MS command is able to override the GCS request and FG command.
- MS_clear: Executes GCS request or FG command when there is no potential flight conflict. All previous requests would be canceled when a flight conflict was confirmed. At this point, the value of MS_clear variable is false, and the values of all command variables are false.

Fig 4 described the state chart of flight control system. «*TimedProcessing*» stereotype showed that the dynamic model supports time-triggered mechanism, and use *on* attribute to specify associated clock of the current model. « *TimedEvent*» stereotype was used to define time events: *requestTimeout* and *detectTimeout*. Event *requestTimeout* described that FG module must generate a new air route within 50ms after receiving user's TC command, otherwise it would trigger timeout transition. Event *detectTimeout* requires MS module to detect and resolve short-term conflict within 10ms, otherwise timeout transition would be triggered.

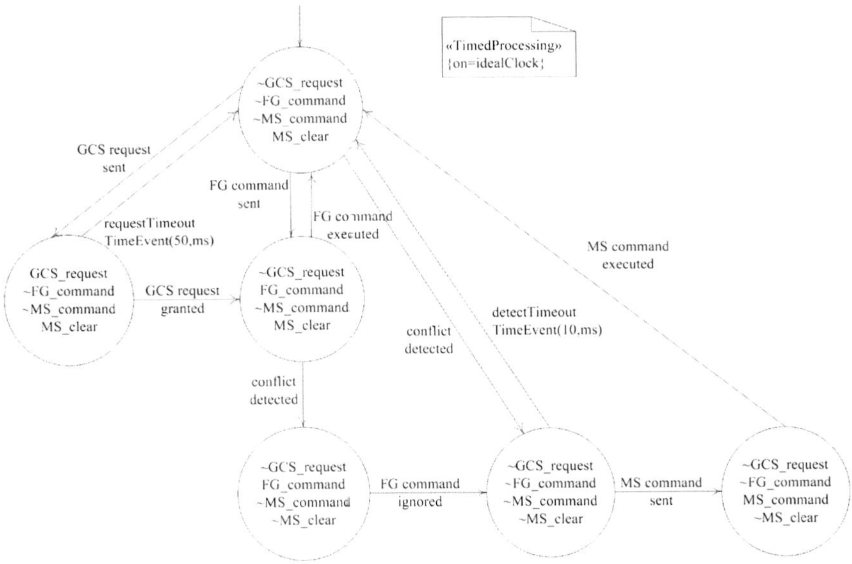

Figure 4: State chart of flight control system.

State chart can be used to describe dynamic behavior triggered by event.

State chart uses state and state transition to describe dynamic behavior model of system for event response, and is widely used for model programming. Comparing with state chart, automaton is formal to analyze recognizable language. As automaton is the foundation of state chart, it could accurately verify behaviors of class[20, 21].

Formal Description based on PTA-OZ

As a graphical modeling language, MARTE works well in establishing the software model for RTES, but it has following deficiencies: 1) As defined in different ways, there are inconsistencies existing among abstract grammar, static semantics and dynamic semantics. 2) MARTE lacks reasoning authentication mechanism. These disadvantages limit MARTE's application field and development, we therefore need to define precise and formal semantics for MARTE.

We proposed a formal integrated model called PTA-OZ[22], which uses Object-Z to describe the static semantics of MARTE and uses probability timed automata(PTA) to define its dynamic semantics. The formal integrated model could mathematically prove whether software models meet the requirements[23], and it could also increase the safety and correctness of software.

Definition 1 A PTA-OZ is a tuple $PO = (A, I, L, P, OZ)$, where:

- A is used to deal with inheritance, lists all parent class using *inherit* clause.
- I is the interface, and consists of channel declarations, which are provided and used by classes.
- L is local methods, which can only be accessed from the inside.
- P is a PTA that maps the state, event and transition of state chart to the attributes and operations of Object-Z.
- OZ is from Object-Z that includes a state schema, an initial schema and several operations.

We designed a transforming algorithm for the implementation of the formal model[24].By mapping the class and state chart of MARTE to Object-Z class and PTA expression in Object-Z format, we created the software model of flight control system through MARTE, and then translated into PTA-OZ model.

Rule 1 In term of the basic transformation rules[25], we could define the transformation rule from MARTE model to PTA-OZ model. 1) MARTE class is translated to Object-Z class of PTA-OZ model. 2) The state chart of MARTE is mapped to PTA expression in Object-Z format. This rule is described as follows:

mapMARTEToPTA_OZ: MARTE→PTA_OZ

∀mar: MARTE•mapMARTEToPTA_OZ (mar) = {po: PTA_OZ |

∀mc:mar.class•∃oz:po.oz•oz = mapMARTEClassToOZ(mc)

∀ms:mar.statechart•∃pta:po.pta•pta = mapMARStateChartToPTA (ms)}

Static Class Transformation.

The class name of MARTE is mapped to the class name of Object-Z. The attributes of MARTE class are translated into state schemas. The association class is translated into the attribute of class. Interface operation invoked by class is translated into a channel schema of PTA-OZ. Interface operation offered by class is translated into a method schema.

Fig 5 showed a class of FG module, which was described in Object-Z format. Depending on class *FG*, association class *CL* was translated into attribute *comm* of class *FG*. The attributes *route*, t_3, *servo, comm* of class *FG* were mapped to state schemas of PTA-OZ model. The operations like *verifyTc, scheduleOperation, sendCommand* provided by class *FG* were translated into methods of PTA-OZ model. The operations like *sendData, dataLink* invoked by the class *FG* were translated into channels of PTA-OZ model.

Figure 5: FG module described in Object-Z class.

Object-Z is a formal language, it can be used to model the static model accurately.

The processing time required by the invariance of the class *FG* should be no more than 50ms. We used *effect+operationname* to specify the operational effect, and used *enable+operationname* to express the operational trigger. For example, in *effect_scheduleOperation,* telecommand *route* releases if and only if the release status is *enabled,* the execution is unblock, and the destination can execute the command. The *guard*condition of operating *enable_sendCommand* is that connection *comm* has been established and servo command has been analyzed.

Dynamic state chart transformation.

As a class, the state chart can describe the behavior of class. In Object-Z, the behavior of class can create model in term of the attributes and operations of class. The attributes show the different statuses of the object, and the operations can change the value of the attributes. The state chart of MARTE consists of state, time event and transition. We thus mainly focus on these compositions to define transformation rules.

We used behavior attributes to create observable states model of object which value is boolean type. If true, object was in behavior state, and was regarded as an *active* state in MARTE. So each state should be mapped to a behavior attribute of Object-Z.

An event is the reception of a signal or the invoking request of an operation[26]. The response to a request can be modeled as receiving operation. Each event of state chart is mapped to the event acceptor operation of Object-Z. If an Object-Z operation was corresponding to a transition, we defined it as the triggered transition operation of event receives operation.

Time event is used to represent transition event triggered by time related factors and state transition in state chart triggered by time. The timing constraints of event in state chart are mapped to the clock constraints annotation on the edge of PTA. In Object-Z, we denoted state transition by comparing clock value with state invariance.

A transition represents either the change of object state or the execution of action. Due to that source state is the condition of transition and the target state is the result of transition, the value of source state is as the precondition of operation, and the value of target state is as the post condition of operation. The source state of transition is mapped to the initial state of behavior attributes in Object-Z, and the target states of transition are mapped to the termination states of behavior attributes.

A function *mapStateMachineToOZ*, which formally describes the transformation rules between state chart and Object-Z, is defined to translate state, time event and transition of state chart into the attributes and operations of Object-Z.

Fig 6 showed a PTA expression in Object-Z format. The state is translated into the behavior attributes of Object-Z class. The initial state of state chart is expressed by the *Init* state schema in Object-Z class, and it is labeled *Ready*. An event is defined as different event receive operations. For example, event *GCSRequestSent* is defined as the operation of sending the *route* data, and causes the state to change from *Ready* state to *Request* state. Time event *requestTimeout* represents the transition event triggered by timeout, so that Its time can be realized by operation *timeCount,* and the state will be changed from *Request* state to *Ready*state. All the transitions belong to transition operations of Object-Z class. The behavior attributes of source state and target state are respectively defined as the precondition and post condition of transition operations. Transition operations contain all these effective activities. For example, the source state of transition *transRequesttoFGcmd* is *Request*, the target state is *FGcmd*, and effective activity is *verifyTC*.

FCS_statemachine
↾(GCSRequestSent,GCSRequestGranted,conflictDetected,⋯,
MSCommandExecuted)
↾(requestTimeout,detectTimeout)
[Behavioral state attributes]
Ready:Boolean
Request:Boolean
FGcmd:Boolean
Detect:Boolean
Conflict:Boolean
MScmd:Boolean
INIT
FCS_statemachine
Ready
[Operations derived from the dynamic model]
[Event acceptor operations]
GCSRequestSent≙[route?:TCDataType]∧transReadytoRequest[]
GCSRequestGranted≙transRequesttoFGcmd[]
conflictDetected≙transFGcmdtoDetect[]∨transReadytoConflict[]
……
MSCommandExecuted≙transMScmdtoReady[]
[TimeEvent acceptor operations]
requestTimeout≙[t_3:Chronometric]∧transRequesttoReady[]
detectTimeout≙[t_4:Chronometric]∧transConflicttoReady[]
[Transiton operations]
transReadytoRequest≙[Δ(Request)|Ready∧Request']∧sendRequest
transRequesttoFGcmd≙[Δ(FGcmd)|Request∧FGcmd']∧verifyTC
……
transRequesttoReady≙[Δ(Ready)|Request∧Ready']∧timeCount
……
transMScmdtoReady≙[Δ(Ready)|MScmd∧Ready']∧sendData

Figure 6: PTA expression in Object-Z format.

Dynamic state transition can be described by the state schema in Object-Z.

EXTRACTING REAL-TIME SPECIFICATIONS

The assurance of real-time requirement is the key of verifying software real-time, and is also the foundation for design, verification and realization of real-time reliability[27]. Most of the software real-time problems are caused by the inadequacy of acquiring real-time requirement. Flight control system is a hard real-time system, and it has strict deadlines on task. If the task could not satisfy the response time or response is not in time, it would lead to disastrous consequences.

The real-world software system developed according to natural language specifications is difficult to verify whether the resulting software satisfies the natural specifications[28]. For checking the software model, it is necessary to use a formal and precise symbol to represent the design specifications. Ogawa et al. proposed a goal-oriented analysis method of the requirement specification[29], which uses natural language to specify the specifications, then refines them into linear temporal logic (LTL) formulas and checks them through SPIN model checker. Therefore, model checking always uses LTL to specify properties to unambiguously describe the desired behavior of system. Each formula expresses a specific expectation of software behavior, a set of all formulas describe a consistent pattern of behavior.

Scenario-oriented Requirement Description

At the stages of design and verification, we need to identify the performance scenarios from end to end, which are usually extracted directly from requirements and used to evaluate the system response times[30]. The duration of a single processing or an end-to-end execution usually needs to be described. We can specify time information within the model by marking time-labeled UML2 interaction diagrams.

Scenario-oriented language is able to graphically describe the software requirements, and then be used to verify the properties of design model. The advantages are straightforward and visualization. Message sequence chart (MSC) is widely used in the development field of industry software by International Telecommunication Union(ITU) as the standard and the description language of communication behavior of real-time system. However, MSC is only used to describe the causal relationships among messages, but explain the time partial order constraints of behavior, and clearly distinguish specifications from executable requirements[31, 32]. These drawbacks of MSC limit its expression ability and application. Based on the extension of MSC, Werner Damm and David Harel proposed live sequence chart (LSC) [31], which distinguishes the existential scenario and the universal scenario of system. If the condition of universal scenario was true, the system must execute the scenario described in sequence chart, meaning the universal scenario is suitable to specify the activity of scenario.

Yves Bontemps et al. applied an extension of LSC to air traffic control system[33],and specified scenario-oriented requirements by associating an instance with a class. But LSC still adopts timing constraints in MSC, such as timer and delay interval, turning out that this application is limited.

MARTE extends sequence diagram, and defines timing constraints on sending and receiving events, and could record the start and end time, and also uses value specification language (VSL) to specify timing constraints among events. For overcoming the shortcomings of LSC in time property, we adopted MARTE to enrich the expressive power of LSC, and proposed TLSC method, which could intuitively describe time-enriched property and timing partial order relation of behaviors.

For overcoming the drawbacks of LSC in time property, we proposed TLSC method to intuitively describe time-enriched property and timing partial order relation of behaviors by using value specification language(VSL) to specify timing constraints among events and to extending sequence diagram by using MARTE. The extension by MARTE is that adding timing constraints to sending and receiving events for recording the start and end time.

We still adopted the property *on* of «*TimedProcessing*» stereotype to associate clocks with current TLSC. Sequence diagram is used to specify the interaction behavior among objects, which may be restricted by time factors in time trigger architecture, thus we need to introduce time observation to describe timing constraint. Time observation offers a method to acquire execution time and duration of system. «*TimedInstantObservation*» stereotype acquires the start or end instant and uses operation *@t* to store acquired time in variable *t*. «*TimedDurationObservation*» stereotype can be used to express the duration of event, using $\{t, t+d\}$ to denote that an event starts at t time and ends at $t+d$ time.

Fig 7 showed a scenario-oriented end-to-end requirement for flight control software. In order to reference ideal clock, we use «*TimedInstantObservation*» stereotype of MARTE to express time observation. Similarly, we defined a time observation of UML to associate with receive events of control message, and referred to the same ideal clock. The rules of execution time among modules of flight control software are that the delay time for receiving telecommand is less than 5 *ms*, the calculating time of flight path is less than 50 *ms*, the response time of conflict detection is less than 10 *ms*, the execution time of servo control is less than 10 *ms*, the output delay time of telemetry is less than 5 *ms*. That is to say, the time from sending telecommand to receiving telemetry is no more than 80 *ms*. Thus, we need to define a timing constraint, which shows that the duration between time observation events *stop* and *start* is less than 80 *ms*.

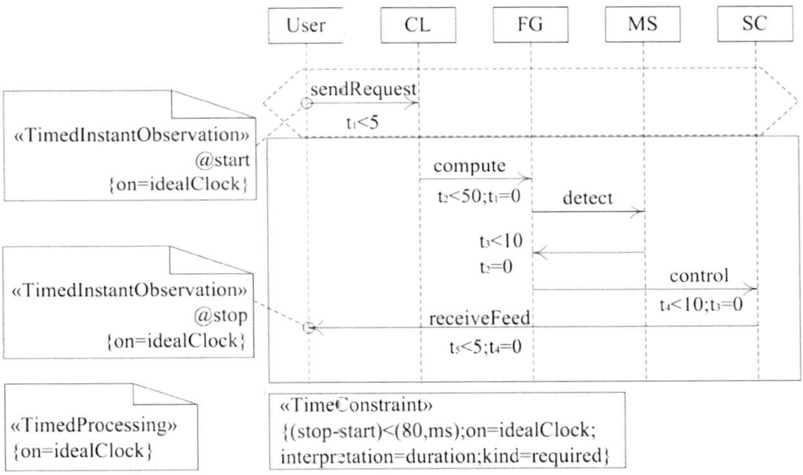

Figure 7: Scenario-oriented requirement for flight control software.

MARTE time model is used to describe the requirement. With timing constraints.

Monitoring Real-time Specification

In the process of software design, it is difficult to design a bug-free system, so we need to employ model checking to find the bugs, which can be used to verify whether software model meets design specification. It is difficult to write bug-free specifications, since we do not know whether the system specification could fully capture the design expectation of software.

Although graphical TLSC could intuitively express timing partial order relation of behaviors, and is suited to describe customer requirement by software engineer, it could not be used to verify the system specification. In the scenario-oriented software engineering, temporal logic is widely applied to describe the software requirements, but it is not realistic to require software engineer to intuitively use temporal logic formula to specify software requirement. Therefore, we tried to extract time property formula from software requirement of flight control system described by TLSC. Firstly, we gave the formal definition of TLSC[34].

Definition 2 A TLSC is a tuple TLSC = $<I, Loc, E, C, \delta, Mode, inv, \mu>$, where

- I is a set of instances.
- Loc is a set of locations.
- E is a set of events, and it contains two events condition Con and message Msg, that is, $E = Con \cup Msg$.
- C is a finite set of clock variables.
- δ: $E \rightarrow Loc$ is an event mapping function which maps each event to a location.
- $Mode$: $E \rightarrow \{cold, hot\}$ is a behavior mapping function which identifies each event with a provisional or mandatory behavior.
- inv:$Loc \rightarrow \Phi(C)$ is a timing constraint mapping function, by which each location $\langle i,l \rangle$ is given assigns timing constraint $inv(l)$ called location invariance.
- μ:$E \rightarrow \Phi(C)$ is a time interval mapping function, it defines the time interval of event occurrence.

Trace-based semantic adopts finite or infinite state sequence to describe the relation of state transition. Using the form of trace-based semantic, precise meaning of software behavior could be reflected, and temporal logic formula could be extracted from TLSC. Here we gave the trace-based semantic of universal chart in TLSC.

Definition 3 Let a CUT sequence $r = (cut_0,v_0), (cut_1,v_1),\ldots, (cut_k,v_k)$ be an execution of TLSC, where cut_i denotes a mapping of current locations of all the instances, and v_i denotes the clock interpretation of current state. cut_0 is the starting point and clock interpretation $v_0 = 0$, cut_k is the terminal point, and $(cut_i,v_i) = succ((cut_{i-1},v_{i-1}),<i, l_i>)$ $(i = 0,1,\ldots,k-1)$. The set of all runs is denoting to $Runs$. We use $r^k = \{r|\forall r \in Runs \wedge |r| = k\}$ to denote the sub path of run r with k-path, and use $Path(cut_i,v_i) = \{r|\forall r \in Runs \wedge cut_0 = cut_i\}$ to denote a path of a run starting at (c_i,v_i). An execution trace, which is the trace of a CUT sequence, is denoted by $\pi = trace(r)$

$$cut_0 \xrightarrow{\pi_0} cut_1 \xrightarrow{\pi_1} \cdots \xrightarrow{\pi_{k-1}} cut_k$$

Then $\pi = \pi_0, \pi_1, \ldots, \pi_{k\text{-}1}$ denotes the events that trigger the state transition, and

$$\pi_i = \begin{cases} \delta(i, l_i) & \mathit{if}\,(cut_i, v_i) = succ((cut_{i-1}, v_{i-1}), \langle i, l_i \rangle) \\ \varepsilon & else \end{cases}$$

In term of execution trace, we define the trace-based language of TLSC *tl*, that is

$$L = \{\pi \mid \exists r \in Runs(tl) \wedge r = (cut_0, v_0), \ldots, (cut_k, v_k)\ s.t.\ \pi = trace(r)\}$$

In the universal chart, all runs must satisfy the given scenario. If executions *r* of TLSC are in the same sub chart, the relation between formulas is logical conjunction. If executions *r* are in the different sub charts, the relation is logical implication. Algorithm 1 showed that temporal formulas corresponding to different message in sub chart were combined into an algorithm about ACTL formula.

Algorithm1 combined Generating (ϕ_{msg1},ϕ_{msg2})

if type(ϕ_{msg1}) = pre-chart **then**
    if type(ϕ_{msg2}) = pre-chart **then**
        $\phi = \neg\phi_{msg2} \mathrm{U}\ (\phi_{msg1}(\mathrm{X}\phi_{msg2}))$
    elseif type(ϕ_{msg2}) = main-chart **then**
        $\phi = \phi_{msg1} \rightarrow (\mathrm{X}\phi_{msg2})$
    endif
elseif type(ϕ_{msg1}) = main-chart **then**
    if type(ϕ_{msg2}) = pre-chart **then**
        $\phi = \phi_{msg1}$
    elseif type(ϕ_{msg2}) = main-chart **then**
        $\phi = \neg\phi_{msg2} \mathrm{U}\ (\phi_{msg1}(\mathrm{X}\phi_{msg2}))$
    endif
endif
return(ϕ)

Universal chart can be used to express the mandatory scenario. If the event in pre-chart was activated, there must have response event in main chart. Hence in term of Algorithm 1, we could get the ACTL formula corresponding to TLSC as follow

$$AG\Big(\Big(\bigwedge_{\forall p_i \in Msg_p} {\phi'}_{p_i,succ(p_i)} \wedge \bigwedge_{\substack{\forall m_i \in Msg_m, \\ p_j = Max_p(i_j)}} {\phi'}_{p_j,m_i} \wedge \bigwedge_{\substack{\forall p_i \in Msg_p, \\ p_j = Max_p(i_j)}} \neg\chi_{p_i,p_j}\Big)$$

$$\rightarrow \Big(\bigwedge_{\forall m_i \in Msg_m} {\phi'}_{m_i,succ(m_i)} \wedge \bigwedge_{m_j = Max_m(i_j)} AF^{inv+u} m_j \wedge \bigwedge_{\substack{\forall e_i \in Msg, \\ m_j = Max_m(i_j)}} \neg\chi_{e_i,m_j}\Big)\Big)$$

Where *Msg* is the set of messages, $succ(m)$ denotes the immediate successor of message m. ${\phi'}_{e_i,e_j} = \neg e_j \cup e_i$ is order attribute and it shows that message e_j will not occur until e_i occurs. $\chi_{e_i,e_j} = (\neg e_i \wedge e_j) \cup (e_i \wedge X((\neg e_i \wedge e_j) \cup e_i))$ is uniqueness property and denotes that message e_i occurs twice before e_j. We can also use optimization strategies to improve the algorithm performance[35].

Using Algorithm 1, we could extract temporal logic formula of real-time property from TLSC for flight control system as showed in Fig 7. After sending message *sendRequest* to UAV from GCS, each module began to work, and FG module computed the flight path, MS module detected conflict, and SC module sent servo command. We could get the temporal logic formula of real-time property from scenario-oriented TLSC as follow

$$AG(A(\neg compute \wedge \neg detect \wedge \neg control) \cup sendRequest) \rightarrow AF^{t<80} receiveFeed)$$

REAL-TIME RELIABILITY ANALYSIS

In the verification of PTA-OZ model, we could check the correctness of grammar and type in Object-Z part, and make sure that all the operations strictly use state model. By using the existing formal tools Z/EVES and PVS, specification could be checked and analyzed in Z form. We could automatically extract corresponding burden of proof for Object-Z specification according to a certain rule, and then test by inputting them to Z/EVES. Through strictly type examination, we could analyze specifications in Object-Z form, and locate the inconsistent information between specifications and requirements.

However, Object-Z is only suitable for data refinement, and does not support the structure similar to program language. Hence, there is semantic gap between Object-Z and program language, while PTA-OZ model can overcome the shortcoming and realize operation refinement through verifying the correctness of operation.

PTA model could be used to express the state transition diagram of flight control system. We could create mathematics model of real-time reliability by applying Markov process to achieve the state transition probability matrix of system. There are three status types of real-time reliability: *up* denotes that system is in working, *down* denotes that system shuts down, *danger*denotes that some transient failures have occurred but have not yet caused system shutdown.

There are various kinds of sensors in UAV for receiving signal, data or command. The performance of sensors is a gradual recession process, thus reduce the reliability of hardware devices. The failure of sensors will cause the software failure of FG module. Though the reliability assessment of hardware devices, the reliability of sensors will reduce after working 1000 *h*, and will down to 0 after working 1500 *h*. In flight control system, software module will reboot to rectify the transient fault. If the system was in sensor failure, FG module was unable to read data from the sensor, meanwhile the system would be forced to skip the current cycle. If the number of skipped cycles exceeded a threshold value, then flight control system would fail and emergency instructions or self-destruct would start.

Fig 8 showed the expected time of each status within T unit time described in logarithm form. Since the requirement of total time from sending telecommand to receiving telemetry is no more than 80 *ms*, Fig 8(a) showed the expected time of different system states within 80 *ms*. Fig 8(b)showed the expected time of different system states within 1*h* when UAV carries out a short-term mission. The expected time in failure status gradually increases, but it is still less than the working time. Fig 8(c) showed that the expected time of *down* status will increase significantly while UAV carries out a long-term mission. As shown in Fig 8, the failure status of software caused by hardware fault would gradually increase along with the execution time increase. Thus we could improve the design method of software through enhancing the reliability of hardware.

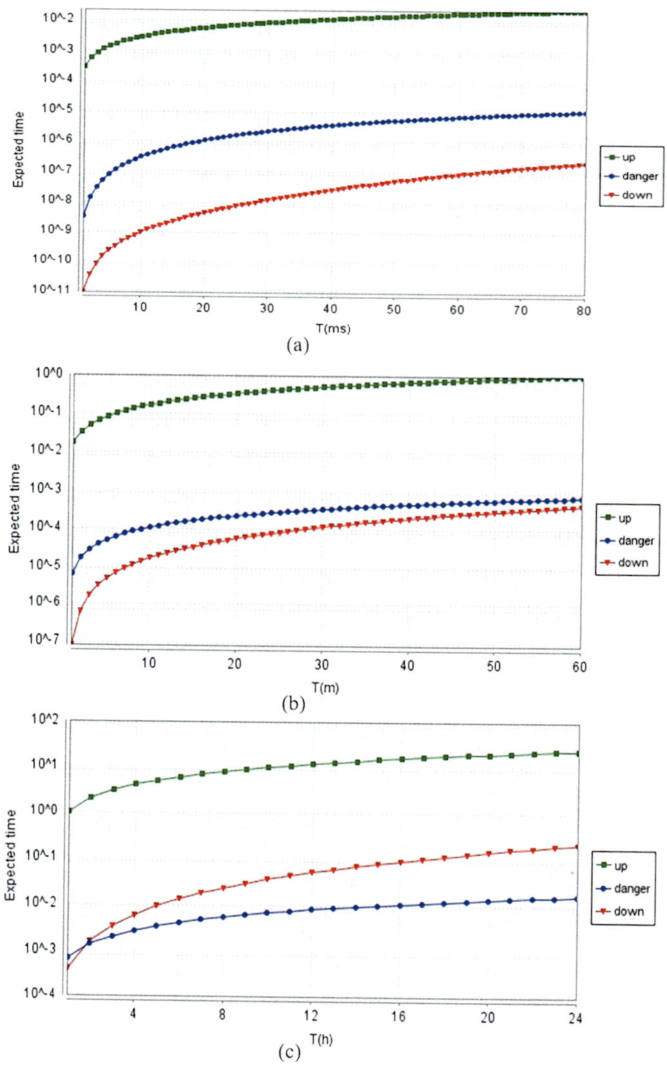

Figure 8: The expected time of each status within T unit time described in logarithm form.

(a) The expected time within 80ms. (b) The expected time within 60m, (c) The expected time within 24h. (a)Within 80ms, the probability of system shutdown is smaller. (b) As time goes on, the danger status goes up. The UAV is fit to carry out a short-term mission. (c)The reliability of hardware determines UAV whether can perform tasks for a long time.

The integrated framework for UAV flight control development can execute real-time simulation[1]. It adopts real-time operating system, does real-time monitoring by GCS, and executes the embedded software code in real-time. Compared with similar method[1], we can accurately calculate the expected time of each status. The result showed that UAV is highly reliable when it carries out a short-term mission and it is not suiteable for a long-term mission.

The system reliability depends on the threshold value K, Table 1 showed the expected time of system states with danger and up. When the value of K increases, the expected time both increase. The increasing of expected time in up is significantly higher than in danger. The different value of K also effects the system reliability. The reliability probability of processor-in-the-loop was given in Fig 9. The increasing value of K makes the reliability probability to stabilize.

Table 1: The Expected time in states "danger" and "up"

K	Expected time	
	danger(hrs)	up(days)
1	0.29	420.78
2	0.39	559.40
4	0.45	651.25
8	0.46	664.53
16	0.46	664.74

doi:10.1371/journal.pone.0167168.t001

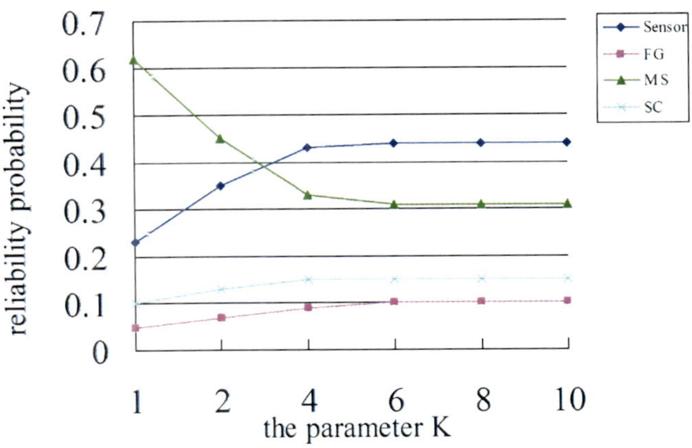

Figure 9: The reliability probability of each processor.

With the increasing K value, the reliability probability became stable.

CONCLUSIONS

Compared with existing integrated framework[1,36,37], we used graphics modeling language MARTE to create software model of flight control, and transformed static structure and dynamic behavior models into formal integrated framework PTA-OZ through defined transformation strategies. We specially focused on the model and verification of time property, which is not considered by most integration framework. The different processes such as analysis, modeling, transforming and verification in proposed framework are tightly-coupled.

For modeling and verification of the real-time reliability of UAV flight control system, we have mainly done following works. Combined with DO-178C standard, we studied model-based method, object-oriented technology and formal method in the framework of software development, and propose a formal PTA-OZ model, which can formalize MARTE model in an object-oriented way by transformation rules. To eliminate the difference in the description of the real-time property formula among software engineers, we proposed an extracting method of temporal logic formula from TLSC, which could automatically generate real-time specification. By verifying the real-time reliability of software model, we could analyze its status type at different time periods.

In order to meet the airworthiness certification, we proposed a design, development and validation framework for UAV flight control system. To begin with, we used MARTE to create the time property model, then translated it into PTA-OZ model. Eventually we could analyze and verify the real-time reliability of UAV flight control system by existing formal verification tools.

ACKNOWLEDGMENTS

We thank Professor Zhuang Yi at Nanjing University of Aeronautics and Astronautics, China, for her helpful comments on this article.

AUTHOR CONTRIBUTIONS

- **Conceptualization:** HX.
- **Data curation:** HX.
- **Formal analysis:** HX.
- **Funding acquisition:** PW.
- **Investigation:** PW.
- **Methodology:** HX.
- **Project administration:** HX.
- **Resources:** HX.
- **Software:** HX.
- **Supervision:** PW.
- **Validation:** PW.
- **Visualization:** PW.
- **Writing – original draft:** HX.
- **Writing – review & editing:** PW.

REFERENCES

1. Paw YC, Balas GJ. Development and application of an integrated framework for small UAV flight control development. Mechatronics. 2011;21(5):789–802.
2. Song H, Rawat D, Jeschke S, Brecher C. Cyber-Physical Systems: Foundations, Principles and Applications Waltham, MA, USA: Elsevier; 2016.
3. Jeschke S, Brecher C, Meisen T, Özdemir D, Eschert T. Industrial Internet of Things: Cybermanufacturing Systems. Switzerland: Springer; 2016.
4. Pouryazdan M, Kantarci B, Soyata T, Song H. Anchor-Assisted and Vote-Based Trustworthiness Assurance in Smart City Crowdsensing. IEEE Access. 2016;4:529–41.
5. Souyris J, Wiels V, Delmas D, Delseny H. Formal verification of avionics software products. the 16 International Symposium on Formal Methods; Toulouse, France: Springer; 2009. p. 532–46.

6. Bingfeng X, Zhiqiu H, Jun H, Xiaofeng Y. Model-driven safety dependence verification for componet-based airborne software supporting ariworthiness certification. Acta Aeronautica et Astronautica Sinica. 2012;33(5):796–808.
7. Gigante G, Pascarella D. Formal methods in avionic software certification: the DO-178C perspective. 5th International Symposium ON ISoLA 2012, Part II, LNCS 7610; Heraklion, Crete, Greece: Springer-Verlag; 2012. p. 205–15.
8. Moy Y, Ledinot E, Delseny H, Wiels V, Monate B. Testing or Formal Verification: DO-178C Alternatives and Industrial Experience. IEEE Software. 2013;30(3):50–7.
9. Cofer D. Model checking: cleared for take off. 17th International SPIN Workshop; Enschede, The Netherlands Springer; 2010. p. 76–87.
10. Jacklin SA, Lowry MR, Schumann JM, Gupta PP, Bosworth JT, Zavala E, et al. Verification, validation, and certification challenges for adaptive flight-critical control system software. American Institute of Aeronautics and Astronautics (AIAA) Guidance, Navigation, and Control Conference and Exhibit2004. p. 1–10.
11. Sreemani T, Atlee JM. Feasibility of model checking software requirements: A case study. Proceedings of the eleventh annual Conference on Computer Assurance: systems integrity, software safety, process security; Gaithersburg, Maryland: Institute of Electrical and Electronics Engineers; 1996. p. 77–88.
12. Pingree PJ, Mikk E, Holzmann GJ, Smith MH, Dams D. Validation of mission critical software design and implementation using model checking. Proceedings of the 21st Digital Avionics Systems Conference; Piscataway, New Jersey: IEEE; 2002. p. 6A4-1–6A4-12.
13. Segev E, Goldshlager S, Miller H, Shua O, Sher O, Greenberg S. Evaluating and comparing simulation verification vs. formal verification approach on block level design. Proceedings of the 2004 11th IEEE International Conference on Electronics, Circuits and Systems; Tel Aviv, Israel: IEEE; 2004. p. 515–8.
14. Cofer D, Whalen M, Miller S. Software model checking for avionics systems. Proceedings of 27th Digital Avionics Systems Conference;

St. Paul, Minnesota: IEEE; 2008. p. 5D-1-5D-8.

15. Whalen M, Cofer D, Miller S, Krogh B, Storm W. Integration of Formal Analysis into a Model-Based Software Development Process. 12th International Workshop on Formal Methods for Industrial Critical Systems; Berlin, Germany: Springer; 2007. p. 68–84.
16. Tafazoli M. A study of on-orbit spacecraft failures. Acta Astronautica. 2009;64(2):195–205.
17. Li W, Song H. ART: An Attack-Resistant Trust Management Scheme for Securing Vehicular Ad Hoc Networks. IEEE Transactions on Intelligent Transportation Systems. 2016;17(4):960–9.
18. Yu H, Talpin J-P, Besnard L, Gautier T, Marchand H, Le Guernic P. Polychronous controller synthesis from MARTE CCSL timing specifications. 9th IEEE/ACM International Conference on Formal Methods and Models for Co-design; Cambridge, UK: IEEE; 2011. p. 21–30.
19. Posadas H, Penil P, Nicolas A, Villar E. System synthesis from UML/MARTE models: The PHARAON approach. Proceedings of the 2013 Electronic System Level Synthesis Conference; Austin, Texas, USA: IEEE; 2013. p. 1–8.
20. Kim S-K, Carrington D. A formal metamodeling approach to a transformation between the UML state machine and Object-Z. 4th International Conference on Formal Engineering Methods; Shanghai, China: Springer-Verlag; 2002. p. 548–60.
21. Kim S-K, Burger D, Carrington D. An MDA approach towards integrating formal and informal modeling languages. International Symposium of Formal Methods Europe; Newcastle, UK: Springer; 2005. p. 448–64.
22. Haiyang X, Yi Z, Jingjing G. A Formal Modeling Method for Embedded Software Architecture. Acta electronica sinica. 2014;42(8):1515–21.
23. Guan T, Wang Y, Duan L, Ji R. On-Device Mobile Landmark Recognition Using Binarized Descriptor with Multifeature Fusion. Acm Transactions on Intelligent Systems & Technology. 2015;7(1):1–29.
24. Zhang Y, Guan T, Duan L, Wei B, Gao J, Mao T. Inertial sensors

supported visual descriptors encoding and geometric verification for mobile visual location recognition applications. Signal Processing. 2015;112:17–26.

25. Haiyang X, Yi Z. A Formal Transformation Approach for Embedded Software Modeling. Journal of Software. 2014;9(4):807–13.
26. Wang Z, Yu J, He Y, Guan T. Affection arousal based highlight extraction for soccer video. Multimedia Tools & Applications. 2014;73(1):519–46.
27. Wei B, Guan T, Duan L, Yu J, Mao T. Wide area localization and tracking on camera phones for mobile augmented reality systems. Multimedia Systems. 2014;21(4):1–19.
28. Rozier KY. Linear temporal logic symbolic model checking. Computer Science Review. 2011;5(2):163–203.
29. Ogawa H, Kumeno F, Honiden S. Model checking process with goal-oriented requirements analysis. Proceedings of the 15th Asia-Pacific Software Engineering Conference Beijing, China: IEEE; 2008. p. 377–84.
30. Jiang Y, Song H, Wang R, Gu M. Data-Centered Runtime Verification of Wireless Medical Cyber-Physical System. IEEE Transactions on Industrial Informatics. 2016;PP(99):1-.
31. Damm W, Harel D. LSCs: breathing life into message sequence charts. Formal Methods in System Design. 2001;19(1):45–80.:
32. Marelly R, Harel D, Kugler H. Multiple instances and symbolic variables in executable sequence charts. ACM SIGPLAN Notices. 2002;37(11):83–100.
33. Bontemps Y, Heymans P, Kugler H. Applying LSCs to the specification of an air traffic control system. Second Workshop on Scenarios and State Machines: Models, Algorithms, and Tools; Portland, Oregon: IEEE; 2003. p. 1–7.
34. Haiyang X, Yi Z, Jingjing G. Monitoring time property in time-sensitive LSC. Journal of Systems Engineering and Electronics. 2015;26(4):857–67.
35. Wei B, Guan T, Yu J. Projected Residual Vector Quantization for ANN Search. IEEE Multimedia. 2014;21(21):41–51.

36. Li D, Li F, Huang X, Lai Y, Zheng S. A model based integration framework for computer numerical control system development. Robotics and Computer-Integrated Manufacturing. 2010;26(4):333–43.
37. Mazzolini M, Brusaferri A, Carpanzano E, editors. An integrated framework for Model-based Design and Verification of discrete automation solutions. IEEE International Conference on Industrial Informatics; 2011.

5 COMPUTATIONAL MODELING, FORMAL ANALYSIS, AND TOOLS FOR SYSTEMS BIOLOGY

Ezio Bartocci[1], **Pietro Lió**[2]

[1] Faculty of Informatics, Technische Universität Wien, Vienna, Austria
[2] Computer Laboratory, University of Cambridge, Cambridge, United Kingdom

ABSTRACT

As the amount of biological data in the public domain grows, so does the range of modeling and analysis techniques employed in systems biology. In recent years, a number of theoretical computer science developments have enabled modeling methodology to keep pace. The growing interest in systems biology in executable models and their analysis has necessitated the borrowing of terms and methods from computer science, such as formal analysis, model checking, static analysis, and runtime verification. Here, we discuss the most important and exciting computational methods and tools currently available to systems biologists. We believe that a deeper understanding of the concepts and theory highlighted in this review will produce better software practice, improved investigation of complex biological processes, and even new ideas and better feedback into computer science.

INTRODUCTION

Computer science is currently central to a huge range of scientific areas. In its early days, its task was simply to translate a model expressed in a mathematical language into a computer program simulating that model. The field has progressed since then, yielding new domain-specific programming languages that are able to directly model a physical process.

In both cases, the computational implementation is perceived as a necessary methodological step for systems biologists, because the simple execution of a program provides an in silico numerical evaluation of hypotheses, avoiding the use of complex analytical methods and considerably reducing the costs of expensive in vivo or in vitro experiments.

Recently, the dichotomies between mathematical and computational models have also been subject to a debate (see also [1,2]) about whether or not the difference between them arises primarily from their ability to be directly executed [1] or from the different purposes and approaches adopted by scientists [2].

The novel concepts and principles (and well-designed tools) developed within the computer science community are accompanied by a domain-specific terminology (for example, executable models, expressivity, abstraction, model checking, reachability analysis, formal verification, and static analysis) that is scarcely known in other scientific communities such as systems biology. The introduction and assimilation of these concepts in fields other than computer science may back-propagate new ideas to computer scientists.

Recent works have discussed in detail how the methods borrowed from computer science have already benefited and can further benefit various problems in biology [1–6]. With respect to these previous research and review papers, our effort focuses on discussing how the use of newly developed tools could facilitate the understanding of the concepts, practice, and terminology acquisition in the current language of systems biologists. Furthermore, this review will take the further step of communicating the usefulness of using a temporal-logic framework for systems biologists who are looking beyond correlation toward event causality or patterns occurring in biological signals.

A nonexhaustive literature review, which is nonetheless an aid to understanding current progress in the field, is then presented.

COMPUTATIONAL MODELING

In the last decade, the area of systems biology has benefited greatly from computational models and techniques previously adopted only in computer science to assess the correctness and safety of a program. In this context, the design of a biological model becomes equivalent to developing a computer program. Various programming languages, often biological domain-specific, provide a means of describing the instruction sequence specifying the control flow of a biological process.

The syntax of the language defines the ways the symbols may be combined to create well-formed sentences or instructions. This specification is often represented in a textual way (i.e., a process calculus, rule-based system), but in several cases (i.e., Petri nets, state charts, etc.), a graphical representation is also available. This helps the user to visualize the process with diagrams displaying the flow of the species in the reactions or the change in the internal states. The semantics reveals the meaning of the syntactically valid instructions by describing the behavior of the model and how it should be executed by the computer. It is also possible that a model specified using a particular language syntax may be executed using different language semantics: for example, a set of chemical reactions rules can be executed using a continuous semantics (ordinary differential equations [ODEs] on molecular concentrations) or a stochastic semantics (on the number of molecules), depending on the level of approximation and/or complexity [7] that we may want to achieve. For example, COPASI [8,9] is a tool for numerical simulation and analysis of biochemical networks for both their continuous and stochastic dynamics.

In the following, we discuss the key features of the main computational modeling approaches that have fallen on fertile ground in systems biology. Fig 1 provides simple examples, inspired by case studies reported in the literature, of the modeling approaches considered.

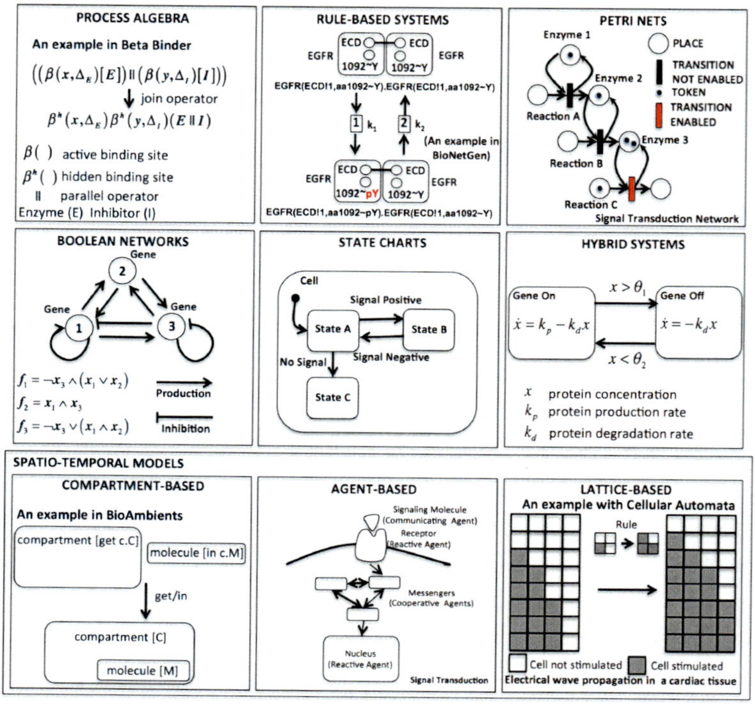

Figure 1: Most relevant examples of computational modeling approaches introduced with toy examples.

Related tools are listed in Table 1. References for the examples are as follows: process algebras [12], compartment-based systems [21], rule-based systems [22], statecharts [23], hybrid systems [24], Boolean networks [25], Petri nets [26], agent-based models [27], lattice-based models [28].

Process Algebras

In recent years, computer scientists have intensively investigated the use of process algebras (PAs) for the modeling and the analysis of biological systems [10–14]. The expressive power of PAs (see Fig 1: first row, first column) allows formal specification, without any ambiguity about the interactions, communications, and synchronizations between a collection of concurrent processes (also called agents). The reason for the interest in PAs for systems biology is that biological systems can be considered as concurrent reactive systems, where biological species can be modeled as processes interacting with each other. Another important feature of PAs in the modeling of complex (often multiscale) biological systems is their compositionality, which offers the possibility of defining the whole system, starting from the specification of its subcomponents. Furthermore, PAs usually permit formal reasoning about equivalences between processes. The leading examples of PAs in computational systems biology include Beta-Binders/BlenX [12], SPiM [15–17], Bio-PEPA [13], sCCP [18], and BioShape [19,20]. PA specifications are usually employed as intermediate models that are then executed or translated in other computational models using different semantics: continuous differential (ODEs), stochastic (Continuous Time Markov Chains), or abstract (transitions systems).

Rule-based Systems

Rule-based modeling (see Fig 1: first row, second column) has gained a lot of attention among biologists, because its notation is very similar to the chemical reaction representation used in systems biology to model biochemical interactions between molecular species. Consider, for example, the classical enzymatic reaction where an enzyme (E) binds a substrate (S) and produces a product (P) by releasing the enzyme (E). This can be expressed in a very compact and concise description by using two simple rules:

1. $E + S \leftrightarrows ES$
2. $ES \rightarrow E + P$

One important feature of this modeling technique is that rules, unlike equations, are independent units, so they can be easily changed or modified. Furthermore, the simple syntax of rule-based models can be stored in a file as a human-readable text and can be edited and visualized using a graph representation. This makes rule-based modeling friendly for users without specialized mathematical or computer science skills. Rule-based models can then be translated, using different semantics, to generate other computational models in order to provide a quantitative (i.e., the amount of a species in time) [22,29] prediction or a qualitative (i.e., where time is abstracted away) understanding of the system's emergent behavior. For these reasons, many rule-based modeling languages and tools, such as BIOCHAM [30,31], Kappa [32], BioNetGen [22,33], have become very popular among systems biologists in the recent years and have been intensively utilized in concrete case studies [34–36]. We refer to [3] for a more exhaustive review of rule-based modeling.

Petri Nets

A Petri net (see Fig 1: first row, third column) is a directed graph whose vertices can be divided into two disjointed sets (bipartite graph), a set of nodes called "transitions" (meaning events that may occur, i.e., reactions), graphically represented by bars, and a set of nodes called "places" (meaning the conditions for a reaction to occur, such as the presence of a molecule), graphically represented by circles. Arrows interconnect these nodes, showing the direction of flow, with this main rule: a place node can be connected only to a transition node and vice versa. The data (i.e., species) are generally represented as "tokens", signified by black marks. The tokens are consumed from the input places through the transitions and then created in the output places. A transition "fires" whenever it is enabled by the presence of some tokens in one of the places directly connected to it. A concurrent semantics specifies the evolution in time of the token distribution. This modeling framework was introduced by Carl Adam Petri in 1962 with the purpose of describing chemical processes [37], but then was also intensively employed in computer science to specify and analyze concurrent and distributed systems. It is not surprising that this intuitive and graphical modeling style is popular among computational systems biologists [26,38–40] to describe biochemical reaction systems, where the tokens are interpreted as single molecules of the species involved. The Petri net formalism, as shown also in [41], provides a natural framework in which both qualitative (given by the static structural topology of the Petri nets) and quantitative (given by the time evolution of the token distribution) analysis are tightly integrated. Important tools for Petri nets used in computational biology are Snoopy [26], MARCIE [42], GreatSPN [43,44], and Pathway Logic Assistant [45,46].

Boolean/Qualitative Networks

Boolean networks (see Fig 1: second row, first column) were first introduced by Kauffman [25] and then by Thomas [47,48]. They are often used to approximate the dynamics of genetic regulatory networks by considering genes either activated (true state) or deactivated (false state). A Boolean network is defined in terms of Boolean variables, each one updated by a Boolean function that determines the next truth value state given the inputs from a subset of those variables. This modeling technique, even though it usually introduces a coarse approximation by neglecting intermediate states, is widely employed to analyze the robustness and stability of genetic regulatory networks. For instance, by generating initial random configurations, it is possible, by executing this model, to detect singleton attractors (also called fixed points), where the system is stable. Relevant tools for Boolean networks analysis in systems biology are GINsim [49–51], BoolNet [52], and BNS [53,54]. Qualitative networks, introduced recently in [55], extend the Boolean network, allowing its elements to assume a finite number of possible values. This feature provides biologists with more flexibility than just Boolean values and enhances the variety of behaviors that it is possible to model with this formalism. The tool for modeling and analysis of qualitative networks is Bio Model Analyzer (BMA) [56].

Statecharts

Another natural way to model the dynamics of a biological system is to specify the sequence of the states characterizing its behavior [23]. For example, when a phosphate group is added to some proteins, their functional behavior can change to a phosphorylated state, enabling other potential protein—protein interactions. A system remains in a state until the occurrence of some event (e.g., the activation or inhibition of a gene) moves its internal behavior from one state to another. This characteristic makes a biological system a multiscale reactive system in which event-driven concurrent interactions, occurring at different levels (molecular, cellular, tissue, organ, or population level) or between levels and with different timing and order, determine its emergent behavior. The statecharts notation (see Fig 1: second row, second column) is then a suitable formalism to present, in a graphical representation, the interdependence among the states of a reactive system. Several slightly different versions of these state diagrams have been proposed with different semantics.

The statecharts introduced by Harel [57] have been the most popular among biologists because they offer appropriate constructs (hierarchy of states with transitions, events, conditions, orthogonal regions, etc.) to handle the complexity of modeling biological systems. The classic statecharts notation, in fact, would require one to specify any possible combination of parameters as a distinct state, leading to an explosion of the number of states. Among the tools for statecharts, the most relevant in systems biology is IBM Rational Rhapsody [58,59].

Hybrid Systems

Hybrid systems [60] (see Fig 1: second row, third column) extend the state-based discrete representation previously mentioned with a continuous dynamics (generally ODEs) in each state (or mode). Hybrid modeling techniques [24] are gaining more and more attention in systems biology [61] for their ability to capture the behavior of biological systems that exhibit clear switching characteristics. In particular, sigmoidal switches occur everywhere in biological models: molecular (an example is the sigmoidal behavior exhibited by Hill-type kinetics), cellular, tissue, organ, and population models. Hybrid modeling is generally suitable to combine qualitative (given by the discrete state) and quantitative (given by the continuous dynamics) information [62]. In the last decade, several hybrid system identification (hybridization) methods have been proposed in the literature [63–66] to approximate complex nonlinear dynamics with piecewise-linear [67,68] or piecewise-multi-affine functions [66,69–71], making such models amenable to formal analysis [60,66–71] and improving large-scale simulation of multicellular ensembles [72–74]. It is noteworthy that widely used mathematical platforms, such as Matlab [75] and Simulink [76,77], enable the user to model and simulate hybrid systems. Other relevant tools for hybrid systems modeling in biology are Rovergene [71], BioDivine [69,78,79], Breach [80,81], dReach [82,83], and S-TaLiRo [84].

Spatio-temporal Models

Continuous state deterministic spatiotemporal systems (see Fig 1: third row) are generally formulated in terms of "reaction-diffusion" systems taking the form of semilinear parabolic partial differential equations (PDE). In the discrete state setting, compartment-based models (i.e., membrane computing), agent-based models, and lattice-based computational models (i.e., cellular automata, cellular Potts) have been employed to simulate the collective behavior of cellular structures. All of these models display a wide range of behaviors emerging from local and nonlocal interactions such as traveling waves (i.e., cardiac tissue) [85], Turing patterning [86,87], and spirals [88,89].

Compartment-based models.

Biological systems are generally organized in compartments (i.e., cell membrane, cell nucleus, organelle), exchanging molecules between them according to certain rules. Compartment-based models (see Fig 1: third row, first column) are specialized to capture several biological characteristics, such as the dynamic rearrangements of the compartments (a typical behavior observed in the mitochondria) and the transport of molecules between them.

The study of the membranes separating the compartments has also initiated a new area within computer science called membrane computing, which aims to discover new bio-inspired computational paradigms, such as the P Systems [90]. However, these models are more suitable for the theory of computation than for modeling in systems biology.

Another relevant modeling framework is BioAmbients [91], a process algebra enriched with special operators able to specify merging, splitting, and communication between compartments. BAM [92,93] is a tool for executing stochastic BioAmbients. BioAmbients evolved into Brane Calculus [94], which offers a specially designed language to describe the dynamic behavior of membranes. Whereas, in BioAmbients, the ambient (i.e., compartment) plays an active role in dictating which processes may enter or exit from it, Brane Calculus offers a different perspective, in which the membranes have the control and play the role of coordinators. To the best of our knowledge, there is not yet an implementation available for it.

Agent-based models.

Agent-based models [95,96] (see Fig 1: third row, second column) consider a collection of autonomous decision-making entities, called agents, which individually sense the environment and make decisions on the basis of a set of rules. Although, at the simplest level, an agent-based model consists of a system of agents and the relationships between them, it can still exhibit complex behavior patterns in terms of changes and adaptation in response to environmental challenges or to neighboring agent behaviors (for example, competition or collaboration).

Because all individuals in a population are explicitly represented, they can have unique histories and behaviors. More complex agent-based models sometimes incorporate sophisticated learning and adaptation rules based on neural networks, evolutionary algorithms, or other techniques. The single-cell-based models represent one of the most promising aspects, in which agents have many cellular functional and structural features and behavior, inching toward reality and enabling the detection of phenomena at different intermediate scales of biosystems.

Cell-based models can express important behavioral characteristics of a cell, such as the dynamics of its replication and information on each stage of its development (i.e., cell geometry, size, and mechanical properties).

A single-cell-based model should be able to understand how stage-dependent cell—cell interactions at microscopic scale will lead to cell—tissue interactions and stage heterogeneity at mesoscopic level and mechanical properties of the tissue at macroscopic level. Models could be implemented using FLAME [27,97] and REPAST [28,98], for example.

Lattice-based models.

A lattice (see Fig 1: third row, third column), which defines a regular repeated graph, formed by identical n-dimensional closed grid sites and characterized by periodic or fixed boundary conditions in each direction, is particularly suited for systems description of interconnected processes at the molecular, cellular, and the tissue or organ level. These natural levels can approximately be connected to a microscopic (molecule motion and interactions), mesoscopic (cell division and motion, cell—cell interactions, cell-matrix), and macroscopic scale (tissue and organ mechanical properties), respectively.

Cellular automata [99] are discrete dynamic systems—discrete in space, time, and state. Cellular pattern formation can be seen as arising from short-range (such as adhesive forces and cell—cell signaling) and long-range (such as mechanical stress fields or diffusing chemicals) interactions. A Bethe lattice (or Cayley tree) [100] is a hierarchically ordered, cycle-free network without ends that has been applied to immunological (idiotypic) networks.

In multiscale lattice-based models, we can observe what happens at almost all scales, from the whole organism down to the molecular level; however, putting things together in order to obtain real understanding is much more difficult and involves scaling up and homogenization of models across multiple spatial scales and related asymptotic techniques for the analysis of multiple time scales. This problem could be overcome by using energetic considerations, such as in the cellular Potts model (also termed the Glazier Graner-Hogeweg model), which are based on the stochastic Monte Carlo method on a regular lattice [101,102]. The objects, either discrete generalized cells (unicellular organisms, clusters of cells, individual cells) or continuous fields (such as gradients of nutrients or small molecules), are associated with an energy description of processes such as cell—cell adhesion or cell—nutrient interaction. Lattice rearrangements, which simulate the evolution of the system, are driven by the energy minimization of a Hamiltonian function.

A very general and flexible framework for Potts model development is CompuCell3D [103,104], which has been used to model a variety of anatomical and pathological conditions at cell, tissue, and organ levels. This framework succeeds in combining both a rigorous energetic and mechanical treatment of the process with an intuitive and insightful biological description. There is growing interest in network ensembles approaches. Multilayer networks and, in particular, multiplex networks (in which different networks share the same nodes) could be analyzed using network entropies to evaluate and quantify the correlations between interdependent networks. For example, in biological systems, gene, protein, and metabolite networks have strong correlations and interdependencies that cannot be fully pictured in terms of single graphs [105].

FORMAL ANALYSIS

The modeling languages presented in the previous section play a key role in supporting the rigorous specification of the mechanisms observed experimentally, helping scientists in the formulation of new hypotheses. Once a model is constructed, a suitable tool can parse the syntax of its specification and interpret it according to the semantics of the chosen modeling language. A model can also undergo a process of compilation that automatically translates it into a computer program simulating the biological process under investigation. The generated program can be used to predict the emergent behavior of a system with certain initial conditions. This contributes to the testing procedure and to reducing the number of costly experiments, concentrating all efforts and resources only on those that promise to reveal novel, interesting mechanisms.

Another advantage is the possibility of inheriting several methods and tools that are commonly developed and employed within the computer-aided verification community to formally check the correctness of a program's behavior. In the context of systems biology, these methods are becoming very useful for reasoning and analyzing models, validating new experimental results, automatically checking behaviors of interest, and identifying the inputs or parameters of the system enforcing a desired behavior.

The formal verification of a program consists of proving that its execution satisfies a given specification of the possible behaviors it should display. In the following, we will first present some logic-based languages used to specify temporal behavioral properties rigorously and concisely.

These languages, first developed within computer science, are now also employed in several case studies of systems biology to model recurrent patterns in biological signals or simply the order of relevant biological events. We will then discuss three well-established formal verification techniques designed first to verify programs and now widely employed to analyze biological models: model checking [6,70,71,106–110], runtime verification [80,111–116], and static analysis [93,117–119].

Temporal Logics

Temporal logics [120–123] are very concise languages for rigorously specifying the occurrence of specific temporal behaviors. One of the most popular temporal logics is Linear Temporal Logic (LTL), introduced by Pnueli in 1977 [120] to reason about the order of events occurring during the execution of a program. The LTL syntax is given by the grammar shown in Fig 2a. The basic proposition p indicates a Boolean value that may express the relationship between a state variable of the system and a value for a particular time instant. For example, we can specify that the concentration of the specie x_1 is greater than or equal to a certain threshold $r(x_1 \geq r)$ or that a specific biological event e (e.g., phosphorylation) should occur. More complex logical formulas can be obtained by combining propositions using logical operators such as or (V) and not (¬). The other classical logical operators such as and (Λ) and implication (→) can be derived by combining the previous two, as shown in Fig 2b.

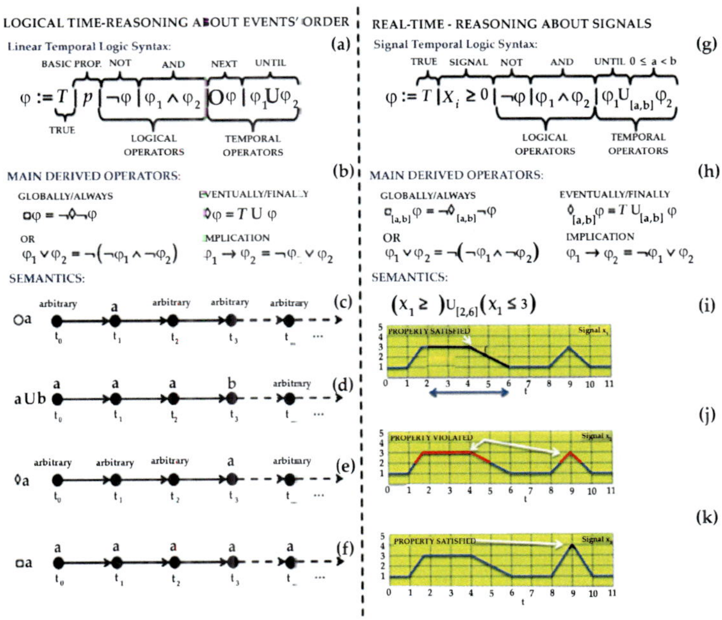

Figure 2: Examples of temporal logics.

Comparison between the main features of the LTL (left) and Signal Temporal Logic (STL) (right) in terms of syntax (top), operators (middle), and semantics (bottom); the black circles represents a propositional state, and the arrows represent the next step in time.

The LTL syntax also includes two temporal operators: the next (○) operator, which means that a formula φ should hold in the next step (see Fig 2c), and the until (u) operator, which requires a formula φ_1 to hold until a formula φ_2 becomes true (see Fig 2d).

From the until operator, it is possible to derive other very suitable temporal operators: the eventually (◇) operator specifies that a formula φ will finally become true at some point (see Fig 2e), and the always (□) operator states that a formula φ should remain true forever (see Fig 2f). The combination and the nesting of the basic propositions with the logical and temporal operators allow the specification of several different types of temporal behaviors.

The most common temporal patterns are:

1. Reachability properties, in which an event will finally happen. For example, we can express the property «the event of protein A production (event $A_{\uparrow}$) will finally occur" with the LTL formula $\varphi = \diamond A_{\uparrow}$. This specification does not guarantee that the same event will happen again after it has occurred.
2. Liveness properties, in which an event will always finally happen. This specification guarantees that the same event will also happen again after it has occurred. For example, the property "always the event of the degradation of protein A (event $A_{\downarrow}$) implies eventually the activation of gene B (event $B_{\uparrow}$)" [124] can be specified with the LTL formula $\varphi = \square(A_{\downarrow} \rightarrow \diamond B_{\uparrow})$.
3. Safety/invariant properties, in which a system will always satisfy a certain requirement. For example, the property "the number of the osteoclasts, the cells degrading/digesting the bone matrix, x_{oc} during bone remodeling will be always less than a particular concentration c" [107] can be specified with the LTL formula $\varphi = \square p$ with $p = (x_{oc} \leq c)$.
4. Stability properties, special cases of liveness properties, in which eventually an invariant property will hold. For example, the property "finally the skin cell proliferation x_c will reach a stable level l" [125] can be expressed with the LTL formula $\varphi = \diamond\square p$ with $p = |x_c - l| \leq \varepsilon$.
5. Oscillatory properties. For example, the property «the concentration of a protein x_p is oscillating between two levels t_a, t_b with $t_a < t_b$" can be written as the LTL formula $\varphi = \square((p_1 \rightarrow \diamond p_2) \wedge (p_2 \rightarrow \diamond p_1)$, with $p_1 = x_p \leq t_a$ and $p_2 = x_p \geq t_b$

LTL operates on a single path of the model execution, and a temporal property can be formulated only for one possible trajectory of the system. Other temporal logics such as computational tree logic (CTL) [126] and CTL* [127] have in their syntax special quantifiers that enable the specification of properties over all the possible trajectories or branches in time: universal quantifier (∀) specifies that a nested formula should be true for all the possible trajectories, while the existential quantifier (∃) requires the formula to hold in at least one of the possible trajectories.

All the aforementioned temporal logics consider only the temporal order of the events and not the actual time at which they really occur. For example, it is not possible to specify that a formula should hold after two units of time and before three and a half units of time. Even if we decide to discretize the time, recording all the events at each time step, the syntax of these logics is not equipped to deal directly with the specification of real-time intervals.

Real-time temporal logics [128–131] overcome these limits by using a continuous time semantics and embedding a time interval in the until temporal operator.

The Signal Temporal Logic (STL) [131,132] is an example of a real-time temporal logic suitable for many biological case studies [115,116,133–135]. STL extends LTL with the continuous time semantics and with predicates over real variables (see Fig 2g and 2h).

Fig 2i shows how the until operator of the STL syntax is enriched with the possibility of specifying a continuous time interval [a, b] within which the first formula φ_1 should hold until $\varphi_2$holds. STL operates on a continuous piecewise representation of a sampled signal. As illustrated in Fig 2j and 2k, the STL semantics uses interpolation to determine the point between two samples where the formula will start to hold or to be violated.

STL has two possible semantics: a qualitative semantics returning a yes/no answer to the question of whether the system satisfies or violates the specification, and a quantitative semantics also providing a measure of robustness [111,113] of how much the system violates or satisfies the specification. Negative robustness implies property violation, while positive robustness implies property satisfaction. As we discuss later in this section, this value can be used to guide the parameter synthesis of a biological model with unknown parameters.

Model Checking

Model checking is an automatic formal verification technique able to check the emergence of a particular behavior in a biological model. This technique operates over a discrete time model with a finite number of states, called a Kripke structure [136], where the execution of a model triggers a sequence of events determining the truth value of the propositions of a temporal logic formula. A Kripke structure is a special labeled graph in which the nodes represent the reachable states generated by executing the biological model, and the edges represent the state transitions. A labeling function maps each node to the set of propositions that hold in the corresponding reachable state. A transition relation specifies the set of possible successors for each state.

Each node always has a successor or a loop transition starting and ending in the same state, representing nonterminating computations where the evaluation of the atomic propositions does not change (also called fixed point). Suitable user-friendly tools can translate the biological models specified with one of the formalisms presented in the previous section into a Kripke structure representation that can be analyzed with very efficient model checkers such as NuSMV [137,138] or CADP [139]. The main drawback of this technique is that the number of states of a model usually grows exponentially in the number of its parameters, giving rise to the state explosion problem. In order to tackle this, the majority of model checkers do not explicitly represent the states, but represent sets of states symbolically [140,141]. For example, the states and the transition relation of a Kripke structure can be encoded as a binary decision diagram (BDD) [140], a very compact acyclic graph data structure used to represent a Boolean function as well as sets or relations in general. The logical operations required by model checking are then interpreted as operations over sets and implemented by polynomial-time graph manipulation algorithms [140] directly on this representation of sets. The works of Bryant [140] on BDDs and of McMillan [141] on symbolic model checking provide more details on the symbolic approach.

Model checking techniques have also been extended to many other computational models that can be regarded as Kripke structures, such as continuous- and discrete-time Markov chains (CTMC and DTMC) (by adding probabilities) [6], Petri nets [41], hybrid systems (by adding continuous dynamics) [142], and spatial lattice-based models (using the quad-tree representation) [88]. In the case of CTMC and DTMC, the analysis may benefit from using probabilistic model checkers such as PRISM [6,143,144], which provide a real number in the interval of [0,1] corresponding to the probability that the system model will satisfy the property of interest. The algorithm used to calculate this probability can return either the exact solution [123], if it operates directly on the structure of the Markov chains, or an approximated solution, when it measures statistically [145] the probability of satisfying a property for a set of samples, generated using a Monte Carlo simulation of the system model. This statistical approach can be applied not only to the classical DTMC and CTMC models, but also to stochastic hybrid systems [146], in which the continuous dynamics are calculated by integration and the discrete transitions are chosen non-deterministically by following a probability distribution.

Runtime Verification/Monitoring

Another way to overcome the state explosion problem of model checking is to focus the analysis on a single execution trace instead of performing an exhaustive verification. Runtime verification is a lightweight yet powerful verification technique that aims to check whether the current execution of a program (i.e., the time series of the concentration of the protein expression during a gene regulatory network simulation) satisfies or violates a property of interest.

The emergent property is still specified in terms of a LTL formula or one of its extensions, but in this case only a single behavior is evaluated. Monitoring does not require a system model but only a set of observable, discrete, or continuous signals that can be collected during a wet-lab experiment or generated by numerical simulation. As previously mentioned, in the last decade, LTL has been extended to specify properties of real-valued variables defined over dense real time. A pioneering example of LTL with predicates expressed in terms of constraints over reals is LTL($\mathbb{R}$), presented in [147,148], and then implemented to monitor numerical simulations of biological models in BIOCHAM [108].

In addition, STL [131] extends LTL with a continuous time semantics and with predicates over real variables and is implemented in the Breach [80] and S-TaLiRo [84,149] tools. In these tools, the evaluation of the

STL formula robustness for a particular trajectory through monitoring is used in combination with sensitivity-based analysis techniques [107,114,115,135] or stochastic-based optimization techniques [116,149] to steer the simulation of a biological model toward the parameter regions in which it would display the property of interest.

Static Analysis

As the term "static" indicates, this analysis is performed on the static description of the model without actually executing it. The principles of static analysis originated in the field of compiler optimization. Nowadays, this approach is widely employed in software verification, its key role being to detect potentially vulnerable code in safety-critical applications.

While model checking generally needs to explore all the states originated by executing the semantics of the model, static analysis operates on the syntactic level of the specification or by using abstract interpretation [150] over finite approximations of the possible model executions [151]. Static analysis can reveal important information regarding the model specification (e.g., the control structure, the flow of species concentrations, the interactions among species), without performing all of the underlying concrete calculations. In the last decade [117], static analysis has also become a useful technique to analyze biological models [93,118,119]. In [93], the authors successfully employ this technique to analyze biological pathways. Given a formal model in BioAmbients of the LDL degradation pathway, the authors compute a fine over-approximation of the possibly infinite reaction sequences that the model specifies. This approximation is "safe", meaning that all the reaction sequences that do not appear in the analysis are not possible.

Static analysis is crucial for dealing with the complexity of real systems (see also [118,119] for other important examples in systems biology), in which model checking all the reaction sequences will fail, owing to the state explosion problem. However, it is not as precise as executing the model: it is not possible to guarantee that all the reachable states in the over-approximation are also reachable in the original model's behavior.

In some cases (see, for example, the Rovergene tool [71]), static analysis and model checking techniques are combined. The first constructs an abstract domain using suitable abstractions. The second provides a logical framework to search in the abstract domain if a set of states is not reachable. This guarantees that they will never occur in the original model's behavior. Examples of this analytic approach can be found in several case studies: genetic networks [71], loss of cardiac cell excitability [66], and bone remodeling [107]. Static analysis has also been used in [152] to relate different semantics and formalisms used for describing reaction systems.

TOOLS

We now use the concepts previously discussed as a guide to choosing among the several tools available.

Fig 3 and Table 1, though not purporting to be complete, present a selection of software closely related to the topics discussed in this review. In Fig 3, we classify the listed tools by the computational modeling language, the supported semantics of execution, and the formal analysis that can be performed, based on the literature. We also specify if the tool supports a mechanism to tune the model's parameters, guided by the formal analysis.

Tool	Modeling Language											Execution			Formal Analysis			
	Agent-based	Boolean/Qualitative Networks	Biochemical Networks	Compartment-based	Hybrid Systems	Lattice-based	Markov Chains	Petri Nets	Process Algebra	Rule-based	State Charts	Continuous Semantics	Discrete/Boolean Semantics	Stochastic Semantics	Model Checking	Parameter Synthesis	Runtime Verification / Monitoring	Static Analysis
BAM [79]				✓					✓					✓				✓
BETAWB [11]									✓			✓	✓	✓				✓
BIOCHAM [29]										✓		✓	✓	✓	✓	✓	✓	✓
BIODIVINE [60, 136]			✓		✓		✓					✓	✓	✓	✓	✓		✓
BIONETGEN [21] + BIOLAB [137]										✓		✓		✓	✓			
BIO-PEPA WB [12]									✓			✓		✓	✓			✓
BOOLNET [45]		✓											✓	✓				
BMA [48]		✓											✓		✓			
BNS [46]		✓											✓		✓			
BREACH [68]					✓							✓				✓	✓	
COMPUCELL3D [87]	✓					✓								✓				
COPASI [8]			✓									✓		✓		✓		
dREACH [69]					✓							✓			✓	✓		
FLAME [26]	✓													✓				
GINSIM [138]		✓											✓		✓			
GREATSPN [40]								✓				✓	✓	✓	✓			
IBM RATIONAL RHAPSODY [50]											✓		✓					
KASIM [30] + KASA										✓		✓		✓				✓
MATHWORKS SIMULINK [67]					✓							✓						
PATHWAY LOGIC [41]								✓					✓		✓			
PRISM [6]							✓							✓	✓	✓		
ROVERGENE [62]					✓								✓		✓	✓		✓
SNOOPY [25] + MARCIE [39]								✓				✓	✓	✓	✓			
SPIM [14]									✓					✓				
S-TALIRO [70]					✓							✓		✓		✓	✓	
REPAST [27]	✓													✓				

Figure 3: Summary of the features for the selected tools.

Tools are classified by the supported computational modeling language, their execution semantics, and the formal analysis that can be performed, based on the literature.

Table 1: Summary of the main case studies in systems biology for the listed tools

Tool	Main case studies
BAM [92]	LDL degradation pathway [93]
BetaWB [12]	The MAPK biochemical pathway [12], cell-cycle [11]
BIOCHAM [30]	Mammalian cell cycle control [34], G protein-coupled receptor kinases [31]
BioDivine [69,78]	Genetic regulatory networks [79]
BioNetGen [22] + BioLab [33]	HMGB1 signal pathway [35] Analysis of T-cell receptor signaling pathway [33]
Bio-PEPA WB [13]	Plant circadian clock [14]
BoolNet [52]	Genetic networks [52]
BMA [56]	Biological signaling networks [55]
BNS [53]	Cell cycle sequence of fission yeast [54]
Breach [80]	Collagen proteolysis [115], Cellular iron homeostasis network [81]
CompuCell3D [103]	Vertebrate segmentation and somite formation [104]
COPASI [8]	Biochemical networks [9]
dReach [82]	Cardiac cell hybrid models [83]
FLAME [27]	Sperm behavior [97]
GINsim [49]	Diversity and plasticity of Th cell types [50]
	MAPK network on cancer cell fate decision [51]
GreatSPN [43]	Signal transduction pathways for angiogenesis [44]
IBM Rational Rhapsody [58]	T-cell activation with statecharts [59]
KaSim [32]	EGFR signaling [36]
Mathworks Simulink [76]	Heart model for pacemaker verification [77]
Pathway Logic [45]	Sporulation initiation in *B. subtilis* [46] MAPK signaling network [46] EGF stimulation network [45]
PRISM [6]	Biological signaling pathways [6,143,144], bone pathologies [107]
Rovergene [71]	Synthetic transcription cascade [71], myocyte excitability [66], bone remodeling [107]
Snoopy [26] + MARCIE [42]	Systems and synthetic biology [41]
SPiM [15]	Modeling of the EGFR network [16], MHC class I peptide optimization [17]
S-TaLiRo [84]	Modeling of the insulin-glucose regulatory system [149]
REPAST [28]	Bone remodeling [98]

doi:10.1371/journal.pcbi.1004591.t001

While each modeling language was developed to solve a real problem, different modeling languages may map into the same program. Knowledge of the syntax is needed in order to carry out static analysis. The executable program, on the other hand, is no longer syntax-dependent. Quantitative analysis (i.e., simulation), which considers the time dimension, is then performed on the output produced by the program.

In the second column of Table 1 (main case studies), references to some applications are presented. The large variety of tools will accommodate the current rich interdisciplinary and multidisciplinary systems biology scenarios. Scientists with different backgrounds may have different initial preferences and later move in various directions, generating the conditions for extensive exchange of ideas and methodological innovations.

CONCLUSIONS AND VISION

The growing availability of large amounts of data (i.e., big data) will allow models to be tested very finely. Spatial data could be collected in three dimensions (thanks, perhaps, to microscope imaging advances), capturing the formation of patterns, niches, molecular associations, and multiscale features. The time dimension could range from molecular events (for example, DNA mutations or epigenetic changes) to organism development, circadian, species evolution, and other meaningful periodicities.

The development of new, efficient tools will motivate others to generate new computational models or to improve the existing ones. This will increase the community of scientists sharing their knowledge through standardized computational models reproducing numerically the behavior of the biological process under investigation. With computational modeling acquiring better capacity to describe biological systems and processes at a level useful for prediction and to suggest experiments, it will trigger a useful feed-forward process with experimental biologists.

The tools described in this paper can already accommodate different complexly structured properties of biological processes and could be used separately or in different combinations and architectures. This will enable biologists to answer complex questions. For example, temporal logics, in particular, will have a profound impact in systems biology by helping to transform cause—effect relationships into objects that can be manipulated both mathematically and computationally. In epistatic control, temporal logics can be used to model two or more causal factors as interacting mechanistically with respect to the observed phenomenon. Doing so will establish powerful connections, with reasoning based on logic and statistics and the mechanisms and processes that underlie the observed behavior.

One future interesting research direction that we envision is the extension of the current formal analysis techniques and temporal logics to the spatial domain. For example, understanding how a spatial pattern emerges from the biochemical level acting at the cellular level (i.e., morphogenesis in developmental biology) is currently very challenging because of both the high computational complexity required by the spatiotemporal modeling and the lack of a suitable specification language to specify the spatiotemporal patterns of interest [86,87,153].

Furthermore, the rapid progress of modern technologies for healthcare has led to a new generation of devices called medical cyber-physical systems [154], in which smart and collaborative computational elements control the biological systems. Examples include pacemakers, biocompatible and implantable devices, insulin pumps, electro-anatomical mapping and intervention, robotic prosthetics, and neurostimulators. Here, the computational modeling of the biological part is indispensable to the development of efficient and safe controlling devices. Furthermore, the successful application of formal analysis techniques and tools to verify the correct and safe behavior of these systems will have an economic impact on our society by reducing warranty, liability, and certification costs. We believe that the concepts and the computational tools described here represent core elements of computational description, particularly in the framework of systems biology, and will have some relevance to both newcomers and experts.

REFERENCES

1. Fisher J, Henzinger TA. Executable cell biology. Nat Biotechnol. 2007 Nov;25(11):1239–1249. pmid:17989686
2. Hunt CH, Ropella GEP, Park S, Engelberg J. Dichotomies between computational and mathematical models. Nature Biotechnology. 2008;26(7):737–738. pmid:18612289
3. Hlavacek WS, Faeder JR, Blinov ML, Posner RG, Hucka M, Fontana W. Rules for Modeling Signal-Transduction Systems. Sci STKE. 2006;2006(344):re6. pmid:16849649
4. Fisher J, Harel D, Henzinger TA. Biology As Reactivity. Commun ACM. 2011 Oct;54(10):72–82.
5. Fisher J, Piterman N. The executable pathway to biological networks. Brief Funct Genomics. 2010 Jan;9(1):79–92. pmid:20118126
6. Kwiatkowska M, Norman G, Parker D. Probabilistic Model Checking for Systems Biology. In: Symbolic Systems Biology. Jones and Bartlett; 2010. p. 31–59.
7. Gay S, Soliman S, Fages F. A graphical method for reducing and relating models in systems biology. Bioinformatics. 2010;26(18).
8. Hoops S, Sahle S, Gauges R, Lee C, Pahle J, Simus N, et al.

COPASI—a COmplex PAthway SImulator. Bioinformatics. 2006 Dec;22(24):3067–3074. pmid:17032683

9. Sahle S, Gauges R, Pahle J, Simus N, Kummer U, Hoops S, et al. Simulation of Biochemical Networks using Copasi—A Complex Pathway Simulator. In: Proc. of WSC 06: the Winter Simulation Conference. IEEE; 2006. p. 1698–1706.
10. Priami C, Regev A, Shapiro E, Silverman W. Application of a stochastic name-passing calculus to representation and simulation of molecular processes. Information Processing Letters. 2001;80(1):25–31.
11. Dematté L, Priami C, Romanel A. The BlenX Language: A Tutorial. In: Formal Methods for Computational Systems Biology 2008: 8th International School on Formal Methods for the Design of Computer, Communication, and Software Systems. vol. 5016 of LNCS. Springer-Verlag; 2008. p. 313–365.
12. Dematté L, Priami C, Romanel A. The Beta Workbench: a computational tool to study the dynamics of biological systems. Brief Bioinform. 2008;9(5):437–449. pmid:18463130
13. Ciocchetta F, Hillston J. Bio-PEPA: A framework for the modelling and analysis of biological systems. Theoretical Computer Science. 2009;410(33–34):3065–3084.
14. Guerriero ML, Pokhilko A, Fernandez AP, Halliday KJ, Millar AJ, Hillston J. Stochastic properties of the plant circadian clock. J R Soc Interface. 2012 Apr;9(69):744–756. pmid:21880617
15. Phillips A, Cardelli L. Efficient, Correct Simulation of Biological Processes in the Stochastic Pi-calculus. In: Proc. of CMSB 2007: The 6th Conference on Computational Methods in Systems Biology. vol. 4695 of LNCS. Springer; 2007. p. 184–199.
16. Wang DY, Cardelli L, Phillips A, Piterman N, Fisher J. Computational modeling of the EGFR network elucidates control mechanisms regulating signal dynamics. BMC Syst Biol. 2009;3:118. pmid:20028552
17. Dalchau N, Phillips A, Goldstein LD, Howarth M, Cardelli L, Emmott S, et al. A peptide filtering relation quantifies MHC class I peptide optimization. PLoS Comput Biol. 2011 Oct;7(10):e1002144. pmid:22022238

18. Bortolussi L, Policriti A. Modeling Biological Systems in Stochastic Concurrent Constraint Programming. Constraints. 2008;13(1–2):66–90.
19. Bartocci E, Corradini F, Di Berardini MR, Merelli E, Tesei L. Shape Calculus. A Spatial Mobile Calculus for 3D Shapes. Scientific Annals of Computer Science. 2010;20(1):2010.
20. Bartocci E, Cacciagrano DR, Di Berardini MR, Merelli E, Tesei L. Timed Operational Semantics and Well-Formedness of Shape Calculus. Scientific Annals of Computer Science. 2010;20(33):2010.
21. Regev A, Panina EM, Silverman W, Cardelli L, Shapiro E. BioAmbients: an abstraction for biological compartments. Theoretical Computer Science. 2004;325(1):141–167.
22. Faeder JR, Blinov ML, Hlavacek WS. Rule-Based Modeling of Biochemical Systems with BioNetGen. Methods in Molecular Biology. 2009;500:113–167. pmid:19399430
23. Fisher J, Harel D. On Statecharts for Biology. In: Symbolic Systems Biology: Theory and Methods. Jones & Bartlett Publishers; 2010.
24. Bortolussi L, Policriti A. Hybrid Systems and Biology. In: Formal Methods for Computational Systems Biology. vol. 5016 of LNCS. Springer; 2008. p. 424–448.
25. Kauffman S. Metabolic stability and epigenesis in randomly constructed genetic nets. J Theor Biology. 1969 Mar;22:437–467.
26. Heiner M, Herajy M, Liu F, Rohr C, Schwarick M. Snoopy—A Unifying Petri Net Tool. In: Proc. of Petri Nets 2012: the 33rd International Conference on Application and Theory of Petri Nets. vol. 7347 of LNCS. Springer; 2012. p. 398–407.
27. Richmond P, Walker DC, Coakley S, Romano DM. High performance cellular level agent-based simulation with FLAME for the GPU. Briefings in Bioinformatics. 2010;11(3):334–347. pmid:20123941
28. North MJ, Collier NT, Vos JR. Experiences creating three implementations of the REPAST agent modeling toolkit. ACM Trans Model Comput Simul. 2006 Jan;16(1):1–25.
29. John M, Lhoussaine C, Niehren J, Versari C. Biochemical Reaction Rules with Constraints. In: Proc. of ESOP 2011: the 20th European Symposium on Programming. vol. 6602 of Lecture Notes in

Computer Science. Springer Berlin Heidelberg; 2011. p. 338–357.

30. Chabrier-Rivier N, Fages F, Soliman S. The Biochemical Abstract Machine BIOCHAM. In: Proc. of CMSB 2005: the 3rd International Conference on Computational Methods in Systems Biology. vol. 3082 of LNCS. Springer; 2005. p. 172–191.

31. Heitzler D, Durand G, Gallay N, Rizk A, Ahn S, Kim J, et al. Competing G protein-coupled receptor kinases balance G protein and β-arrestin signaling. Mol Syst Biol. 2012;8:590. pmid:22735336

32. Danos V, Feret J, Fontana W, Harmer R, Krivine J. Rule-Based Modelling of Cellular Signalling. In: Proc. of CONCUR 2007: 18th International Conference on Concurrency Theory. vol. 4703 of LNCS. Springer Berlin Heidelberg; 2007. p. 17–41.

33. Clarke EM, Faeder JR, Langmead CJ, Harris LA, Jha SK, Legay A. Statistical Model Checking in BioLab: Applications to the Automated Analysis of T-Cell Receptor Signaling Pathway. In: Proc. of CMSB 2008: the 6th International Conference on Computational Methods in Systems Biology. vol. 5307 of LNCS. Springer; 2008. p. 231–250.

34. Chabrier-Rivier N, Chiaverini M, Danos V, Fages F, Schächter V. Modeling and querying biomolecular interaction networks. Theor Comput Sci. 2004;325(1):25–44.

35. Gong H, Zuliani P, Komuravelli A, Faeder JR, Clarke EM. Analysis and verification of the HMGB1 signaling pathway. BMC Bioinformatics. 2010;11 Suppl 7:S10. pmid:21106117

36. Feret J, Danos V, Krivine J, Harmer R, Fontana W. Internal coarse-graining of molecular systems. Proceedings of the National Academy of Sciences. 2009;106(16):6453–6458.

37. Petri CA, Reisig W. Petri net. Scholarpedia. 2008;3(4):6477.

38. Cordero F, Horváth A, Manini D, Napione L, Pierro MD, Pavan S, et al. Simplification of a complex signal transduction model using invariants and flow equivalent servers. Theor Comput Sci. 2011;412(43):6036–6057.

39. Koch I, Junker BH, Heiner M. Application of Petri Net theory for modelling and validation of the sucrose breakdown pathway

in the potato tuber. Bioinformatics. 2005;21(7):1219–1226. pmid:15546934

40. Blätke MA, Heiner M, Marwan W. Predicting Phenotype from Genotype through Automatically Composed Petri Nets. In: Proc. of CMSB 2012: the 10th International Conference on Computational Methods in Systems Biology. vol. 7605 of LNCS; 2012. p. 87–106.
41. Heiner M, Gilbert D, Donaldson R. Petri Nets for Systems and Synthetic Biology. In: Formal Methods for Computational Systems Biology 2008: 8th International School on Formal Methods for the Design of Computer, Communication, and Software Systems. No. 5016 in Lecture Notes in Computer Science. Springer; 2008. p. 215–264.
42. Heiner M, Rohr C, Schwarick M. MARCIE—Model Checking and Reachability Analysis Done Efficiently. In: Application and Theory of Petri Nets and Concurrency. vol. 7927 of LNCS. Springer Berlin Heidelberg; 2013. p. 389–399.
43. Baarir S, Beccuti M, Cerotti D, De Pierro M, Donatelli S, Franceschinis G. The GreatSPN tool: recent enhancements. SIGMETRICS Perform Eval Rev. 2009;36(4):4–9.
44. Napione L, Manini D, Cordero F, Horváth A, Picco A, Pierro M, et al. On the Use of Stochastic Petri Nets in the Analysis of Signal Transduction Pathways for Angiogenesis Process. In: Proc. of CMSB 2009: the 7th Conference on Computational Methods in Systems Biology. vol. 5688 of LNCS; 2009. p. 281–295.
45. Talcott C, Dill DL. The Pathway Logic Assistant. In: Proceedings of the Workshop Computational Methods in Systems Biology (CMSB); 2005. p. 228–239.
46. Tiwari A, Talcott C, Knapp M, Lincoln P, Laderoute K. Analyzing Pathways using SAT-based Approaches. In: Proc. of AB 2007: the 2nd Intl. Conf. on Algebraic Biology. vol. 4545 of LNCS. Springer; 2007. p. 155–169.
47. Thomas R, Kaufman M. Multistationarity, the basis of cell differentiation and memory. II. Logical analysis of regulatory networks in terms of feedback circuits. Chaos. 2001;11(1):180–195.

pmid:12779452

48. Thomas R, Kaufman M. Multistationarity, the basis of cell differentiation and memory. I. Structural conditions of multistationarity and other nontrivial behavior. Chaos. 2001 Mar;11(1):170–179. pmid:12779451
49. Chaouiya C, Naldi A, Thieffry D. Logical modelling of gene regulatory networks with GINsim. Methods Mol Biol. 2012;804:463–479. pmid:22144167
50. Naldi A, Carneiro J, Chaouiya C, Thieffry D. Diversity and plasticity of Th cell types predicted from regulatory network modelling. PLoS Comput Biol. 2010;6(9):e1000912. pmid:20824124
51. Grieco L, Calzone L, Bernard-Pierrot I, Radvanyi F, Kahn-Perles B, Thieffry D. Integrative modelling of the influence of MAPK network on cancer cell fate decision. PLoS Comput Biol. 2013 Oct;9(10):e1003286. pmid:24250280
52. Mussel C, Hopfensitz M, Kestler HA. BoolNet—an R package for generation, reconstruction and analysis of Boolean networks. Bioinformatics. 2010 May;26(10):1378–1380. pmid:20378558
53. Dubrova E, Teslenko M. A SAT-Based Algorithm for Finding Attractors in Synchronous Boolean Networks. IEEE/ACM Transactions on Computational Biology and Bioinformatics. 2011;8(5):1393–1399. pmid:21778527
54. Davidich MI, Bornholdt S. Boolean Network Model Predicts Cell Cycle Sequence of Fission Yeast. PLoS ONE. 2008;3(2):e1672. pmid:18301750
55. Schaub MA, Henzinger TA, Fisher J. Qualitative networks: a symbolic approach to analyze biological signaling networks. BMC Syst Biol. 2007;1:4. pmid:17408511
56. Benque D, Bourton S, Cockerton C, Cook B, Fisher J, Ishtiaq S, et al. BMA: Visual Tool for Modeling and Analyzing Biological Networks. In: Proc. of CAV 2012: the 24th International Conference on Computer Aided Verification. vol. 7358 of LNCS. Berlin, Heidelberg: Springer-Verlag; 2012. p. 686–692.
57. Harel D. Statecharts: A Visual Formalism for Complex Systems. Sci Comput Program. 1987;8(3):231–274.

58. Harel D, Gery E. Executable object modeling with statecharts. Computer. 1997;30(7):31–42.
59. Kam N, Cohen IR, Harel D. The Immune System as a Reactive System: Modeling T-Cell Activation With Statecharts. In: Proc. HCC 2001: Human-Centric Computing Languages and Environments. IEEE Computer Society; 2001. p. 15–22.
60. Alur R, Courcoubetis C, Henzinger TA, Ho PH. Hybrid Automata: An Algorithmic Approach to the Specification and Verification of Hybrid Systems. In: Hybrid Systems. vol. 736 of LNCS. Springer; 1993. p. 209–229.
61. Bartocci E, Bortolussi L, Smolka SA. Hybrid Systems and Biology. Information and Computation. 2014;236:1–2.
62. Fromentin J, Eveillard D, Roux O. Hybrid modeling of biological networks: mixing temporal and qualitative biological properties. BMC Syst Biol. 2010;4:79. pmid:20525331
63. Asarin E, Dang T, Girard A. Hybridization methods for the analysis of nonlinear systems. Acta Informatica. 2007;43(7):451–476.
64. Dang T, Maler O, Testylier R. Accurate hybridization of nonlinear systems. In: Proc. of HSCC 2010: the 13th ACM International Conference on Hybrid Systems: Computation and Control. ACM; 2010. p. 11–20.
65. Dang T, Testylier R. Hybridization domain construction using curvature estimation. In: Proc. of HSCC 2011: the 14th International Conference on Hybrid Systems: computation and control. ACM; 2011. p. 123–132.
66. Grosu R, Batt G, Fenton F, Glimm J, Le Guernic C, Smolka SA, et al. From Cardiac Cells to Genetic Regulatory Networks. In: Proc. of CAV 2011: the 14th International Conference on Computer Aided Verification. vol. 6806 of LNCS. Springer Berlin / Heidelberg; 2011. p. 396–411.
67. Ghosh R, Tomlin C. Lateral Inhibition through Delta-Notch Signaling: A Piecewise Affine Hybrid Model. In: Proc. of HSCC 2001: the 4th International Workshop on Hybrid Systems: Computation and Control. vol. 2034 of LNCS. Springer; 2001. p. 232–246.
68. Ghosh R, Tiwari A, Tomlin C. Automated Symbolic Reachability

Analysis; with Application to Delta-Notch Signaling Automata. In: Proc. of HSCC 2003: the 6th International Workshop on Hybrid Systems: Computation and Control. vol. 2623 of LNCS. Springer; 2003. p. 233–248.

69. Barnat J, Brim L, Cerná I, Drazan S, Fabriková J, Lánk J, et al. BioDiVinE: A Framework for Parallel Analysis of Biological Models. In: Proc. of COMPMOD 2009: the 2nd International Workshop on Computational Models for Cell Processes. vol. 6 of EPTCS; 2009. p. 31–45.
70. Batt G, Belta C, Weiss R. Temporal Logic Analysis of Gene Networks under Parameter Uncertainty. IEEE Trans of Automatic Control. 2008;53:215–229.
71. Batt G, Yordanov B, Weiss R, Belta C. Robustness analysis and tuning of synthetic gene networks. Bioinformatics. 2007;23(18):2415–2422. pmid:17660209
72. Bartocci E, Cherry EM, Glimm J, Grosu R, Smolka SA, Fenton FH. Toward real-time simulation of cardiac dynamics. In: Proc. of CMSB 2011: the 9th International Conference on Computational Methods in Systems Biology. ACM; 2011. p. 103–112.
73. Bartocci E, Corradini F, Di Berardini MR, Entcheva E, Smolka SA, Grosu R. Modeling and simulation of cardiac tissue using hybrid I/O automata. Theoretical Computer Science. 2009;410(33–34):3149–3165.
74. Bartocci E, Corradini F, Entcheva E, Grosu R, Smolka S. CellExcite: an efficient simulation environment for excitable cells. BMC Bioinformatics. 2008;9(Suppl 2):S3. pmid:18387205
75. The MathWorks I. MATLAB; 2015. Natick, Massachusetts, United States.
76. The MathWorks I. Simulink; 2015. Natick, Massachusetts, United States.
77. Chen T, Diciolla M, Kwiatkowska MZ, Mereacre A. A simulink hybrid heart model for quantitative verification of cardiac pacemakers. In: Proc. of HSCC 2013: the 16th International Conference on Hybrid Systems: Computation and Control. ACM; 2013. p. 131–136.
78. Brim L, Ceska M, Drazan S, Safránek D. Exploring Parameter Space of Stochastic Biochemical Systems Using Quantitative Model

Checking. In: Proc. of CAV 2013: the 25th International Conference on Computer Aided Verification 2013, Saint Petersburg, Russia, July 13–19, 2013. Proceedings. vol. 8044 of LNCS. Springer; 2013. p. 107–123.

79. Barnat J, Brim L, Krejci A, Streck A, Safránek D, Vejnar M, et al. On Parameter Synthesis by Parallel Model Checking. IEEE/ACM Trans Comput Biology Bioinform. 2012;9(3):693–705.

80. Donzé A. Breach, A Toolbox for Verification and Parameter Synthesis of Hybrid Systems. In: Proc. of CAV 2010: the 22nd International Conference on Computer Aided Verification. vol. 6174 of LNCS. Springer Berlin; 2010. p. 167–170.

81. Mobilia N, Donzé A, Moulis JM, Fanchon E. A Model of the Cellular Iron Homeostasis Network Using Semi-Formal Methods for Parameter Space Exploration. In: Proc. of HSB 2012: First International Workshop on Hybrid Systems and Biology. vol. 92 of EPTCS; 2012. p. 42–57.

82. Kong S, Gao S, Chen W, Clarke E. dReach: δ-Reachability Analysis for Hybrid Systems. In: Proc. of TACAS 2015: the 21st International Conference on Tools and Algorithms for the Construction and Analysis of Systems. vol. 9035. Springer Berlin Heidelberg; 2015. p. 200–205.

83. Liu B, Kong S, Gao S, Zuliani P, Clarke EM. Parameter Synthesis for Cardiac Cell Hybrid Models Using δ-Decisions. In: Proc. of CMSB 2014: the 12th International Conference on Computational Methods in Systems Biology. vol. 8859 of LNCS; 2014. p. 99–113.

84. Annapureddy YSR, Liu C, Fainekos GE, Sankaranarayanan S. S-TaLiRo: A Tool for Temporal Logic Falsification for Hybrid Systems. In: Proc. of TACAS 2011: the 17th International Conference on Tools and Algorithms for the Construction and Analysis of Systems. vol. 6605 of LNCS. Springer; 2011. p. 254–257.

85. Murthy A, Bartocci E, Fenton FH, Glimm J, Gray R, Smolka SA, et al. Curvature analysis of cardiac excitation wavefronts. In: Proceedings of the 9th International Conference on Computational Methods in Systems Biology. CMSB '11. New York, NY, USA: ACM; 2011. p. 151–160.

86. Gol EA, Bartocci E, Belta C. A formal methods approach to pattern synthesis in reaction diffusion systems. In: Proc. of CDC 2014: the IEEE 53rd Annual Conference on Decision and Control; 2014. p. 108–113.

87. Haghighi I, Jones A, Kong Z, Bartocci E, Grosu R, Belta C. SpaTeL: A Novel Spatial-temporal Logic and Its Applications to Networked Systems. In: Proc. of HSCC '15: the 18th International Conference on Hybrid Systems: Computation and Control. ACM; 2015. p. 189–198.

88. Grosu R, Smolka SA, Corradini F, Wasilewska A, Entcheva E, Bartocci E. Learning and detecting emergent behavior in networks of cardiac myocytes. Communications of the ACM. 2009;52(3):97–105.

89. Bartocci E, Singh R, von Stein FB, Amedome A, Caceres AJJ, Castillo J, et al. Teaching cardiac electrophysiology modeling to undergraduate students: laboratory exercises and GPU programming for the study of arrhythmias and spiral wave dynamics. Advances in Physiology Education. 2011;35(4):427–437. pmid:22139782

90. Paun G, Rozenberg G. A guide to membrane computing. Theoretical Computer Science. 2002;287(1):73–100. Natural Computing.

91. Regev A, Panina E, Silverman W, Cardelli L, Shapiro E. BioAmbients: an abstraction for biological compartments. Theoretical Computer Science. 2004;325(1):141–167. Computational Systems Biology.

92. Muganthan VA, Phillips A, Vigliotti MG. BAM: BioAmbient machine. In: Proc. of ACSD 2008: the 8th International Conference on Application of Concurrency to System Design. IEEE; 2008. p. 45–49.

93. Pilegaard H, Nielson F, Nielson HR. Pathway analysis for BioAmbients. J Log Algebr Program. 2008;77(1–2):92–130.

94. Cardelli L. Brane Calculi. In: Proc. of CMSB 2004: the international Conference, Computational Methods in Systems Biology. vol. 3082 of LNCS. Springer; 2004. p. 257–278.

95. Merelli E, Armano G, Cannata N, Corradini F, d'Inverno M, Doms A, et al. Agents in bioinformatics, computational and systems biology. Briefings in Bioinformatics. 2007;8(1):45–59. pmid:16772270

96. Bartocci E, Cacciagrano D, Cannata N, Corradini F, Merelli E, Milanesi L, et al. An agent-based multilayer architecture for bioinformatics grids. NanoBioscience, IEEE Transactions on. 2007;6(2):142–148.

97. Burkitt M, Walker DC, Romano DM, Fazeli A. Modelling sperm behaviour in a 3D environment. In: Proc. of CMSB 2011: the 9th International Conference on Computational Methods in Systems Biology; 2011. p. 141–149.

98. Paoletti N, Liò P, Merelli E, Viceconti M. Multilevel Computational Modeling and Quantitative Analysis of Bone Remodeling. IEEE/ACM Trans Comput Biology Bioinform. 2012;9(5):1366–1378.

99. Deutsch A, Dormann S. Cellular Automaton Modeling of Biological Pattern Formation: Characterization, Applications, and Analysis. Genetic Programming and Evolvable Machines. 2007 Mar;8(1):105–106.

100. Bethe HA. Statistical Theory of Superlattices. Proceedings of the Royal Society of London Series A, Mathematical and Physical Sciences. 1935;150(871):552–575.

101. Zaki MH, Tahar S, Bois G. Computing cancer software models of complex tissues and disease are yielding a better understanding of cancer and suggesting potential treatments. Nature. 2012;491:s62–s63.

102. Scianna M, P L, editor. Cellular Potts Models: Multiscale Developments and Biological Applications. Chapman Hall/CRC Press; 2013.

103. Izaguirre JA, Chaturvedi R, Huang C, Cickovski TM, Coffland J, Thomas GL, et al. COMPUCELL, a multi-model framework for simulation of morphogenesis. Bioinformatics. 2004;20(7):1129–1137.

104. Hester SD, Belmonte JM, Gens JS, Clendenon SG, Glazier JA. A Multi-cell, Multi-scale Model of Vertebrate Segmentation and Somite Formation. PLoS Comput Biol. 2011;7(10):e1002155. pmid:21998560

105. Menichetti G, Remondini D, Bianconi G. Correlations between weights and overlap in ensembles of weighted multiplex networks. Phys Rev E. 2014;90:062817.

106. Bartocci E, Corradini F, Merelli E, Tesei L. Detecting synchronisation of biological oscillators by model checking. Theoretical Computer Science. 2010;411(20):1999–2018.
107. Bartocci E, Liò P, Merelli E, Paoletti N. Multiple Verification in Complex Biological Systems: The Bone Remodelling Case Study. T Comp Sys Biology. 2012;14:53–76.
108. Calzone L, Fages F, Soliman S. BIOCHAM: an environment for modeling biological systems and formalizing experimental knowledge. Bioinformatics. 2006;22(14):1805–1807. pmid:16672256
109. Batt G, Bergamini D, de Jong H, Garavel H, Mateescu R. Model Checking Genetic Regulatory Networks Using GNA and CADP. In: Proc. of SPIN 2004: the 11th International SPIN Workshop on Model Checking Software. vol. 2989 of LNCS; 2004. p. 158–163.
110. Rizk A, Batt G, Fages F, Soliman S. Continuous valuations of temporal logic specifications with applications to parameter optimization and robustness measures. Theoretical Computer Science. 2011;412(26):2827–2839.
111. Fainekos G, Pappas G. Robust Sampling for MITL Specifications. In: Proc. of FORMATS 2007: the 5th International Conference on Formal Modeling and Analysis of Timed Systems. vol. 4763 of LNCS. Springer; 2007. p. 147–162.
112. Rizk A, Batt G, Fages F, Soliman S. On a Continuous Degree of Satisfaction of Temporal Logic Formulae with Applications to Systems Biology. In: Proceedings of the 6th International Conference on Computational Methods in Systems Biology. CMSB '08. Berlin, Heidelberg: Springer-Verlag; 2008. p. 251–268.
113. Donzé A, Maler O. Robust Satisfaction of Temporal Logic over Real-Valued Signals. In: Proc. of FORMATS 2010: the 8th International Conference on Formal Modeling and Analysis of Timed Systems. vol. 6246 of LNCS. Springer; 2010. p. 92–106.
114. Donzé A, Clermont G, Langmead CJ. Parameter Synthesis in Nonlinear Dynamical Systems: Application to Systems Biology. Journal of Computational Biology. 2010;17(3):325–336. pmid:20377448
115. Donzé A, Fanchon E, Gattepaille LM, Maler O, Tracqui P.

Robustness analysis and behavior discrimination in enzymatic reaction networks. PLoS ONE. 2011;6(9):e24246. pmid:21980344

116. Bartocci E, Bortolussi L, Nenzi L, Sanguinetti G. System design of stochastic models using robustness of temporal properties. Theor Comput Sci. 2015;587:3–25.
117. Nielson F, Nielson HR, Priami C, Rosa D. Static Analysis for Systems Biology. In: Proc. of the Winter International Synposium on Information and Communication Technologies. WISICT '04. Trinity College Dublin; 2004. p. 1–6.
118. Danos V, Feret J, Fontana W, Krivine J. Abstract interpretation of cellular signalling networks. In: Proc. of VMCAI'2008: the Ninth International Conference on Verification, Model Checking and Abstract Interpretation. vol. 4905 of LNCS. Springer, Berlin, Germany; 2008. p. 83–97.
119. Feret J. Reachability Analysis of Biological Signalling Pathways by Abstract Interpretation. In: Proc. of ICCMSE'2007: the International Conference of Computational Methods in Sciences and Engineering. No. 963.(2) in American Institute of Physics Conference Proceedings. American Institute of Physics; 2007. p. 619–622.
120. Pnueli A. The temporal logic of programs. Foundations of Computer Science, IEEE Annual Symposium on. 1977;0:46–57.
121. Clarke EM, Emerson E. Design and synthesis of synchronization skeletons using branching time temporal logic. In: Proc. of Logics of Programs, Workshop. vol. 131 of LNCS. Springer Berlin; 1982. p. 52–71.
122. Hansson H, Jonsson B. A Logic for Reasoning about Time and Reliability. Formal Asp Comput. 1994;6(5):512–535.
123. Aziz A, Sanwal K, Singhal V, Brayton R. Model-checking continuous-time Markov chains. ACM Trans Comput Logic. 2000 Jul;1(1):162–170.
124. Batt G, Belta C, Weiss R. Model Checking Liveness Properties of Genetic Regulatory Networks. In: Proc. of TACAS 2007: the 13th International Conference on Tools and Algorithms for the Construction and Analysis of Systems. vol. 5016 of LNCS. Springer-Verlag; 2007. p. 323–338.

125. Cook B, Fisher J, Krepska E, Piterman N. Proving Stabilization of Biological Systems. In: Proc. of VMCAI 2011: the 12th International Conference on Verification, Model Checking, and Abstract Interpretation. vol. 6538 of LNCS. Springer; 2011. p. 134–149.
126. Clarke EM, Emerson EA, Sistla AP. Automatic Verification of Finite-state Concurrent Systems Using Temporal Logic Specifications. ACM Trans Program Lang Syst. 1986;8(2):244–263.
127. Emerson EA, Halpern JY. «Sometimes» and «Not Never» Revisited: On Branching Versus Linear Time Temporal Logic. J ACM. 1986;33(1):151–178.
128. Alur R, Henzinger TA. Real-time Logics: Complexity and Expressiveness. In: LICS; 1990. p. 390–401.
129. Alur R, Henzinger TA. A Really Temporal Logic. J ACM. 1994;41(1):181–204.
130. Alur R, Feder T, Henzinger TA. The Benefits of Relaxing Punctuality. J ACM. 1996;43(1):116–146.
131. Maler O, Nickovic D. Monitoring Temporal Properties of Continuous Signals. In: Proc. of FORMATS/FTRTFT 2004: joint International Conferences on Formal Modeling and Analysis of Timed Systmes and Formal Techniques in Real-Time and Fault-Tolerant Systems. vol. 3253 of LNCS; 2004. p. 152–166.
132. Donzé A, Maler O, Bartocci E, Nickovic D, Grosu R, Smolka SA. On Temporal Logic and Signal Processing. In: Proc. of ATVA 2012, the 10th International Symposium on Automated Technology for Verification and Analysis. vol. 7561 of Lecture Notes in Computer Science. Springer; 2012. p. 92–106.
133. Bartocci E, Bortolussi L, Sanguinetti S. Data-driven Statistical Learning of Temporal Logic Properties. In: Proc. of FORMATS 2014: the 12th International Conference on Formal Modeling and Analysis of Timed Systems. vol. 8711 of LNCS; 2014. p. 23–37.
134. Bufo S, Bartocci E, Sanguinetti G, Borelli M, Lucangelo U, Bortolussi L. Temporal Logic Based Monitoring of Assisted Ventilation in Intensive Care Patients. In: Proc. of ISoLA 2014: the 6th International Symposium on Leveraging Applications of Formal Methods, Verification and Validation. Part II. vol. 8803 of Lecture Notes in Computer Science. Springer; 2014. p. 391–403.

135. Bartocci E, Bortolussi L, Nenzi L. A Temporal Logic Approach to Modular Design of Synthetic Biological Circuits. In: Computational Methods in Systems Biology. vol. 8130 of Lecture Notes in Computer Science. Springer Berlin Heidelberg; 2013. p. 164–177.
136. Kripke S. Semantical Considerations on Modal Logic. Acta Philosophica Fennica. 1963;16:83–94.
137. Cimatti A, Clarke EM, Giunchiglia F, Roveri M. NuSMV: A New Symbolic Model Checker. STTT. 2000;2(4):410–425.
138. Nusser-Stein S, Beyer A, Rimann I, Adamczyk M, Piterman N, Hajnal A, et al. Cell-cycle regulation of NOTCH signaling during C. elegans vulval development. Mol Syst Biol. 2012;8:618. pmid:23047528
139. Garavel H, Lang F, Mateescu R, Serwe W. CADP 2010: A Toolbox for the Construction and Analysis of Distributed Processes. In: Proc. of TACAS 2011: the 17th International Conference on Tools and Algorithms for the Construction and Analysis of Systems. vol. 6605. Springer; 2011. p. 372–387.
140. Bryant RE. Graph-Based Algorithms for Boolean Function Manipulation. IEEE Trans Computers. 1986;35(8):677–691.
141. Burch JR, Clarke EM, McMillan KL, Dill DL, Hwang LJ. Symbolic Model Checking: 1020 States and Beyond. Inf Comput. 1992;98(2):142–170.
142. Ahmad J, Bourdon J, Eveillard D, Fromentin J, Roux O, Sinoquet C. Temporal constraints of a gene regulatory network: Refining a qualitative simulation. Biosystems. 2009;98(3):149–159. pmid:19446002
143. Calder M, Vyshemirsky V, Gilbert D, Orton RJ. Analysis of Signalling Pathways Using Continuous Time Markov Chains. T Comp Sys Biology. 2006;4220:44–67.
144. Heath J, Kwiatkowska M, Norman G, Parker D, Tymchyshyn O. Probabilistic model checking of complex biological pathways. Theoretical Computer Science. 2008;319(3):239–257.
145. Jha SK, Clarke EM, Langmead CJ, Legay A, Platzer A, Zuliani P. A Bayesian Approach to Model Checking Biological Systems. In: Proc. of CMSB 2009: the 7th International Conference on Computational Methods in Systems Biology. vol. 5688 of Lecture

Notes in Computer Science. Springer; 2009. p. 218–234.

146. Zuliani P, Baier C, Clarke EM. Rare-event verification for stochastic hybrid systems. In: HSCC. ACM; 2012. p. 217–226.

147. Antoniotti M, Policriti A, Ugel N, Mishra B. Model building and model checking for biochemical processes. Cell Biochemistry and Biophysics. 2003;38:271–286. pmid:12794268

148. Calzone L, Chabrier-Rivier N, Fages F, Soliman S. Machine learning biochemical networks from temporal logic properties. Transactions on Computational Systems Biology VI. 2006; p. 68–94.

149. Sankaranarayanan S, Fainekos G. Simulating Insulin Infusion Pump Risks by In-Silico Modeling of the Insulin-Glucose Regulatory System. In: Proc. of CMSB 2012: the 10th Conference on Computational Methods in Systems Biology. vol. 7605 of LNCS; 2012. p. 322–341.

150. Cousot P, Cousot R. Abstract interpretation: a unified lattice model for static analysis of programs by construction or approximation of fixpoints. In: Proc. of POPL '77: the 4th ACM SIGACT-SIGPLAN symposium on Principles of programming languages. ACM; 1977. p. 238–252.

151. Paulev L, Magnin M, Roux O. Static analysis of Biological Regulatory Networks dynamics using abstract interpretation. Math Struct in Comp Science. 2012;22:651–685.

152. Fages F, Soliman S. Abstract interpretation and types for systems biology. Theor Comput Sci. 2008;403(1):52–70.

153. Bartocci E, Bortolussi L, Milios D., Nenzi L., Sanguinetti G. Studying Emergent Behaviours in Morphogenesis using Signal Spatio-Temporal Logic. In: Proc. of HSB 2015: the 4th International Workshop on Hybrid Systems Biology. vol. 9271 of LNCS. Springer; 2015. p. 156–172

154. Bartocci E, Gao S, Smolka SA. Proc. of ISoLA 2014: the 6th International Symposium on Leveraging Applications of Formal Methods, Verification and Validation. Part II. In: Medical Cyber-Physical Systems—(Track Introduction). vol. 8803 of Lecture Notes in Computer Science. Springer; 2014. p. 353–355.

6 PETRI NET AND PROBABILISTIC MODEL CHECKING BASED APPROACH FOR THE MODELLING, SIMULATION AND VERIFICATION OF INTERNET WORM PROPAGATION

Misbah Razzaq, Jamil Ahmad

Department of Computational Sciences, Research Center for Modeling & Simulation (RCMS), National University of Sciences and Technology (NUST), Islamabad, Pakistan

ABSTRACT

Internet worms are analogous to biological viruses since they can infect a host and have the ability to propagate through a chosen medium. To prevent the spread of a worm or to grasp how to regulate a prevailing worm, compartmental models are commonly used as a means to examine and understand the patterns and mechanisms of a worm spread. However, one of the greatest challenge is to produce methods to verify and validate the behavioural properties of a compartmental model. This is why in this study we suggest a framework based on *Petri Nets*and *Model Checking* through which we can meticulously examine and validate these models. We investigate *Susceptible-Exposed-Infectious-Recovered (SEIR)* model and propose a new model *Susceptible-Exposed-Infectious-Recovered-Delayed-Quarantined (Susceptible/Recovered) (SEIDQR(S/I))* along with hybrid quarantine strategy, which is then constructed and analysed using *Stochastic Petri Nets* and *Continuous Time Markov Chain*. The analysis shows that the hybrid quarantine strategy is extremely effective in reducing the risk of propagating the worm. Through *Model Checking*, we gained insight into the functionality of compartmental models. *Model Checking* results validate simulation ones well, which fully support the proposed framework.

INTRODUCTION

Internet Worm

Since the discovery of the first internet worm in 1988 viz. *Morris* Worm, systems running on networks are more prone to digital threats [1]. The safety and security of the internet have been compromised particularly by worms that exploit zero hour vulnerabilities. The sudden advancement of computer technologies and network applications have become a potential haven for malicious software programs. The propagation behaviour of worms on internet can somewhat be correlated with biological diseases [2, 3]. Some notable worms including *Code Red* and *Nimda* attacked hundreds of thousands of computers in 2001 [4, 5]. *Blaster* worm (2003) employed sequential scanning to find its targets [6]. *SQL Slammer* infected more than ninety percent vulnerable computers within 10 minutes in 2003 [7]. Witty worm was the first wide spreading worm that damaged infected hosts [8]. *Storm* worm infected thousands of computers in 2007 [9]. *Conficker* was detected in November 2008 is the largest known worm since *SQL Slammer* [10]. Worm propagation speed is directly proportional to the bandwidth and automatic mitigation is the only solution to stop their propagation because manual countermeasures are very slow. Network intrusion detection techniques are used for this purpose and can be divided into two categories: signature based and anomaly based. Every technique has its own pros and cons. Signature based techniques cannot detect unknown worms while anomaly based techniques have high false positive rates [11]. Recently, Entropy measure methods have been proposed [12–15] to study the robustness and complexity of the network.

Existing Models

Worm propagation models are used to understand propagation behaviour in order to develop appropriate defence mechanisms against future attacks [16]. A variety of worm propagation models have been proposed to study the worm's spread and the effectiveness of defensive strategies. Most of the these models [5, 17, 18] are based on the Kermack-Mckendrick model. By the use of worm propagation models, Anderson and May have thoroughly explained the behavioural nature of biological diseases and parasites that can lead to the propagation of infectious diseases in human population [19]. By applying the same method, via using the epidemiological models for disease propagation we can monitor and study the behaviour of worms throughout a network [20]. The Susceptible-Exposed-Infectious-Recovered-Susceptible (SEIRS) model presented by Mishra and Saina have latent and temporary periods that identify the propagation of a common worm [21]. Based on the Susceptible-Exposed-Infectious-Recovered (SEIR) model, Dong et al. proposed a computer virus propagation model and studied the dynamical behaviour including local asymptotical stability and local Hopf bifurcation of a computer virus model using time delay as a bifurcating parameter [22]. L.-X. Yang and X. Yang, examined the dynamics of the virus propagation, once infected systems are running on the network with positive chance [23]. Under human intervention Gan et al. examined the computer virus propagation behaviour [24]. Ren et al. gave a new computer virus dispersion model and studied different dynamic behaviour of the model [25]. Quarantine is common and an effective way of containing the worms [7]. The use of quarantine containment method has produced some extraordinary results, successfully regulating diseases [7, 19–26]. Wang et al. combined both a dynamic quarantine strategy and a vaccination in an epidemic model and referred this new model as SEIQV model [27]. Zou et al. proposed a new model with dynamic quarantine strategy based on two-factor model [7]. Xia et al. proposed a new model with direct immunization [28]. Xia et al. examined the SIRS model to determine the effect of non uniform transmission [29]. Xia et al. proposed a new epidemic model with infection delay and propagation vector [30]. Sanz et al. proposed a new framework to study the dynamics of concurrent diseases [31]. Wang et al. comprehensively reviewed the latest work on the spatial meta population [32]. Cattuto et al. presented a scalable framework to monitor the social interaction and study the dynamics of face to face interaction [33]. Zhang et al. studied the contact network from temporal point of view [34]. Driessche et al. presented a SIRI model for a disease with relapse [35]. Driessche et al. developed a SEIRI compartmental model [35].

Our Contribution

According to our knowledge, previous studies have not taken into account the effect of time delay in detecting worm and applying countermeasures on susceptible, exposed and infectious hosts. To cope with this delay, delayed state is introduced in the proposed model. To make our results more realistic, we have introduced a transition from recovered to susceptible and infected state because a network can never be worm free as there is always a chance of re-infection. Our proposed model is based on the hybrid intrusion detection, which combine features of both signature based and anomaly based techniques. According to the above description, we have presented a Susceptible-Exposed-Infectious-Recovered-Delayed-Quarantined (Susceptible/Recovered) "SEIDQR(S/I)" worm propagation model by modifying *Susceptible-Exposed-Infectious-Recovered (SEIR)*, to study the behaviour of worm's spread and to analyse the effectiveness of a quarantine strategy through *Model Checking*. This work presents the framework for studying worm's propagation and validating the compartmental models. We have used *Petri Nets* and Model Checking to look closely at the behaviour of the model. *Stochastic Petri Net (SPN)* of the *SEIDQR(S/I)* is constructed and simulated in *Snoopy*Tool. *Continuous Time Markov Chain (CTMC)* of the model is generated in *PRISM* model checker to formally verify the behavioural properties of the model. The *Charlie* tool is used to analyse qualitative properties of the *SPN*. Through *SPN* we have created many experiments and have studied the impact of different parameters and classes on the system. According to our knowledge, framework based on *Petri Nets* and *Model Checking* has not been previously proposed for this purpose. Our paper presents the first approach in this direction. This framework offers promising advantages in terms of qualitative and quantitative analysis of compartmental models.

Structure of the Paper

The rest of the paper has been structured in the following manner: Section 2 gives an overview of the proposed *SEIDQR(S/I)* model and illustrates the *SPN* and *CTMC* of the proposed model. In section 3, we show the simulations using *Snoopy* tool, quantitative analysis using *PRISM*model checker and qualitative analysis using *Charlie* tool. It also shows the analysis of the hybrid quarantine strategy through *PRISM* model checker. We discuss the methodology and results in section 4. Conclusions are drawn on the basis of results in section 5. A list of abbreviations is provided at the end of this article.

METHODS

This research is an exploratory study on how worms propagate and how their parameters have an effect on their propagation speed. Worm propagation models are used to understand propagation behaviour in order to develop appropriate defence mechanisms against future attacks. Current worm propagation modelling techniques are based on complex differential equations. *Petri Nets* formalism can be used to develop worm propagation models with less complexity [36]. What is advantageous is that it is not such a laborious task to develop worm propagation models using *Petri Nets*. We can also look closely at the behaviour of the model through *Model Checking* and this offers promising advantages in terms of qualitative and quantitative analysis. Fig 1 presents the structure of the proposed framework.

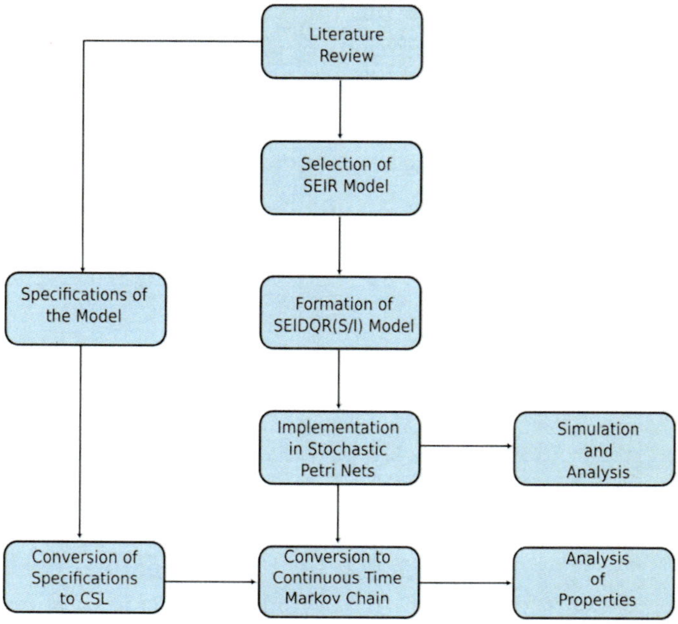

Figure 1: Flow chart of the Proposed Framework.

After reviewing literature, *SEIR* model is selected and a new *SEIDQR(S/I)* is proposed by modifying SEIR model. *SPN* of the proposed model is constructed and analysed in *Snoopy* and *Charlie*, after which the system is converted to *CTMC* and specifications are encoded in CSL for quantitative analysis in *PRISM* model checker.

Model Formulation

Taking into account the worms having exploited zero day vulnerabilities, the host could not be immunized by the usually effective and reliable safety patches. Susceptible hosts initially face an incubation period (exposed) prior to becoming infectious, for this reason people may try placing countermeasures as a precautionary attempt to immunize the exposed and infectious host. However, this can be time consuming and potentially aggravate the harm caused by worms if they are unknown. Due to the existence of the delays, the infectious hosts are put through a temporary state (delayed) before quarantining and recovery. We introduced delayed stage prior to the quarantined stage in order to compensate for the delays experienced by the hosts.

It is important to note that there is no permanent immunity in the real network. The only immunity a node achieves in a real network is temporary, for this reason we must observe the real phenomena of possible re-infection. In order to address this issue, a node reverts to the susceptible and infectious compartment again in the proposed model.

Quarantine strategy is dependent on two types of intrusion detection systems, which can be categorized as misuse and anomaly intrusion detection. They both have their pros and cons but misuse intrusion detection systems recognizes the attack behaviour of potential threats with its broad database constructed of known attack behavioural patterns. This is beneficial to an extent but with regards to unknown worms variants, it fails to recognize them as a threat by not having the data of their behavioural patterns. On the contrary, anomaly detection systems are able to recognize abnormal behavioural patterns which help in the detection of unknown worms and their variants. The quarantine strategy proposed in this study is based on both, anomaly and misuse intrusion detection system. Although, anomaly detection technique can detect unknown worms, it is accompanied by false-positive rates and because of that two transitions have been added with rates n_1 and n_2 from susceptible and exposed classes (See Fig 2).

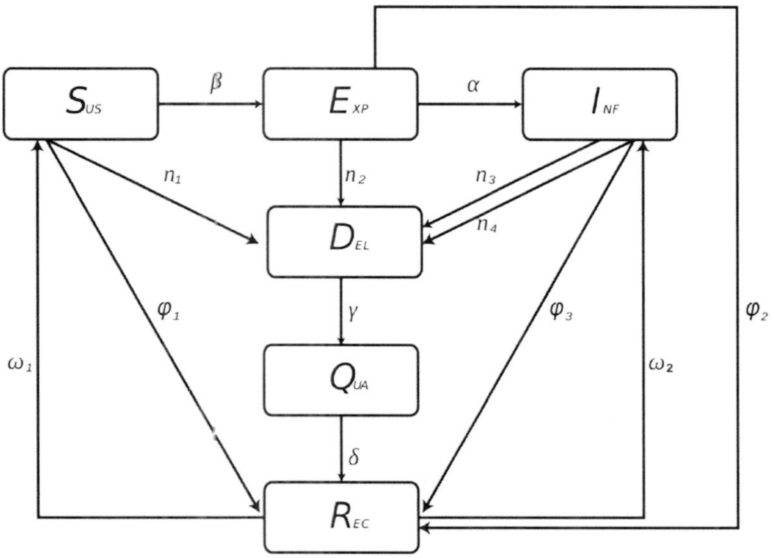

Figure 2: The states and the transitions of *SEIDQR(S/I)* **model.**

The rectangles represent the compartments and the arrows represent the movement of hosts from one compartment to another. The labels on the rectangles indicate the type of compartment i.e. susceptible, exposed, infectious, delayed, quarantined and recovered. The labels on the arrows indicate the rate of transmission of hosts from one compartment to another.

According to the above description, we have proposed a *SEIDQR(S/I))* model with hybrid quarantine strategy. Presumably, the host will be in one of the following compartments: Susceptible Compartment (S_{US}), Exposed Compartment (E_{XP}), Infectious Compartment (I_{NF}), Delayed Compartment (D_{EL}), Quarantined Compartment (Q_{UA}) and Recovered Compartment (R_{EC}) with initial condition $N = S_{US}(t_0) + E_{XP}(t_0) + I_{NF}(t_0) + D_{EL}(t_0) + Q_{UA}(t_0) + R_{EC}(t_0)$. Here, $S_{US}(t_0)$, $E_{XP}(t_0)$, $I_{NF}(t_0)$, $D_{EL}(t_0)$, $Q_{UA}(t_0)$ and $R_{EC}(t_0)$ represents the number of susceptible nodes, exposed nodes, infectious nodes, delayed nodes, quarantined nodes and recovered nodes at time instant t_0. Fig 2 represents the proposed *SEIDQR(S/I)* model. β is the rate of transfer from susceptible to exposed compartment. α is the rate of transfer from exposed to infectious compartment. Parameters used in the proposed model are listed in Table 1.

Table 1: Notations and Explanation

Notation	Explanation
N	Total size of population
$S_{US}(t)$	Number of susceptible nodes at time instant *t*
$E_{XP}(t)$	Number of exposed nodes at time instant *t*
$I_{NF}(t)$	Number of infectious nodes at time instant *t*
$D_{EL}(t)$	Number of delayed nodes at time instant *t*
$Q_{UA}(t)$	Number of quarantined nodes at time instant *t*
$R_{EC}(t)$	Number of recovered nodes at time instant *t*
β	Rate of transfer from susceptible to exposed compartment
α	Rate of transfer from exposed to infectious compartment
γ	Quarantined rate of delayed nodes
δ	Recovery rate of quarantined nodes
n_1	Delayed rate of susceptible nodes
n_2	Delayed rate of exposed nodes
n_3	Delayed rate of infectious nodes with anomaly detection
n_4	Delayed rate of infectious nodes with signature based detection
φ_1	Rate of transfer from susceptible to recovered compartment
φ_2	Rate of transfer from exposed to recovered compartment
φ_3	Rate of transfer from infectious to recovered compartment
ω_1	Rate of transfer from recovered to susceptible compartment
ω_2	Rate of transfer from recovered compartment to infectious compartment

doi:10.1371/journal.pone.0145690.t001

Petri Nets

Petri Nets theory was originated from Carl Adam's Publications in 1962. *Petri Nets* are a powerful graphical and mathematical tool used to describe systems and their behaviour. We can analyse behavioural properties of the system using *Petri Nets* with relative ease [37].

Petri Net is a bipartite graph consisting of places in one partite and transitions in another. Places and transitions are connected through directed edges. If there is a directed arc from place p to a transition t then p is the input place of the transition t. If there is a directed arc from transition t to a place p then p is the output place of the transition t. If every input place of a transition contains token then transition is fire-able. Firing of a transition consist of removing a token from every input place and adding a token to every output place of a transition. Firing of transition results into the new marking of the *Petri Net*, for example to reach marking M_z from M_y, there exist a firing sequence S [38].

Standard Petri Net.

"A *Standard Petri Net* [37] is defined by 5 − *tuple* $\langle P, T, F, W, M_0\rangle$ where;

- P is a finite set of places $\{p_1, p_2, \ldots, p_m\}$
- T is a finite set of transitions $\{t_1, t_2, \ldots, t_m\}$
- $F \subseteq (P \times T) \cup (T \times P)$ is a set of arcs
- W is a weight function of arcs
- M_0: is initial marking $P \rightarrow \{0, 1, 2, \ldots\}$

where $P \cap T = \emptyset$ and $P \cup T \neq \emptyset$". The example in Fig 3 illustrates the definition of the *Standard Petri Net*.

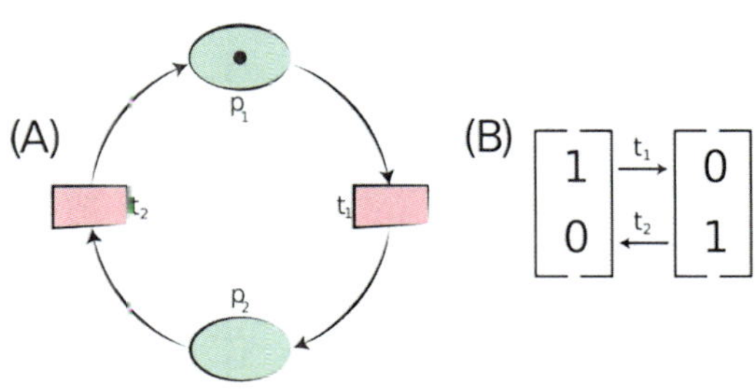

Figure 3: Example of a *Standard Petri Net*.

(A) A *Petri Net* consists of a set of places $\{p_1, p_2\}$, set of transitions $\{t_1, t_2\}$ and an initial marking M_0 consisting of one token in place p_1. In this example, the weight of the arcs are not specified so every arc weighs 1. The enabling degree of a transition is determined by number of times a transition can be fired without depositing a token again to the input place of a transition through self-loop. In case of above example t_1 is 1 enabled and t_2 is 0 enabled from the initial marking M_0. (B) The reachability graph obtained from initial marking M_0 of the *Petri Net*. A reachability graph consist of set of places which can be reached from M_0 and arcs which are labelled with enabled transitions. This graph shows one cycle: $(1, 0) \rightarrow (0, 1) \rightarrow (1, 0)$ and contains no deadlock. To reach marking $M_1 = (0, 1)$ from the marking $M_0 = (1, 0)$, a firing sequence S consist of a transition t_1 once and transition t_2 zero time.

Stochastic Petri Net.

"A *Stochastic Petri Net (SPN)* [39] is defined by 6 – *tuple* $\langle P, T, F, W, M_0, \Omega \rangle$ where P, T, F, W, M_0 are same as described in the definition of the *Standard Petri Net* and Ω represents the function $\Omega : T \rightarrow \mathbb{R}_{\geq 0}$ which assigns rate to the transition $t \in T$ according to the negative exponential distribution function". The evolution of Stochastic *Petri Net* is described by a *Continuous Time Markov Chain (CTMC)* and a state of a *CTMC* represents the one marking of the *Petri Net*. In other words, *CTMC* represents the reachability graph of the *Petri Net* [39].

The example in Fig 4 illustrates the definition of the *Stochastic Petri Net*. There are several behavioural properties of *Petri Nets* [37, 38, 40] and some of these are described below:

- Reachability: This property is used to study dynamic properties of the system. A marking M_k is reachable from an initial marking M_0 if there exists a firing sequence from M_0 to M_k.
- Liveness: A live *Petri Net* is a deadlock free *Petri Net* and from any marking, there exists a firing sequence which contain all transitions.
- Reversibility: This property ensures that there will always be a way back to the initial marking M_0 from all reachable markings commencing from M_0.

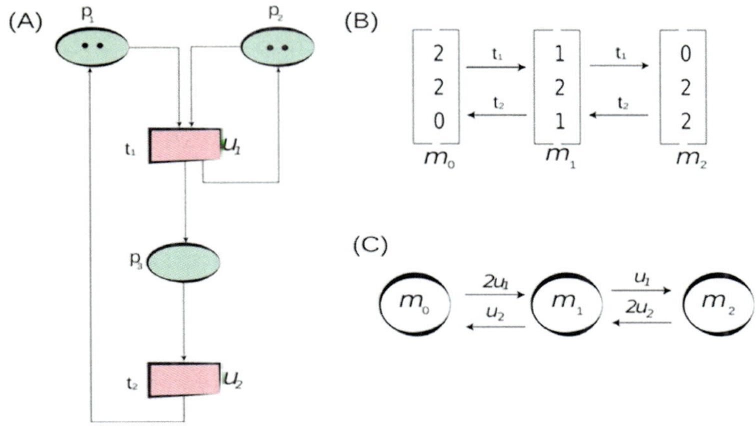

Figure 4: Example of a *Stochastic Petri Net.*

(A) A *SPN* consists of a set of places $\{p_1, p_2, p_3\}$, set of transitions $\{t_1, t_2\}$, rates μ_1, $\mu_2$and an initial marking $M_0 = (2, 2, 0)$. In case of this example t_1 is 2 enabled and t_2 is 0 enabled from the initial marking M_0. (B) The reachability graph obtained from initial marking M_0 of the *Petri Net*. (C) The *Markov Chain* obtained from the reachability graph in (B). Every reachable marking of the *SPN* is associated with a state of the *Markov Chain* and a transition between states is labelled with the product of the enabling degree and rate.

SPN of the proposed model.

We have presented an approach through which we can model network epidemiological systems through *Petri Nets* with relative ease. *Petri Net* modelling of the real system is sometimes called Condition-Event net. *Petri Net* places are used to identify conditions of the system and transitions represent the flow from one condition to another. An event can only occur if all the conditions are satisfied i.e., input places are marked with sufficient tokens.

We are using *SPN* to model our proposed system because we can easily generate *CTMC*though *SPN* as *SPNs* are isomorphic to *CTMC* [39]. To model an *SEIDQR(S/I)* as a *SPN*, we need to represent the host population which consist of different compartments. For this purpose, places are used to represent the states or compartments of the system i.e. susceptible, exposed, infectious, delayed, quarantined and recovered.

Hosts are represented by the tokens and dynamic part of *SEIDQR(S/I)* is modelled by transitions labelled as $t_1, t_2, t_3, t_4, t_5, t_6, t_7, t_8, t_9, t_{10}, t_{11}, t_{12}, t_{13}$ and these transitions originate the flow of hosts from one state to another with specified rate. Fig 5 illustrates the *SPN* of the proposed model.

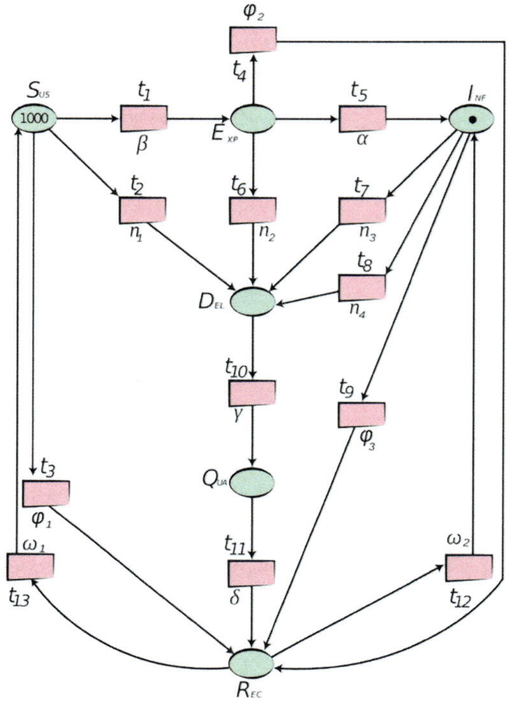

Figure 5: The *SPN* **of the** proposed model.

The *SPN* of the proposed model consists of a set of places $P = \{S_{US}, E_{XP}, I_{NF}, D_{EL}, Q_{UA}, R_{EC}\}$ and set of transitions $T = \{t_1, t_2, t_3, t_4, t_5, t_6, t_7, t_8, t_9, t_{10}, t_{11}, t_{12}, t_{13}\}$ and initial marking $M_0 = (1000, 0, 1, 0, 0, 0)$.

Model Checking

Testing or simulation-based system analysis techniques are not effective as compared to automatic model-based verification approaches [41]. Model checking, in particular, is a more powerful tool capable of exploring a whole state space. [42]. A model checker is used to examine whether the model of a system which is specified in some modelling formalism such as *Petri Nets*, meets the requirements of a system which are usually encoded in some temporal logic such as CTL (Computation

Tree Logic) or PCTL (Probabilistic Computation Tree Logic) [43]. Fig 6 explains the *Model Checking* process.

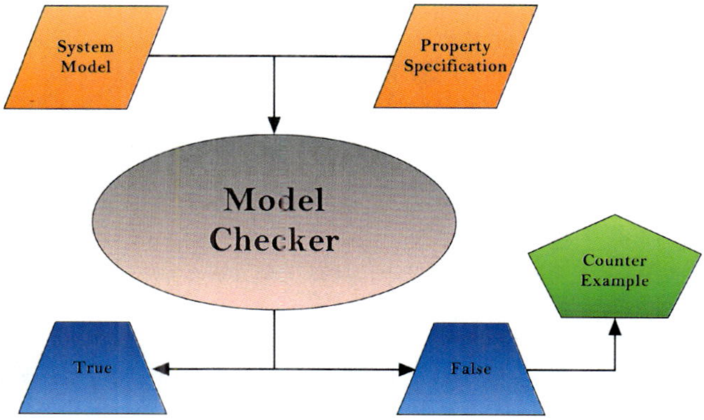

Figure 6: *Model Checking* **Process.**

Model checker takes the system model and property specification as input and generates two types of output: (1) true which means property is satisfied (2) false with counter example which means property is not satisfied.

Probabilistic Model Checking.

Probabilistic Model Checking is a variant of a formal verification method and is used for analysing and modelling a system which shows stochastic behaviours. There are two types of outputs of a probabilistic model checker: (1) 'True' signifying that the property is satisfied or 'False' signifying the property is dissatisfied. (2) 'Numerical Number' indicating the probability or expected time [44]. The *Model Checking* approach used in this study is probabilistic which is based on *CSL*. *PRISM* model checker is used for this purpose because *PRISM* supports *CTMCs* with *Continuous Stochastic Logic (CSL)*.

Continuous Stochastic Logic.

The temporal logic used in *CTMCs* is *CSL* which is based on both CTL and PCTL [45, 46]. It can specify path based, reward based as well as traditional properties [44]. The syntax of *CSL*is as follows:

$$\phi ::= true \mid a \mid \neg\phi \mid \phi_1 \wedge \phi_2 \mid (P_{\sim p}[\phi_1 \cup^I \phi_2] \mid S_{\sim p}[\phi] \mid R_{\sim r}[F\phi]$$

Where a represents the atomic proposition, $\sim \in \{>, \geq, <, \leq\}$, $p \in [0, 1]$, I is an interval of $\mathbb{R}_{\geq 0}$ and $r \in \mathbb{R}_{\geq 0}$.

CSL formulae are evaluated over the *CTMC* states. A formula $s \models \phi$ indicates that ϕ is true in state s of *CTMC* model. *CSL* contains all standard operators from propositional logic: true (all states satisfy); atomic propositions (true in all states labelled with a); negation ($\neg\phi$ is true in all states in which ϕ does not hold) and conjunction ($\phi_1 \wedge \phi_2$) (will be true in a state in which both ϕ_1 and ϕ_2 hold). We can drive other standard operators like disjunction and implication from these standard operators.

Furthermore, *CSL* includes probabilistic operators P and S. Both probabilistic operators include probability bound $\sim p$. We write $P_{\sim p}[\Psi]$ to indicate the *CSL* formula Ψ is true in a state s if the probability of *CSL* path formula meets the bound $\sim p$. The S operator is used to verify the steady state behaviour of the *CTMC* in long run.

CSL also has another operator R to calculate those properties which require expected value of reward. $R_{\sim r}[F\phi]$ is used to calculate the accumulated value of the expected reward before a state is reached where ϕ is satisfied. [44, 47].

CTMC of the Proposed Model.

We have chosen a *Probabilistic Model Checking* approach because it provides both probabilistic analysis and conventional reachability. Through *Probabilistic Model Checking*, we will be able to accumulate accurate answers as compared to approximate solutions obtained through simulation. State space explosion is the only drawback of *Probabilistic Model Checking*[41].

We initiated the model definition, writing keyword *ctmc* in the beginning, to explicitly mention the type of probabilistic model used in this study. Then we mentioned the sequence of possible values upheld by state variables S_{US}, E_{XP}, I_{NF}, D_{EL}, Q_{UA} and R_{EC}. In our case, we choose to let them vary between 0 and upper-limit labelled as Max. It is not necessary to specify upper-limits using parameters, but it helps to maintain the clarity of the model. Then, we labelled the module enclosing the transition rules as *SEIDQRSI*. After mentioning state variable names and defining their range within square brackets, keyword *init* is used to define the initial value of the variable. Then, we gave the definition of transition rules β, α, γ, δ, n_1, n_2, n_3, n_4, φ_1, φ_2, φ_3, ω_1, ω_2. The list of transition rules are separated from the list of conditions using a symbol –>. We end the module by writing the keyword *endmodule*. We specified a reward structure by writing a reward rule between keywords *rewards* and *endrewards*.

We encoded behavioural properties in *CSL* in order to verify against the proposed model. Some of these behavioural properties are listed below:

- Expected number of hosts at any time instant *t*.
- Probability of reaching the maximum number of infectious hosts
- Invariance principle

RESULTS

In this section, first we present the simulation results obtained through the *Snoopy* tool and then the verification results obtained through *PRISM* and *Charlie* tools.

Simulation Using Snoopy

Here we present the simulation results of the *Snoopy* tool. Initial values of the network are: $N = 1001$, $S_{US}(0) = 1000$, $E_{XP}(0) = 0$, $I_{NF}(0) = 1$, $D_{EL}(0) = 0$, $Q_{UA}(0) = 0$, $R_{EC}(0) = 0$, $\beta = 0.7$, $\alpha = 0.66$, $\gamma = 0.9$, $\delta = 0.8$, $n_1 = 0.01$, $n_2 = 0.01$, $n_3 = 0.01$, $n_4 = 0.02$, $\varphi_1 = 0.001$, $\varphi_2 = 0.005$, $\varphi_3 = 0.004$, $\omega_1 = 0.0001$ and $\omega_2 = 0.0001$.

Fig 7 shows dynamic behaviour of the proposed model with implementation of the quarantine strategy. It shows the behaviour of all states of the proposed system with respect to time. The results predict that the proposed system is asymptotically stable. In addition, It also shows that recovered class has a powerful impact on all other classes of the network. Initially, it can be seen clearly that infection is of a lesser degree but with time it increases gradually. We observe over time that $R_{EC}(t)$ increases whereas $I_{NF}(t)$ decreases. We also notice that we still have some infected nodes at 100th time unit, which proves our assumption that real network can never be completely free from infection. It also shows the important role of the quarantine strategy. The quarantined computers are kept under observation and treated with anti-virus software.

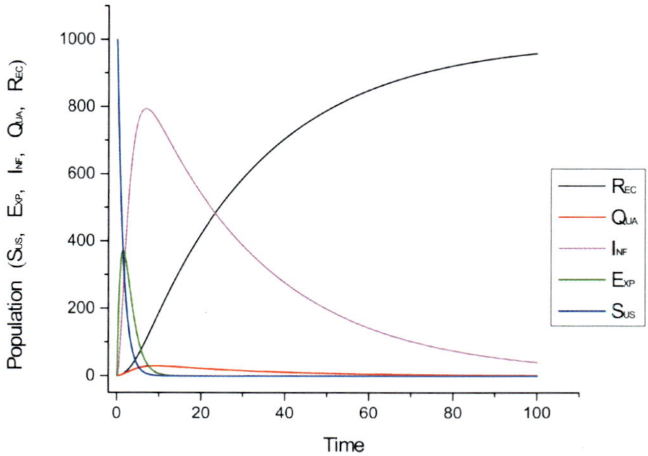

Figure 7: Dynamical behaviour of the proposed system.

Fig 8 shows the behaviour of the proposed model without implementation of any containment strategy. We see in Fig 8 that infectious hosts are diminishing very slowly and recovery process is slow as well. Fig 7 shows the behaviour of the model's entities of the proposed system using quarantine strategy. We see from Fig 7 that infectious hosts are diminishing sharply when we applied quarantine strategy.

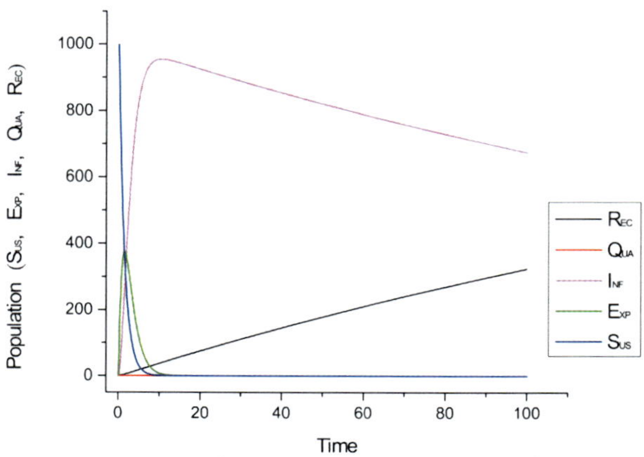

Figure 8: Dynamical behaviour of the proposed system without Quarantine.

Fig 9 shows the relationship among quarantine, susceptible, exposed and infectious compartments. Fig 9 shows the results of susceptible, exposed and infectious classes with respect to the quarantine class. We observe in this figure that nodes from these classes (Susceptible, Exposed and Infectious) are recovering quickly with application of the quarantine strategy.

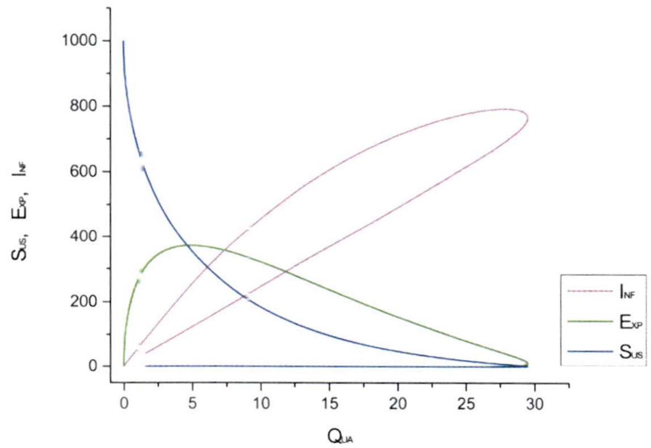

Figure 9: Quarantine effect on different compartments.

Fig 10 shows the impact of quarantine over infectious compartment. Fig 10 shows the behaviour of infectious class with and without quarantine implementation. We observe that when hosts are infected then quarantine is very effective solution.

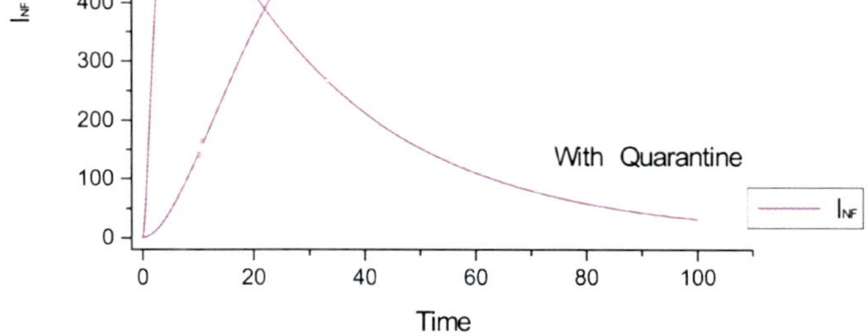

Figure 10: Dynamic behaviour of infectious class with and without quarantine.

Fig 11 shows the behaviour of susceptible compartment with respect to recovered compartment. Fig 11 shows the relationship between recovered and susceptible compartments. We can observe decrease in susceptible nodes when recovered nodes are increasing. It shows that as time passes, recovered hosts increases gradually. It means susceptibility towards worm decreases with time.

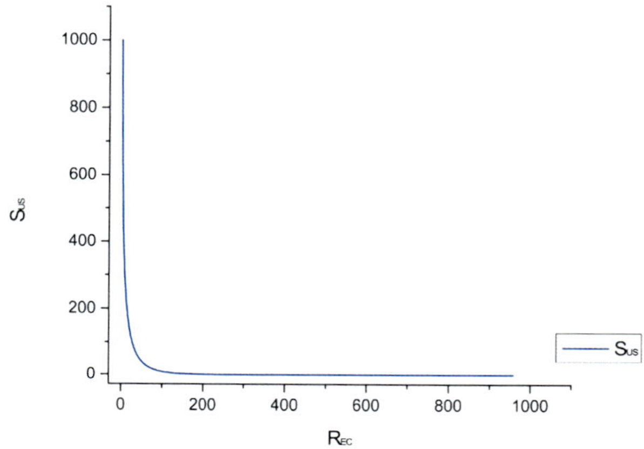

Figure 11: Behaviour of susceptible versus recovered compartment.

For next analysis, all parameters are same except these: $\gamma = 0.01$, $\delta = 0.1$, $n_1 = 0.001$, $n_2 = 0.001$, $n_3 = 0.001$ *and* $n_4 = 0.002$.

Fig 12 shows the impact of infection rate on the performance of the proposed system. We see in Fig 12 that the worm is spreading quickly in the whole network and nodes are becoming infectious with high pace when infection rate is higher than the recovery rate.

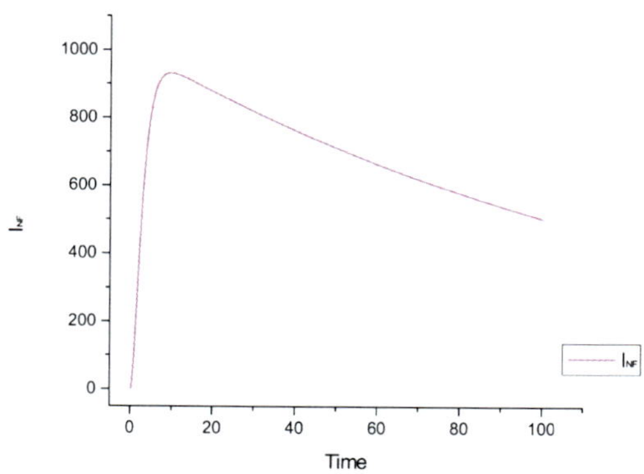

Figure 12: Behaviour of infectious compartment when infection rate is greater than the recovery rate.

Verification Results

This section contains the verification results of the proposed system. In the context of several applications, formal methods have been used to understand and characterize the behaviour of population models. *Probabilistic Model Checking* is a fully automated formal method for verifying quantitative properties of systems that exhibit stochastic behaviour. It is based on the exhaustive searching of the state space. We can check various behavioural properties regarding time and probabilities through *Probabilistic Model Checking* [44].

For quantitative analysis, we have developed a *CTMC* in *PRISM* model checker. The logic used is *Continuous Stochastic Logic (CSL)* which is an extension of Probabilistic Computation Tree Logic (PCTL). PCTL itself is a variant of CTL (Computation Tree Logic) where the path quantifiers (A and E) are replaced by a probabilistic operator (P) [44]. We can also use the keyword "filter" to customize the *PRISM* properties. Filters are represented using the following form:

filter(*op*, *prop*), where *op* denotes the operation we want to perform and *prop* denotes the property we want to verify [48].

For analysis purpose, the parameters in the experiments are defined as: $N = 10$, $S_{US}(0) = 9$, $E_{XP}(0) = 0$, $I_{NF}(0) = 1$, $D_{EL}(0) = 0$, $Q_{UA}(0) = 0$, $R_{EC}(0) = 0$, $\beta = 0.7$, $\alpha = 0.66$, $\gamma = 0.9$, $\delta = 0.8$, $n_1 = 0.01$, $n_2 = 0.01$, $n_3 = 0.02$, $n_4 = 0.03$, $\varphi_1 = 0.001$, $\varphi_2 = 0.005$, $\varphi_3 = 0.004$, $\omega_1 = 0.001$ and $\omega_2 = 0.001$.

We have checked a list of behavioural properties in *PRISM* and some of these are illustrated below:

- $P = ?\ [F\ I_{NF} = 0]$
  This formula inquires, "what is the probability that infection will be eradicated eventually?". This property is verified with probability 1. It means that retreat of the infection is unavoidable. The probability of reaching the state where infected individuals are 0s is 1.
- $P = ?\ [F\ R_{EC} > S_{US}]$
  This represents the probability that recovered individuals will be greater than susceptible individuals. In other words, it means that most of the population is infected at certain points of time. This property is verified with probability 1 in the proposed model

which means that most of the population first became infected at certain times and then eventually recovered.

- $P = ?\ [F \leq 10\ I_{NF} = N/2]$
  It shows the probability that half of the population will be infected within 10 time units. The results shows that there is a 99 percent chance of infection spreading in half of the population within 10 time units.
- $P = ?\ [F \leq 10\ I_{NF} \geq S_{US}]$
  This property inquires, "what is the probability that infected nodes will exceed the susceptible nodes within 10 time units?". This property shows how the worm is spreading in the initial period of time. There is a 99 percent chance that infected individuals will exceed the susceptible within 10 time units.
- $P = ?\ [F \leq 10\ I_{NF} = N]$
  It represents the probability that the whole network will be infected within 10 time units. There is only a 12 percent chance of the infection spreading in every computer within this time.
- $P \geq 1\ [G\ (S_{US} + E_{XP} + I_{NF} + D_{EL} + Q_{UA} + R_{EC}) = N]$
  This property represents the very important principle "Invariance". It represents the probability that sum of all nodes will be equal to the size of the population. This should be the case in our proposed model because the population can never be negative. Since our model is based on closed population, this property should globally hold and the result shows that it is true in the proposed model.
- $R = ?\ [F\ I_{NF} = 0]$
  This property inquires, "what is the expected time for a network to be eventually infection free?". The expected time for the extinction of the worm is 58 time units.
- $filter(forall, P \geq 1\ [F\ R_{EC} = N])$
  This states that we will eventually reach a state, initiating from any reachable state, where all hosts are recovered with probability 1. This property is true in the proposed model.
- $S = ?\ [I_{NF} = 0]$
  This property represents the long run probability (steady state) of the worm's extinction from the network. The result obtained through this property shows that there is a 70 percent chance of the worm being neutralized. This shows that network is never

going to be infection free, there will always be a chance of re-infection. Model checking results successfully validates the simulation results.

These behavioral properties allow us to know if behavior of *SEIDQR(S/I)* model is stable and valid at every instance of time.

Verification of Hybrid Quarantine Strategy using PRISM.

In order to analyze the effectiveness of the quarantine strategy through *Model Checking*, the parameters in the experiments are same as defined in the above section.

Table 2 summarises the results of *Model Checking* with and without quarantine strategy based on these parameters. Model checking validates the use of quarantine strategy in worm containment. We have compared results in three scenarios. In the first scenario, we have checked the probability of the whole network becoming infectious within 10 time units. It shows a huge difference in results with and without quarantine implementation. When we have implemented quarantine strategy it shows that there is only a 12 percent chance of spreading the worm in the whole population within 10 time units but without quarantine it spreads rapidly. Without applying the quarantine strategy there is a 74 percent chance of the infection spreading throughout the whole population within 10 time units. In second scenario, we have inquired, "what are the chances that half of the population will be infected within 10 time units?". In that particular case probability is equal in both cases with and without quarantine strategy. In third scenario, we have investigated the chances of the network becoming infection free within 100 time units. In case of the quarantine strategy, there is a 91 percent chance that whole network will be infection free within the specified time limit. In case of without the quarantine strategy, there is a 0 percent chance that whole network will be infection free within 100 time units. Table 3 summarises the results of *Model Checking* with and without quarantine strategy based on the above mentioned parameters except that population size is 26 now, susceptible hosts are 25 and infectious host is 1. In the first study, we have checked the probability of the worm infecting the whole population within 10 time units. The probability of the infection spreading across the whole population after implementing the quarantine strategy was minimal, on the contrary, without the use of the quarantine strategy the probability of infection increased by 40 percent. In the second experiment, we discovered that the probability of the infection spreading to half of the population was 0.9999 within 10 time units, with or without the implementation of the quarantine strategy. In the third experiment, we have discovered that with the implementation of the quarantine strategy, almost 69 percent of the population was infection free within 100 time units but the percentage was considerably less without quarantine. This analysis indicates the significance of implementing mitigation techniques in the initial stages of an infection which otherwise would be incredibly difficult to control and may cause severe harm to the majority of the hosts and this will be very costly. The results in Tables 2 and 3 shows the importance of implementing the hybrid quarantine strategy. It also enlightens the fact that within a larger population the speed of a worm's spread gradually decelerates with time. The results reported in Tables 2 and 3 also indicates that smaller population recovered quickly as compared to the larger population.

Table 2: Results with and without Quarantine for sample size 10

Property	Probabilities With Quarantine	Probabilities Without Quarantine
$P = ?\ [F \leq 10\ I_{NF} = N]$	0.1207	0.7412
$P = ?\ [F \leq 10\ I_{NF} = N/2]$	0.9999	0.9999
$P = ?\ [F \leq 100\ I_{NF} = 0]$	0.9131	0.0029

doi:10.1371/journal.pone.0145690.t002

Table 3. Results with and without Quarantine for sample size 26

Property	Probabilities With Quarantine	Probabilities Without Quarantine
$P = ?\ [F \leq 10\ I_{NF} = N]$	0.0013	0.3972
$P = ?\ [F \leq 10\ I_{NF} = N/2]$	0.9999	0.9999
$P = ?\ [F \leq 100\ I_{NF} = 0]$	0.6849	0.0016

doi:10.1371/journal.pone.0145690.t003

Verification of Qualitative Properties using Charlie.

The reachability graph is strongly connected which means that the graph is homogeneous. Each pair of markings are reachable from one another. Since the proposed system (compartmental model) is homogeneous therefore, the reachability graph is homogeneous. This reachability graph indicates that all markings of the model always end up in a cycle which also states that the system is deadlock free, reversible and live. This model ensures the invariance principle which means that population will never be negative. This property can be ensured by P-invariant and is verifiable in our model. Fig 13 shows the reachability graph of the *SPN*.

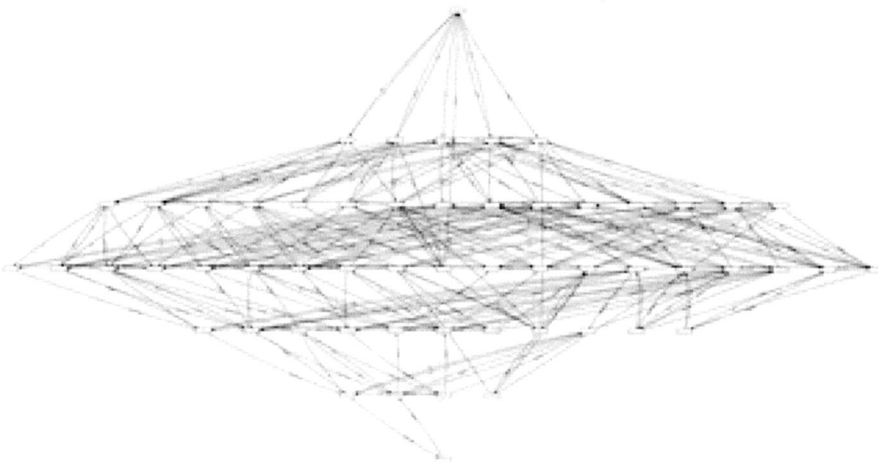

Figure 13: Reachability Graph.

Fig 13 shows the reachability graph consisting of a total of 56 unique markings and 273 transitions with initial marking $M_0 = (2, 0, 1, 0, 0, 0)$.

DISCUSSION

In this work we have proposed a new model called *SEIDQR(S/I)* model which was based on the delays experienced by the hosts before worm containment and possible reinfection probability. We presented modelling of a compartmental model via *Petri Net* approach. Moreover, in order to study the dynamic behaviour of the proposed model we used two types of analysis techniques: *Simulation* and *Probabilistic Model Checking*.

It is important to model and study the behaviour of the system before resulting to deployment. Sometimes, models are developed after deployment as well in order to study the dynamics of the systems. The domain of communication systems are full of queries regarding cost and efficiency etc.. In order to resolve these problems it requires the construction and study of analytical and simulation models before the development and deployment of the systems. It is necessary to develop models for qualitative and quantitative understanding of the systems.

The nature of traffic between communication systems is unpredictable and therefore, it is typical to develop a stochastic model to represent such systems [39]. Therefore, in this study we have used *SPN* to construct models. Mathematical models have been conventionally used for analysis of worm propagation. However, these models rely on unreasonable assumptions [39] and cannot be formally verified. In this work, we have used the *SPN* to model worm propagation. Then, *CTMC* of the proposed model is constructed in *PRISM* model checker.

Our results are comparable to Mishra and Tyagi [49] where dynamical behaviour is achieved after quarantining 50 nodes. Our model encapsulated a population of 1000 nodes and generated results more accurately by quarantining 30 nodes while retaining similar behavioural curves, as that of Mishra and Tyagi [49].

The analysis of the *CTMC* strongly validates the results obtained through simulation of the *SPN*, which makes the proposed framework valid for application in the field of epidemiology. The analysis obtained through *Model Checking* also supports assumption that real network is never infection free. There is always a chance of possible re-infection. We have already showed this through simulation of the *SPN*. We verified the structural property of the *SPN*through *Charlie* tool. Since the proposed model is homogeneous, it should be strongly connected and this was confirmed through *Charlie* tool. We have also verified some behavioural properties of the *SPN* such as reachability, liveliness, reversibility and deadlock freeness through *Charlie* tool.

A major disadvantage of the modelling approach is the computational cost of the method. In order to evaluate quantitative properties via the *Probabilistic Model Checking* method, it requires a reasonable amount of time (in hours). To overcome this computational obstacle we had to limit our sample size to the maximum of 26 hosts. A possible solution to this problem is to use *Approximate Model Checking* [50]. However, *Probabilistic Model Checking* offers promising outcomes in the analysis of dynamics of compartmental models and therefore, it is worth further investigation.

CONCLUSION AND FUTURE WORK

In this paper, we have proposed a framework to formally verify and validate the compartmental models via model checking and simulation. The proposed framework can be applied to any epidemiological compartmental network model. Beginning with the development of a *SEIDQR(S/I)* model in *Petri Nets* and *PRISM*, we were able to get insight into how *SEIDQR(S/I)* works. On the basis of proposed methodology, we were able to simulate as well as investigate the *SEIDQR(S/I)* model through queries encoded in *CSL*. By varying different parameters of the proposed model, we verified its behavioural properties. Using this approach, we checked certain situations through these properties such as when the worm's infection will be at its peak point, its duration and so on and so forth. The *Petri Net* approach described here has allowed us to perform modelling of the system easily and quickly as compared to other analysis methods. According to this work, we have come to the conclusion that quarantine strategies are extremely effective in reducing the risk of propagating the worm and, in fact, have an outstanding effect in regulating it. *Probabilistic model checking* allowed us to explore many behavioural properties of our model. The proposed approach is applicable for both understanding worm propagation and developing more challenging worm defence strategies. There are many factors that effect worm propagation such as delay, bandwidth and activity of device in the network, which cannot be neglected and will be taken into consideration in our future works. We will use Entropy based measure to compute different properties of the proposed model and will counter verify it with *Probablistic Model Checking Approach* in the futrue work. Since negative exponential distribution is used to generate stochastic transitions, sensitivity analysis of the proposed model will be performed in the next study.

ACKNOWLEDGMENTS

The authors would like to thank Muhammad Tariq Saeed for his support and guidance in this study.

AUTHOR CONTRIBUTIONS

Conceived and designed the experiments: MR JA. Performed the experiments: MR JA. Analyzed the data: MR JA. Contributed reagents/materials/analysis tools: MR JA. Wrote the paper: MR JA.

REFERENCES

1. Feily M, Shahrestani A, Ramadass S. A survey of botnet and botnet detection. In: Emerging Security Information, Systems and Technologies, 2009. SECURWARE'09. Third International Conference on. IEEE; 2009. p. 268–273.
2. Anderson RM, May RM. Infectious diseases of humans. vol. 1. Oxford University Press, Oxford; 1991.
3. Zhu Q, Yang X, Ren J. Modeling and analysis of the spread of computer virus. Communications in Nonlinear Science and Numerical Simulation. 2012;17(12):5117–5124.
4. Li P, Salour M, Su X. A survey of internet worm detection and containment. Communications Surveys & Tutorials, IEEE. 2008;10(1):20–35.
5. Zou CC, Gong W, Towsley D. Code red worm propagation modeling and analysis. In: Proceedings of the 9th ACM conference on Computer and communications security. ACM; 2002. p. 138–147.
6. Bailey M, Cooke E, Jahanian F, Watson D. The blaster worm: Then and now. Security & Privacy, IEEE. 2005;3(4):26–31.
7. Zou CC, Gong W, Towsley D. Worm propagation modeling and analysis under dynamic quarantine defense. In: Proceedings of the 2003 ACM workshop on Rapid malcode. ACM; 2003. p. 51–60.
8. Shannon C, Moore D. The spread of the witty worm. Security & Privacy, IEEE. 2004;2(4):46–50.
9. Mukamurenzi NM. Storm worm: A p2p botnet. 2008.
10. Shin S, Gu G. Conficker and beyond: a large-scale empirical study. In: Proceedings of the 26th Annual Computer Security Applications Conference. ACM; 2010. p. 151–160.

11. Kabiri P, Ghorbani AA. Research on Intrusion Detection and Response: A Survey. IJ Network Security. 2005;1(2):84–102.
12. Chen Z, Dehmer M, Emmert-Streib F, Shi Y. Entropy of Weighted Graphs with Randi c Weights. Entropy. 2015;17(6):3710–3723.
13. Chen Z, Dehmer M, Shi Y. A Note on Distance-based Graph Entropies. Entropy. 2014;16(10):5416–5427.
14. Cao S, Dehmer M, Shi Y. Extremality of degree-based graph entropies. Information Sciences. 2014;278:22–33.
15. Chen Z, Dehmer M, Shi Y. Bounds for degree-based network entropies. Applied Mathematics and Computation. 2015;265:983–993.
16. Misslinger S. Internet worm propagation. Technische University Munchen. 2003.
17. Chen Z, Gao L, Kwiaty K. Modeling the spread of active worms. In: INFOCOM 2003. Twenty-Second Annual Joint Conference of the IEEE Computer and Communications. IEEE Societies. vol. 3. IEEE; 2003. p. 1890–1900.
18. Zou CC, Gong W, Towsley D, Gao L. The monitoring and early detection of internet worms. IEEE/ACM Transactions on Networking (TON). 2005;13(5):961–974.
19. Anderson R, May R. Population Biology of Infectious Diseases. 1982. Springer-Verlag, New York.
20. Mishra BK, Saini D. Mathematical models on computer viruses. Applied Mathematics and Computation. 2007;187(2):929–936.
21. Mishra BK, Saini DK. SEIRS epidemic model with delay for transmission of malicious objects in computer network. Applied Mathematics and Computation. 2007;188(2):1476–1482.
22. Dong T, Liao X, Li H. Stability and Hopf bifurcation in a computer virus model with multistate antivirus. Abstract and Applied Analysis. Hindawi Publishing Corporation; 2012.
23. Yang LX, Yang X. Propagation behavior of virus codes in the situation that infected computers are connected to the Internet with positive probability. Discrete Dynamics in Nature and Society. 2012.

24. Gan C, Yang X, Liu W, Zhu Q, Zhang X. Propagation of computer virus under human intervention: a dynamical model. Discrete Dynamics in Nature and Society. 2012.
25. Ren J, Yang X, Zhu Q, Yang LX, Zhang C. A novel computer virus model and its dynamics. Nonlinear Analysis: Real World Applications. 2012;13(1):376–384.
26. Yao Y, Guo L, Guo H, Yu G, Gao Fx, Tong Xj. Pulse quarantine strategy of internet worm propagation: modeling and analysis. Computers & Electrical Engineering. 2012;38(5):1047–1061.
27. Wang F, Zhang Y, Wang C, Ma J, Moon S. Stability analysis of a SEIQV epidemic model for rapid spreading worms. Computers & Security. 2010;29(4):410–418.
28. Xia C, Liu Z, Chen Z, Yuan Zz. SIRS epidemic model with direct immunization on complex networks. Control and Decision. 2008;23(4):468.
29. Xia C, Sun S, Liu Z, Chen Z, Yuan Z. Epidemics of SIRS model with nonuniform transmission on scale-free networks. International Journal of Modern Physics B. 2009;23(09):2203–2213.
30. Xia C, Wang L, Sun S, Wang J. An SIR model with infection delay and propagation vector in complex networks. Nonlinear Dynamics. 2012;69(3):927–934.
31. Sanz J, Xia CY, Meloni S, Moreno Y. Dynamics of interacting diseases. Physical Review X. 2014;4(4):041005.
32. Wang L, Li X. Spatial epidemiology of networked metapopulation: An overview. Chinese Science Bulletin. 2014;59(28):3511–3522.
33. Cattuto C, Van den Broeck W, Barrat A, Colizza V, Pinton JF, Vespignani A. Dynamics of person-to-person interactions from distributed RFID sensor networks. PloS one. 2010;5(7):e11596. pmid:20657651
34. Zhang Y, Wang L, Zhang YQ, Li X. Towards a temporal network analysis of interactive WiFi users. EPL (Europhysics Letters). 2012;98(6):68002.
35. Van den Driessche P, Zou X. Modeling relapse in infectious diseases. Mathematical biosciences. 2007;207(1):89–103. pmid:17112547
36. Thomas R, d'Ari R. Biological feedback. CRC press; 1990.

37. Murata T. Petri nets: Properties, analysis and applications. Proceedings of the IEEE. 1989;77(4):541–580.
38. David R, Alla H. Discrete, continuous, and hybrid Petri nets. Springer Science & Business Media; 2010.
39. Bhat AA. Stochastic Petri Net Models of Service Availability in a PBNM System for Mobile Ad Hoc Networks. Virginia Polytechnic Institute and State University; 2004.
40. Lu N. Power system modeling using Petri nets. Rensselaer Polytechnic Institute; 2002.
41. Kwiatkowska M, Norman G, Parker D. Quantitative analysis with the probabilistic model checker PRISM. Electronic Notes in Theoretical Computer Science. 2006;153(2):5–31.
42. Baier C, Katoen JP. Principles of model checking. vol. 26202649. MIT press Cambridge; 2008.
43. Clarke EM, Grumberg O, Peled D. Model checking. MIT press; 1999.
44. Kwiatkowska M, Norman G, Parker D. Probabilistic model checking for systems biology. 2011.
45. Aziz A, Sanwal K, Singhal V, Brayton R. Model-checking continuous-time Markov chains. ACM Transactions on Computational Logic (TOCL). 2000;1(1):162–170.
46. Aziz A, Sanwal K, Singhal V, Brayton R. Verifying continuous time Markov chains. In: Computer Aided Verification. Springer; 1996. p. 269–276.
47. Kwiatkowska M, Norman G, Parker D. Probabilistic Model Checking for Systems Biology. In: Symbolic Systems Biology. Jones and Bartlett; 2010. p. 31–59.
48. Property Specification;. Accessed May 20, 2015. http://www.prismmodelchecker.org/manual/PropertySpecification/AllOnOnePage/.
49. Mishra BK, Tyagi I. Defending against Malicious Threats in Wireless Sensor Network: A Mathematical Model. International Journal of Information Technology and Computer Science (IJITCS). 2014;6(3):12.

50. Katoen JP. Abstraction of probabilistic systems. In: Formal Modeling and Analysis of Timed Systems. Springer; 2007. p. 1–3.

7 DESIGN AND ANALYSIS OF A PETRI NET MODEL OF THE VON HIPPEL-LINDAU (VHL) TUMOR SUPPRESSOR INTERACTION NETWORK

Giovanni Minervini[1], Elisabetta Panizzoni[1], Manuel Giollo[1,2], Alessandro Masiero[1], Carlo Ferrari[2], Silvio C. E. Tosatto[1]

[1] Dept. of Biomedical Sciences, University of Padua, Padua, Italy

[2] Dept. of Information Engineering, University of Padua, Padua, Italy

ABSTRACT

Von Hippel-Lindau (VHL) syndrome is a hereditary condition predisposing to the development of different cancer forms, related to germline inactivation of the homonymous tumor suppressor pVHL. The best characterized function of pVHL is the ubiquitination dependent degradation of Hypoxia Inducible Factor (HIF) via the proteasome. It is also involved in several cellular pathways acting as a molecular hub and interacting with more than 200 different proteins. Molecular details of pVHL plasticity remain in large part unknown. Here, we present a novel manually curated Petri Net (PN) model of the main pVHL functional pathways. The model was built using functional information derived from the literature. It includes all major pVHL functions and is able to credibly reproduce VHL syndrome at the molecular level. The reliability of the PN model also allowed in silico knockout experiments, driven by previous model analysis. Interestingly, PN analysis suggests that the variability of different VHL manifestations is correlated with the concomitant inactivation of different metabolic pathways.

INTRODUCTION

Pathological deregulation of cellular pathways often results in a family of complex and correlated diseases commonly termed cancer [1]. Cancer is a multi factorial disease where different causes contribute to its development. Several computational methods have been developed to explore the functional pathways involved in tumorigenesis. Some of them focus on differential gene expression between healthy and pathologic tissues [2]–[3], on protein-protein interaction network analysis [4]–[5] or on molecular dynamics simulations [6]. Other methods approach the disease through discretization of pathological components that result in tumor [7]. All of these approaches are very powerful when the variables related to the disease, although complex, are well known and studied. A multi-factorial disease can be approached by means of mathematical theory, building a theoretical model where cell components are connected with each other. In biology, several problems were dealt with network theory [8]–[9]. A network is a group of objects strongly inter-connected with each other (e.g. proteins and enzymes of a pathway or animals belonging to interacting populations). Their construction and subsequent simulation is made via mathematical analysis of the connections between nodes found in the system and their time-dependent behavior [10]. A biological network is generally composed of proteins, nucleic acids and cofactors connected by biological reactions such as protein complex formation or enzyme activity regulation [10]. Von Hippel-Lindau syndrome (VHL) [11] is a good study case to test the network theory applied to cancer due to the similar medical history and pathological phenotype that patients share. While hereditary cancers represent only a small part of all human tumors, their investigation represents a challenge to understand the pathway leading to tumor formation. In 2010, Heiner et al. first approached VHL using the so-called Petri Net (PN) simulation networks [12]. Their work, inspired by a previous theoretical model of cellular oxygen-related pathways [13] [14], was a preliminary investigation of the core oxygen sensing system and its connection with VHL onset. Heiner and coworkers proposed three different functional modules responsible for hypoxia network control and for HIF-1α degradation [12]. In other words, they theorized that hereditary forms of cancer, such as different manifestations of VHL, are the result of different and concomitantly compromised metabolic pathways.

Von Hippel-Lindau Disease

Von Hippel-Lindau protein (pVHL) is the product of the von Hippel-Lindau gene, located in the short arm of 3rd chromosome, and constantly transcribed in both fetal and adult tissues [15]. Mutations of pVHL are related to a pathological outcome termed VHL syndrome, an inherited form of cancer [16]. VHL syndrome is characterized by cysts and tumors growing in specific parts of the organism [16]–[17]. It is considered a severe autosomal dominant genetic condition with inheritance of one person in over 35,000 [18]. The tumor injuries, which can be either benign or malign, are usually located in the retina, adrenal glands, epididymis, central nervous system, kidneys and pancreas [19]. As a genetic disorder, VHL syndrome follows Knudson's two hit principle. A copy of the gene is mutated in the germ line, but the other gene copy still produces a functional protein. Complete protein inactivation appears during life due to somatic inactivation of the remaining functional copy [20]. On the contrary, mutations occurring during early fetal formation result in unsuccessful development [21]. The pVHL gene has 11,213 base pairs including three exons [18] and the final transcript is a protein commonly present in two isoforms: pVHL30 and pVHL19, of 213 and 160 residues respectively. Neither isoform contains a known enzymatic domain, but rather appears to serve as a multipurpose adapter protein engaging in multiple protein-protein interactions [22]. pVHL structure is organized in an α- and β-domain and its stability was demonstrated to be ensured by direct interaction with other proteins such as Elongins B and C [23]. Both Elongin B and C are also required for the best characterized function of pVHL, the ubiquitination dependent degradation of Hypoxia Inducible Factor (HIF) via the proteasome [24]. However, pVHL is considered a multipurpose protein due to its high number of known interactors. At the time of writing, the IntAct database [25] presents more than 200 different interaction partners, with some of them competing for the same Elongin binding site. Indeed, pVHL was found in different cellular compartments and seems to be involved in many different cellular processes such as apoptosis, cell proliferation, survival and motility [26]. Considering the huge number of interactors and multiple cellular localizations, many different functions have been described or hypothesized, such as regulation of cytoplasmic microtubules during mitosis [27] and endothelial extracellular matrix deposition [28]. On the other hand, considering the huge number of players involved in VHL syndrome and the lack of reliable kinetic data, a PN based approach may be a preferable option for an entire VHL pathway simulation.

Petri Net for Interaction Pathways

Since their invention, by Carl Adam Petri in the early sixties, PNs were mostly used to describe technical systems, but later the utility in describing biological and biochemical functions has also been demonstrated [29]. PNs were successfully used in many studies to describe biological networks [30], such as the regulation and etiopathology in human Duchenne Muscular Dystrophy [31] and the hypoxia response network [12]. PNs are qualitative mathematical models that can graphically represent many object types, not only metabolites but also different protein states and are useful to simulate networks where not only metabolites are involved. Indeed, PNs can be a powerful tool to study all concurrent interactions in a specific pathway, even if the proteins or kinetics are not well-known. Due to the large number of different pVHL functions involved in VHL disease progression, we decided to extend the PN based analysis of [12] increasing the number of considered protein-protein interactions. We generated a novel manually curated PN model of the entire VHL regulation system collecting data from the literature and including the signaling pathways and glucidic metabolism. In order to build a realistic network, literature from both biochemical experiments and *in silico*predictions were used as source. It was decided to build a PN with only confirmed pVHL interactions whose function was also known. The resulting PN was validated using an analysis of specific properties as suggested by previous studies using the same method [29]. After validating the PN structure, *in silico* knock outs of specific proteins were done in order to observe the different network behaviors and the resulting biological effect.

METHODS

The network was designed in the Snoopy PN framework (version 2, revision 1.13) [32], respecting the mathematical PN formalism as described in [12]–[33]. PN were demonstrated to be useful in describing discrete and concurrent processes in a simple graphical representation [30] and have been used to describe biomedical processes due to their capacity of representing sequential steps in a process. PN modeling methods are actively used to describe, simulate, analyze, and predict the behavior of biological systems. The Snoopy PN framework provides an extensible multi-platform framework to design, animate, and simulate Petri nets [32]. We chose Snoopy to facilitate future extensions of the VHL pathway presented here. Among different available PN types a standard PN was chosen to limit the number of variables. Both Charlie and PInA analyzers were used for PN analysis and validation (34). Further, *in silico* knock out experiments were used to test the biological reliability of the model. Structural model validation was made by analysis of the T-invariants to demonstrate whether the system was covered by T-invariants and to confirm the biological meaning of each invariant. The use of T- and P-invariants is given by their own properties: they are a set (of transitions or places, respectively) that allow the reproduction of the same state after *n* transformations. A P-invariant represents a set of places where the number of tokens is constant and independent on the firing rate. A T-invariant instead represents a set of transitions that cyclically comes back to show the same initial set. Biologically a P invariant can represent the process of regulating a protein, whereas T invariants can represent cyclical biochemical transformations such as metabolic reactions. To this end, the computed invariants were grouped in Maximal Common Transition Sets (MCTS) and Clusters, the former based on occurrence of specific sets of transition inside the various T-invariants, and the latter based on similarities between T-invariants. Different numbers of clusters will be defined depending on the resulting square matrix. Where MCTS create disjunctive nets, Clusters merge together similar T-invariants. Behavioral validation was made by selectively deleting tokens inside the model, imitating possible biological disruptions such as disease-causing mutations. The resulting network behavior was compared to what is reported in the literature. Total runtime for invariants computation were less than ten seconds on a mainstream Linux x86 workstation. The Snoopy framework for PN construction, Charlie and PInA tools for analysis are available at the website (URL: http://www-dssz.informatik.tu-cottbus.de/DSSZ/Software). Finally, the model was used to simulate the network behavior through visual inspection of both token movement and accumulation in specific parts of the network.

RESULTS

Notations and Assumptions

The PN built here focuses on pVHL interactions that were already proven by biochemical experiments and reported in the literature. We chose to model a realistic VHL disease pathways based on confirmed literature data, including all known VHL functions, VHL related signal pathway and glucidic metabolism. The final PN is composed of 323 places and 238 transitions, connected by 801 arcs. Places are mainly proteins and enzymes, while some represent DNA or small molecular substrates such as glucose and cofactors (e.g. ATP). In a few cases, places are used to represent a whole group of changes generated by DNA transcription, (e.g. p_32 and p_33 or Et_eff1 and Et_eff2). Transitions instead symbolize complex formation between two proteins or post-translational modifications. Output transitions stand for degradation or movement to other parts of the cell or organism to complete their functions (e.g. degrad_1 and degrad_2) whereas input transitions show the generation of a substrate or protein. In order to simplify the design of such a large network, we decided to use macro nodes to group reactions representing complex molecular pathways such as signaling pathways or secondary signal cascades. The whole process is merged into a single node with a given name to allow visual inspection only in case of need. From the top level all transitions can still be found in a hierarchical lower layout level. Logic nodes were used for places participating in many reactions throughout the network such as ATP and ADP (7 logical copies each) or NAD and NADH (4 logical copies each). A total nesting depth of two was chosen to model macro nodes. Special arcs were not used while we chose to model the permanent presence of some objects using double arcs (e.g. for elob, eloc and places standing for enzymatic activity). In case of proteins which are actively degraded, it was preferred to create an input transition simulating constant production (or synthesis) and an output for consumption. This is the case for pkcz2, Jade1, pVHL and HIF-1α. As can be seen from Figures 1 to 3, which represent the entire model, two major nodes can be immediately identified: pVHL and vcb, the complex made by pVHL and the two elongins. Another relevant part is the glucidic metabolism, modeled due to its hypoxia induced regulation. It is represented in detail in Figure 2.

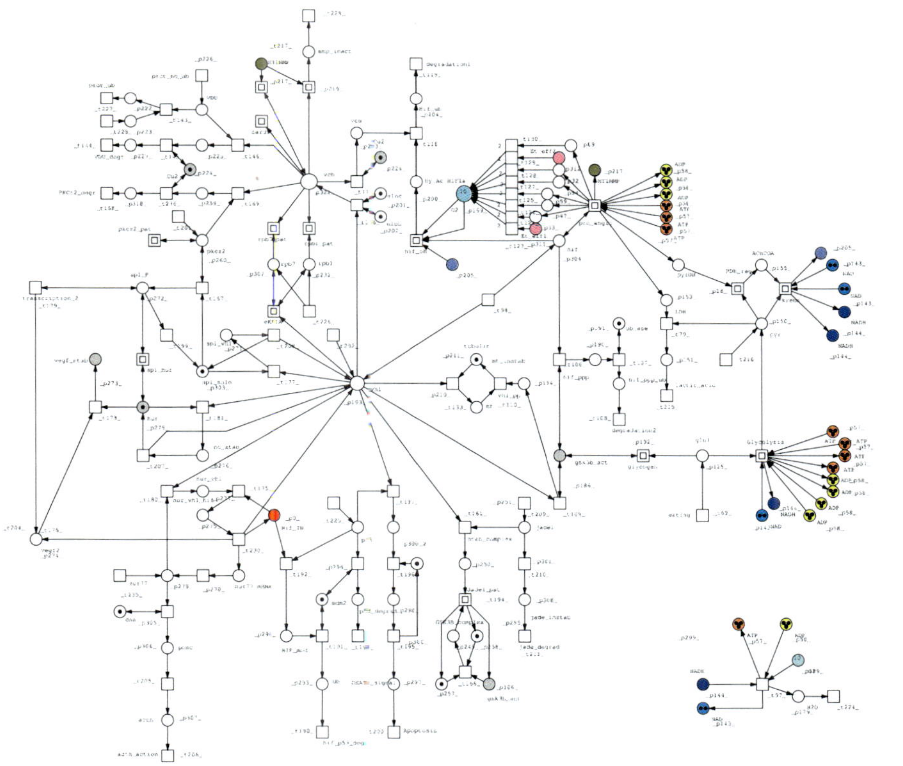

Figure 1: Top level model.

The colors of some tokens were arbitrarily chosen to give a clearer identification of the central nodes (ATP, Vcb and oxygen) or for nodes involved in more reactions such as GSK3β. The group of nodes in the bottom left is not disconnected from the central body of the network thanks to the presence of logic nodes for ATP synthesis (t_97).

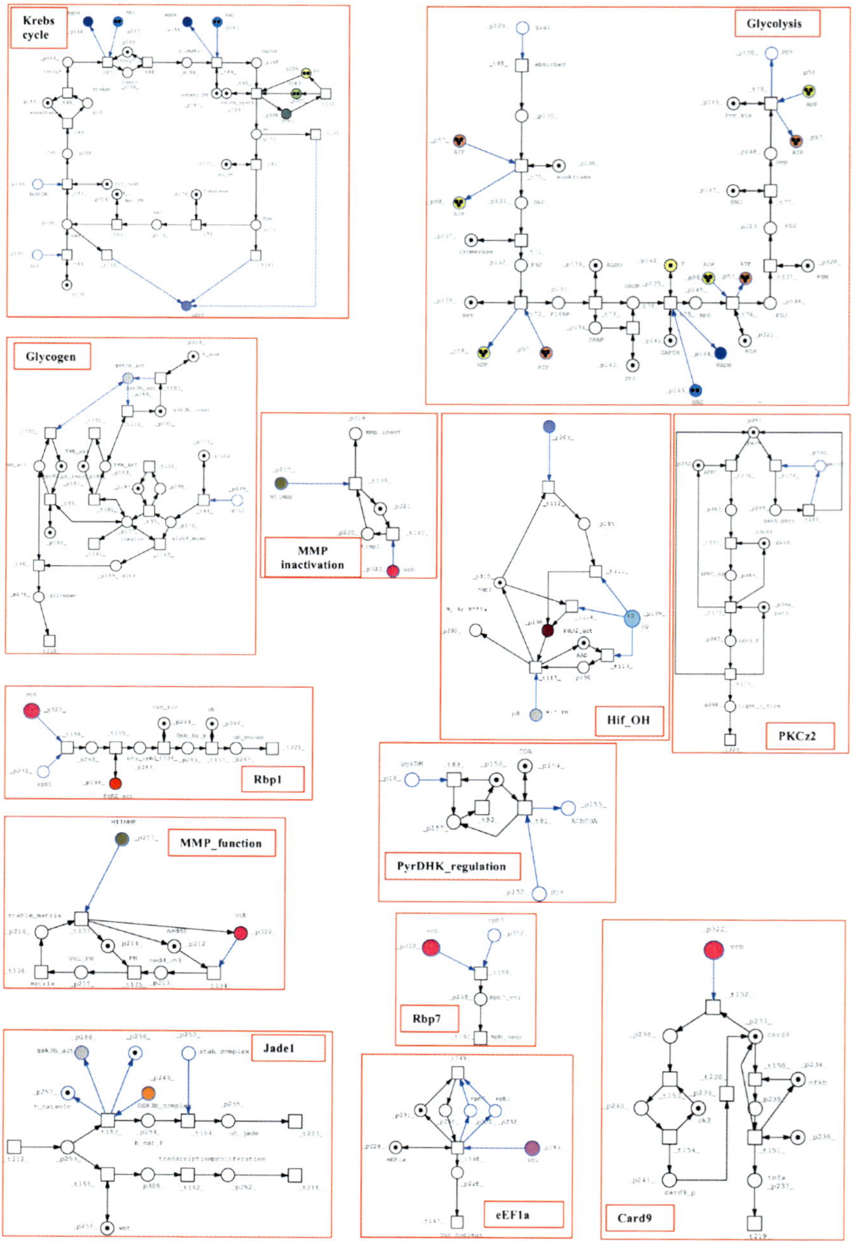

Figure 2: Lower hierarchical PN levels.

Pathways from the top level are grouped in macro-nodes (functional subordinated layer), in particular glucidic metabolism and various VHL functions.

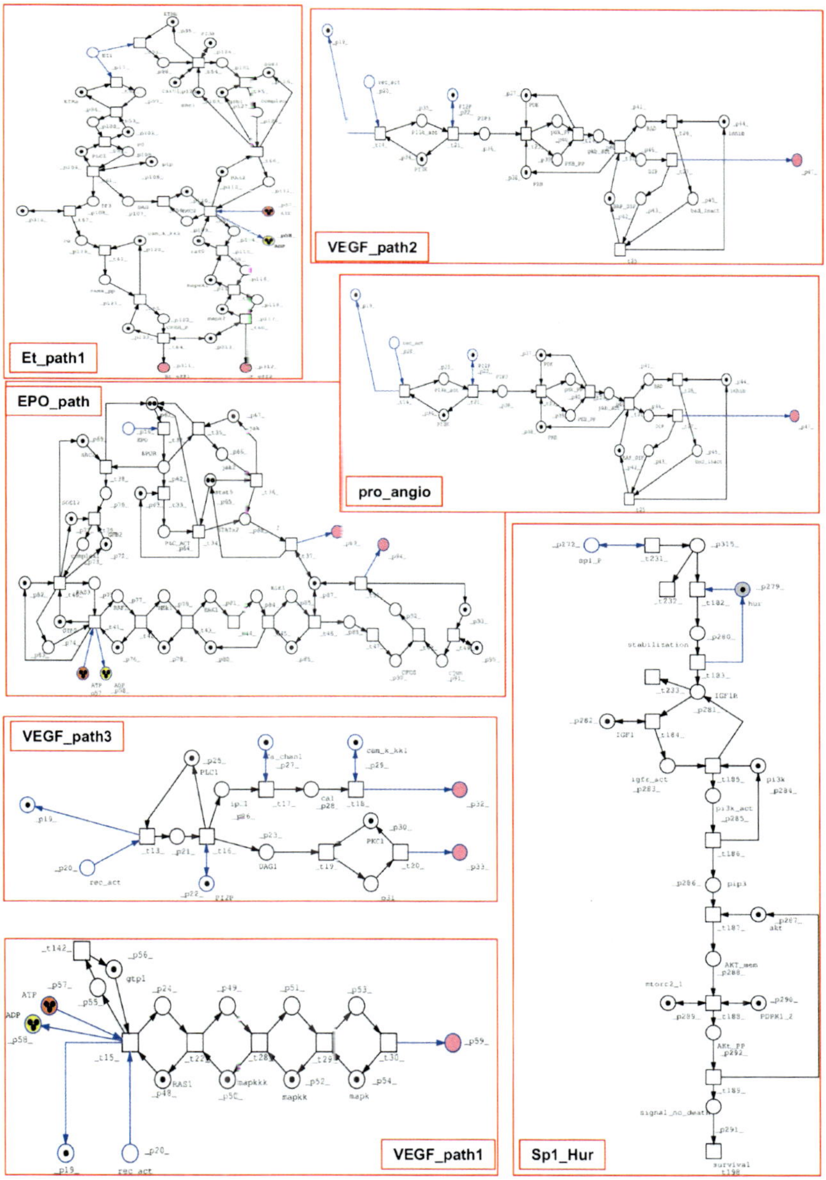

Figure 3: Lower hierarchical PN levels, in particular HIF-1α regulation and HIF-1α-dependent pro-angiogenic signaling.

VEGF and EPO pathways are at a lower hierarchical level than the pro_angio macro-node.

HIF-1α Transcription Activity

The HIF-1α transcription factor stimulates proliferation of endothelial cells to create new blood vessels during localized or broad hypoxia. In human, it is present as three different paralogs: HIF-1α, HIF-2α and HIF-3α. The sequence is quite conserved between the former two, whereas the latter is slightly shorter and seems to have completely different functions compared to the other two [33]–[34]. Both HIF-1α and -2α stimulate DNA transcription but the exact products of this activity are still poorly understood. In our model, only HIF-1α *in vivo* activity was considered. It cannot be excluded that other biological effects depend on the second paralog. Indeed, both have a pro-angiogenetic function and are degraded by pVHL via proline-directed hydroxylation. HIF is a heterodimer of HIF-1α and HIF-1β, the latter being also termed Aryl hydrocarbon Receptor Nuclear Translocator (ARNT). We started from the transcription activity of HIF due to its regulation is the most studied pVHL function. Our model, as expected from literature data, shows that HIF-1α enters the nucleus when not degraded by pVHL. It subsequently binds HIF-1β to form the HIF heterocomplex which interacts with DNA. Our model correctly simulates the increased affinity of HIF towards DNA. Transcription is enhanced by some co-factors binding both subunits of HIF and other proteins such as p300, Creb and cjun. This takes place in a specific DNA promoter sequence termed Hypoxia Response Element (HRE). Furthermore, during transcription some pro-angiogenic factors are produced: Vascular Endothelial Growth Factor (VEGF), Endothelin (ET) and Erythropoietin (EPO). All described pathways are in agreement with previous observations reported in [35].

Metabolic Processes

HIF-1α transcription activity includes some proteins which are dependent on oxygen but involved in other pathways (e.g. oxidative metabolism) or completely independent (e.g. metallo-proteinase MT1MMP). Further, HIF-1α stimulates production of proteins involved in the glucidic pathway. The final product of the metabolism is adenosine triphosphate (ATP), a molecular form of energy, composed by adenosine, an adenine ring connected to a ribose sugar, and three phosphate moieties. When a phosphate moiety is hydrolyzed it releases energy, used by cells for enzymatic reactions. The glucidic metabolism is composed of glycolysis, Krebs cycle, glycogen formation and respiratory chain with ATP synthesis. Glucose is absorbed in cells by enzymatic glucose transporters (GLUT), which carry the molecule to the location inside the cell where the metabolism takes place [36]. There are many isoforms of these transporters: GLUT1 is present in all cells and in particular in erythrocytic membranes, neurons and glia [37]. GLUT2, located in both liver and pancreatic beta cells, is characterized by low affinity for glucose, hence it requires a higher glucose concentration to be activated [38]. Right after eating, glucose concentration increases, thereby quickly activating them. GLUT2 stimulates production of insulin, a hormone regulating the plasmatic glucose concentration. Glucose plasmatic concentration can also increase due to an opposite pathway, originating from liver glycogen being decomposed into glucose and reaching systemic circulation. GLUT3 is mostly present in neurons, whereas GLUT4 is the insulin activated transporter located in myocytes, adipocytes and cardiomyocytes [36]–[39]. In our model, we chose to exclude GLUT3 due to its specific role in neuronal cells. Glycolysis occurs in the cytoplasm and during this process each glucose molecule is phosphorylated, consuming two molecules of ATP, then divided into two smaller molecules. Further modifications of these two molecules result in new ATP production. The molecule obtained at the end of glycolysis is pyruvate, which can be again modified through three different pathways. It can be decarboxylated and linked to Co-enzyme A to form acetyl-Co-enzyme A. It can then be carboxylated to obtain oxalacetate, or transformed through lactate dehydrogenase into lactic acid. Pyruvate can also be generated by other metabolic pathways, like protein or fatty acid disruption and amino-acid modifications. Acetyl-CoA and oxalacetate are the molecules used in the following glucidic metabolism process, the Krebs cycle, taking place in the mitochondrial matrix. The Krebs cycle starts with acetyl-CoA and oxalacetate merging to create citric acid, which continues undergoing modifications until oxalacetate is formed again. During the process some co-enzymes are modified. Decarboxylation of pyruvate to form acetyl-CoA already transforms a NAD+ (Nicotinamide Adenine Dinucleotide) in NADH (reduced form), afterwards obtaining one more of ATP, GTP, $FADH_2$ (Flavin Adenine Dinucleotide) and three more NADH per pyruvate molecule entering the Krebs cycle. The redox co-enzymes are considered electron transporters. During metabolic reactions they reduce themselves and get electrons (and protons) to oxidize the substrate of the enzymatic reaction. Electrons taken during the glucose metabolism are then used in the respiratory chain taking place in the internal mitochondrial membrane. The respiratory chain consists in transporting electrons through enzymes called cytochromes and others co-enzymes, characterized by the capability to receive and donate electrons. NADH ($FADH_2$) is oxidized again by cytochromes going back to the form of NAD (or FAD). Electrons gained through oxidation are used to reduce half a molecule of oxygen into water, releasing more energy. The $FADH_2$ and NADH redox chain establishes a chemical potential causing the push of protons outside the internal membrane towards the inter-membrane space, which stays between the mitochondrial inner and outer membrane. This also causes a higher concentration of protons outside the inner membrane. The resulting gradient causes the tendency of protons to enter the cell. The final step is ATP-synthetase, formed by a channel that allows protons to enter, pushed by the gradient, allowing the enzyme to change conformation and make its reaction. This kinetic energy is converted into ATP. In our model, the glycolytic and Krebs cycles were described in detail, represented at the hierarchical second level by the coarse transition Glycolysis. The respiratory chain was instead merged into a single node (t_97). We chose to represent creation and consumption of ATP in order to show the effects of lower and higher oxygen concentration on the network. On the other hand, oxygen consumption for ATP synthesis during the respiratory chain creates a flow of oxygen in the model. Oxygen is not the only connection between glucidic metabolism and hypoxia. Indeed, HIF-1α transcription activity enhances the transcription of many GLUT isoforms (such as 1, 3 and 9) and the pyruvate dehydrogenase kinase, which determines the pyruvate dehydrogenase (PyrDH) inactivation and consequent Acetyl-CoA formation from pyruvate. Finally, Lactate dehydrogenase is also produced, to ensure an alternative compound, creating energy needed for cell survival [36]–[40].

pVHL-dependent Processes

Some interactors can bind pVHL in regions interacting with Elongin C. These are HuR, Nur77, p53 and Jade1. Nur77 has a complex function and its role in pVHL tumor suppressor activity is still not entirely clear.

Nur77 can bind pVHL, inhibiting Elongin binding while allowing HIF-1α binding. Its transcription is stimulated by HIF-1α itself, and pVHL-HIF-1α-Nur77 complex formation stabilizes the transcription activity of HIF-1α by inhibiting the pVHL-dependent degradation [41]. Another Nur77 function is the stimulation of proopiomelanocortin (POMC) transcription, which is a precursor for adrenocorticotropic hormone (ACTH) formation. This hormone has an important stress response function, stimulating cortisol production and other neurotransmitters from the adrenal glands, to enhance the organism reaction to danger and stress *stimuli* e.g. increase of gluconeogenesis and muscle mass. An excess of this hormone can cause desensitization of its receptors for feedback down-regulation and thus muscular weakness, tiredness, hyperglycemia and osteoporosis [42]. p53 can bind to pVHL avoiding the degradation of this tumor suppressor. Instead, it stimulates the apoptotic signal cascade via the p300 co-activator, which stimulates production of proteins enhancing the cell programmed death. If p53 cannot bind pVHL, two more mechanisms are described in the model. One is its modification and degradation by Mdm2 and the other is the pVHL-independent degradation of HIF-1α. Interaction with Mdm2 is needed in both cases [43]–[44]. Jade1 is a short-lived protein whose main function is to stimulate the phosphorylation-dependent degradation of β-catenin. This is a subunit of the cadherin protein complex acting as an intracellular signal transducer in the Wnt signaling pathway. It seems that β-catenin is able to stop cell division via a contact-dependent inhibition signal, whereas in Wnt signaling it is also involved in proliferative transcription. When Wnt is not present, β-catenin can be phosphorylated by Glycogen Synthetase Kinase, type 3β (GSK3β) in complex with APC (Adenomatous Polyposis Coli) and Axin. β-catenin can interact with Jade1 and be only successfully degraded after this interaction [45]. Related functions are represented in the macro node Jade1_pat. GSK3β seems to be a protein involved in many different pathways. GSK3β is involved in Glycogen Synthetase deactivation and can even phosphorylate pVHL and HIF-1α. In the case of HIF-1α, it generates a pVHL-independent degradation pathway, where phosphorylation allows ubiquitination, whereas in the case of pVHL, it inhibits pVHL stabilization of microtubules [46].

Structural Model Analysis

Based also on previous observations of Heiner et al., [47], in 2008 Grunwald et al., demonstrated that PN can be used to describe large and complex metabolic pathways [31]. They postulated the following set of minimal rules that a PN should satisfy to be considered biologically reliable: (1) the network should be entirely connected, (2) the network should be covered by T-invariants, and (3) each T-invariant and P-invariant should have a biological meaning. The model described here was tested with respect to what previously done by Grunwald and co-workers [31] and resulted to be covered by T-invariants, connected, homogeneous and each place has a pre-transition and a post-transition. Transitions without pre- or post-places were used to simulate the system interface to the surroundings. The network is alive, in other words, it continues to work forever, with all transitions contributing to the net behavior forever, and no dead transitions. The MCTS and Cluster analysis were used due to the large number of T- and P-invariants included in the model. Both methods are used in PN theory to reduce the complexity connected with such a large network and to reduce the errors connected with manual investigation. From the 238 transitions present at the beginning in the model, 393 T-invariants were computed without considering 10 trivial invariants. The latter consist in a pair of transitions that usually represent a forward and backward reaction, such as the active and inactive state of a protein. Trivial invariants could be erased to reduce the dimension of the network without disturbing the overall system when the interest is focused on the steady state behavior [12]. T-invariants were grouped into 44 Clusters using the Tanimoto coefficient with similarity threshold of 65%, as described in [31]. Only 11 of these 44 comprised more than one T-invariant. The three biggest Clusters are C9, composed of 144 T-invariants, C8 of 72 and C11 of 64 T-invariants. Separation into clusters allows easier analysis of networks pathways represented by each T-invariant, since they are grouped by similarity, specifically the common transitions by which they are composed.

Cluster C8

Cluster C8 groups all transitions included in HIF-1α pathways, including transcription, signaling cascades, degradation via pVHL, p53 and GSK3β, and eventually the Krebs cycle. For the EPO signaling pathway, two transitions (t_35 and t_36) are not included which cause Jak activation and consequent Stat5 activation to stimulate DNA transcription. Matrix stability regulation is also part of the cluster due to the destabilization induced by HIF-1α transcription of metallo-proteinase (MMP), transitions from t_134 to t_140. The largest T-invariant in C8 is Inv_280 (93 transitions) while the smallest is Inv_377 (81 transitions). The differences between T-invariants show the possibility of alternative pathways inside the model. For example, the VEGF dependent signal cascade can proceed in three different ways: t_13, t_14 and t_15, which lead to the pathways being merged in the coarse nodes Vegf_path3, Vegf_path2 and Vegf_path1, respectively. The occurrence rate in C8 is 24 transitions for each path. The Endothelin, VEGF and Erythropoietin pathways are not in conflict and occurring together. Disaggregation of the matrix via MMPs is present in 18 T-invariants, whereas inhibition of these proteins, i.e. matrix stabilization, is present in the remaining 54 transitions. Regarding the Krebs cycle, 47 T-invariants have t_91, of which only 24 reach t_92 and t_93, representing the last three steps of the cycle: succinate to fumarate, fumarate to malate, and malate to oxalacetate. All the malate being produced is used to regenerate oxalacetate. Degradation of HIF-1α occurs in any T-invariant of the cluster. The pVHL-dependent degradation of HIF-1α is always present (transitions t_116 to t_119). In 19 T-invariants degradation takes place via p53 (t_191 to t_193) or, alternatively, via phosphorylation by GSK3β in another 17 T- invariants. Two of the three pathways can be present in the same T-invariant, as in Inv_227, where degradation via pVHL and degradation via p53 are both present. This was considered as the HIF-1α dependence on the lack of degradation by these proteins. All three degradation pathways never appear in the same T-invariant. The p53 and GSK3β paths are never present together but each of them is accompanied by pVHL-dependent proteasomal degradation. Inv_377 lacks the EPO signaling pathway but is the only one in this cluster to have t_34, t_33 and t_37. These invariants have all input and output transitions. For example, t_202 the second input for pVHL, is present in only 18 invariants. Other inputs are t_98, always present, leading to formation of HIF-1α and pVHL, t_192, producing p53 and t_216, representing other pyruvate generating metabolic pathways. The latter is also present in each invariant allowing formation of the pyruvate needed for Krebs cycle progression.

Cluster C9

Cluster C9 is the largest cluster in our model and includes 144 T-invariants. It is characterized by complete EPO pathway abrogation which goes through formation of the Shc-Grb-Sos complex and the consequent mapk-dependent phosphorylation cascade. Transition t_127, representing EPO effects on oxygen production, is absent. In its place, t_35 and t_36 are considered, which are present in 72 T-invariants. In cluster C9, the largest T-invariants are Inv_278 and Inv_279 (74 transitions) while the shortest ones are Inv_101, Inv_105, Inv_144 and Inv_148 with 65 transitions each.

Cluster C10

Cluster C10, composed of 52 T-invariants, is characterized by the presence of glycolysis between many transitions grouped in the cluster. This is also the cluster containing the most populated T-invariant of all computed 393 non-trivial T-invariants. This is Inv_245, including 101 transitions and covering almost half of the whole model. Cluster C10 also includes Inv_125, the shortest invariant of this model, composed by 85 transitions due to lack of the Krebs cycle. Another difference with the other three major clusters is that here both EPO paths are present, specifically, the Jak pathway belongs to 4 T-invariants and Shc-Grb-Sos is observed throughout the cluster. Vegf_path1 seems to be more common in this cluster, being present in 36 T-invariants, whereas the other two are present 12 times each. This time they are present even in the same invariant, as for Inv_60, Inv_129, Inv_172 and Inv_215, with both t_13 and t_15, and Inv_142, Inv_185 and Inv_228 with t_14 and t_15 and all subsequent signaling appearing at the same time. Despite glycolysis being present in all cluster invariants, the Krebs cycle appears only in 11 cases. p53-dependent degradation of HIF-1α occurs in 11 cases while the phosphorylation-dependent one appears in 13. An input transition has been added with respect to the other major clusters so far analyzed (i.e. t_69_eating) without which glycolysis could never take place.

Cluster C11

Cluster C11 is composed of 64 T-invariants. Only part of the EPO pathway is described here, with the major difference that the Krebs cycle is completely abrogated while Prolyl Hydroxylase type 2 (PHD2) regulation by oxalacetate is included. HIF-1α interaction with Nur77 and transcription of VEGF by Sp1 are also present. t_80 (transformation of pyruvate in oxalacetate) is not present in the first 42 cluster T-invariants. Nur77 interaction with HIF-1α is present only in 8 T-invariants, specifically Inv_87 to Inv_94. Sp1 transcription activity is appearing in twice the amount, including the same 8 invariants just mentioned. VEGF transcription via Sp1 activity is aPKCζ2 phosphorylation dependent, which does however not appear in the cluster. When VEGF is synthesized, it is subsequently stabilized by Hur, followed by t_178 and Hur is recreated to allow other functions. Indeed, it is one of the few places without input transition but with a token that goes forward and backward again. Compared to the other clusters, C11 also shows one less transition in the coarse PHD regulation node, specifically t_81, which shows the transformation of pyruvate by pyrDH into acetyl-Coenzyme A, needed for the Krebs cycle. The four clusters C-8 to C12 are very similar to each other, as can be seen from the distance tree in Figure 4. They all contain the HIF-1α transcription activity and signaling pathways caused by EPO, VEGF and the HIF-1α degradation options. They include the effects of other transcription activity products, like metallo-proteinase and pyruvate dehydrogenase kinase, which regulate the activation state of PyrDH. All include part of the glucidic metabolism but not Glycogen formation itself. Other five clusters from C12 to C16 have a smaller number of T-invariants and fewer transitions present in each invariant. They do not include transcription activity but are only formed by the VEGF and glycolytic pathways. The information contents of these clusters turned out to be uninformative and their analysis was not included. The same applies to clusters composed by 1–3 T-invariants. Finally, some transitions are not present in the clusters and not listed in the T-invariants because trivial invariants were excluded from cluster analysis. These transitions are shown in Table 1 with their respective biological meaning.

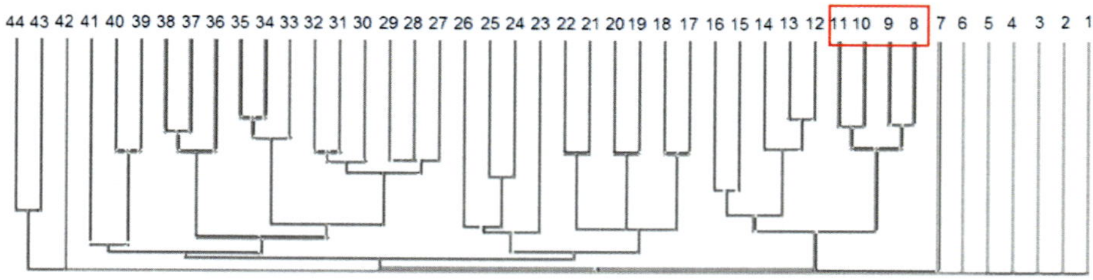

Figure 4: PinA Distance Matrix clustering, using Tanimoto coefficient and 65% threshold of.

The numbers indicates clusters. In C8, C9, C10, C11 are highlighted a red square.

Table 1: List of Trivial T-invariants excluded from calculation with their associated biological meaning

Trivial T-Invariants	ID transitions	Biological Meaning
TInv_1	t_99, t_100	Glycongen Synthase regulation
TInv_2	t_101, t_102	Pkb regulation
TInv_3	t_103, t_132	GSK3β active-inactive state
TInv_4	t_174, t_222	Par6 inactivation via aPKCζ2
TInv_5	t_177, t_208	VHL binding to Sp1
TInv_6	t_167, t_199	Sp1 phosphorylation and dephosphorylation
TInv_7	t_0, t_2	Hif transport in and out of nucleus
TInv_8	t_0, t_234	Hif inhibition via FIH
TInv_9	t_181, t_207	Hur inhibition via VHL
TInv_10	t_231, t_232	IGFR mRNA production and destruction

doi:10.1371/journal.pone.0096986.t001

MCTS Analysis

Another way to group invariants is by the amount of single transitions present in them. Maximal common transition set (MCTS) analysis provides a PN decomposition into non-overlapping subnets, sharing parts of the same T-invariants [29]. In a biochemical network, MCTS could be interpreted as enzyme subsets operating together under steady state conditions, computed based on the support of a T-invariant. MCTS computation does not consider stoichiometric relations, describing exclusively sets of reactions present in a maximal number of T-invariants resulting shared by different signaling pathways [48]. A total of 40 non-trivial MCTS were identified, with results and related biological means shown in Table 2. Some transitions do not belong to a non-trivial MCTS, because their occurrence has no similarity with other transitions and they create separate MCTS (specifically: t_69, t_82, t_91, t_94, t_98, t_114, t_116, t_120, t_121, t_122, t_179, t_202, t_209, t_212, t_216, t_225 and t_229). MCTS define transitions that always take place together, but are not necessarily connected, thus representing disjunct building blocks constituting the network. Considering both analyses, a table was automatically built in PInA [29] showing a correlation between clusters and MCTS. Transitions (t) or MCTS (M) are compared to evaluate how many T-invariants clusters cover the selected M or t (if the transition is not already part of the MCTS, as listed above). The more covered a transition or set is, the more central it could be considered for the network behavior. Recently, a network coarsening method based on abstract dependent transition sets (ADT) was presented [49]. It is formulated without the requirement of pre-computation of the T-invariants and is a tool commonly used for the decomposition of large biochemical networks into smaller subnets. Due to the manually designed nature of our model, we preferred to maintain a logic hierarchy based on metabolic pathways in order to maintain the network centered on pVHL and its interaction. The MCTS calculation results shows that the most covered set by cluster T-invariants is M20 with 358 T-invariants covering all transitions in the set, indicating that this MCTS corresponds to more T-invariants than the others. All transition sets are an important link to the others, as tokens pass through these transitions more often. A transition not present in any set but most covered by T-invariants is t_98, which is also the most frequently occurring transition, see Figure 5. The 10 most occurring transitions are listed in the Table 3.

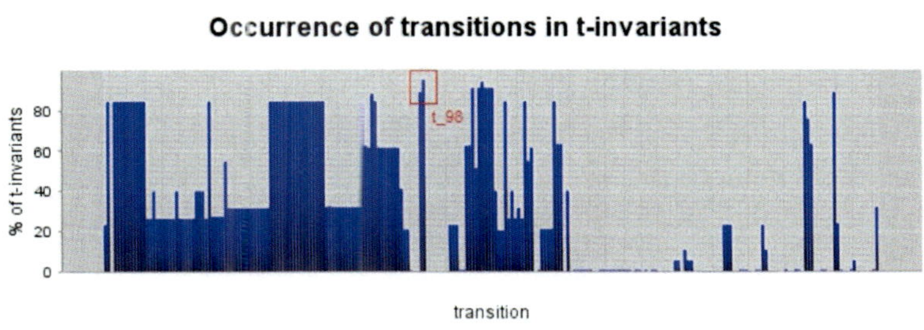

Figure 5: Transitions occurrence T-invariants.

Transitions are ordered by name and t_98 is highlighted in red.

Table 2: List of MCTS and transitions from PInA

MCTS	ID Transitions
MCTS 1 (M1)	t_0, t_190, t_191, t_192;
MCTS 2 (M2)	t_1, t_3, t_4, t_5, t_6, t_7, t_8, t_9, t_10, t_11, t_12, t_32, t_51, t_52, t_53, t_54, t_55, t_56, t_57, t_58, t_59, t_60, t_61, t_62, t_63, t_64, t_65, t_66, t_67, t_79, t_83, t_123, t_129, t_138, t_215;
MCTS 3 (M3)	t_2, t_99, t_100, t_101, t_102, t_103, t_132, t_167, t_174, t_181, t_199,_177, t_207, t_208, t_222, t_232, t_234;
MCTS 4 (M4)	t_13, t_16, t_17, t_18, t_19, t_20, t_124, t_128;
MCTS 5 (M5)	t_14, t_21, t_23, t_24, t_25, t_26, t_27, t_31, t_126;
MCTS 6 (M6)	t_15, t_22, t_28, t_29, t_30, t_125, t_142;
MCTS 7 (M7)	t_33, t_34;
MCTS 8 (M8)	t_35, t_36;
MCTS 9 (M9)	t_37, t_130;
MCTS 10 (M10)	t_38, t_39, t_40, t_41, t_42, t_43, t_44, t_45, t_46, t_47, t_48, t_49, t_50, t_127;
MCTS 11 (M11)	t_68, t_70, t_71, t_72, t_73, t_74, t_75, t_76, t_77, t_78, t_237;
MCTS 12 (M12)	t_80, t_111, t_112;
MCTS 13 (M13)	t_81, t_84, t_85, t_86, t_87, t_88, t_89, t_90, t_131;
MCTS 14 (M14)	t_92, t_93;
MCTS 15 (M15)	t_95, t_104, t_141;
MCTS 16 (M16)	t_96, t_105, t_218;
MCTS 17 (M17)	t_97, t_224;
MCTS 18 (M18)	t_106, t_107, t_108;
MCTS 19 (M19)	t_109, t_110, t_133;
MCTS 20 (M20)	t_113, t_115, t_117, t_118, t_119;
MCTS 21 (M21)	t_134, t_135, t_136, t_137;
MCTS 22 (M22)	t_139, t_140, t_217;
MCTS 23 (M23)	t_143, t_227, t_228;
MCTS 24 (M24)	t_144, t_145, t_146;
MCTS 25 (M25)	t_147, t_148, t_149;
MCTS 26 (M26)	t_150, t_151, t_219;
MCTS 27 (M27)	t_152, t_153, t_154, t_220;
MCTS 28 (M28)	t_155, t_156, t_157, t_158, t_159, t_160, t_221, t_226;
MCTS 29 (M29)	t_161, t_163, t_164, t_166, t_213;
MCTS 30 (M30)	t_162, t_165, t_214;
MCTS 31 (M31)	t_168, t_169, t_201, t_236;
MCTS 32 (M32)	t_170, t_171, t_172, t_173, t_223;
MCTS 33 (M33)	t_175, t_176, t_180, t_230;
MCTS 34 (M34)	t_178, t_203;
MCTS 35 (M35)	t_182, t_183, t_231, t_233;
MCTS 36 (M36)	t_184, t_185, t_186, t_187, t_188, t_189, t_198;
MCTS 37 (M37)	t_193, t_194;
MCTS 38 (M38)	t_195, t_196, t_197, t_200;
MCTS 39 (M39)	t_204, t_205, t_206, t_235;
MCTS 40 (M40)	t_210, t_211;

doi:10.1371/journal.pone.0096986.t002

Table 3: Ranking of the 10 most occurring transitions with biological meaning and percentage of occurrence

Rank	Transitions	Biological meaning	Occurrence %
1	t_98	Input transition for Hif and VHL	95.165
2	t_116	Interaction of VHL with Elongin B and C	94.148
3	t_113	Activation by oxygen of ARD	94.094
4	t_115	Acetylation and hydroxilation of Hif	94.094
5	t_117	Interaction of complex Vcb with Cu2	94.094
6	t_118	Interaction of complex Vcb with modified Hif	94.094
7	t_119	Degradation VHL dependent of Hif	94.094
8	t_97	ATP formation	89.059
9	t_224	Water Output transition	89.059
10	t_82	Pyruvate Dehydrogenase inactivation	88.041

doi:10.1371/journal.pone.0096986.t003

P-invariant Analysis

Although the network is not covered by P-invariants, it has 130 P-invariants. 47 of these are trivial P-invariants, comprising a single place, connected with double arcs to imitate an activator arc function. Another object represented with double arcs is the enzymatic activity catalyzing a reaction and immediately going back to the steady state. P-invariants show places or sets of places where token numbers always remain equal and do not move outside the subnetwork induced by the P-invariant in the initial marking. In other words, they do not grow nor diminish. The remaining P-invariants are mostly located in signal transduction pathways, such as situations in which a protein is sequestered from its function and then goes back after a second reactivation mechanism. This scenario is present in p_41, p_42 and p_45 located in invariant P_58. It is important to notice that ATP and ADP, as well as NAD and NADH, are modeled as P-invariants. P_90, P_91 and t_97 are able to transform ATP and ADP. More in general, all energy consuming transitions are considered to be backward transitions of invariants. Invariants not related to signal transduction are places located in the Hur system, where Hur is removed from its function by pVHL. This is a good approximation for sequential modifications that momentarily activate proteins. Afterwards, Hur can go back and stabilize VEGF to increase its transcription activity.

In Silico Knock Out Experiments

The previously described clustering and MCTS analysis for T-invariants allowed us to identify the most common transitions and to understand which transitions can be depleted in our knock out experiments in order to get the most important biological effect. The knock out experiments were performed erasing selected transitions or tokens and observing which transitions or MCTS become inactivated. Considering our results and the literature, we decided to knock out the following pathway elements: (i) pVHL, (ii) HIF1α alone and with Sp1, (iii) t_98, (iv) PHD2, (v) MCTS1, (vi) t_97 and (vii) GSK3β. In the following, we describe the effect of each knock out scenario on our model.

(i) pVHL knock out. Degradation of HIF-1α is not completely depleted due to presence of both p53- and GSK3β-dependent alternative degradation pathways. All other processes usually inhibited by pVHL take place in an uncontrolled way, including creation of VEGF via Sp1 transcription activity and increased matrix regulation due to lack of fibronectin crosslinking. Hur resulted constantly activated and nur77 can stimulate synthesis of Proopiomelanocortin, precursor for the Adrenocorticotropic hormone. Card9 increases release of tumor necrosis factor, and NF-kB when not inhibited by pVHL. Instead, Jade1 is unable to survive long enough to inhibit β–catenin, generating a proliferation signal with Wnt. Lactic acid is also not produced due to LDH enzyme production being HIF-1α transcription activity dependent.

(ii) HIF-1α knock out. VEGF is still created thanks to Sp1, thus oxygen is still generated even if in lower proportion. If HIF-1α and Sp1 are both knocked out at the same time, oxygen is quickly consumed and the metabolism is soon unable to proceed. Lactic acid is not produced due to LDH enzyme production being HIF-1α transcription activity dependent. Glycolysis and glycogen are produced normally and the metabolism is not inhibited by PyrDH negative regulation and lactic acid formation. Since pVHL is present, other tumor suppressor activities are enabled, except for proteasomal degradation of HIF-1α due to the substrate being non-existent.

(iii) HIF-1α and pVHL double knock out. This generates a situation where the metabolism is normal but oxygen regeneration is less productive, with only Sp1 acting for transcription. Due to absence of pVHL, all proliferation-stimulating processes are active, causing an unbalanced consumption of resources. Our model shows that this condition is compatible with cell growth and multiplication, but new blood vessel generation is consistently slower and glucidic metabolism appears principally based on the glycolysis reaction. Similar activity reduction applies to both tight junction and cellular external matrix (ECM) pathway regulation. It cannot be excluded that some observed effects could be mitigated by both HIF-2α and HIF-3α activity *in vivo.*

(iv) PHD2 knock out. The protein is involved in pVHL mediated and oxygen dependent degradation of HIF-1α. Further, PHD2 is involved in hydroxylation of the RNA polymerase II subunit Rpb1 to allow its translocation to less chromatin-concentrated areas of the nucleus. When it is knocked out, HIF-1α degradation can continue via alternative pathways as seen in the pVHL knock out experiment and there is more RNA polymerase II activity, even if rpb7 can still be inactivated by pVHL.

(v) MCTS1 knock out. MCTS1 groups some reactions involved in the HIF-1α p53-dependent degradation pathway (Table 2). To perform this knock out, we erased the necessary token in mdm2, making the precondition insufficient to enable the MCTS transitions. p53 is not degraded and can continue its proapoptotic signal. On the other hand, a HIF-1α degradation mechanism is also knocked out resulting in an increased HIF-1α transcription activity.

(vi) t_97 knock out. This is the ATPase transition, allowing the model to imitate oxygen consumption for ATP synthesis. If this transition is inactive, oxygen accumulates infinitely and ATP is not regenerated after few simulation steps. At the beginning, ATP is formed during the first step of glycolysis but afterwards it is consumed again. At some point, these reactions do not have any ATP available to allow the system to re-balance the consumed ATP. After few simulation steps, oxygen reaches a high level due to slower consumption in the PHD2 regulation process. Biologically, this means that the metabolism stops and the cell is not able to create energy to survive. There is no accumulation other than glucose in the model. A few oxygen creation processes are blocked as well due to absence of ATP, e.g. t_15, t_41 and t_57.

(vii) GSK3β knock out. This enzyme is involved in negative glycogen synthetase (GS) regulation and is inactivated when phosphorylated. When GSK3β is knocked out, glycogen is continuously produced due to the enzyme remaining in an active state. In a real organism there are alternative forms of

GSK3β which can inactivate GS, hence the effect will be less sharp. GSK3β is also involved in the degradation of HIF-1α, causing its phosphorylation and following ubiquitination. It is also involved in the degradation of β-catenin, where it is responsible for primary phosphorylation. If knocked out, even if Jade1 can be stabilized by pVHL, the effect will be similar to a knock out of Jade1, where β-catenin is free to continue proliferation stimulating transcription activity.

DISCUSSION

We started from a core model of hypoxia response [12] and extended the original network with functional data derived from the literature in order to represent a complete description of the pVHL interaction pathway according to current knowledge. VHL syndrome is characterized by the formation of tumors and cysts affecting different organism districts and tissues. Indeed, pVHL is a tumor suppressor whose functions are connected to inhibition of proliferation and survival, growth and stability of extracellular matrix and microtubules, as well as cell polarity and migration. The IntAct database reports more than 200 suspected pVHL interactors and for most of them interaction and function details remain largely unknown. We chose to model the pVHL interactions in a credible cellular context with many protein activities occurring at the same time. The main idea was to create a novel manually curated PN description of the entire VHL disease pathway, including glucidic metabolism and signaling pathways. The model was designed as a standard PN and is composed of 238 transitions and 323 places, connected by 801 edges. A biologically realistic PN model needs to be covered by T-invariants, meaning each transition in the model has to be included in a T-invariant, and each invariant needs to have a biological meaning [31]–[47]. We used the T-invariant analysis to validate the reliability of the model. We computed a total of 393 T-invariants, plus 10 trivial invariants, which were excluded from analysis. These were grouped into 44 Clusters and, through use of T-invariants, transitions were grouped into 40 MCTS. The model obtained is connected, covered by T-invariants with each invariant holding a biological meaning. MCTS analysis was used to identify the most frequent crucial transitions occurring in the model. This specific subset was further used to plan *in silico* knock out experiments and for the model validation and analysis of expected biological behavior. The model was then used to perform *in silico* knock out experiments inactivating specific transitions during qualitative network analysis. Our results showed that the model is able to represent important transitions reflecting real biological outcomes, i.e. transitions involving species such as oxygen or ATP are correctly inactivated under certain circumstances as expected from the bibliographic data. Biological energy-related reactions (e.g. ATP production from ADP) were modeled as P-invariants. Although the network is intentionally not covered by P-invariants, P-invariant analysis was used to verify all modeled energy consuming transitions. Both the ATP and NADH balances appeared constant during the simulation, with irrelevant P-invariants located in the Hur system. This approximation was used to verify the Hur-dependent regulation of VEGF, with results in accordance with [50]. The specific pVHL knock out suggests that this protein alone is not sufficient for complete HIF-1α inactivation. Indeed, other concurrent HIF-1α degradation pathways promote a sort of cell cycle regulation backup. On the contrary, simple deletion of pVHL turned out to be sufficient to increase all its other inhibitory functions, showing similar effects to pathological VHL symptoms. Indeed, ECM destabilization increases cell migration to other areas, promoting metastasis outbreak in case of tumor cells. Further, pVHL-dependent inhibition of tight junction formation by aPKCζII participates in an easier cellular detachment. The interactions of Nur77 could be considered a good example for pathological effects. It is a stimulator of Proopiomelanocortin production, a precursor for the Adrenocorticotropic hormone. If excessively released, it promotes an overproduction of adrenergic neurotransmitters by adrenal glands. Coming at clinical condition known as Cushing syndrome. On the very long term, Nur77 deregulation is known to cause tumors of the pituitary and adrenal glands [51], [52]. This happens in pheochromocytoma, which is one of the main VHL disease manifestations. We speculate that continuous VEGF transcription, even in situations where HIF-1α (but not Sp1) is knocked out, could be the explanation for clinical studies where VEGF-targeting drugs have turned out to be effective in kidney cancer treatment as reported in [53]. Although we used only confirmed data from the literature, Nur77 may be involved in other regulation systems which were not considered in our model. The transitions for pVHL fibronectin stabilization show a behaviour which is coherent with biochemical experiments, illustrating a complete abrogation of ECM stabilization and an increased matrix metallo-proteinase action. Although the results are encouraging, the presented model will need further improvements since standard PNs do neither allow a complete transition control nor enzymatic activity modulation. Nevertheless, thanks to its manual curation our model can be used to plan new *in vitro* and *in vivo*experiments. The results are convincing enough to suggest our model as a comprehensive pathway model to simulate the main pVHL functions.

ACKNOWLEDGMENTS

The authors are grateful to Stefano Moro and to members of the BioComputing UP lab for insightful discussions.

AUTHOR CONTRIBUTIONS

Conceived and designed the experiments: GM CF ST. Performed the experiments: GM EP MG. Analyzed the data: EP MG AM. Contributed reagents/materials/analysis tools: ST. Wrote the paper: GM EP ST.

REFERENCES

1. Soga T (2013) Cancer metabolism: Key players in metabolic reprogramming. Cancer Sci 104: 275–281.
2. Golub TR, Slonim DK, Tamayo P, Huard C, Gaasenbeek M, et al. (1999) Molecular classification of cancer: class discovery and class prediction by gene expression monitoring. Science 286: 531–537.
3. Thomas JG, Olson JM, Tapscott SJ, Zhao LP (2001) An efficient and robust statistical modeling approach to discover differentially expressed genes using genomic expression profiles. Genome Res 11: 1227–1236
4. Leonardi E, Murgia A, Tosatto SCE (2009) Adding structural information to the von Hippel-Lindau (VHL) tumor suppressor interaction network. FEBS Lett 583: 3704–3710.
5. Leonardi E, Martella M, Tosatto SCE, Murgia A (2011) Identification and in silico analysis of novel von Hippel-Lindau (VHL) gene variants from a large population. Ann Hum Genet 75: 483–496.

6. Minervini G, Masiero A, Moro S, Tosatto SCE (2013) In silico investigation of PHD-3 specific HIF1-α proline 567 hydroxylation: A new player in the VHL/HIF-1α interaction pathway? FEBS Lett. 587(18): 2996–3001.
7. Wu M, Liu L, Hijazi H, Chan C (2013) A multi-layer inference approach to reconstruct condition-specific genes and their regulation. Bioinforma Oxf Engl: 1–12. doi:10.1093/bioinformatics/btt186.
8. Almaas E (2007) Biological impacts and context of network theory. J Exp Biol 210: 1548–1558.
9. Weitz JS, Benfey PN, Wingreen NS (2007) Evolution, interactions, and biological networks. PLoS Biol 5: e11
10. Proulx SR, Promislow DEL, Phillips PC (2005) Network thinking in ecology and evolution. Trends Ecol Evol 20: 345–353.
11. Mahon PC, Hirota K, Semenza GL (2001) FIH-1: a novel protein that interacts with HIF-1alpha and VHL to mediate repression of HIF-1 transcriptional activity. Genes Dev 15: 2675–2686.
12. Heiner M, Sriram K (2010) Structural analysis to determine the core of hypoxia response network. PloS One 5: e8600
13. Kohn KW, Riss J, Aprelikova O, Weinstein JN, Pommier Y, et al. (2004) Properties of switch-like bioregulatory networks studied by simulation of the hypoxia response control system. Mol Biol Cell 15: 3042–3052.
14. Yu Y, Wang G, Simha R, Peng W, Turano F, et al. (2007) Pathway switching explains the sharp response characteristic of hypoxia response network. PLoS Comput Biol 3: e171
15. Stolle C, Glenn G, Zbar B, Humphrey JS, Choyke P, et al. (1998) Improved detection of germline mutations in the von Hippel-Lindau disease tumor suppressor gene. Hum Mutat 12: 417–423.
16. Gnarra JR, Tory K, Weng Y, Schmidt L, Wei MH, et al. (1994) Mutations of the VHL tumour suppressor gene in renal carcinoma. Nat Genet 7: 85–90.
17. Latif F, Tory K, Gnarra J, Yao M, Duh FM, et al. (1993) Identification of the von Hippel-Lindau disease tumor suppressor gene. Science 260: 1317–1320.

18. Kim WY, Kaelin WG (2004) Role of VHL gene mutation in human cancer. J Clin Oncol Off J Am Soc Clin Oncol 22: 4991–5004.
19. Vortmeyer AO, Huang SC, Pack SD, Koch CA, Lubensky IA, et al. (2002) Somatic point mutation of the wild-type allele detected in tumors of patients with VHL germline deletion. Oncogene. 14 21(8): 1167–70.
20. Knudson AG Jr (1971) Mutation and cancer: statistical study of retinoblastoma. Proc Natl Acad Sci U S A 68: 820–823.
21. Gnarra JR, Ward JM, Porter FD, Wagner JR, Devor DE, et al. (1997) Defective placental vasculogenesis causes embryonic lethality in VHL-deficient mice. Proc Natl Acad Sci U S A 94: 9102–9107.
22. Frew IJ, Krek W (2008) pVHL: a multipurpose adaptor protein. Sci Signal 1: pe30
23. Schoenfeld AR, Davidowitz EJ, Burk RD (2000) Elongin BC complex prevents degradation of von Hippel-Lindau tumor suppressor gene products. Proc Natl Acad Sci U S A 97: 8507–8512.
24. Semenza GL (1999) Regulation of mammalian O2 homeostasis by hypoxia-inducible factor 1. Annu Rev Cell Dev Biol 15: 551–578.
25. Kerrien S, Aranda B, Breuza L, Bridge A, Broackes-Carter F, et al. (2012) The IntAct molecular interaction database in 2012. Nucleic Acids Res 40: D841–846.
26. Frew IJ, Krek W (2007) Multitasking by pVHL in tumour suppression. Curr Opin Cell Biol 19: 685–690.
27. Thoma CR, Toso A, Gutbrodt KL, Reggi SP, Frew IJ, et al. (2009) VHL loss causes spindle misorientation and chromosome instability. Nat Cell Biol 11: 994–1001.
28. Tang N, Mack F, Haase V (2006) pVHL function is essential for endothelial extracellular matrix deposition. Mol Cell 26. doi:10.1128/MCB.26.7.2519.
29. Sackmann A, Heiner M, Koch I (2006) Application of Petri net based analysis techniques to signal transduction pathways. BMC Bioinformatics 7: 482.
30. Chaouiya C (2007) Petri net modelling of biological networks. Brief Bioinform 8: 210–219.

31. Grunwald S, Speer A, Ackermann J, Koch I (2008) Petri net modelling of gene regulation of the Duchenne muscular dystrophy. Biosystems 92: 189–205.

32. Rohr C, Marwan W, Heiner M (2010) Snoopy–a unifying Petri net framework to investigate biomolecular networks. Bioinforma Oxf Engl 26: 974–975.

33. Maynard MA, Evans AJ, Hosomi T, Hara S, Jewett MAS, et al. (2005) Human HIF-3alpha4 is a dominant-negative regulator of HIF-1 and is down-regulated in renal cell carcinoma. FASEB J Off Publ Fed Am Soc Exp Biol 19: 1396–1406.

34. Li QF, Wang XR, Yang YW, Lin H (2006) Hypoxia upregulates hypoxia inducible factor (HIF)-3alpha expression in lung epithelial cells: characterization and comparison with HIF-1alpha. Cell Res 16: 548–558.

35. Smith TG, Robbins PA, Ratcliffe PJ (2008) The human side of hypoxia-inducible factor. Br J Haematol 141: 325–334.

36. Richardson SM, Knowles R, Tyler J, Mobasheri A, Hoyland JA (2008) Expression of glucose transporters GLUT-1, GLUT-3, GLUT-9 and HIF-1alpha in normal and degenerate human intervertebral disc. Histochem Cell Biol 129: 503–511.

37. Vannucci SJ, Maher F, Simpson IA (1997) Glucose transporter proteins in brain: Delivery of glucose to neurons and glia. Glia 21: 2–21.

38. Takeda J, Kayano T, Fukomoto H, Bell GI (1993) Organization of the human GLUT2 (pancreatic beta-cell and hepatocyte) glucose transporter gene. Diabetes 42: 773–777.

39. Heather LC, Pates KM, Atherton HJ, Cole MA, Ball DR, et al.. (2013) Differential Translocation of FAT/CD36 and GLUT4 Coordinates Changes in Cardiac Substrate Metabolism During Ischemia and Reperfusion. Circ Heart Fail. doi:10.1161/CIRCHEARTFAILURE.112.000342.

40. Kim J, Tchernyshyov I, Semenza GL, Dang CV (2006) HIF-1-mediated expression of pyruvate dehydrogenase kinase: a metabolic switch required for cellular adaptation to hypoxia. Cell Metab 3: 177–185.

41. Kim BY, Kim H, Cho EJ, Youn HD (2008) Nur77 upregulates HIF-alpha by inhibiting pVHL-mediated degradation. Exp Mol Med 40: 71–83.
42. Choi J-W, Park SC, Kang GH, Liu JO, Youn H-D (2004) Nur77 activated by hypoxia-inducible factor-1alpha overproduces proopiomelanocortin in von Hippel-Lindau-mutated renal cell carcinoma. Cancer Res 64: 35–39.
43. Roe J-S, Youn H-D (2006) The positive regulation of p53 by the tumor suppressor VHL. Cell Cycle Georget Tex 5: 2054–2056.
44. Fels DR, Koumenis C (2005) HIF-1alpha and p53: the ODD couple? Trends Biochem Sci 30: 426–429.
45. Berndt JD, Moon RT, Major MB (2009) Beta-catenin gets jaded and von Hippel-Lindau is to blame. Trends Biochem Sci 34: 101–104.
46. Hergovich A, Lisztwan J, Thoma CR, Wirbelauer C, Barry RE, et al. (2006) Priming-Dependent Phosphorylation and Regulation of the Tumor Suppressor pVHL by Glycogen Synthase Kinase 3. Mol Cell Biol 26: 5784–5796.
47. Heiner M, Koch I, Will J (2004) Model validation of biological pathways using Petri nets–demonstrated for apoptosis. Biosystems 75: 15–28.
48. Bortfeldt RH, Schuster S, Koch I (2011) Exhaustive analysis of the modular structure of the spliceosomal assembly network: a petri net approach. Stud Health Technol Inform 162: 244–278.
49. Heiner M (2009) Understanding Network Behavior by Structured Representations of Transition Invariants. Algorithmic Bioprocesses. Natural Computing Series. Springer Berlin Heidelberg. 367–389. Available: http://link.springer.com/chapter/10.1007/978-3-540-88869-7_19.
50. Zhu JL, Kaytor EN, Pao CI, Meng XP, Phillips LS (2000) Involvement of Sp1 in the transcriptional regulation of the rat insulin-like growth factor-1 gene. Mol Cell Endocrinol 164: 205–218.
51. Okabe T, Nawata H (1998) [Functional role of nur77 family in T-cell apoptosis and stress response]. Nihon Rinsho Jpn J Clin Med 56: 1734–1738.

52. Murphy EP, Conneely OM (1997) Neuroendocrine regulation of the hypothalamic pituitary adrenal axis by the nurr1/nur77 subfamily of nuclear receptors. Mol Endocrinol Baltim Md 11: 39–47.
53. Tabernero J (2007) The Role of VEGF and EGFR Inhibition: Implications for Combining Anti–VEGF and Anti–EGFR Agents. Mol Cancer Res 5: 203–220.

8 CONSTRUCTION AND EXPERIMENTAL VALIDATION OF A PETRI NET MODEL OF WNT/β-CATENIN SIGNALING

Annika Jacobsen[1,2,3], Nika Heijmans[4], Folkert Verkaar[3,5], Martine J. Smit[3,5], Jaap Heringa[1,2,3], Renée van Amerongen[4], K. Anton Feenstra[1,2,3]

[1] Centre for Integrative Bioinformatics (IBIVU), VU University Amsterdam, Amsterdam, The Netherlands
[2] Department of Computer Science, VU University Amsterdam, Amsterdam, The Netherlands
[3] Amsterdam Institute for Molecules, Medicines and Systems, VU University Amsterdam, Amsterdam, The Netherlands
[4] Section of Molecular Cytology and Van Leeuwenhoek Centre for Advanced Microscopy, Swammerdam Institute for Life Sciences, University of Amsterdam, Amsterdam, The Netherlands
[5] Division of Medicinal Chemistry, VU University Amsterdam, Amsterdam, The Netherlands

ABSTRACT

The Wnt/β-catenin signaling pathway is important for multiple developmental processes and tissue maintenance in adults. Consequently, deregulated signaling is involved in a range of human diseases including cancer and developmental defects. A better understanding of the intricate regulatory mechanism and effect of physiological (active) and pathophysiological (hyperactive) WNT signaling is important for predicting treatment response and developing novel therapies. The constitutively expressed CTNNB1 (commonly and hereafter referred to as β-catenin) is degraded by a destruction complex, composed of amongst others AXIN1 and GSK3. The destruction complex is inhibited during active WNT signaling, leading to β-catenin stabilization and induction of β-catenin/TCF target genes. In this study we investigated the mechanism and effect of β-catenin stabilization during active and hyperactive WNT signaling in a combined *in silico* and *in vitro* approach. We constructed a Petri net model of Wnt/β-catenin signaling including main players from the plasma membrane (WNT ligands and receptors), cytoplasmic effectors and the downstream negative feedback target gene *AXIN2*. We validated that our model can be used to simulate both active (WNT stimulation) and hyperactive (GSK3 inhibition) signaling by comparing our simulation and experimental data. We used this experimentally validated model to get further insights into the effect of the negative feedback regulator AXIN2 upon WNT stimulation and observed an attenuated β-catenin stabilization. We furthermore simulated the effect of APC inactivating mutations, yielding a stabilization of β-catenin levels comparable to the Wnt-pathway activities observed in colorectal and breast cancer. Our model can be used for further investigation and viable predictions of the role of Wnt/β-catenin signaling in oncogenesis and development.

INTRODUCTION

The Wnt/β-catenin signaling pathway is crucial for regulating cell proliferation and differentiation during embryonic development, while in adults it helps control tissue homeostasis and injury repair in stem cell maintenance [1, 2]. Extracellular WNT ligands activate signaling leading to CTNNB1 (commonly and hereafter referred to as β-catenin) stabilization, nuclear translocation, interaction with TCF/LEF transcription factors [3] and induction of β-catenin/TCF target genes [4] (Fig 1B). A critical feature of Wnt/β-catenin signaling is the inhibition of a 'destruction complex' which degrades the constitutively expressed β-catenin (Fig 1A) [5].

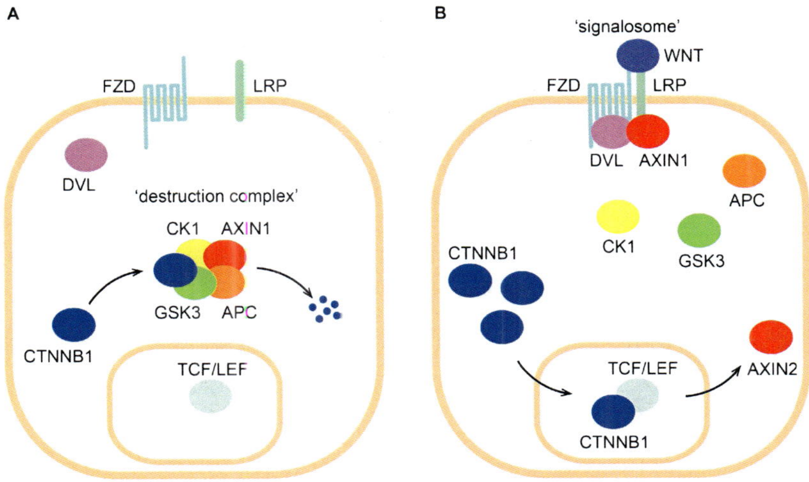

Figure 1: Illustration of Wnt/β-catenin signaling.

(A) In the absence of an external WNT stimulus β-catenin (referred to by its official gene name CTNNB1 in the figure) is continuously degraded by a 'destruction complex' consisting of AXIN1, adenomatous polyposis coli (APC), casein kinase 1 (CK1) and glycogen synthase kinase 3 (GSK3). (B) Extracellular WNT interacts with the membrane-bound receptors frizzled (FZD) and lipoprotein receptor-related protein (LRP). Dishevelled (DVL) interacts with the intracellular tail of FZD and sequesters AXIN1 to the plasma membrane forming a so-called 'signalosome'. The ensuing depletion of the cytoplasmic pool of AXIN1 inhibits the formation of the destruction complex. β-catenin thereby stabilizes and translocates to the nucleus, where it interacts with TCF/LEF transcription factors activating transcription of specific target genes, including the negative feedback regulator *AXIN2*.

The destruction complex consists of two scaffolding proteins, AXIN1 and adenomatous polyposis coli (APC), and two kinases, casein kinase 1 (CK1) and glycogen synthase kinase 3 (GSK3). β-catenin is phosphorylated by CK1 and GSK3 [6, 7] and thereafter presented to the proteasome for ubiquitination [8] and degradation (Fig 1A). Extracellular WNT binds to and activates the 7 transmembrane receptor, Frizzled (FZD) [9], and the co-receptor, lipoprotein receptor-related protein (LRP5/6) [10]. The intracellular tail of FZD interacts with Dishevelled (DVL) through an incompletely understood mechanism and sequesters

AXIN1 to the cell membrane [11] forming a so-called 'signalosome' [12]. This leads to depletion of the cytoplasmic pool of the destruction complex component AXIN1, which in turn inhibits the formation of the destruction complex itself (Fig 1B). It is not fully understood whether only AXIN1 or more destruction complex components are sequestered to the cell membrane during WNT signaling. Indeed, a study by Li *et al.* [13] showed that AXIN1 does not dissociate from the other destruction complex components during WNT signaling.

The inhibition of the destruction complex leads to β-catenin stabilization and nuclear translocation. Nuclear β-catenin interacts with TCF/LEF transcription factors [14] forming the β-catenin/TCF transcriptional (co)activator complex. A collection of more than 100 genes induced by β-catenin/TCF transcription is listed on the WNT homepage [15]. The specific subset of genes induced, however, strongly depends on tissue type and developmental stage [16]. Several of these target genes are feedback regulators, where *AXIN2* is of particular interest. First, *AXIN2* is a universal β-catenin/TCF target gene and as such it is believed to faithfully report Wnt-pathway activity in multiple tissues [17, 18]. Second, AXIN2 encodes a functional homolog of the destruction complex component AXIN1 [19] and mediates an auto-inhibitory feedback loop. Although AXIN1 and AXIN2 share functional similarities, they are only partially redundant *in vivo* due to their different expression patterns [20]: *AXIN1* is constitutively expressed [21], whereas *AXIN2* is induced during active Wnt/β-catenin signaling [18, 22]. The AXIN2 negative feedback is believed to be important for the tight spatio-temporal regulation of Wnt/β-catenin signaling [23]. However, the exact regulatory role of AXIN2 remains an open question.

Deregulated Wnt/β-catenin signaling caused by genetic alterations can have major developmental consequences, and is the leading cause of colorectal carcinogenesis [24]. The most common colorectal cancer mutation is found in APC [25, 26]. Different APC inactivating mutations lead to different levels of Wnt-pathway activity e.g. higher β-catenin stabilization is seen in colorectal cancer compared to breast cancer (as reviewed in [27]). Other rarer colorectal cancer mutations [28] are found in AXIN1 [29], AXIN2 [30, 31] and β-catenin [32, 33]. As a common mode of action, these oncogenic mutations cause hyperactive WNT signaling [34].

Investigating the mechanism and effect of β-catenin stabilization during physiological (active) and pathophysiological (hyperactive) WNT signaling is crucial for developing effective treatment, both in the field of cancer research and regenerative medicine. *In vitro* experiments in which cells are stimulated with WNT are generally assumed to represent active signaling, whereas downstream oncogenic mutations represent hyperactive signaling. Inhibition of GSK3 using small molecule inhibitors is widely used to activate WNT signaling during cellular reprogramming and in embryonic stem cell cultures [35, 36]. Inhibition of GSK3 inhibits the destruction complex, which can be interpreted as similar to the effects of oncogenic mutations. Several quantitative mathematical models of Wnt/β-catenin signaling have been created as reviewed in [37, 38] to facilitate these investigations. The first model [39] described the cytosolic interactions in WNT signaling based on data from experiments using *Xenopus* extracts. Later models included amongst other, extensions with (i) AXIN2 feedback, explaining effects of mutations in colorectal cancer [40]; (ii) AXIN2 feedback and another negative upstream feedback, demonstrating how these feedbacks ensure robust oscillations [41]; (iii) WNT inhibitors, secreted Frizzled-related protein and Dickkopf, which showed a synergistic effect on β-catenin accumulation [42]; (iv) effects of different target gene regulations induced by different WNT and APC concentrations [43]; (v) the interplay between adhesive and transcriptional functions of β-catenin [44] and (vi) data from experiments using mammalian cells, showing significant differences in AXIN levels [45]. However, constructing such quantitative models remains a challenge, because they require detailed information on e.g. protein concentrations and reaction rates. In addition to being dependent on large experimental efforts, these data are particularly difficult to obtain for a signaling pathway that does not involve a typical kinase cascade. Consequently, these models include many estimated parameters, which limits their scale of applicability [37]. Petri net models, on the other hand, use coarse-grained data describing currently known interactions and relative protein levels [46, 47]. A clear advantage of this is that such coarse-grained data are more readily available, and much easier to obtain. Coarse-grained Petri net models thus expand the scale of applicability for future modeling purposes, including extensions to novel signaling components or pathways.

Here we have used a combined computational and experimental approach to build the first Petri net model of Wnt/β-catenin signaling. Compared to the aforementioned mathematical models, it includes a larger number of core Wnt-pathway components. Most importantly, we have included a signaling module that captures the interactions occurring at the cell membrane. As a result, our model allows both physiological (i.e. WNT ligand induced) and pathophysiological (i.e. induced by oncogenic mutations in downstream signaling components) to be captured. Furthermore, our model offers the possibility of including the negative feedback by AXIN2. We used the model to explain how active signaling upon WNT stimulation and hyperactive signaling upon GSK3 inhibition leads to different levels of β-catenin stabilization. We corroborated our observations from the model using data from TCF/LEF luciferase reporter assays and Western blot analysis. We then used the experimentally validated model to explore plausible modes of action of β-catenin stabilization as a result of negative feedback by activating expression of AXIN2 upon WNT stimulation, or due to APC inactivating mutations that are known to play a key role in oncogenesis of colorectal and breast cancer.

RESULTS

Building a Petri Net Model for Wnt/β-Catenin Signaling

A Petri net model can be graphically represented with two types of nodes: 'places', describing the biological components, and 'transitions', describing the activity between the biological components, which can be constructed based on known interaction data. The places are denoted with 'tokens', which describe the relative availability of the biological component. Tokens are assigned on the basis of existing data from the literature, typically relative protein levels. Places and transition are connected by weighted arcs that are important for the flow of the network. [48–50] (see Materials and Methods for a detailed explanation of Petri nets).

We created a Petri net model of Wnt/β-catenin signaling to investigate the mechanism and effect of β-catenin stabilization under physiological (e.g. embryonic development) and pathophysiological (e.g. cancer) conditions based on the literature as described in details below (Fig 2). The model describes the interactions between the core proteins in the pathway with a focus on capturing the immediate behavior of β-catenin stabilization following destruction complex inactivation. Therefore the degradation of β-catenin by the destruction complex is specifically included in the model, while no changes in the production/degradation rate of the other proteins needed to be assumed. Likewise, the gene expressions of *β-catenin* (encoding β-catenin), but also of *AXIN2*, a negative feedback target gene of the Wnt-pathway, are also specifically included in the model. Production and degradation of all other proteins are assumed to have similar rates and are therefore omitted, such that the token levels of these proteins remain the same throughout the simulation (as detailed in Materials and Methods).

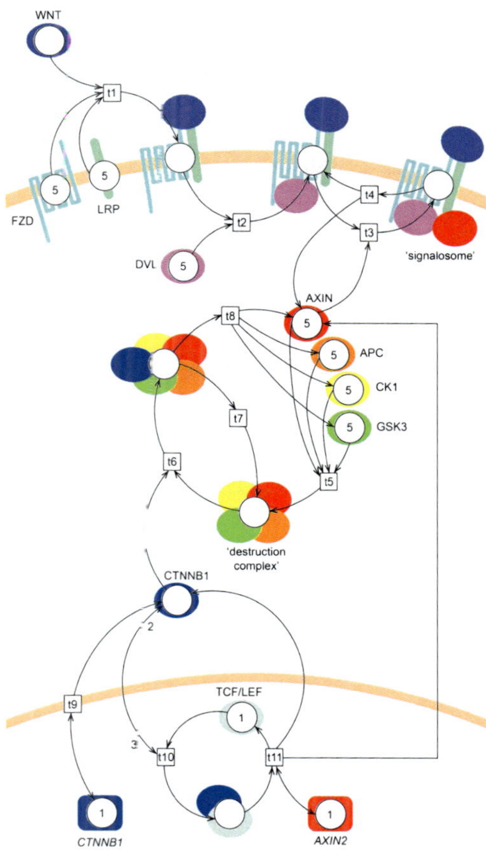

Figure 2: Petri net model of Wnt/β-catenin signaling.

The model consists of 18 places (circles, representing gene or protein states), 11 transitions (boxes, representing protein complex formation, and dissociation, translocation or gene expression) and 41 arcs (arrows, representing the direction of flow of the tokens). WNT initiates signaling by binding to FZD and LRP (t1), forming the WNT/FZD/LRP complex. DVL and AXIN1 then interact with this complex intracellularly (t2 and t3, respectively) forming a so-called 'signalosome'. The signalosome dissociates (with a rate of once every 10 steps) into WNT/FZD/LRP/DVL and AXIN1 (t4). Note that β-catenin is referred to by its official gene name CTNNB1 in the figure. The β-catenin protein is produced every step (t9) by the *β-catenin* gene. AXIN1, APC, CK1 and GSK3 interact (t5) and form a 'destruction complex'. The destruction complex binds β-catenin (t6) to mark it for degradation. The destruction complex is then either reused (t7) for another round of β-catenin degradation or dissociates (t8) into its components AXIN1, APC, CK1 and GSK3. Alternatively, β-catenin may interact with TCF/LEF in the nucleus (t10), leading to transcriptional activation of *AXIN2* (t11). Initial token levels are 0 (not shown), 1 or 5 (depicted in the places). Most arc weights are 1 (not shown), except for the nuclear translocation and interaction of β-catenin to TCF/LEF transcription factors, which has an incoming arc weight of 3 and an outgoing arc weight of 2 (depicted on the arcs).

The final model consists of 18 places (circles, representing gene or protein states), 11 transitions (boxes, representing protein complex formation, dissociation, translocation or gene expression) and 41 arcs (arrows, representing the direction of flow of the tokens). In the model, WNT initiates signaling extracellularly by binding to its transmembrane receptors FZD and LRP (t1), forming the WNT/FZD/LRP complex. DVL interacts with the intracellular tail of FZD when present in the WNT/FZD/LRP complex (t2), forming the WNT/FZD/LRP/DVL complex. DVL thereafter sequesters AXIN1 to the membrane (t3) forming the signalosome consisting of WNT, FZD, LRP, DVL and AXIN1. In the model we have not specifically included the contribution of GSK3 and CK1 in the formation of the signalosome, because these two multi-tasking kinases are generally assumed not to be rate-limiting in the cell [24, 39]. Further, AXIN1 is the only destruction complex constituent that binds to the signalosome in the model. The signalosome dissociates once every 10 steps (t4) into the WNT/FZD/LRP/DVL complex and

AXIN1 in order to incorporate a lower dissociation- than formation-rate of the signalosome. The destruction complex, which sequesters β-catenin unless WNT induces signalosome formation, is formed (t5) by AXIN1, APC, CK1 and GSK3. In the model, β-catenin binding to the destruction complex leads to degradation of β-catenin (t8 and t7), and the destruction complex is then either reused (t7) for another round of β-catenin degradation or dissociates (t8) to AXIN1, APC, CK1 and GSK3. In the model, β-catenin protein is produced every step (t9) following transcription of the *-catenin* gene, and either binds the destruction complex (t6) or translocates to the nucleus, where it interacts with TCF/LEF (t10) to activate transcription of *AXIN2* (t11). Since AXIN1 and AXIN2 are functional homologs [19], they are modeled as one protein entity (depicted as 'AXIN'). Further, we do not distinguish between the cytoplasmic and nuclear pool of β-catenin in the model. This allowed the nuclear translocation and TCF/LEF interactions to be modeled as one transition (t10).

The initial token level of the protein places were set to 5 (with exceptions described below) in order to have a concise but sufficiently large pool of the protein tokens for the model to work with. Higher levels had no effect, and lower levels restricted the expressiveness of the model, i.e. too coarse-grained. The initial token level of the β-catenin protein place and all protein complexes (WNT/FZD/LRP, WNT/FZD/LRP/DVL, signalosome, destruction complex-β-catenin and TCF/LEF-β-catenin) were set to 0, because these are produced throughout the simulation and are assumed to be initially absent. The initial token level of TCF/LEF was set to 1 which gives the lowest rate of TCF/LEF-β-catenin interaction, and hence the induction of low levels of AXIN2 [51]. A parameter sweep of initial token levels of TCF/LEF confirmed that higher initial token levels resulted in a stronger response and higher AXIN2 levels. Initial token levels of the gene places, *β-catenin* and *AXIN2*, were set to 1 and kept at these values since these genes are always presumed to be present. In our model this means that *AXIN2* is induced only when the TCF/LEF-β-catenin complex is present and *β-catenin* is induced once every step, because there is nothing implemented to restrain this induction (β-catenin levels are instead regulated by the destruction complex).

Most arc weights were set to 1, which means that the model dynamics rely on its connectivity. This has been proven successful using

Petri net modeling of MAPK and AKT signaling cascades [46, 47, 52]. An exception to this was applied when implementing fractional arc weights to represent a lower transition rate (i.e. the dissociation of the signalosome, the effects of different APC mutations and the induction of AXIN2) and when implementing a higher interaction affinity of β-catenin to the destruction complex than to TCF/LEF. For the latter the arc weight from β-catenin to t10 (i.e. its translocation to the nucleus and subsequent interaction with TCF/LEF) was set to 3, and the arc weight from t10 to β-catenin was set to 2. From the model point of view this means that for t10 to fire, the β-catenin place needs to be occupied by 3 tokens, but only 1 is consumed (See Fig 2). These weights were chosen because it is generally assumed that β-catenin accumulates in the cytoplasm before it translocates to the nucleus and binds TCF/LEF (as reviewed in [53]). This assumption is based on the higher interaction affinities of β-catenin to the destruction complex compared to TCF/LEF (as reviewed in [54]), which means that β-catenin will interact with TCF/LEF when the β-catenin levels begin to increase because the destruction complex is unable to keep up with the degradation. In order to implement the lower dissociation rate of the signalosome, the ingoing and outgoing arcs of t4 were implemented with a fractional arc weight of 0.1, which represents a firing rate of once every 10 steps. Further, we implemented a constraint on the transition to ensure that it does not fire more than once every step. Parts of this initial setup were changed accordingly to mimic the different conditions of Wnt/β-catenin signaling simulated in this study (see below).

Active Signaling upon WNT Stimulation

We simulated WNT stimulation to predict the level of β-catenin stabilization during active signaling. To this end we ran a series of simulations with different initial WNT token levels (ranging from 0 to 5) without AXIN2 feedback (i.e. the arc weight from t11 to AXIN was set to 0). As shown in Fig 3A, we observed four different β-catenin response levels depending on the initial WNT token level. A flat β-catenin response was seen for WNT = 0, 1 or 2. For WNT = 3, 4 or 5, we observed a delay in the initial increase of β-catenin, which eventually increased linearly with a slope depending on the WNT level. The β-catenin stabilization was low for WNT = 3 and moderate for WNT = 4 and 5. Maximal WNT stimulation (WNT = 5) led to a stabilization of ~60 β-catenin tokens.

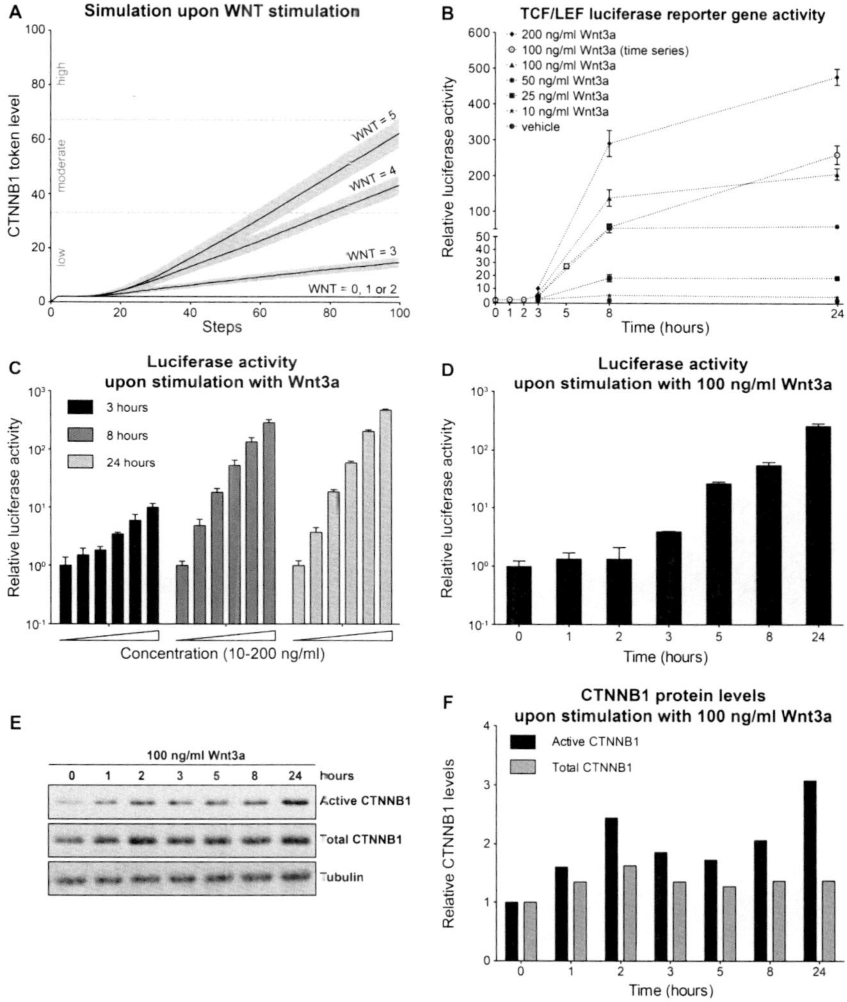

Figure 3: Model simulation and experimental validation of Wnt-pathway activation upon WNT stimulation.

(A) β-catenin (referred to by its official gene name CTNNB1 in the figure) token levels predicted by our model with initial WNT token levels ranging from 0 to 5. For WNT = 0, 1 or 2, we observed a flat β-catenin response. For WNT = 3, 4 and 5 β-catenin increases from low to moderate levels. (B) Graph combining the results from panels C and D to allow easy comparison to the modeling results depicted in panel

(A), showing dose- and time-dependent activation of a Wnt/β-catenin responsive TCF/LEF luciferase reporter in HEK293T^{WOO} cells. For all curves with black data points (corresponding to panel C), luciferase activity was plotted relative to the vehicle control (not shown), which was set at 1 for each of the three time points (3, 8 and 24 hours). For the curve with white data points (corresponding to panel D), luciferase activity was plotted relative to the vehicle control, which was set at 1 for the t = 0 hours condition. (C) Reporter assay in HEK293T^{WOO} cells, showing dose-dependent activation at 3, 8 and 24 hours after stimulation with purified Wnt3a (same concentrations as depicted in B). (D) Reporter assay in HEK293T^{WOO} cells, showing time-dependent activation upon treatment with 100 ng/ml of Wnt3a. Values were plotted relative to the vehicle control, which was set at 1 for t = 0 hours. (E) Western blot from the experiment depicted in (D), showing total and active (i.e. non-phosphorylated) β-catenin levels. Since the soluble, signaling pool of β-catenin constitutes only a minor fraction of the total pool of β-catenin, the use of antibody against active β-catenin ensures that only the pool involved in WNT signaling is visualized. Tubulin was used as a loading control. (F) Quantification of the Western blot shown in (E). Total and active β-catenin levels were normalized to tubulin. The increase in either total or active β-catenin levels was plotted relative to time point 0, for which the normalized levels were set to 1. Experiments were repeated two (C) or three (D-F) times. A representative experiment is shown.

To compare the response predicted by our model to the biological response of cells treated with Wnt3a, we measured β-catenin activation by both Western blot analysis and TCF/LEF luciferase reporter assay (Fig 3B–3F). Although the former directly detects β-catenin levels, the latter faithfully reports Wnt/β-catenin signaling [55] and remains the most sensitive and robust method to quantify Wnt/β-catenin signaling to date [15, 56, 57]. Furthermore, it allows high-throughput analyses of Wnt-pathway activation (i.e. a comparison of multiple doses and time points within the same experiment). To validate the β-catenin levels predicted upon WNT stimulation by our model, we treated HEK293T^{WOO} cells (carrying a stably integrated β-catenin/TCF luciferase reporter) with increasing concentrations of purified, commercially available, Wnt3a for 3, 8 and 24 hours. These experiments reproduce the dose- and time-dependent increase of TCF/LEF reporter gene activity predicted by our model (Fig 3B and 3C). To directly link the results from the reporter gene assay to an increase in β-catenin protein levels, we repeated the experiment for one level of WNT stimulation (100 ng/ml purified Wnt3a) for a more extensive time series, including additional earlier time points, and analyzed the results by performing both a TCF/LEF reporter gene assay (Fig 3B and 3D) and quantitative Western blot analysis (Fig 3E and 3F), which allows direct, albeit less sensitive, detection of β-catenin protein levels. Both the transcriptional reporter assay and the measurement of β-catenin protein levels show a time-dependent increase (Fig 3D–3F). Direct comparison of the two readouts reveals the inherent limitations of each of the two experimental systems: The change (i.e. fold increase) in TCF/LEF reporter activity is more pronounced than, but slightly delayed compared to, the change in β-catenin protein levels. Our Petri net model (Fig 3A) shows the same qualitative effect: a consistent rise in β-catenin levels. As such, our model more closely mimics the luciferase response (i.e. activation of an artificial reporter gene).

Hyperactive Signaling upon GSK3 Inhibition

To predict the level of β-catenin stabilization during hyperactive signaling by a downstream perturbation, we next simulated our model upon GSK3 inhibition. We ran a series of simulations with different initial GSK3 token levels (ranging from 5 to 0), where 5 initial tokens represents wildtype (i.e. no Wnt-pathway activity) and 0 corresponds to complete inhibition (hyperactive signaling). The simulations revealed that the response levels depend on initial GSK3 token levels (see Fig 4A). For GSK3 = 3, 4 or 5, we observed a flat β-catenin response. A linear increase in β-catenin levels with a slope depending on GSK3 levels was seen for GSK3 = 0, 1 or 2. This corresponds to β-catenin degradation ranging from no degradation to 1 or 2 β-catenin tokens degraded per three simulation steps, respectively. Consequently, β-catenin stabilization was low for GSK3 = 2, moderate for GSK3 = 1 and high for GSK3 = 0. Complete GSK3 inhibition led to a stabilization of 100 β-catenin tokens.

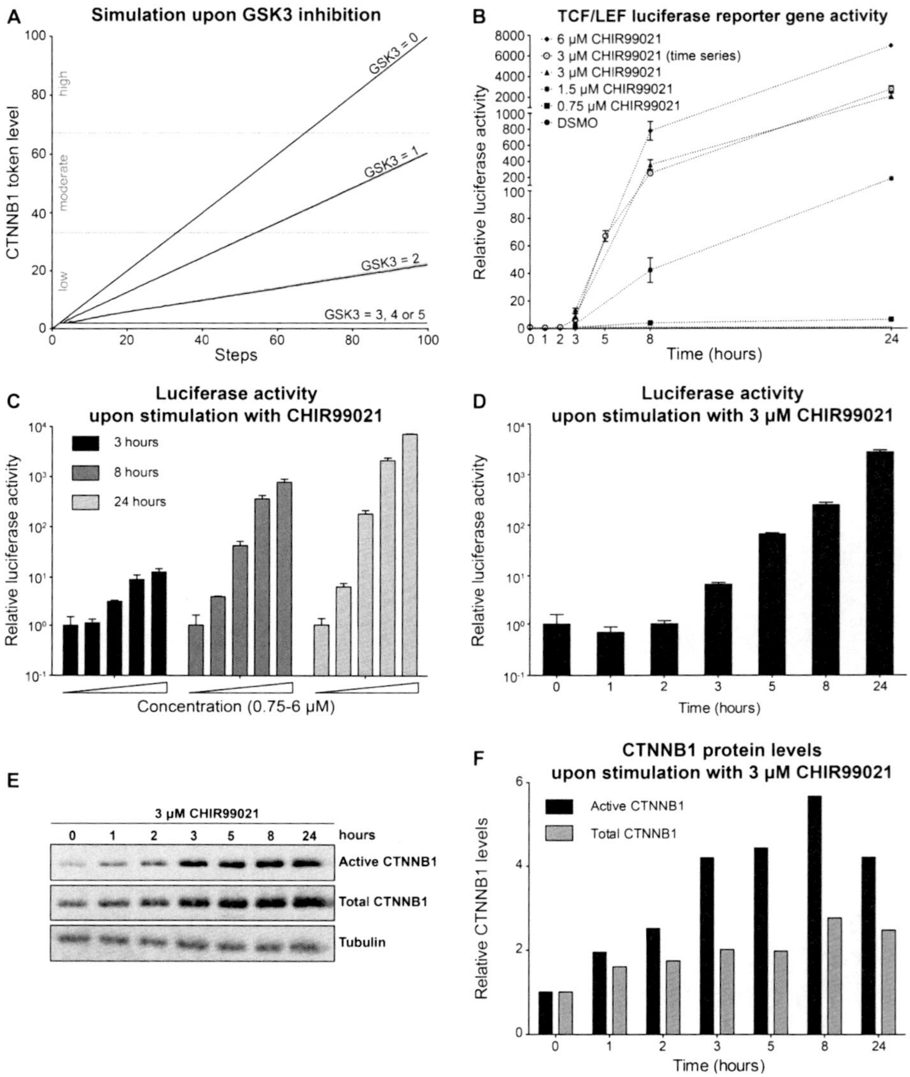

Figure 4: Model simulation and experimental validation of Wnt-pathway activation upon GSK3 inhibition.

(A) β-catenin (referred to by its official gene name CTNNB1 in the figure) token levels predicted by our model with initial GSK3 token levels ranging from 0 to 5. For GSK3 = 3, 4 or 5, we observed a flat β-catenin response. For GSK3 = 0, 1 or 2 β-catenin increases to low, moderate or high levels, respectively. (B) Graph combining the results from panels C and D to allow easy comparison to the modeling results depicted in panel (A), showing dose- and time-dependent activation of a Wnt/β-catenin responsive TCF/LEF luciferase reporter in HEK293T^{WOO} cells. For all curves with black data points (corresponding to panel C), luciferase activity was plotted relative to the vehicle control (not shown), which was set at 1 for each of the three time points (3, 8 and 24 hours). For the curve with white data points (corresponding to panel D), luciferase activity was plotted relative to the vehicle control, which was set at 1 for the t = 0 hours condition. (C) Reporter assay in HEK293T^{WOO} cells, showing dose-dependent activation at 3, 8 and 24 hours after stimulation with CHIR99021 (same concentrations as depicted in B). (D) Reporter assay in HEK293T^{WOO} cells, showing time-dependent activation upon treatment with 3 μM CHIR99021. Values were plotted relative to the DMSO control, which was set at 1 for t = 0 hours. (E) Western blot from the experiment depicted in (D), showing total and active (non-phosphorylated) β-catenin levels. Tubulin was used as a loading control. (F) Quantification of the Western blot shown in (E). Total and active β-catenin levels were normalized to tubulin. The increase in either total or active β-catenin levels was plotted relative to time point 0, for which the normalized levels were set to 1. Experiments were repeated two (C) or three (D-F) times. A representative experiment is shown.

To validate the coarse-grained β-catenin levels predicted by our model upon GSK3 inhibition, we stimulated HEK293T^{WOO} cells with increasing concentrations of CHIR99021, one of the most potent and selective GSK3 inhibitors available to date [58], over a broad time range (3, 8 and 24 hours). The measured TCF/LEF reporter gene activity confirmed the dose- and time-dependent increase upon GSK3 inhibition (Fig 4B and 4C) predicted by our model (Fig 4A). As with the Wnt3a treatment, here we also performed a TCF/LEF reporter gene assay and quantitative Western blot analysis side by side for one of the treatment conditions (3 μM CHIR99021) for multiple time points. The 3 μM CHIR99021 concentration was chosen in order to achieve a near maximal GSK3 inhibition or Wnt-pathway activation. An increase in both active (i.e. non-phosphorylated) and total (i.e. both phosphorylated and non-phosphorylated) β-catenin is apparent after 1 hour, whereas an increase in the signal of the luciferase reporter assay can only be detected after 3 hours. Furthermore, the dynamic range of the Western blot analysis is limited compared to the reporter gene assay, allowing us to measure at most a 4-fold increase in β-catenin levels in the former, but up to a 10^4 fold increase in Wnt-pathway activity in the latter (Fig 4D–4F).

Predictions of Hyperactive Signaling by APC Inactivating Mutations

The most common colorectal oncogene, *APC*, perturbs downstream WNT signaling. Different APC mutations exist that result in truncated proteins negatively influence the formation of the destruction complex to different degrees. As a result, the different APC mutations lead to different levels of β-catenin stabilizations. According to a recent review [27], the β-catenin signaling activity (β-catenin reporter activity) was low (between 10–20%) for APC mutations in breast tumors, versus moderate to high (between 20–100%) in colorectal tumors.

We used our validated model to explore if the effect of these APC mutations might be explained by different rates of destruction complex formation. We implemented the effect of the APC mutations by decreasing the rate of the destruction complex formation ranging from no production at all to production every 20, 10 and 5 steps. In Fig 5 we observed four different response levels for the different APC mutations, where stabilization of β-catenin levels went from low to high depending on this rate of destruction complex formation. Comparing these token levels to the β-catenin signaling activities reviewed in [27], the three highest β-catenin stabilizations would correspond to hyperactive signaling by APC mutations in colorectal tumor formation (moderate and high β-catenin token levels), whereas the lowest β-catenin stabilization would correspond to the effects by APC mutations as observed in breast tumor formation (low β-catenin token levels).

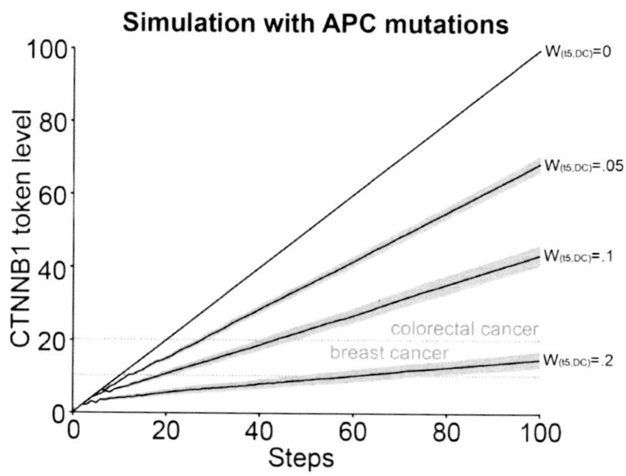

Figure 5: Model prediction of Wnt-pathway hyperactivation by APC inactivating mutations.

β-catenin (referred to by its official gene name CTNNB1 in the figure) token levels predicted by our model with four different APC mutations (weight on the arc going from t5 to the destruction complex (DC) set at 0.2, 0.1, 0.05 and 0, respectively). Moderate and high β-catenin stabilizations might correspond to the effects by mutations in colorectal tumor formation and the low β-catenin stabilizations might correspond to the effects by mutations in breast tumor formation.

Predictions of Active Signaling upon WNT Stimulation with AXIN2 Feedback

In our model *AXIN2* is induced by β-catenin/TCF transcription and increases the cytoplasmic pool of AXIN, which under certain conditions, e.g. WNT stimulation, is the limiting factor for β-catenin degradation. However, our experimental dataset obtained using Wnt3a stimulation showed no obvious decrease in β-catenin levels that might be due to this negative feedback (Fig 3E and 3F). It should be noted that in this experimental setting (100 ng/ml Wnt3a), the Wnt-pathway is likely still activated at supra-physiological levels. Moreover, the WNT ligand remains present throughout the experiment. *In vivo*, however, physiological Wnt-pathway activation is strictly regulated both due to the WNT concentration gradient and due to the tight spatio-temporal control of Wnt gene expression. Under these circumstances, lower levels of Wnt/β-catenin signaling are likely to occur and, as a result, part of the regulation may be due to the AXIN2 auto-inhibitory feedback loop. Therefore, it may be the ratio between the WNT and AXIN2 levels that is crucial to the regulatory role of AXIN2. We therefore used our model to get further insights into the effect of the AXIN2 feedback and explored a spectrum of possible β-catenin stabilizations under different WNT and AXIN2 levels. We ran a series of simulations with different initial WNT token levels: 3, 4 or 5, which showed increased β-catenin stabilization in Fig 3A, and with different AXIN2 feedback strengths: the arc weight from t11 to AXIN was varied from 0 for no feedback to 0.15 for maximum feedback. As shown in Fig 6, we observed three different spectra of β-catenin stabilizations depending on the different initial WNT token levels. The highest β-catenin stabilizations (solid lines in Fig 6) were identical to those observed in Fig 3A (without AXIN2 feedback). At high feedback, the β-catenin stabilization is lowered, and a maximum appears after which the β-catenin level declines (dashed lines in Fig 6). The lowest β-catenin stabilizations displayed three different peak responses. For the peak responses, the height of the peak and the duration of the response depended on initial WNT token levels. Maximal β-catenin stabilization comes later in the simulation for higher initial WNT token levels.

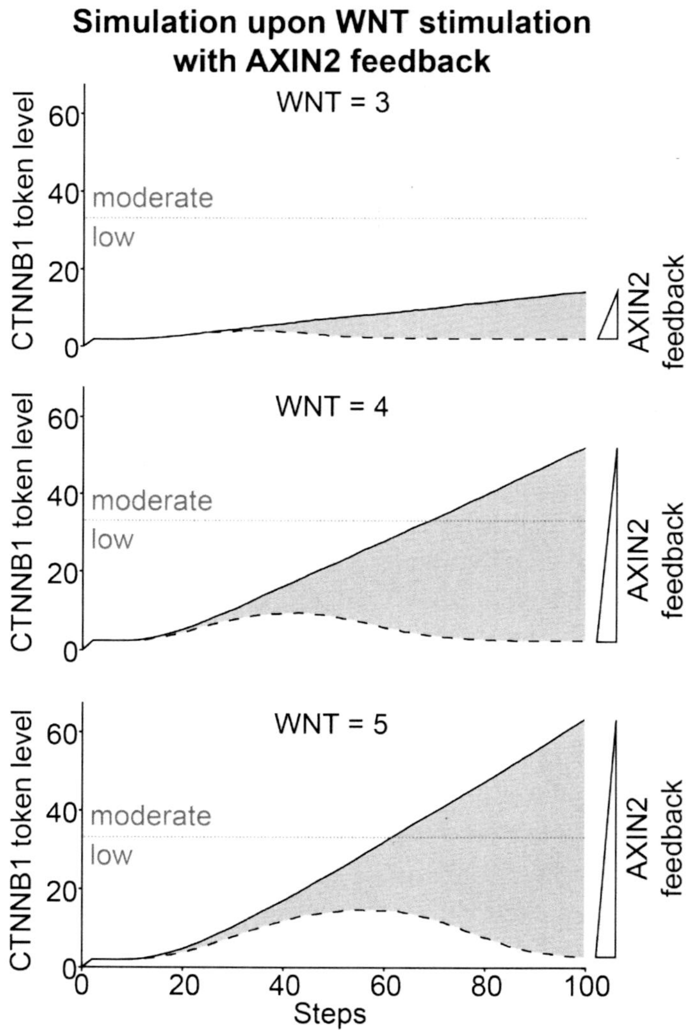

Figure 6: Model prediction of Wnt-pathway activation upon WNT addition with AXIN2 feedback.

β-catenin (referred to by its official gene name CTNNB1 in the figure) token levels predicted by our model with arc weight from t11 to AXIN varied from 0 (no feedback; solid lines) to 0.15 (high feedback, dashed lines), and initial WNT token levels at 3, 4 and 5 (top, middle and bottom panels, respectively). We observed three spectra of β-catenin stabilizations depending on initial WNT levels. The highest β-catenin stabilizations correspond to simulations without AXIN2 feedback (solid lines), whereas with high AXIN2 feedback the β-catenin stabilization was attenuated (dashed lines).

DISCUSSION

In spite of more than 30 years of study, the Wnt/β-catenin signaling pathway still holds many questions. The molecular details of how an external WNT stimulus results in the stabilization of transcriptionally active β-catenin/TCF complexes remain incompletely understood and, in some cases, a topic of debate [59]. The Petri net model presented in this paper allows us to investigate downstream effects of Wnt/β-catenin signaling under physiological and pathophysiological conditions. The core of the model describes the current state of knowledge as summarized in the introduction. The coarse-grained nature of the interaction and protein level data used to build our model allowed us to include the interactions at the plasma membrane, which is lacking from currently existing quantitative models as reviewed in [37, 38]. Of note, AXIN1 is the only destruction complex component sequestered to the plasma membrane during Wnt/β-catenin signaling in our model. For now we ignored the actions of GSK3 at the plasma membrane, where it phosphorylates LRP5/6 to create the AXIN1 binding site and where, in turn, the kinase itself may be inhibited [60, 61]. Furthermore, we considered free cytoplasmic and nuclear β-catenin as a single pool in the model. More detailed experimental data on subcellular compartmentalization of β-catenin (or any other signaling component) would allow us to refine our Petri net model, which easily allows incorporation of such detail. For instance, at present our model only considers the active (i.e. unphosphorylated), rather than the total pool of β-catenin, which would also include the β-catenin present in the adhesion complexes in the cell membrane.

Our Petri net model for Wnt/β-catenin signaling was constructed based on known interactions of signaling components described in the literature, thereby capturing the current state of knowledge in the field. To validate the model, we generated our own experimental data. This allowed a direct comparison of physiological (i.e. WNT stimulation) and pathophysiological (i.e. GSK3 inhibition) activation of the pathway in the same cell line, using time points and analyses best suited for connecting our experimental data and the Petri net modeling predictions.

Our model predicts a dose- and time dependent response for both WNT stimulation and GSK3 inhibition (Figs 3A and 4A). This is confirmed by the experimental data (Figs 3B, 3C, 4B and 4C). The main discrepancy between the simulated and the experimental data is the time-delay that is predicted in response to WNT stimulation compared to GSK3 inhibition (compare Figs 3A–4A). Indeed, activation of Wnt/β-catenin signaling is known to be a slow event (unlike the activation of MAPK signaling for instance, which occurs within a matter of minutes) [62–64]. However, we did not detect this delay in β-catenin accumulation by either TCF/LEF luciferase reporter assay (compare Fig 3B–3D to Fig 4B–4D) or Western blot analysis (compare Fig 3E and 3F to Fig 4E and 4F). We believe this is mainly due to experimental limitations. Given that a subtle increase in β-catenin protein levels can be detected approximately one hour after stimulation with either Wnt3a (Fig 3E and 3F) or CHIR99021 (Fig 4E and 4F), any delay in activation of the Wnt-pathway must occur prior to that time point. Detecting this delay would require assays with superior spatio-temporal resolution. The delay predicted by our model upon WNT stimulation (Fig 3A) can be explained by the fact that formation of the signalosome occurs a few steps into the simulation, whereas inhibition of GSK3 is a one-step event, and that the transitions for signalosome formation (i.e. pathway activation) and destruction complex formation (i.e. pathway inhibition) compete for AXIN1. Thus, when AXIN1 is sequestered to the plasma membrane, less cytoplasmic AXIN1 is available for formation of the destruction complex. To what extent these events contribute to Wnt-pathway activation under experimental conditions remains unknown, owing to the absence of tools to study the exchange of endogenous AXIN1 between these two pools. Our results do suggest that competition over AXIN1 between the destruction complex and the signalosome may well be important also under physiological conditions.

The time-delay together with the continuous sequestration and dissociation of AXIN1 to the signalosome leads to prediction of higher stabilization of β-catenin for complete GSK3 inhibition compared to maximal WNT stimulation, where the difference is almost two-fold (compare Figs 4A–3A). We observe a similar difference when measuring TCF/LEF reporter gene activity: the highest concentration of CHIR99021 activates the reporter approximately 10-fold higher than the highest concentration of Wnt3a tested (compare Fig 4B–4D to Fig 3B–3D). Comparing protein levels, instead of transcriptional activation, shows a much smaller difference: 2-fold higher β-catenin at most when cells are stimulated with CHIR99021 versus Wnt3a (compare Fig 4E and 4F to Fig 3E and 3F). Although it is tempting to conclude that this data again confirms the predictions of our model, it should be stressed that the different experimental modes of Wnt-pathway activation cannot be compared directly. This is because they are achieved by different molecules (i.e. purified Wnt3a versus a synthetic small-molecule GSK3 inhibitor) with different intrinsic activities and chemical properties such as half-life and stability in the tissue culture medium, which may greatly impact on the experimental outcome. At the same time, we may speculate that the observed differences reflect real differences in sensitivity of the Wnt-pathway. In this case, our experimental findings might be explained by the fact that the more physiological means of pathway activation by Wnt3a is more likely to be subject to negative feedback control via AXIN2 induction than the more artificial perturbation by CHIR99021 inhibition of GSK3 at the level of the destruction complex.

AXIN2 is one of the few comprehensive globally expressed WNT target genes and is thought to act as a negative regulator to Wnt/β-catenin signaling [17, 18]. The degree to which AXIN2 attenuates WNT signaling and the actual spatio-temporal regulatory role of AXIN2 is still a topic of debate. Indeed, when we incorporate this negative feedback loop in the model upon WNT stimulation, our simulations predict that Wnt-pathway activity is attenuated (at certain levels of AXIN2 induction), and ultimately returns to baseline levels (dashed lines in Fig 6). Importantly, in the model the feedback from AXIN2 only negatively influences stabilized β-catenin levels when AXIN1 is the limiting factor. This is the case when AXIN1 is deprived from the cytoplasm by sequestration to the signalosome (i.e. upon WNT stimulation). This is why we are able to observe a negative effect from the AXIN2 feedback upon WNT stimulation in our model (Fig 6), but not by GSK3 inhibition (Fig 4A) or

APC inactivating mutations (Fig 5). It should be noted however, that on the timescale used for the experiments, we do not observe complete feedback inhibition by AXIN2 (Fig 3B–3F). This might be due to the relatively low level of *AXIN2* induction in the cells used for these experiments [51] in combination with supra-physiological levels of Wnt-pathway activation achieved upon stimulation with purified Wnt3a. However, it could also be due to the fact that AXIN1 is not the limiting factor in the cells used for this study. Previously, a study of Wnt/β-catenin signaling in *Xenopus laevis* showed that AXIN1 is 1000-fold lower than the other components of the destruction complex [39] and has therefore been considered the natural limiting factor. However, a recent study of Wnt/β-catenin signaling in mammalian cells showed that the concentrations of the components of the destruction complex were on the same range [45]. Therefore, we cannot exclude the possibility that AXIN1 is not the limiting factor in the cells used for this study. Unfortunately, the current experimental tools, most notably Western blot analysis of endogenous β-catenin levels, are not robust, high-throughput and sensitive enough to resolve this issue. However, by using our model we were able to predict and visualize spectra of β-catenin stabilization, which showed that the ratio between the WNT and AXIN2 levels are important for the degree of feedback observed (Fig 6). The two most notable observations were that, for high WNT levels, a higher level of AXIN2 was needed to reach baseline β-catenin levels and, for low WNT levels, a baseline β-catenin level is reached early. Based on these predictions we can speculate whether the AXIN2 negative feedback only has an effect on low WNT levels and whether the regulatory role of this is to insure a faster on/off switch of Wnt-pathway activity. At present, in both our simulations and current experimental setting the cells are continuously exposed to Wnt3a. During normal development cells may essentially only receive a short pulse of WNT stimulation, given that the hydrophobic WNT proteins either do not travel far from their production source or are quickly sequestered by responsive cells. Indeed, in vivo Wnt-pathway activity shows dynamic on and off switches during development [23, 65, 66]. Examples of these are the restriction of Wnt/β-catenin responsive cells to the crypt, but not to the villus sections of the intestinal epithelium, and oscillation of WNT signaling as part of the mouse segmentation clock. By including protein degradation and different sources of WNT protein in our model, such oscillations might also be simulated.

In conclusion, our Petri net model of Wnt/β-catenin signaling provides insight on the mechanisms leading to different levels of β-catenin stabilization upon WNT stimulation and GSK3 inhibition corroborated by TCF/LEF luciferase assay and Western blot analysis. It should be stressed that the simulations show a coarse-grained output per step and we cannot directly map token levels to the relative activities in the TCF/LEF luciferase reporter assay nor to the β-catenin levels measured by Western blot analysis. Furthermore, we also cannot directly map a simulation step in the model to an experimental timescale. Despite these limitations, our model resembles Wnt/β-catenin signaling to the extent that it captures the logic of the interactions and reflects the sequence of events of pathway activation and repression by various mechanisms. In this way, our model can be used to simulate and predict both physiological and pathophysiological WNT signaling. Thus, this modeling exercise has allowed us to study the mechanisms and effects of Wnt/β-catenin signaling under different conditions, as well as the effects of protein- and pathway-modifications that are known to influence this pathway in many types of cancer.

MATERIALS AND METHODS

Petri Net Modeling

We built a Petri net model of Wnt/β-catenin signaling describing known components, actions and interactions, well established in literature, in a logical way. A Petri net consists of two types of nodes, 'places' and 'transitions', and is connected by directed edges called 'arcs'. A place represents an entity (e.g. gene or protein), whereas a transition indicates the activity occurring between the places (e.g. gene expression or complex formation). Places can only link to transitions and vice versa (i.e., a Petri net is a bipartite graph). The direction of the arcs is important for the flow of the network. An arc goes from an input place to a transition, and from a transition to an output place. Places contain 'tokens', indicating the availability of the corresponding entity, while arcs have a weight, denoting the amount of tokens to consume from an input place or to produce to an output place. If the token levels of all input places of a transition fulfill the requirement of (i.e. are equal to or higher than) the weights of the respective arcs, the transition is enabled. Only enabled transitions can be executed, leading to transfer (consumption/production) of tokens between places. Note that if two (or more) enabled transitions share an input place, they may be in competition if available token levels do not allow simultaneous execution of both (or all). In our model, AXIN, β-catenin and the destruction complex with β-catenin bound, are each input places for two transitions (t3/t5, t6/t10 and t7/t8, respectively). The initial token levels and the arc weights are generally restricted to be integer values. However, to represent a lower firing rate of a transition (i.e. a rate-limiting step) a fractional arc weight is implemented.

Gene expression is modeled such that one arc goes from the gene-place to the transcriptional-transition, one arc goes from the transcriptional-transition to the gene-place, and one arc goes from the transcriptional-transition to the protein-place. Gene-places are initiated with 1 token and when the transcriptional-transition of a gene is enabled the token is produced both in the protein-place and in the gene-place itself. This way the token can be reused for another round of gene expression, reflecting the fact that the gene (DNA) is needed, but is not consumed during expression.

Active and Hyperactive Conditions in the Model

We modeled active and hyperactive signaling upon WNT stimulation and GSK3 inhibition, respectively, and used these conditions to validate the model with experimental data (see below). Inhibition of GSK3 inhibits formation of the destruction complex, which we interpret to be similar to oncogenic perturbations. Therefore, for modeling purposes, GSK3 inhibition was used to mimic hyperactive signaling. For GSK3 inhibition we varied the initial token level of GSK3, respectively, from 0 to 5. For WNT stimulation we varied the initial token level of WNT from 0 to 5 and removed the AXIN2 feedback (the arc weight from t11 to AXIN was set to 0). The experimentally validated model was used to predict the level of β-catenin stabilization with the AXIN2 negative feedback upon WNT stimulation and APC inactivating mutations, respectively. Upon WNT stimulation with the AXIN2 feedback we varied the initial token level of WNT (3, 4 and 5) and the arc weight from t11 to AXIN (0 (no feedback) and 0.15 (maximal feedback)). The maximal feedback of 0.15

was chosen based on the criteria that it should i) show a peak response and ii) return to basal level for all initial WNT token levels (3, 4 and 5). This arc weight represents a firing rate of three times every 20 steps. Thus, the simulation for each initial WNT token level produced two β-catenin stabilization curves (i.e. no feedback and maximal feedback). The area between these two curves was used to explain the spectra of β-catenin stabilizations at intermediate levels of *AXIN2* induction. APC mutants have decreased binding affinity to the other components of the destruction complex to different degrees. We implemented this by reducing the formation of the destruction complex i.e. the weight on the arc going from the complex-formation-transition (t5) to the destruction complex (production) was decreased to 0, 0.05, 0.1 and 0.2. In addition, we incorporated arcs going from the complex-formation-transition to the individual destruction complex components (i.e. AXIN1, APC, GSK3 and CK1) with arc weights of 1 minus the production-weight to equally decrease the consumption. The implemented arc weight of 0 represents no production of the destruction complex (i.e. a complete null mutation). The implemented fractional arc weights of 0.05, 0.1 and 0.2 represent a production of the destruction complex once every 20, 10 and 5 steps, respectively.

Simulations

The model was simulated with maximally parallel execution, cf. our previous work [47], where the maximum possible number of enabled transitions are executed at each simulation step. This mimics the behavior in the cell, where typically many interactions happen at the same time. Two or more transitions can compete over one input place, as mentioned above. If this place only contains enough tokens to enable one of the transitions, but not both, a conflict occurs which is resolved by randomly drawing one of the competing transitions to execute. This makes the simulations non-deterministic.

For each condition we simulated the total β-catenin token levels, i.e. free β-catenin and β-catenin bound to the destruction complex or TCF/LEF, respectively, over 100 steps repeated 100 times. To account for variations in token levels due to the non-deterministic nature of the model, the mean and standard deviation of the β-catenin token levels over the 100 simulations were calculated for each step. These 100 steps represent the (early) time scale of β-catenin accumulation and the final token count represents the stabilized β-catenin level measured in experiments. The simulation steps describe the sequence of events and should not be linearly translated to time units. Similarly, the token level is a coarse-grained quantitative representation of actual protein levels and should not be linearly translated to a concentration. Instead, for analysis of the simulations we observe relative differences of β-catenin token levels over steps between simulations (i.e. different conditions and dosages). To validate the model we compared the relative β-catenin token levels predicted by our model simulations to the relative Wnt-pathway activities measured in the experiment (see below), where we distinguish between 'low', 'moderate' and 'high' levels. A Python script was written to run the simulations and is available together with the model in pnml format via http://www.ibi.vu.nl/downloads/WNTmodel/.

Cell Lines

HEK293T^{WOO} (WNT OFF/ON) cells were generated by transfecting HEK293T cells with a 7xTcf-FFluc//SV40-Puro^{R} (7TFP) reporter plasmid (a gift from Christophe Fuerer, [67]). Following puromycin selection to obtain stable integrants, individual clones were assessed for their response to Wnt-pathway activation. The clone with the highest dynamic range was used for the experiments depicted in Figs 3 and 4.

Cell Culture and Stimulation

HEK293T^{WOO} cells were cultured in Dulbecco's Modified Eagle Medium: Nutrient Mixture F-12 (DMEM/F12) supplemented with 10% FCS and 1% Penicillin/Streptomycin (GIBCO, Life Technologies) in 5% CO_2 at 37°C. These cells respond to activation of the Wnt/β-catenin signaling pathway by expressing firefly luciferase, since the firefly luciferase in the 7TFP construct is driven by the 7xTcf promoter, which contains 7 repeats of the TCF/LEF transcription response element. Cells were plated the day prior to stimulation in a 96 well-plate at a density of 20.000 cells per well. Cells were stimulated with different concentrations (10–200 ng/ml) of purified Wnt3a protein (RnD) dissolved in 0.1% BSA in PBS, or with different concentrations (750 nM-6 μM) CHIR99021 (BioVision) dissolved in DMSO, for different amounts of time (1–24 hours). At the indicated time points following stimulation, cells were lysed in 20 μl of Passive Lysis Buffer (Promega) and cell lysate from the same experiment was used for both the luciferase assay (3 wells per condition) and Western blot analysis (the remainder of the 3 wells, pooled per lane).

Western Blot Analysis

Protein concentration was measured using the Pierce BCA Protein Assay Kit (Thermo Fisher Scientific). Equal amounts of protein were run on an 8% SDS-PAGE gel. Proteins were transferred to a nitrocellulose membrane (Bio-Rad) and blocked with TBS Odyssey Blocking Buffer (LI-COR Biosciences, diluted 1:1 in TBS prior to use). Primary antibodies directed against active β-catenin (Cat# 8814S, Cell Signaling, 1:1000), total β-catenin (Cat# 610153, BD Biosciences, 1:2000) and α-Tubulin (Cat# T9026, Sigma-Aldrich, 1:500) were diluted in blocking buffer supplemented with 0.1% Tween-20 (TBS-T). Staining was performed overnight at 4°C. Membranes were washed in TBS-T followed by incubation with secondary antibodies (IRDye 680LT (Cat# 926–68021) or IRDye 800CW (Cat# 926–32212) (LI-COR), 1:20000 in TBS-T) for 2 hours. Membranes were washed in TBS-T and incubated in TBS prior to scanning at 700 nm and 800 nm using an Odyssey Fc (LI-COR Biosciences). Image Studio™ Lite 4.0 software (LI-COR Biosciences) was used to quantify relative protein levels. Background correction was performed according to the manufacturer's instructions (median of pixels, top/bottom border width of 3).

Luciferase Assay

To measure the activity of firefly luciferase (and hence Wnt-pathway activity), 10 μl of cell lysate was transferred to a black 96-well Optiplate (Perkin Elmer). The SpectraMax L Microplate Luminometer was used to inject 50 μl Luciferase Assay Reagent II (Promega) per well followed by measurement of firefly luciferase activity.

ACKNOWLEDGMENTS

We thank Vivienne Woo for helping to establish and characterize the HEK293T 7TCF reporter cell line.

AUTHOR CONTRIBUTIONS

Conceived and designed the experiments: AJ NH FV MJS JH RvA KAF. Performed the experiments: AJ NH. Analyzed the data: AJ NH FV MJS JH RvA KAF. Contributed reagents/materials/analysis tools: AJ NH JH RvA KAF. Wrote the paper: AJ NH JH RvA KAF.

REFERENCES

1. Clevers H, Nusse R. Wnt/β-catenin Signaling and Disease. Cell. 2012;149: 1192–205. pmid:22682243
2. Cadigan KM, Peifer M. Wnt Signaling from Development to Disease: Insights from Model Systems. Cold Spring Harbor perspectives in biology. 2009;1: a002881. pmid:20066091
3. Henderson BR, Fagotto F. The ins and outs of APC and β-catenin nuclear transport. EMBO Rep. 2002;3: 834–9. pmid:12223464
4. Mosimann C, Hausmann G, Basler K. β-catenin hits chromatin: regulation of Wnt target gene activation. Nature reviews Molecular cell biology. 2009;10: 276–86. pmid:19305417
5. Stamos JL, Weis WI. The β-catenin Destruction Complex. Cold Spring Harbor perspectives in biology. 2013;5: a007898. pmid:23169527
6. Amit S, Hatzubai A, Birman Y, Andersen JS, Ben-Shushan E, Mann M, et al. Axin-mediated CKI phosphorylation of β-catenin at Ser 45: a molecular switch for the Wnt pathway. Genes & development. 2002;16: 1066–76.
7. Ikeda S, Kishida S, Yamamoto H, Murai H, Koyama S, Kikuchi A. Axin, a negative regulator of the Wnt signaling pathway, forms a complex with GSK-3β and β-catenin and promotes GSK-3β-dependent phosphorylation of β-catenin. EMBO J. 1998;17: 1371–84. pmid:9482734
8. Aberle H, Bauer A, Stappert J, Kispert A, Kemler R. β-catenin is a target for the ubiquitin–proteasome pathway. EMBO J. 1997;16: 3797–804. pmid:9233789
9. Bhanot P, Brink M, Samos CH, Hsieh J-C, Wang Y, Macke JM, et al. A new member of the frizzled family from Drosophila functions

as a Wingless receptor. Nature. 1996;382: 225–30. pmid:8717036

10. Tamai K, Semenov M, Kato Y, Spokony R, Liu C, Katsuyama Y, et al. LDL-receptor-related proteins in Wnt signal transduction. Nature. 2000;407: 530–5. pmid:11029007
11. Schwarz-Romond T, Metcalfe C, Bienz M. Dynamic recruitment of axin by Dishevelled protein assemblies. Journal of cell science. 2007;120: 2402–12. pmid:17606995
12. Bilic J, Huang Y-L, Davidson G, Zimmermann T, Cruciat C-M, Bienz M, et al. Wnt Induces LRP6 SIgnalosomes and Promotes Dishevelled-Dependent LRP6 Phosphorylation. Science. 2007;316: 1619–22. pmid:17569865
13. Li VS, Ng SS, Boersema PJ, Low TY, Karthaus WR, Gerlach JP, et al. Wnt Signaling through Inhibition of β-catenin Degradation in an Intact Axin1 Complex. Cell. 2012;149: 1245–56. pmid:22682247
14. Behrens J, von Kries JP, Kühl M, Bruhn L, Wedlich D, Grosschedl R, et al. Functional interaction of β-catenin with the transcription factor LEF-1. Nature. 1996;382: 638–42. pmid:8757136
15. Nusse R. Howard Hughes Medical Institute and the Department of Developmental Biology at Stanford University, California, USA; 2016. Available: http://web.stanford.edu/group/nusselab/cgi-bin/wnt/.
16. Buchert M, Athineos D, Abud HE, Burke ZD, Faux MC, Samuel MS, et al. Genetic Dissection of Differential Signaling Threshold Requirements for the Wnt/β-catenin Pathway In Vivo. PLoS genetics. 2010;6: e1000816. pmid:20084116
17. Lustig B, Jerchow B, Sachs M, Weiler S, Pietsch T, Karsten U, et al. Negative Feedback Loop of Wnt Signaling through Upregulation of Conductin/Axin2 in Colorectal and Liver Tumors. Molecular and cellular biology. 2002;22: 1184–93. pmid:11809809
18. Jho Eh, Zhang T, Domon C, Joo CK, Freund JN, Costantini F. Wnt/β-Catenin/Tcf Signaling Induces the Transcription of Axin2, a Negative Regulator of the Signaling Pathway. Molecular and cellular biology. 2002;22: 1172–83. pmid:11809808
19. Behrens J, Jerchow B-A, Würtele M, Grimm J, Asbrand C, Wirtz R, et al. Functional Interaction of an Axin Homolog, Conductin,

with β-Catenin, APC, and GSK3β. Science. 1998;280: 596–99. pmid:9554852

20. Chia IV, Costantini F. Mouse Axin and Axin2/Conductin Proteins Are Functionally Equivalent In Vivo. Molecular and cellular biology. 2005;25: 4371–6. pmid:15899843
21. Zeng L, Fagotto F, Zhang T, Hsu W, Vasicek TJ, Perry WL, et al. The Mouse Fused Locus Encodes Axin, an Inhibitor of the Wnt Signaling Pathway That Regulates Embryonic Axis Formation. Cell. 1997;90: 181–92. pmid:9230313
22. Leung JY, Kolligs FT, Wu R, Zhai Y, Kuick R, Hanash S, et al. Activation of AXIN2 expression by β-catenin-T cell factor. A feedback repressor pathway regulating Wnt signaling. The Journal of biological chemistry. 2002;277: 21657–65. pmid:11940574
23. Aulehla A, Herrmann BG. Segmentation in vertebrates: clock and gradient finally joined. Genes & development. 2004;18: 2060–7.
24. MacDonald BT, Tamai K, He X. Wnt/β-catenin signaling: components, mechanisms, and diseases. Developmental cell. 2009;17: 9–26. pmid:19619488
25. Polakis P. Wnt Signaling in Cancer. Cold Spring Harbor perspectives in biology. 2012;4: a008052. pmid:22438566
26. Anastas JN, Moon RT. WNT signalling pathways as therapeutic targets in cancer. Nature reviews Cancer. 2013;13: 11–26. pmid:23258168
27. Albuquerque C, Bakker ER, van Veelen W, Smits R. Colorectal cancers choosing sides. Biochimica et biophysica acta. 2011;1816: 219–31. pmid:21855610
28. Fearon ER. Molecular Genetics of Colorectal Cancer. Annual review of pathology. 2011;6: 479–507. pmid:21090969
29. Satoh S, Daigo Y, Furukawa Y, Kato T, Miwa N, Nishiwaki T, et al. AXIN1 mutations in hepatocellular carcinomas, and growth suppression in cancer cells by virus-mediated transfer of AXIN1. Nat Genet. 2000;24: 245–50. pmid:10700176
30. Liu W, Dong X, Mai M, Seelan RS, Taniguchi K, Krishnadath KK, et al. Mutations in AXIN2 cause colorectal cancer with defective mismatch repair by activating β-catenin/TCF signalling. Nat Genet. 2000;26: 146–7. pmid:11017067

31. Mazzoni SM, Fearon ER. AXIN1 and AXIN2 variants in gastrointestinal cancers. Cancer letters. 2014;355: 1–8. pmid:25236910
32. Morin PJ, Sparks AB, Korinek V, Barker N, Clevers H, Vogelstein B, et al. Activation of β-Catenin–Tcf Signaling in Colon Cancer by Mutations in β-Catenin or APC. Science. 1997;275: 1787–90. pmid:9065402
33. Rubinfeld B, Robbins P, El-Gamil M, Albert I, Porfiri E, Polakis P. Stabilization of β-Catenin by Genetic Defects in Melanoma Cell Lines. Science. 1997;275: 1790–2. pmid:9065403
34. Klaus A, Birchmeier W. Wnt signalling and its impact on development and cancer. Nature reviews Cancer. 2008;8: 387–98. pmid:18432252
35. Ying QL, Wray J, Nichols J, Batlle-Morera L, Doble B, Woodgett J, et al. The ground state of embryonic stem cell self-renewal. Nature. 2008;453: 519–23. pmid:18497825
36. Li Y, Zhang Q, Yin X, Yang W, Du Y, Hou P, et al. Generation of iPSCs from mouse fibroblasts with a single gene, Oct4, and small molecules. Cell research. 2011;21: 196–204. pmid:20956998
37. Lloyd-Lewis B, Fletcher AG, Dale TC, Byrne HM. Toward a quantitative understanding of the Wnt/β-catenin pathway through simulation and experiment. Wiley interdisciplinary reviews Systems biology and medicine. 2013;5: 391–407. pmid:23554326
38. Kofahl B, Wolf J. Mathematical modelling of Wnt/β-catenin signalling. Biochem Soc Trans. 2010;38(5): 1281–5. pmid:20863299
39. Lee E, Salic A, Krüger R, Heinrich R, Kirschner MW. The Roles of APC and Axin Derived from Experimental and Theoretical Analysis of the Wnt Pathway. PLoS biology. 2003;1: E10. pmid:14551908
40. Cho K-H, Baek S, Sung M-H. Wnt pathway mutations selected by optimal β-catenin signaling for tumorigenesis. FEBS letters. 2006;580(15): 3665–70. pmid:16764864
41. Wawra C, Kuhl M, Kestler HA. Extended analyses of the Wnt/β-catenin pathway: robustness and oscillatory behaviour. FEBS letters. 2007;581(21): 4043–8. pmid:17678900

42. Kogan Y, Halevi-Tobias Karin E, Hochman G, Baczmanska Anna K, Leyns L, Agur Z. A new validated mathematical model of the Wnt signalling pathway predicts effective combinational therapy by sFRP and Dkk. Biochemical Journal. 2012;444(1): 115–25. pmid:22356261
43. Benary U, Kofahl B, Hecht A, Wolf J. Modeling Wnt/beta-Catenin Target Gene Expression in APC and Wnt Gradients Under Wild Type and Mutant Conditions. Frontiers in physiology. 2013;4: 21. pmid:23508686
44. van Leeuwen IM, Byrne HM, Jensen OE, King JR. Elucidating the interactions between the adhesive and transcriptional functions of β-catenin in normal and cancerous cells. Journal of theoretical biology. 2007;247(1): 77–102. pmid:17382967
45. Tan CW, Gardiner BS, Hirokawa Y, Layton MJ, Smith DW, Burgess AW. Wnt Signalling Pathway Parameters for Mammalian Cells. PloS one. 2012;7: e31882. pmid:22363759
46. Bonzanni N, Garg A, Feenstra KA, Schutte J, Kinston S, Miranda-Saavedra D, et al. Hard-wired heterogeneity in blood stem cells revealed using a dynamic regulatory network model. Bioinformatics. 2013;29: i80–8. pmid:23813012
47. Bonzanni N, Krepska E, Feenstra KA, Fokkink W, Kielmann T, Bal H, et al. Executing multicellular differentiation: quantitative predictive modelling of C.elegans vulval development. Bioinformatics. 2009;25: 2049–56. pmid:19515963
48. Krepska E, Bonzanni, N, Feenstra, A, Fokkink, W, Kielmann, T, Bal, H, Heringa, J. Design Issues for Qualitative Modelling of Biological Cells with Petri Nets. Proceedings of the Formal Methods in Systems Biology 2008, Vol 5054 of LNBI, Springer, Cambridge, UK. 2008: 48–62.
49. Petri CA. Kommunikation mit Automaten. PhD Thesis, Technische Universität Darmstadt, Bonn, Germany. 1962.
50. Reisig CAR, G. Lectures on Petri Nets I: Basic Models, Vol. 1491 and 1492 of LNCS. Springer, Berlin, Germany. 1998.
51. de la Roche M, Worm J, Bienz M. The function of BCL9 in Wnt/beta-catenin signaling and colorectal cancer cells. BMC Cancer. 2008;8: 199. pmid:18627596

52. Ruths D, Muller M, Tseng J-T, Nakhleh L, Ram PT. The Signaling Petri Net-Based Simulator: A Non-Parametric Strategy for Characterizing the Dynamics of Cell-Specific SIgnaling Networks. PloS CB. 2008;4: e1000005.
53. Jamieson C, Sharma M, Henderson BR. Targeting the β-catenin nuclear transport pathway in cancer. Seminars in Cancer Biology. 2014;27: 20–9. pmid:24820952
54. Harris TJC, Peifer M. Decisions, decisions: β-catenin chooses between adhesion and transcription. Trends Cell Biol. 2005;15: 234–7. pmid:15866026
55. Molenaar M, van de Wetering M, Oosterwegel M, Peterson-Maduro J, Godsave S, Vladimir K, et al. XTcf-3 Transcription Factor Mediates β-Catenin-Induced Axis Formation in Xenopus Embryos. Cell. 1996;86: 391–9. pmid:8756721
56. Veeman MT, Slusarski DC, Kaykas A, Louie SH, Moon RT. Zebrafish Prickle, a Modulator of Noncanonical Wnt/Fz Signaling, Regulates Gastrulation Movements. Current Biology. 2003;13: 680–5. pmid:12699626
57. van de Wetering M, Cavallo R, Dooijes D, van Beest M, van Es J, Loureiro J, et al. Armadillo Coactivates Transcription Driven by Product of the Drosophila Segment Polarity Gene dTCF. Cell. 1997;88: 789–99. pmid:9118222
58. Ring DB, Johnson KW, Henriksen EJ, Nuss JM, Goff D, Kinnick TR, et al. Selective GLycogen Synthase Kinase 3 Inhibitors Potentiate Insulin Activation of Glucose Transport and Utilization In Vitro and In Vivo. Diabetes. 2003;52: 588–95. pmid:12606497
59. Verkaar F, Cadigan KM, van Amerongen R. Celebrating 30 Years of Wnt Signaling. Science signaling. 2012;5: mr2. pmid:23233527
60. Davidson G, Wu W, Shen J, Bilic J, Fenger U, Stannek P, et al. Casein kinase 1γ couples Wnt receptor activation to cytoplasmic signal transduction. Nature. 2005;438: 867–72. pmid:16341016
61. Zeng X, Tamai K, Doble B, Li S, Huang H, Habas R, et al. A dual-kinase mechanism for Wnt co-receptor phosphorylation and activation. Nature. 2005;438: 873–7. pmid:16341017

62. Naik S, Piwnica-Worms D. Real-time imaging of β-catenin dynamics in cells and living mice. PNAS. 2007;104:17465–70. pmid:17954915
63. Yokoyama N, Yin D, Malbon CC. Abundance, complexation, and trafficking of Wnt/β-catenin signaling elements in response to Wnt3a. Journal of molecular signaling. 2007;2:11. pmid:17961224
64. Verkaar F, Blankesteijn WM, Smits JF, Zaman GJ. β-Galactosidase enzyme fragment complementation for the measurement of Wnt/β-catenin signaling. FASEB journal: official publication of the Federation of American Societies for Experimental Biology. 2010;24: 1205–17.
65. Gonzalez A, Manosalva I, Liu T, Kageyama R. Control of *Hes7* expression by Tbx6, the Wnt pathway and the chemical Gsk3 inhibitor LiCl in the mouse segmentation clock. PloS one. 2013;8(1): e53323. pmid:23326414
66. Suriben R, Fisher DA, Cheyette BN. Dact1 presomitic mesoderm expression oscillates in phase with Axin2 in the somitogenesis clock of mice. Dev Dyn. 2006;235(11): 3177–83. pmid:17013874
67. Fuerer C, Roel N. Lentiviral Vectors to Probe and Manipulate the Wnt Signaling Pathway. PloS one. 2010;5: e9370. pmid:20186325

9 A PETRI NET MODEL OF GRANULOMATOUS INFLAMMATION: IMPLICATIONS FOR IL-10 MEDIATED CONTROL OF LEISHMANIA DONOVANI INFECTION

Luca Albergante[1], Jon Timmis[1], Lynette Beattie[2], Paul M. Kaye[2]

[1] Department of Computer Science and Department of Electronics, University of York, York, United Kingdom
[2] Center for Immunology and Infection, Department of Biology and Hull York Medical School, University of York, York, United Kingdom

ABSTRACT

Experimental visceral leishmaniasis, caused by infection of mice with the protozoan parasite *Leishmania donovani*, is characterized by focal accumulation of inflammatory cells in the liver, forming discrete "granulomas" within which the parasite is eventually eliminated. To shed new light on fundamental aspects of granuloma formation and function, we have developed an *in silico* Petri net model that simulates hepatic granuloma development throughout the course of infection. The model was extensively validated by comparison with data derived from experimental studies in mice, and the model robustness was assessed by a sensitivity analysis. The model recapitulated the progression of disease as seen during experimental infection and also faithfully predicted many of the changes in cellular composition seen within granulomas over time. By conducting *in silico* experiments, we have identified a previously unappreciated level of inter-granuloma diversity in terms of the development of anti-leishmanial activity. Furthermore, by simulating the impact of IL-10 gene deficiency in a variety of lymphocyte and myeloid cell populations, our data suggest a dominant local regulatory role for IL-10 produced by infected Kupffer cells at the core of the granuloma.

INTRODUCTION

Human visceral leishmaniasis (HVL or Kala azar) is the most severe form of the tropical disease leishmaniasis, and is caused by infection with the protozoan parasites *Leishmania donovani* or *L. infantum* [1]. HVL is a systemic disease, with the intracellular (amastigote) stage of the parasite found predominantly, but not exclusively, in mononuclear phagocytes of the spleen, bone marrow and liver of infected individuals. In the absence of treatment, HVL is usually fatal, with ~40,000 deaths reported annually [2]. However, an estimated 90% of infections do not result in clinical disease. Evidence from epidemiological studies of HIV- *Leishmania* co- infection and from experimental studies indicate an important role for cellular immune mechanisms in controlling sub-clinical infection [3]. Evidence from studies in humans, from murine models of experimental visceral leishmaniasis (EVL) and from the study of canine visceral leishmaniasis (CVL) all point to an important role for T cell-derived cytokines in maintaining the balance of immunity during subclinical disease [4]. Furthermore, in each of these settings, there is evidence to suggest that granulomatous inflammation provides a histopathologic correlate of protective immunity [5]–[7].

The granuloma represents one of the defining tissue responses associated with chronic inflammation following a variety of microbial (e.g. *Schistosoma*, *Mycobacterium*, *Leishmania*) and non-infectious (e.g. autoimmune, prosthetics) insults. Although generally characterized by the focal accumulation of monocytes and T cells, recent data have indicated that a broad range of leucocytes can be found within these specialized microenvironments, including B cells, NK cells, NKT cells, T cells and dendritic cells. In addition, in some but not all cases, granulomas may progress to caseation, most commonly in tuberculosis, whereby neutrophils are seen in high abundance [8]–[12]. In EVL, granuloma formation has been shown to be dependent upon multiple cytokines, with the elimination of intracellular *Leishmania* governed by the balance of cytokines that are able to activate (e.g. IFNγ) or deactivate (e.g. IL-10) local macrophage anti-leishmanial activity [4], [5]. However, the relative functional contribution of different cell types producing similar cytokines, and whether these cells/cytokines exert their effects locally or indirectly (e.g. through upstream regulatory pathways operating outside the granuloma environment) remain as important but unanswered questions.

IL-10 is the best studied of the cytokines that have an inhibitory effect on macrophage leishmanicidal activity and serum IL-10 represents a biomarker of disease severity [13]. The current literature suggests multiple pathways in which IL-10 may operate [14], [15]. For example, expression of *Nos2* in macrophages, a key event in the generation of the leishmanicidal effector molecule nitric oxide, is directly inhibited by IL-10 [16]. Such inhibition may occur through autocrine signaling, with IL-10 being produced by macrophages after direct recognition of parasites or following immune complex binding to macrophage Fc receptors [17], [18]. Alternatively, IL-10 may indirectly regulate effector T cell differentiation and/or activation, e.g. by influencing the ability of macrophages and/or dendritic cells to stimulate T cell IFNγ production [19]. IL-10-producing DCs have been described in chronic EVL [20], [21] and $CD4^+$T cells which produce IL-10 (including natural Tregs, Tr-1 and $CD4^+$ Th1 cells) have all been described in various forms of leishmaniasis in mouse and man [20], [22]–[28]. Given the potentially tissue damaging effects of uncontrolled inflammation, multiple cell populations within the granuloma may also develop self-regulating capacity, again with IL-10 as a component of this response. Thus, $CD4^+IFN\gamma^+$ Th1 cells and NK cells, which produce cytokines directing classical macrophage activation in the early stages of EVL, develop an IL-10-dependent immunoregulatory function as disease progresses [28], [29].

What has remained a considerable experimental challenge, however, has been to determine which of these cellular sources of IL-10 is functionally most potent in the local tissue microenvironment, which cells respond to the IL-10 signals and how this dynamic balance of immune effector and regulatory function evolves throughout the course of infection. In HVL, the invasive nature of the methods needed to address these questions is beyond what is practically or ethically achievable, and even in EVL, current methodology is still wanting. Nevertheless, there is an imperative to more fully understand these and related issues, if the information derived from past and future studies are to be effectively translated into new therapeutic approaches around this and other cytokines [30].

In silico models do not share the same experimental limits of *in vivo* models and allow more direct control on multiple experimental conditions. Computational and mathematical models of the cellular response to granulomatous infection have been developed previously in the context of tuberculosis [31]–[35], sarcoidosis [36] and leishmaniasis [37], but they generally account only for a limited number of leukocyte populations. For example, a recent study used a coloured Petri net approach to model the innate macrophage granuloma that forms during infection of zebrafish with *Mycobacterium* [38]. Here, we describe a stochastic Petri net model of granulomatous inflammation in the liver of mice infected with *L. donovani*, which faithfully reproduces many of the characteristics of experimental infection. Petri nets provide a visual-aided network-oriented modeling process, which simplifies their development and provides visual feedback affording interpretation by a broad audience. Moreover, the underlying mathematical structure of the model can be used to perform a structural validation, which is independent from the actual simulations. This validation assesses different properties of the model and can be used to detect entities that do not interact as intended or actions that will never be performed. These advantages have made stochastic Petri nets popular for the development of systems biology models [38], [39].

We have applied this methodology to gain a greater insight into the potential importance of macrophage deactivation in regulating the outcome of EVL, using this model to simulate the importance of macrophage deactivation mediated through IL-10. Our results indicate that local leishmanicidal activity is most strongly influenced through the action of IL-10 produced by infected Kupffer cells themselves rather than by infiltrating leucocytes. These results provide new insight into how effector mechanisms may be regulated within the granuloma, and a new tool to interpret how pharmacologic interventions may operate.

RESULTS/DISCUSSION

The Essential Features of Granulomatous Inflammation can be reproduced *in silico*

Given the limited modeling work available in the context of EVL, we opted for a high-level population dynamics stochastic Petri net model that characterized many of the entities that are believed to be relevant for the progression of the disease. Figure 1 presents a schematic representation of the model dynamics. The Petri net files are available for use in Snoopy and as a SBML compliant .xml file. We chose to model granulomas as self-contained independently functioning units, i.e. without migration of cells or cytokine from one granuloma to another. Although we acknowledge that such events may occur, current experimental approaches in mice do not allow for these processes to be quantified. We defined a "baseline model" characterized by initial infection in resident Kupffer cells and a set of specific assumptions governing the behavior and inter-relationships between five cytokines (IL-2, IL-4, IL-10, IL-12 and IFNγ), a variety of effector/regulatory $CD4^+$ and $CD8^+$ T cell populations, NK and NKT cells and inflammatory monocytes/DC. Our baseline model does not include other populations of cells identified within granulomas but with less well-established roles in granuloma biology (e.g. B cells; [40]). Each cytokine was also associated with an 'effectiveness' parameter. This permits the same concentration of different cytokines to have different effects on cells, reflecting differences in specific activity, differences in sensitivity of signal transduction pathways and/or different numbers of receptors.

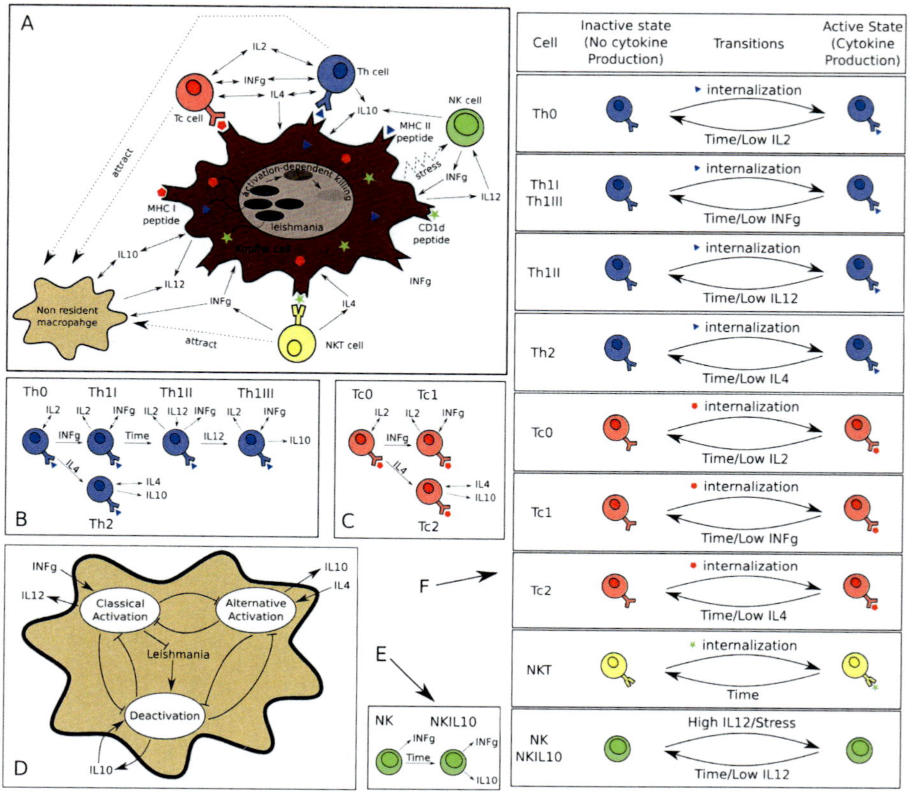

Figure 1: Schematics of the model dynamics.

(**A**) High-level depiction of the interactions among the entities modeled. (**B**) Differentiation of helper T cells. Labels on arrows indicate the conditions for differentiation. Arrows pointing to/originating from a cytokine name indicate that the cytokine is produced/consumed by the cell. (**C**) Differentiation of cytotoxic T cells. Arrow conventions as in panel B. (**D**) Dynamics of activation types in macrophages. *Leishmania* interactions are restricted to Kupffer cells only. Note how different cytokines promote different types of activation and how different types of activation result in the production of different cytokines. (**E**) Differentiation of NK cells. Arrow conventions as in panel B. (**F**) Transitions from/to inactive to/from active states for the modeled leukocytes. This representation stresses the complexity of the model and the degree of interaction among the different cell populations; see Section 1 of Supplementary Information for a more detailed description.

As expected from the central limit theorem [41], the variability in simulated cell number depends on the number of simulations. Therefore, we performed experiments varying the number of independent granulomas. Although the infected liver contains an estimated 500,000 granulomas (based on counting the number of granulomas per unit volume in 2-photon 3D tissue images; data not shown), computational analyses suggested that 50 granulomas for each simulation were sufficient to generate a simulated total tissue parasite burden similar to that observed *in vivo* both in terms of mean and standard deviation (Figure 2A). Past studies on granulomatous inflammation have modeled granulomas as self-sustained microenvironments [34]. While different rationales for this approach exist, no clear biological evidence to support this view is available. Our data indicate that sampling a small subset of independent granulomas is sufficient to characterize the entire tissue response during infection. Although the qualitative variation of parasite burden over time reported by multiple investigators is similar, the absolute parasite burden may vary for a number of factors (e.g. parasite strain, animal husbandry, mouse strain etc.). Therefore, although to validate our model we choose a set of reference data [42], we compared the qualitative characteristics of the data only, and not the absolute quantitative values obtained. While this approach introduces simplifications over the *in vivo* situation, our results indicate that it provides a simple and manageable way to study the phenomenon of parasite killing within granulomas at an organ level.

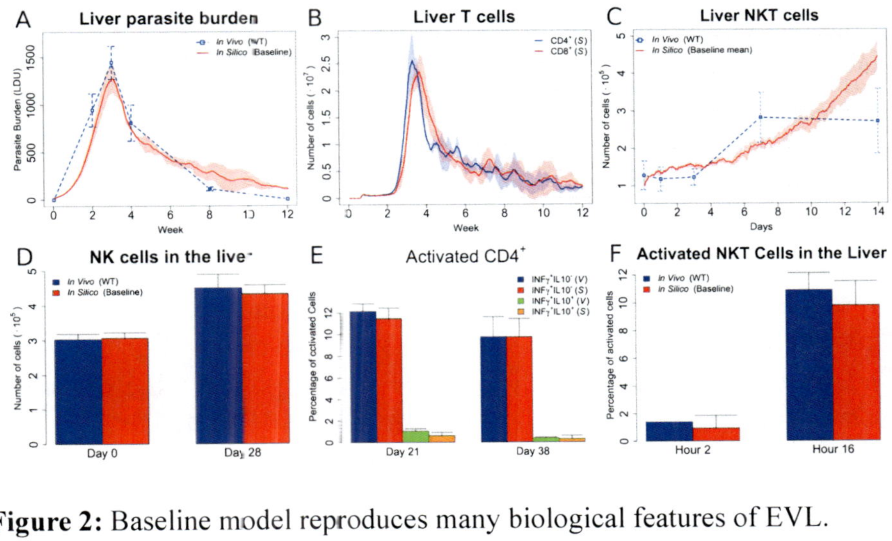

Figure 2: Baseline model reproduces many biological features of EVL.

In all the panels, means and standard deviation are reported. Standard deviation is indicated by error bars or shaded areas (**A**) Organ level parasite burden (compared with [58]). (**B**) Number of $CD4^+$ and $CD8^+$ T cells over the course of infection of *in silico* data. The same plotting convention as panel A is used. (**C**) Number of NKT cells (compared with [59]). The same plotting conventions are used as in panel A. (**D**) **NK** cell number (compared with [29]). (**E**) Percentage of activated $CD4^+$ T cells (compared with unpublished data). (V) and (S) indicate *in vivo* and *in silico*, respectively. (**F**) Percentage of activated NKT cells (compared with [59] and [60]).

To validate our model, we first ran simulations in which key parameters of immune function were measured. Our baseline model produced data that displayed good agreement with the published experimental data, in terms of the number of granuloma $CD4^+$ and $CD8^+$ T cells (Figure 2B); the number of NK cells (Figure 2D); the percentage of activated $CD4^+$ T cells with differing functional activity (Figure 2E) and the frequency of activated NKT cells (Figure 2F). Nevertheless, the model did not predict all parameters of granuloma composition with strict accuracy. For example, there was a disparity in the absolute number of NKT cells within *in silico* granulomas compared to that observed in vivo (Figure 2C). This disagreement is likely due to biological constraints absent from our model, and indicates the importance of additional experimental work. Nevertheless, statistical analysis supports the overall agreement between our simulations and experimental data points in the direction of robust modeling of the immune response.

In silico modeling provides insight into the dynamics of leucocyte dynamics during infection

Since our *in silico* model allows a detailed characterization of the many biological entities involved in the immune response, we decided to explore their dynamics during infection. The number of non-resident phagocytes (Figure 3A), $CD4^+IFN\gamma^+$ T cells (Figure 3B), activated NK cells (Figure 3C), and activated NKT cells (Figure 3F) closely follow the dynamics observed for parasite burden. The number of $CD4^+IFN\gamma^+IL\text{-}10^+$ T cells is very low when compared to $CD4^+IFN\gamma^+IL\text{-}10^-$ T cells in the initial stages of infection, but their numbers become similar at later times (Figure 3B), perhaps suggesting a connection between IL-10-producing Th1 cells and the low level persistence of infection. A striking difference in kinetics is evident when comparing the activation status of non-resident phagocytes (Figure 3D) with resident Kupffer cells (Figure 3E). While in Kupffer cells the presence of parasites promotes a very high level of deactivation, non-resident phagocytes are strongly activated. This observation suggests that limiting the capacity of *Leishmania* to deactivate Kupffer cells could have a strong impact on the immune response. Moreover, while non-resident macrophages become strongly polarized, classical activation and deactivation coexists in Kupffer cells, resulting in a more dynamic and unstable equilibrium. Note that due to the very low rates of inflow and death, the number of Kupffer cells is effectively stable over time (data not shown).

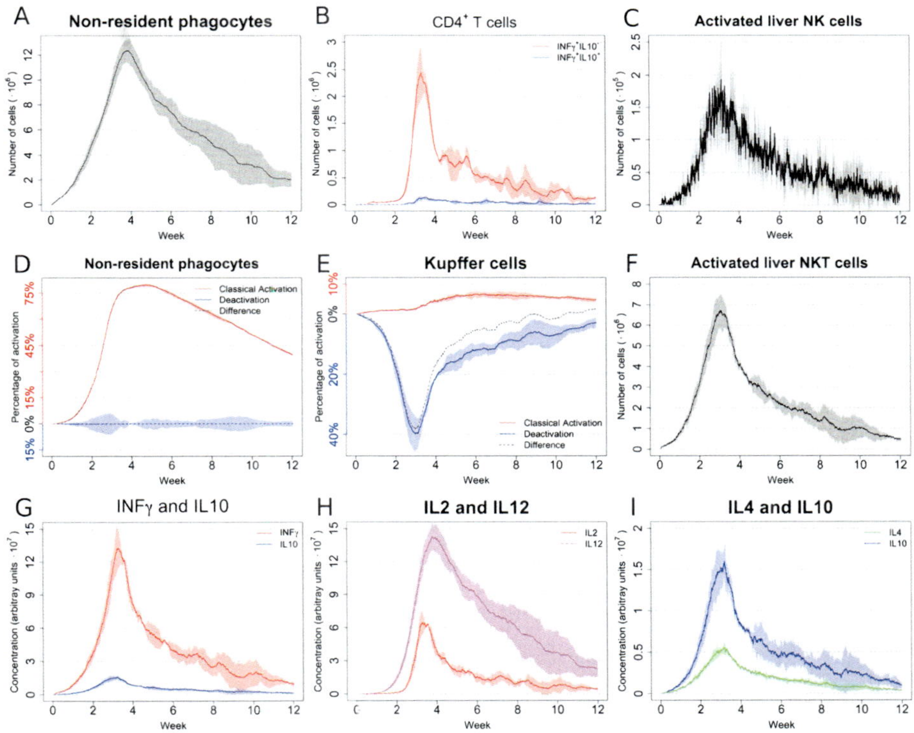

Figure 3: Baseline model allows the exploration of biological quantities difficult to access experimentally.

In all the panels, means and standard deviation (indicated by shaded area around the mean) are reported. All numbers are relative to cells in the liver associated with a granuloma microenvironment. (**A**) Number of granuloma-associated non-resident macrophages. (**B**) Number of differentiated Th1 cells. (**C**) Number of activated NK cells. (**D**) Level of activation and deactivation of non-resident macrophages. (**E**) Level of activation and deactivation of Kupffer cells. (**F**) Number of activated NKT cells. (**G**) Concentration of IFNγ and IL-10. (**H**) Concentration of IL-2and IL-12. (**I**) Concentration of IL-4 and IL-10.

Cytokines are effective only within a limited range. Unfortunately, accessing the concentration of cytokines in the granuloma microenvironment is experimentally beyond reach. Our data suggests that the concentration follows the parasite burden for all the modeled cytokines (Figure 3G–I). Notably, IL-10 concentration is much lower than IFNγ concentration over most of the time course of the infection (Figure 3G). As with the ratio of Th1 cells making IL-10 and those that do not (Figure 3B), the IFNγ: IL10 ratio decreases as peak parasite load is reduced and the rate of decay of liver parasite burden shallows off.

Sensitivity analysis

The various entities included in the model were extensively parameterized, where possible using data extracted directly from the literature or from our own unpublished results. However, other parameters result from modeling decisions and simplifications and were determined by fitting the data. We therefore performed a sensitivity analysis to assess the robustness of the model. Here, we briefly describe the main points elucidated by sensitivity analysis. Following established methodology [43], we sampled the parameter space using Latin hypercube sampling and studied the impact of each parameter on the parasite burden using Partial Rank Correlation Coefficients (PRCC). The effect of parameter variation was assessed on the parasite burden at different stages of the infection. As observed above, parasite burden correlates with most of the modeled aspects of the immune response. Hence, using parasite burden maximizes the information derived from the sensitivity analysis. Wherever possible, parameters were varied according to known biological variability. Additionally, given the stochastic nature of the model, a dummy parameter with no effect on the parasite burden was also included in the analysis. This expedient allowed us to disentangle the impact of the intrinsic variability of the model from the variability due to parameter variation.

The varying model parameters has different impacts on parasite burden. This was to be expected given the differences in the number of leukocytes within and affecting the granuloma microenvironment. Varying the reproduction rate of the parasite, the effectiveness of IFNγ or the production of NKT-derived IFNγ resulted in a strongly varied parasite burden. However, varying the effectiveness of IL-2, the effectiveness of IL-10 and the chemokinetic effect of T cells did not significantly affect parasite burden. Sensitivity analysis confirmed the importance of many of the parameters believed to be the most important in determining the outcome of infection, again supporting the robustness of the model. However, less obvious results were also observed, and various parameters have remarkably different effects on parasite burden at different stages of the infection. This result stresses the complex dynamics that underlie the immune response during EVL and indicates how a cell with exactly the same behavior can potentially have very different degrees of biological significance at different stages of the infection.

Individual granulomas display distinct dynamic behavior

Experimental data on parasite burden in mice is measured on a total organ basis (obtained from impression smears, limiting dilution analysis or quantitative PCR), with no experimental approaches being available to evaluate parasite number over time within individual granulomas. In contrast, our *in silico* model allows us to examine whether there is heterogeneity in parasite burden over time between individual granulomas. We observed that even under the same initial conditions (each granuloma seeded with 4 amastigotes), the peak parasite burden per granuloma varied greatly amongst individual granulomas (i.e. each represented by a single run of the simulation). More importantly, the dynamics of parasite burden displayed a remarkable variability between individual granulomas. Rather simple behaviors (granuloma G1: Figure 4A) coexisted with more complex ones (granuloma G2: Figure 4B). Notably, some granulomas (herein referred to as long-lasting) were characterized by an unexpected long-term equilibrium (granuloma G3; Figure 4C), with alternating high and low levels of parasite burden. Surprisingly, granuloma G1, though most effective at clearing parasites and maintaining effective control over recrudescence had the highest peak primary parasite load. This diversity in the parasite load is accompanied by a similar variation in the number of non-resident phagocytes (Figures 4D–F) and activated NKT cells (Figures 4G–I).

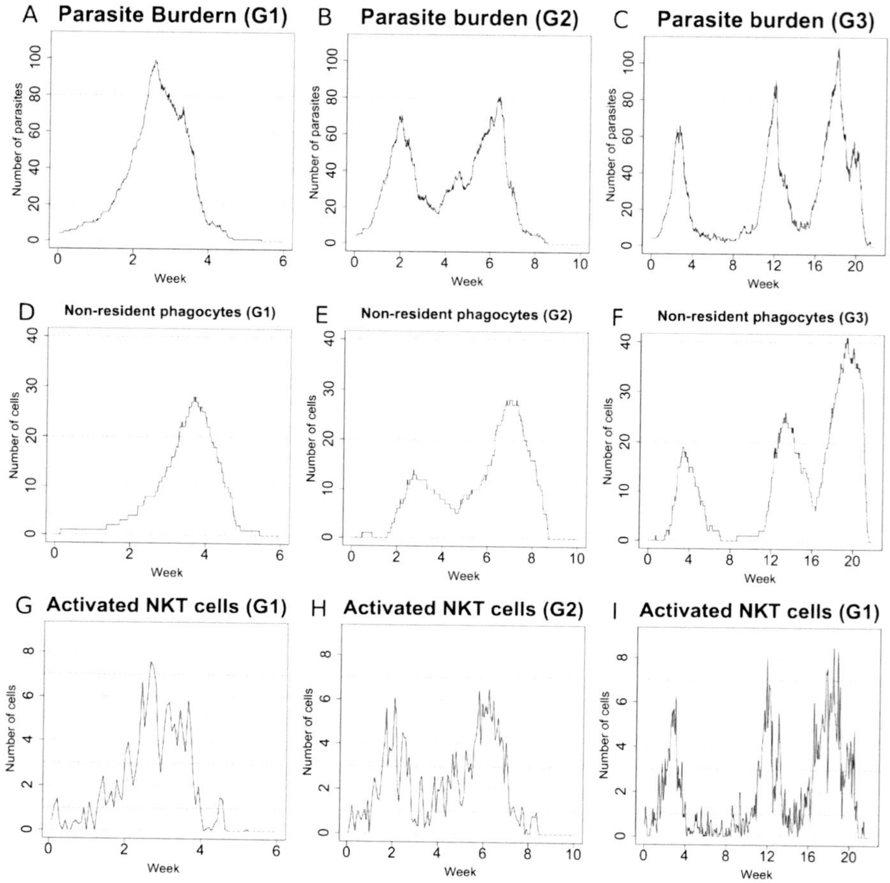

Figure 4: Sample behaviours of different *in silico* **granulomas: 1.**

Number of parasites (**A–C**), number of non-resident phagocytes (**D–F**) and number of activated NKT cells (**G–I**) in sample granulomas. Note how remarkable diversity is observed among the different granulomas, with rather simple dynamics (**G1**) coexisting with more complex ones (**G2**, **G3**) in the simulations. Total organ parasite load can be reflected by the aggregate results from 50 granulomas.

To gain further insights into possible contingencies that can drive the emergence of the different types of granulomas observed, we explored the dynamics of the resident and non-resident phagocytes, the relations between the different populations of Th1 cells and the concentration of cytokines. The levels of classical activation and deactivation of Kupffer cells were comparable in all three granulomas. However, it was notable that the most effective granuloma (G1) was able to reach a relatively high level of activation (~20%) and this was sustained past week 4 with negligible late deactivation (Figure 5A), whereas granulomas G2 and G3 took more time to reach maximal classical activation and the degree of classical KC activation fell more sharply after the primary peak of parasite load concomitant with a degree of deactivation (Figures 5B and 5C). The activation of non-resident macrophages follows a similar trend with a high level of activation reached in granuloma G1 by week 4 (Figure 5D), while granulomas G2 and G3 again did not reach the same level of classical activation in response to the primary peak of parasite load (Figures 5E and 5F). The number of $IFN\gamma^{+}IL\text{-}10^{-}$ T cells was comparable in all 3 granulomas considered (Figures 5G–H). However, $IFN\gamma^{+}IL10^{+}$ T cells were practically absent in granuloma G1 (Figure 5G), while these cells were present in moderately high numbers in granulomas G2 and G3 (Figures 5H and 5I). These findings further support a role for $IFN\gamma^{+}IL10^{+}$ T cells in the persistence of infection. Nevertheless, $IFN\gamma^{+}IL10^{+}$ T cells appear quite late in G3, suggesting that they are not the only factor contributing to delayed clearance. Finally, the cytokine concentration is related to the number of Th1 cells (Figures 5J–L), supporting the importance of T cells in the control of the local environment.

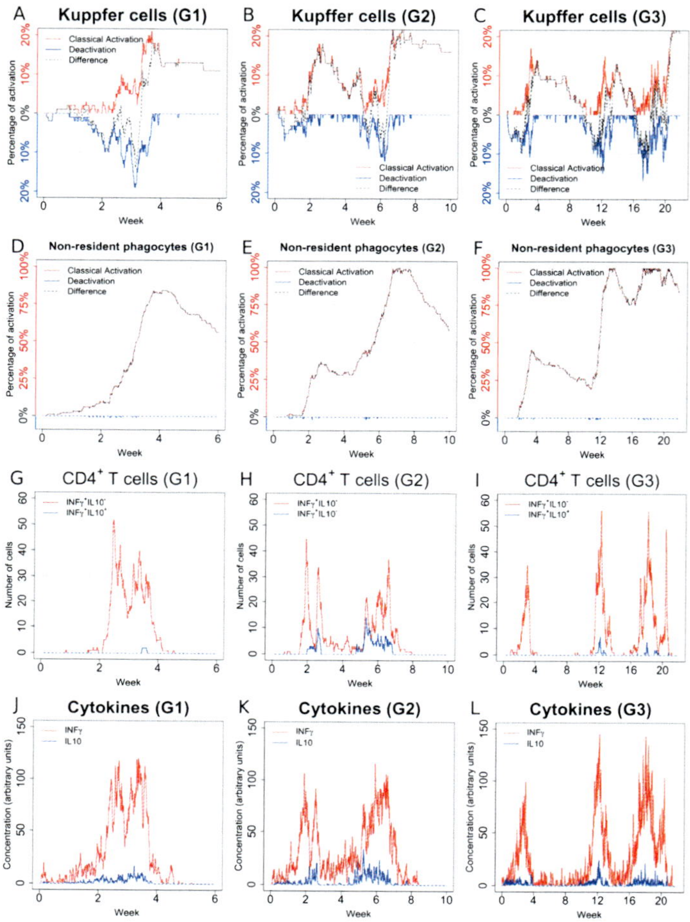

Figure 5: Sample behaviours of different *in silico* **granulomas: 2.**

Level of activation in Kupffer cells (**A–C**; classical activation, red; deactivation, blue; difference, dotted), level of activation in non-resident phagocytes (**D–F**; classical activation, red; deactivation, blue; difference, dotted), number of activated effector Th1 cells (**G–I**; IFNγ^+IL-10$^-$, red; IFNγ^+IL-10$^+$, blue), and cytokine concentration (**J–L**; IFNγ, red; IL-10, blue) in samples granulomas.

From a biological perspective, our results provide the first demonstration that local immune control within granulomas may be variable, with important implications for how the effector response is regulated. In particular, these results suggest that the local environment within the granuloma shapes the effector response and that granulomas may behave as autonomous units of immune function. Conceptually, this model of autonomous units of immunity is supported by recent data that suggests local antigen-specific re-stimulation is required for T cell effector function [44]. Additionally, our model suggests that a limited number of long-lasting granulomas, which would be difficult to detect with standard parasite counting techniques, may provide a reservoir for disease reactivation in murine models of T cell insufficiency [45] and this has implications for the immunological basis of long-term parasite persistence that warrant further exploration. Although we have not extensively investigated this point to date, the small sample of granulomas sampled suggests that those with highest initial peak parasite burden may actually be the most effective at controlling parasite load over the long term.

From a modeling perspective, the diversity of parasite loads seen in individual granulomas obtained in the simulations supports the power of stochastic models: the same Petri net is able to generate widely diverse parasite numbers in different granulomas over time. However, averaging these burdens leads to a quite characteristic (and mostly deterministic) "shape" for graphs of parasite burden determined at an organ level. The emergence of a definite trend from stochastic interactions is not a new theme, and is a founding principle of statistical thermodynamics. However, the emergence of multi-scale behaviors (stochastic for the microenvironment and deterministic at the organ level) indicates the importance of multi-level studies when trying to understand biological processes.

The impact of *in silico* immunodeficiency on the course of infection

Having established that our model recapitulated many of the features of infection seen in immunocompetent mice, we then went on to explore how well we could recapitulate the differing outcomes of infection as seen in cell or cytokine deficient mice. T cells are considered to be the main mediators of cellular immunity against *Leishmania* and not surprisingly, depletion of T cells in our *in silico* model (Figure 6A) led to high parasite burden and a non-healing course of infection, reflecting the course of infection in T cell-deficient mice [5]. The cytokine IFNγ is considered fundamental for the classical activation of macrophages [46] and mice deficient in IFNγ are unable to mount an adequate immune response and are highly susceptible to EVL [5]. Likewise in our model, inhibiting production of IFNγ from all cells capable of producing this cytokine lead to very high parasite burden and to a non-healing infection (Figure 6B). In contrast to IFNγ, IL-10 has a negative impact on host resistance, with IL-10 KO mice or mice treated with anti-IL-10R having enhanced resistance to infection [47], [48]. Our model also indicated an important role for IL-10 in regulating parasite burden, as blocking the production of IL-10 by all leukocytes resulted in a reduced peak parasite burden (Figure 6C), though to a slightly lesser extent compared to that reported in IL-10 KO mice. Overall, however, the model appeared to faithfully recapitulate many of the key features of EVL observed in various immunodeficient mouse models.

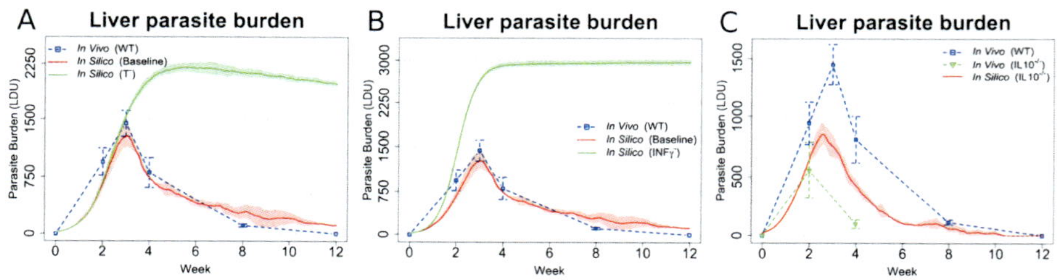

Figure 6: Simulations reflecting gene KO qualitatively reproduce expected changes in disease outcome.

(**A** and **B**) Parasite burden after *in silico* knock out of T cells (A) or IFNγ (B), compared to the results from the baseline model (baseline) and in vivo ([58]; WT). (**C**) *In silico*knock out of IL-10 compared with [58] and data adapted from [61]). In all the panels, means and standard deviation are reported. Standard deviation is indicated by error bars or shaded areas.

KC-derived IL-10 plays a dominant role in regulating granuloma effector function

In EVL, multiple cellular sources of IL-10 have been described, including IL-10-producing CD4[+]Th1 cells [20], NK cells [29], and inflammatory macrophages (monocytes and DCs [20]). Kupffer cells are also well known to produce IL-10 under differing conditions [49], [50]. On the basis that our model was able to demonstrate the effects of global IL-10 deficiency (Figure 6C), we proceeded to conduct a series of predictive studies to identify which cell(s) produced IL-10 with most impact on the effector function of the granuloma (in essence generating a series of conditional cell-specific IL-10 gene deficiencies *in silico*). Our simulation results indicated that removing the capacity of CD4$^+$ IFNγ^+ Th1 cells, inflammatory monocytes/DC, and IFNγ^+ NK cells to make IL-10 all had perceivable but different impacts on parasite burden (Figure 7A). Removing the capacity of CD4$^+$ IFNγ^+ Th1 and NK cells to produce IL-10 did not alter the peak parasite burden, but delayed final stages of parasite clearance. In contrast, removing the capacity of myeloid cells (including KCs and inflammatory DC/monocytes) to produce IL-10 had a much more significant impact on parasite burden evident by a reduction in peak tissue parasite load and a more rapid resolution of infection. Qualitatively, the effect of IL-10 depletion from myeloid cells alone was similar to that of global IL-10 depletion (Figure 6C).

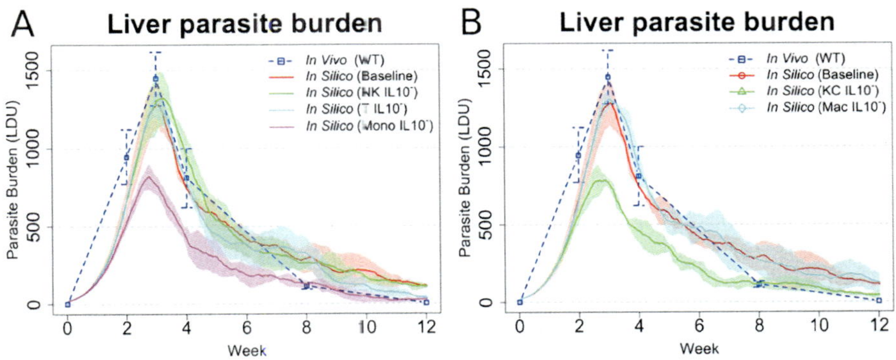

Figure 7: ***In silico*** **cell-specific knock out of IL-10 implicates** Kupffer cell IL-10 production as a major determinant of leishmanicidal activity within granulomas.

(**A**) *In silico* knockout of IL-10 in mononuclear phagocytes (Mono IL-10$^-$), T cells (T IL10$^-$), and NK cells (NK IL10$^-$) compared with baseline *in silico* model and in vivo ([58]; WT). (**B**) *In silico* knockout of IL-10 from Kupffer cells (KC IL10$^-$) and non-resident macrophages/ monocytes/DC (Mac IL10$^-$), compared with baseline *in silico* model and [58]. In all the panels, means and standard deviation are reported. Standard deviation is indicated by error bars or shaded areas.

To further dissect the role of different myeloid cells and the relative contribution of autocrine IL-10 production by infected KC and IL-10 that was derived from inflammatory monocytes/DC, we selectively eliminated IL-10 production by each population. Our results clearly indicated that IL-10 production by KCs had a greater impact on parasite burden compared to IL-10 production by inflammatory monocytes/DC (Figure 7B). Indeed, our model predicts the outcome of KC IL-10 deficiency to be as effective in increasing host resistance as total ablation of IL-10 (Figures 6Cand 7B). Thus, while supporting a role for $IFN\gamma^{+}IL10^{+}$ T cells and $IL\text{-}10^{+}$ NK cells in the regulation of immunity to *L. donovani*, our data suggests that IL-10 production by infected KCs themselves plays the most dominant role in regulating intra-granuloma effector function. This finding is clearly a consequence of the high level of deactivation observed in Kupffer cells at both global (Figure 3E) and local scales (Figures 5A–C), which promotes IL-10 production by these cells.

Concluding remarks

In silico models are increasingly important tools to elucidate complex biological phenomena. However, selecting the adequate level of abstraction and controlling its complexity can be daunting tasks when studying the diverse biological mechanisms used by the vertebrate immune system. Care is needed in building *in silico* models with clear working hypotheses and extensive validation. In comparison to other *in silico* models of granuloma formation, our model provides a systematic view of the course of infection, without sacrificing the complexity and diversity of the immune response. Our model of course contains a number of explicit simplifications and assumptions, and whilst based on the literature, many of these may be open to alternate interpretation or indeed not operate as hard rules. However, an extensive list of the working hypotheses and an assessment of the effect of the different model parameters by sensitivity analysis provides further insight into the working of the model and its robustness. In contrast, a disadvantage of our systemic view is that unlike agent based models [51], Petri net models are not able to elucidate the role played by physical interactions among leucocytes within a spatially defined environment. Additionally, in comparison to simpler deterministic models, our analyses are performed only by means of simulations, thus limiting the exploration of the parameter space.

Notwithstanding these limitations, our current model captures many experimentally determined features of the *Leishmania* granuloma and has provided a number of unique and important insights into the aspects of granuloma function that are currently intractable in vivo. First, our observation that individual granulomas display distinct patterns of effector function over time suggests a novel means for the maintenance of persistent parasites in tissues and has implications for understanding parasite recrudescence. Second, the prediction from our model that autocrine IL-10 production by KCs is a major regulator of leishmanicidal activity within granulomas was unexpected, given the recent attention focused on the production of this cytokine by T cells and NK cells, including from our own work. Importantly, it should be noted that our model only simulates events within the granuloma that lead to the control of parasite load and hence does not take into account the possible regulatory effects of IL-10 outside this environment. For example, our model would not capture possible effects of IL-10 on T cell differentiation occurring in other tissues, but which might affect the quality and/or quantity of T cells that enter into the granuloma microenvironment.

Our model also adds to a growing body of modeling literature on macrophage activation. Macrophages have the capacity to assume different states of functional 'activation' dependent in part upon the cytokine environment to which they are exposed (variously defined as M1 and M2 or as classical and alternate activation, respectively) with profound implications for the control of intracellular pathogens and the regulation of inflammation (reviewed in [52], [53]). The interplay between classical and alternate activation has been previously modeled in the context of tuberculosis [33], [54], [55]. Alternatively activated macrophages (driven by IL-4) are limiting in our model, whereas de-activation resulting from non-cytokine as well as cytokine mediated mechanisms acts as the principal counter balance to classical activation. Nevertheless, taken together these studies are providing novel insights into how macrophage effector function is regulated in a dynamic way over the course of infection and illustrate how changes in the balance of activation phenotypes at the local site can shape the outcome of infection. It remains to be determined whether such information can be harnessed to develop useful and clinically relevant prognostic indicators of disease outcome.

In conclusion, this novel stochastic Petri net model of granuloma formation provides a new tool to complement other approaches to understand the biology of granulomatous inflammation and the determinants of host resistance to *L. donovani*. Whilst our *in silico* studies indicate the potential for enhancing local immunity through disabling IL-10 production in a cell-specific manner, final validation of the predictions made by this model will require the future development of novel KC-specific IL-10 deficient mice.

MATERIALS AND METHODS

Animal experiments

Data on the cellular composition of the *Leishmania* granuloma in mice, collected by real time intravital imaging and the analysis of disaggregated liver tissue, was used for parameterization of the model. Data from the authors› laboratory were collected under license from the UK Home Office (PPL 60/4377). All animal experiments were approved by the University of York Ethical Review Process and studies were conducted in accord with ARRIVE guidelines and the principles of the 3Rs.

Formalism and tools

The model used was developed using stochastic Petri nets and simulated with Snoopy [56]. For each *in silico* experiment, the populations of entities at the organ level were calculated using the averages of 50 independently simulated granulomas and by multiplying these averages by the calculated number of granulomas in the entire liver (5×10^5). *In silico* values displayed in the figures were obtained by averaging the results of 3 experiments under the same conditions, the error bars indicate sample standard deviation. Leishman Donovan Units (LDU) values were obtained by dividing the number of parasites by 10^5 [57].

Dynamics of modeled entities

The number of individuals for any given population was modeled by the number of tokens in the place representing that population. Besides some transitions modeling the time-flow, the firing time for a transition was modeled by a negative exponential distribution. The following entities were considered by the model: Cytokines (IL-2, IL-4, IL-10, IL-12, and IFNγ), mononuclear phagocytes (Kupffer Cells, non-resident macrophages/monocytes/DC), *L. donovani*-derived peptides associating with MHC and non-classical MHC molecules, NK cells, NKT cells, and $CD8^+$ and $CD4^+$ T cells.

Statistical analysis

Statistical analysis was performed on the mean using Student's t-test with Welch's correction for the degrees of freedom. P-value was calculated for equality test.

Sensitivity analysis

Both Latin hypercube sampling and partial rank correlation coefficients are widely used techniques. A formal presentation of these techniques can be found in [43]. Briefly, PRCC characterizes the strength of the linear relationship between two variables after a correction has been made for the linear effects of the other variables considered by the analysis. Additionally, p-value indicates the probability of getting a correlation as large as the observed value by random chance, when the true correlation is zero. P-values lower than 0.05 (or 0.01) were considered indicative of statistical significance.

AUTHOR CONTRIBUTIONS

Conceived and designed the experiments: LA JT LB PMK. Performed the experiments: LA LB. Analyzed the data: LA LB. Contributed reagents/materials/analysis tools: LB PMK. Wrote the paper: LA JT LB PMK. Supervised the study: JT PMK.

REFERENCES

1. Desjeux P (2004) Leishmaniasis: current situation and new perspectives. Comp Immunol Microbiol Infect Dis 27: 305–318.
2. Alvar J, Velez ID, Bern C, Herrero M, Desjeux P, et al. (2012)

Leishmaniasis worldwide and global estimates of its incidence. PLoS One 7: e35671.

3. Kaye PM, Aebischer T (2011) Visceral leishmaniasis: immunology and prospects for a vaccine. Clin Microbiol Infect 17: 1462–1470.
4. Kaye PM, Svensson M, Ato M, Maroof A, Polley R, et al. (2004) The immunopathology of experimental visceral leishmaniasis. Immunol Rev 201: 239–253.
5. Murray HW (2001) Tissue granuloma structure-function in experimental visceral leishmaniasis. Int J Exp Pathol 82: 249–267.
6. Pampiglione S, Manson-Bahr PE, Giungi F, Giunti G, Parenti A, et al. (1974) Studies on Mediterranean leishmaniasis. 2. Asymptomatic cases of visceral leishmaniasis. Trans R Soc Trop Med Hyg 68: 447–453.
7. Sanchez MA, Diaz NL, Zerpa O, Negron E, Convit J, et al. (2004) Organ-specific immunity in canine visceral leishmaniasis: analysis of symptomatic and asymptomatic dogs naturally infected with Leishmania chagasi. Am J Trop Med Hyg 70: 618–624.
8. Brighenti S, Andersson J (2012) Local immune responses in human tuberculosis: learning from the site of infection. J Infect Dis 205 Suppl 2: S316–324.
9. Cancellieri A, Dalpiaz G, Trisolini R, Ricchiuti E, Pesci A (2010) Granulomatous lung disease. Pathologica 102: 464–488.
10. Ramakrishnan L (2012) Revisiting the role of the granuloma in tuberculosis. Nat Rev Immunol 12: 352–366.
11. Schilder AM (2010) Wegener's Granulomatosis vasculitis and granuloma. Autoimmun Rev 9: 483–487.
12. Moore JW, Moyo D, Beattie L, Andrews PS, Timmis J, et al. (2013) Functional complexity of the Leishmania granuloma and the potential of in silico modeling. Front Immunol 4: 35.
13. Verma S, Kumar R, Katara GK, Singh LC, Negi NS, et al. (2010) Quantification of parasite load in clinical samples of leishmaniasis patients: IL-10 level correlates with parasite load in visceral leishmaniasis. PLoS One 5: e10107.
14. Duell BL, Tan CK, Carey AJ, Wu F, Cripps AW, et al. (2012) Recent insights into microbial triggers of interleukin-10 production in the

host and the impact on infectious disease pathogenesis. FEMS Immunol Med Microbiol 64: 295–313.

15. Saraiva M, O'Garra A (2010) The regulation of IL-10 production by immune cells. Nat Rev Immunol 10: 170–181.
16. Gazzinelli RT, Oswald IP, James SL, Sher A (1992) IL-10 inhibits parasite killing and nitrogen oxide production by IFN-gamma-activated macrophages. J Immunol 148: 1792–1796.
17. Kane MM, Mosser DM (2001) The role of IL-10 in promoting disease progression in leishmaniasis. J Immunol 166: 1141–1147.
18. Lucas M, Zhang X, Prasanna V, Mosser DM (2005) ERK activation following macrophage FcgammaR ligation leads to chromatin modifications at the IL-10 locus. J Immunol 175: 469–477.
19. Fiorentino DF, Zlotnik A, Vieira P, Mosmann TR, Howard M, et al. (1991) IL-10 acts on the antigen-presenting cell to inhibit cytokine production by Th1 cells. J Immunol 146: 3444–3451.
20. Owens BM, Beattie L, Moore JW, Brown N, Mann JL, et al. (2012) IL-10-producing Th1 cells and disease progression are regulated by distinct CD11c(+) cell populations during visceral leishmaniasis. PLoS Pathog 8: e1002827.
21. Svensson M, Maroof A, Ato M, Kaye PM (2004) Stromal cells direct local differentiation of regulatory dendritic cells. Immunity 21: 805–816.
22. Anderson CF, Lira R, Kamhawi S, Belkaid Y, Wynn TA, et al. (2008) IL-10 and TGF-beta control the establishment of persistent and transmissible infections produced by Leishmania tropica in C57BL/6 mice. J Immunol 180: 4090–4097.
23. Ansari NA, Kumar R, Gautam S, Nylen S, Singh OP, et al. (2011) IL-27 and IL-21 are associated with T cell IL-10 responses in human visceral leishmaniasis. J Immunol 186: 3977–3985.
24. Belkaid Y, Hoffmann KF, Mendez S, Kamhawi S, Udey MC, et al. (2001) The role of interleukin (IL)-10 in the persistence of Leishmania major in the skin after healing and the therapeutic potential of anti-IL-10 receptor antibody for sterile cure. J Exp Med 194: 1497–1506.

25. Gautam S, Kumar R, Maurya R, Nylen S, Ansari N, et al. (2011) IL-10 neutralization promotes parasite clearance in splenic aspirate cells from patients with visceral leishmaniasis. J Infect Dis 204: 1134–1137.
26. Nylen S, Maurya R, Eidsmo L, Manandhar KD, Sundar S, et al. (2007) Splenic accumulation of IL-10 mRNA in T cells distinct from CD4+CD25+ (Foxp3) regulatory T cells in human visceral leishmaniasis. J Exp Med 204: 805–817.
27. Ranatunga D, Hedrich CM, Wang F, McVicar DW, Nowak N, et al. (2009) A human IL10 BAC transgene reveals tissue-specific control of IL-10 expression and alters disease outcome. Proc Natl Acad Sci U S A 106: 17123–17128.
28. Stager S, Maroof A, Zubairi S, Sanos SL, Kopf M, et al. (2006) Distinct roles for IL-6 and IL-12p40 in mediating protection against Leishmania donovani and the expansion of IL-10+ CD4+ T cells. Eur J Immunol 36: 1764–1771.
29. Maroof A, Beattie L, Zubairi S, Svensson M, Stager S, et al. (2008) Posttranscriptional regulation of Il10 gene expression allows natural killer cells to express immunoregulatory function. Immunity 29: 295–305.
30. O'Garra A, Barrat FJ, Castro AG, Vicari A, Hawrylowicz C (2008) Strategies for use of IL-10 or its antagonists in human disease. Immunol Rev 223: 114–131.
31. Chakravarty SD, Zhu G, Tsai MC, Mohan VP, Marino S, et al. (2008) Tumor necrosis factor blockade in chronic murine tuberculosis enhances granulomatous inflammation and disorganizes granulomas in the lungs. Infect Immun 76: 916–926.
32. Ganguli S, Gammack D, Kirschner DE (2005) A metapopulation model of granuloma formation in the lung during infection with mycobacterium tuberculosis. Math Biosci Eng 2: 535–560.
33. Marino S, Myers A, Flynn JL, Kirschner DE (2010) TNF and IL-10 are major factors in modulation of the phagocytic cell environment in lung and lymph node in tuberculosis: a next-generation two-compartmental model. J Theor Biol 265: 586–598.
34. Ray JC, Flynn JL, Kirschner DE (2009) Synergy between individual TNF-dependent functions determines granuloma performance for

controlling Mycobacterium tuberculosis infection. J Immunol 182: 3706–3717.

35. Ray JC, Wang J, Chan J, Kirschner DE (2008) The timing of TNF and IFN-gamma signaling affects macrophage activation strategies during Mycobacterium tuberculosis infection. J Theor Biol 252: 24–38.
36. Aguda BD, Marsh CB, Thacker M, Crouser ED (2011) An in silico modeling approach to understanding the dynamics of sarcoidosis. PLoS One 6: e19544.
37. Flugge AJ, Timmis J, Beattie L, Kaye PM (2009) Modeling and simulation of granuloma formation in visceral leishmaniasis. IEEE Congress on Evolutionary Computation Trondheim, Norway.
38. Carvalho RV, Kleijn J, Meijer AH, Verbeek FJ (2012) Modeling innate immune response to early Mycobacterium infection. Comput Math Methods Med 2012: 790482.
39. Koch I, Reisig W, Screiber F (2011) Modeling in Systems Biology: The Petri Net Approach. pp. 364.
40. Moore JW, Beattie L, Dalton JE, Owens BM, Maroof A, et al. (2012) B cell: T cell interactions occur within hepatic granulomas during experimental visceral leishmaniasis. PLoS One 7: e34143.
41. Mood A, Graybill F, Boes D (1974) Introduction to the Theory of Statistics. London: McGraw Hill Higher Education. 480 p.
42. Murray HW, Tsai CW, Liu J, Ma X (2006) Responses to Leishmania donovani in mice deficient in interleukin-12 (IL-12), IL-12/IL-23, or IL-18. Infect Immun 74: 4370–4374.
43. Saltelli A, Chan K, Scott EM (2000) Sensitivity Analysis: John Wiley & Sons.
44. Muller AJ, Filipe-Santos O, Eberl G, Aebischer T, Spath GF, et al. (2012) CD4+ T cells rely on a cytokine gradient to control intracellular pathogens beyond sites of antigen presentation. Immunity 37: 147–157.
45. Murray HW, Hariprashad J, Fichtl RE (1996) Models of relapse of experimental visceral leishmaniasis. J Infect Dis 173: 1041–1043.
46. Mosser DM, Edwards JP (2008) Exploring the full spectrum of macrophage activation. Nat Rev Immunol 8: 958–969.

47. Murphy ML, Wille U, Villegas EN, Hunter CA, Farrell JP (2001) IL-10 mediates susceptibility to Leishmania donovani infection. Eur J Immunol 31: 2848–2856.
48. Murray HW, Lu CM, Mauze S, Freeman S, Moreira AL, et al. (2002) Interleukin-10 (IL-10) in experimental visceral leishmaniasis and IL-10 receptor blockade as immunotherapy. Infect Immun 70: 6284–6293.
49. Ellett JD, Atkinson C, Evans ZP, Amani Z, Balish E, et al. (2010) Murine Kupffer cells are protective in total hepatic ischemia/reperfusion injury with bowel congestion through IL-10. J Immunol 184: 5849–5858.
50. Emmanuilidis K, Weighardt H, Maier S, Gerauer K, Fleischmann T, et al. (2001) Critical role of Kupffer cell-derived IL-10 for host defense in septic peritonitis. J Immunol 167: 3919–3927.
51. Alden K, Timmis J, Andrews PS, Veiga-Fernandes H, Coles MC (2012) Pairing experimentation and computational modeling to understand the role of tissue inducer cells in the development of lymphoid organs. Front Immunol 3: 172.
52. Cohen HB, Mosser DM (2013) Extrinsic and intrinsic control of macrophage inflammatory responses. J Leukoc Biol [epub ahead of print].
53. Tugal D, Liao X, Jain MK (2013) Transcriptional control of macrophage polarization. Arterioscler Thromb Vasc Biol 33: 1135–1144.
54. Day J, Friedman A, Schlesinger LS (2009) Modeling the immune rheostat of macrophages in the lung in response to infection. Proc Natl Acad Sci U S A 106: 11246–11251.
55. Cilfone NA, Perry CR, Kirschner DE, Linderman JJ (2013) Multi-scale modeling predicts a balance of tumor necrosis factor-alpha and interleukin-10 controls the granuloma environment during Mycobacterium tuberculosis infection. PLoS One 8: e68680.
56. Rohr C, Marwan W, Heiner M (2010) Snoopy–a unifying Petri net framework to investigate biomolecular networks. Bioinformatics 26: 974–975.

57. Gutierrez Y, Maksem JA, Reiner NE (1984) Pathologic changes in murine leishmaniasis (Leishmania donovani) with special reference to the dynamics of granuloma formation in the liver. Am J Pathol 114: 222–230.

58. Murray HW, Xiang Z, Ma X (2006) Responses to Leishmania donovani in mice deficient in both phagocyte oxidase and inducible nitric oxide synthase. Am J Trop Med Hyg 74: 1013–1015.

59. Amprey JL, Im JS, Turco SJ, Murray HW, Illarionov PA, et al. (2004) A subset of liver NK T cells is activated during Leishmania donovani infection by CD1d-bound lipophosphoglycan. J Exp Med 200: 895–904.

60. Beattie L, Svensson M, Bune A, Brown N, Maroof A, et al. (2010) Leishmania donovani-induced expression of signal regulatory protein alpha on Kupffer cells enhances hepatic invariant NKT-cell activation. Eur J Immunol 40: 117–123.

61. Stanley AC, Zhou Y, Amante FH, Randall LM, Haque A, et al. (2008) Activation of invariant NKT cells exacerbates experimental visceral leishmaniasis. PLoS Pathog 4: e1000028.

10 SHER: A COLORED PETRI NET BASED RANDOM MOBILITY MODEL FOR WIRELESS COMMUNICATIONS

Naeem Akhtar Khan[1], Farooq Ahmad[2], Sher Afzal Khan[3,4]

[1] Faculty of Information Technology, University of Central Punjab, Lahore, Pakistan
[2] Department of Computer Science, COMSATS Institute of information Technology, Lahore, Pakistan
[3] Department of Computer Sciences, Abdul Wali Khan University, Mardan, Pakistan
[4] Faculty of Computing and Information Technology in Rabigh, King Abdul Aziz University, Jeddah, KSA

ABSTRACT

In wireless network research, simulation is the most imperative technique to investigate the network's behavior and validation. Wireless networks typically consist of mobile hosts; therefore, the degree of validation is influenced by the underlying mobility model, and synthetic models are implemented in simulators because real life traces are not widely available. In wireless communications, mobility is an integral part while the key role of a mobility model is to mimic the real life traveling patterns to study. The performance of routing protocols and mobility management strategies e.g. paging, registration and handoff is highly dependent to the selected mobility model. In this paper, we devise and evaluate the Show Home and Exclusive Regions (SHER), a novel two-dimensional (2-D) Colored Petri net (CPN) based formal random mobility model, which exhibits sociological behavior of a user. The model captures hotspots where a user frequently visits and spends time. Our solution eliminates six key issues of the random mobility models, i.e., *sudden stops*, *memoryless movements*, *border effect*, *temporal dependency of velocity*, *pause time dependency*, *and speed decay* in a single model. The proposed model is able to predict the future location of a mobile user and ultimately improves the performance of wireless communication networks. The model follows a uniform nodal distribution and is a mini simulator, which exhibits interesting mobility patterns. The model is also helpful to those who are not familiar with the formal modeling, and users can extract meaningful information with a single mouse-click. It is noteworthy that capturing dynamic mobility patterns through CPN is the most challenging and virulent activity of the presented research. Statistical and reachability analysis techniques are presented to elucidate and validate the performance of our proposed mobility model. The state space methods allow us to algorithmically derive the system behavior and rectify the errors of our proposed model.

INTRODUCTION

Wireless networking has received unprecedented attention from the research community during the last decade due to the fast growth in technology. It has witnessed extensive development and created new horizons of communication. Wireless communication networks have several types, and one example is wireless mesh networks (WMNs) [1]. The mobile hosts (MHs) or simple stations (STAs) in wireless communications have dynamic nature and move in terrain according to different mobility profiles. Mobility models are used to mimic the traveling patterns of mobile hosts. Therefore, an underlying mobility model that dedicates the movement behavior to MH has a direct influence on the performance of these networks. This is due to their characteristics such as dynamic topology, multi-hop communication, security, shared media, entropy measure and eigenvalue measure in complex systems.

Mobility and Mobility Models in Wireless Networks

Mobility models have two broad categories and those are trace based and synthetic mobility models. In general, traces are accurate realistic mobility patterns that are derived from real life scenarios, particularly where a large number of participants are involved. However, new network environments like mobile ad hoc networks (MANETs) or WMNs cannot be easily modeled because they have not been deployed in large scale yet. Hence, researchers proposed various synthetic models without traces where the objective was to capture the characteristics of mobile nodes (MNs) without using traces. Synthetic mobility models attempt to model the mobility of each mobile host (MH) in a simplistic manner based on direction, speed, transition time between home and destination, the length between two points, and distribution of MH positions. A comprehensive study of these synthetic models can be found in [2][3].

The major role of mobility model is to generate the movement patterns according to real life scenarios in simulation based studies. An individual mobility model can be applied into a wide range of systems particularly the dynamics in mobile scenarios are of great interest [4][5]. Moreover, the authenticity of a mobility model depends on how it produces more realistic mobility patterns. A precise and realistic mobility model generates more accurate simulation results to evaluate network parameters. Researchers have developed numerous mobility models offering diverse characteristic in simulation based research. Some models are simplistic and others are based on comprehensive modeling approach to generate realistic travelling patterns. Mobility models can be divided into seven broad categories: (i) individual mobility models, (ii) group mobility models, (iii) flocking mobility, (iv) auto-regressive mobility models, (v) non-recurrent mobility, (vi) virtual game-driven mobility, and (vii) time-variant community mobility [6]. The accuracy of the mobility model is highly dependent on the degree of realism. Some other mobility models are customized for specific scenarios. The most popular random mobility models are random walk mobility model [7] and its variations, random waypoint mobility model (RWP) [8], and random direction mobility model [9]. In recent years, several studies have been published with consensus that existing mobility models such as the well-known random waypoint (RWP) are insufficient to represent realistic mobility patterns. Remarkable effort was made in [10] to compare the evaluation methods and it concluded that 75.5% research is based on simulations and majority of papers (73.8%) implemented well known RWP mobility model. In addition to its wide applicability and popularity, there is broad criticism in numerous studies (e.g., [6][11][12][13][14][15][16][17][18]) on RWP and other random models. The key issues are sudden stops, speed decay, density wave issue, steady state problem, and the so-called border effect phenomena. Moreover, the mobility model does not retain any preceding information; therefore, the memory-less decisions for the next itinerary may generate unrealistic movement patterns. Finally, there is an increasing consensus among the network research community that the existing mobility models are either unrealistic or tailor-made for specific situations, and this causes the degradation of quality of service (QoS) for wireless networks.

To alleviate the above issues, this paper presents a random SHER mobility model based on movement patterns observed from a social and behavioral network for a perspective user. The objective is to enhance the model such that it can monitor the behavior and position of the MHs on a regular basis. If the network has enough information about the MHs attraction points or hotspots, then the model can implement intelligent strategies to accurately predict the MH's current or future location based on previous observations. Consequently, the network can reserve its resources for appropriate time by sending minimum location finding messages.

Traditionally, simulation is a method to conduct wireless networks research because of its numerous benefits. However, the study of literature reflects that newcomer students and researchers often get perplexed in the complexity of simulators and lose their concentration [19]. Formal methods [20] are mathematical-based techniques that have been proven as an appropriate tool for investigation and rectification of the model's attribution and rectification. This approach is typically motivated because of its power to detect inconsistency and reduce the "time to market". Conventional methods have rigorous computer based tool support, which ticks off all possible execution paths throughout the system and reveals virulent concurrent errors that have not been unveiled by implementing other testing strategies. Graphs have also been used as a formal approach and to describe the characteristics and entropy-based measures of complex networks, researchers investigated many graph invariants, e.g. [21][22][23][24].

Colored Petri nets (CPNs) [25][26] are bipartite graphs suitable for development of concurrent discrete events and distributed systems. Many techniques such as timed color token, hierarchical modeling, capacity bounding, priority queues, recursive functions, synchronous, and asynchronous behaviors are used to model these complex systems. CP-nets combine Petri nets [27] and functional programming language Standard ML (SML) [28] to provide a concrete platform to researchers. CPN Tools [29] is a powerful software for modeling and analysis of the CPN models, and is widely accepted and acknowledged by the research community.

The movement patterns of the mobility model play a vital role in the performance evaluation of wireless networks. The literature demonstrates that very few publications can be found that address the mobility issues in a wireless network using CPNs. A magnificent work of Kristensen et al. [30] can be considered as a landmark in CPN based modeling of the network protocols. The authors abstractly described both micro and macro mobility architecture scenarios in ad-hoc networks. Their focus was to develop a model that integrates conventional protocols with ad-hoc network protocols. A valuable contribution of their work is that the CPN model reflects communication and mobility functionality in a single model. The model is appropriate for mobility test cases. The work of Xiong et al. [31] has a profound influence on the mobility in ad-hoc networks. To overcome the dynamically changing topology problem, they proposed a topology approximation (TA) architecture using CPNs. They implemented their proposed mechanism to build a CPN model based on an Ad Hoc on Demand Distance Vector (AODV) routing protocol. Their results showed that TA mechanism exhibits realistic movement characteristics and is able to mimic the dynamic changes of the network topology.

Capturing mobility through CPN is the most challenging activity. Khan et al. [32] presented a CPNs based formal model in the well-known random walk mobility model for WMN without border effect and speed decay problems. The proposed model can be easily modified to generate complex mobility patterns. An elegant CPN based synthetic RWP mobility model was presented in [33]. Despite their contributions, the main limitation is that the proposed model was not able to generate the trajectory of every epoch. In order to produce realistic movement patterns, we implemented RWP mobility model in [34] by removing the border effect and speed decay issues. The model was able to generate different mobility patterns based on the diverse topology. Those patterns can further be used to address the mobility management issues in wireless communication networks. A nice effort was presented in [14] and the authors presented a group mobility model that considers the psychological and sociological behavior of the mobile nodes. The model was able to capture the natural behavior as fork-join and generated the realistic motion of the living creatures. To produce several mobility patterns, the authors in [35] presented a generalized random mobility model including hotspots over one-dimensional terrains. The model had the functionally to capture points that the user had higher probability to spend time. Recently, we introduced an accurate and extendable abstract level hierarchical CPN based formal model of a community based wireless mesh network where a user can move or send data packets [36]. The aim of the proposed CPN model was to elaborate the communication mobility requirements, and this was the first step of the systematic verification in the WMN environment at an abstract level.

Although some of the above efforts were made to model realistic behaviors of the mobility models, no one attempted to cover diverse aspects of the MHs movement compared to the SHER mobility model. A significant difference between SHER and other random or deterministic mobility models is the simplicity and generality. Most of the existing models are implemented in simulators and their underlying mathematical models are complex. On the contrary, our implementation is based on the formal modeling and a new module can easily be added or existing modules can be modified to produce more complex scenarios such as obstacles in the mobility of the nodes.

Research Contributions

The significant contributions of the work presented in this paper can be summarized as follows:

- Temporal dependency of velocity: To select the next epoch parameters and provide steady state, SHER mobility model considers the previous velocity and gradually increase, decrease or remain constant for the next epoch's speed.

- Temporal dependency of destination: To select the next itinerary, SHER mobility model considers previous information; hence, MH's new destination is intelligently dependent on its moving history.
- Sudden stops: The proposed approach provides complete removal of the abrupt stops for MHs.
- Speed decay problem: Our implementation does not exhibit speed decay issue, and the MH's speed remains constant during each trip using the proposed application.
- Pause time dependency: Random pause time after completion of each trip is dependent on the destination location. For example, the pause time for location "A" is more than location "B" and "C" in a priority based method. This type of pause time reflects a more realistic attitude of the mobile user and it is employed in the SHER model.
- Border effect problem: Border effect issue demonstrates that when an MH touches the boundary of terrain, then it bounces to the middle and concentrates. The SHER mobility model avoids this type of behavior.
- Spatial dependency: Spatial dependent behavior of the nodes influenced by previous information can be monitored using our implementation.
- Uniform nodal distribution: On start and during execution, the SHER maintains uniform distribution.
- Mini simulator: The SHER mobility model can be executed in CPN Tools' user friendly environment that is freely available [29]. The SHER mobility model, in an executable *SHER.cpn* file, enables the user to generate numerous different mobility patterns using a single mouse-click, even if a researcher is not much familiar with formal methods or CPNs.

To demonstrate the impact of this model, we validate its functional properties using extensive simulations and state space analysis techniques. The proposed model will provide an encouragement to researchers for the specification, modeling, and verification of communication protocols using CPNs to avoid the complexities of simulators. The rest of the paper is divided into four main sections. Section 2 concentrates the formal modeling of the SHER mobility model using CPN tools. Section 3 examines the state space of the models and verifies the results. We summarized our achievements in Section 4 where we also present our conclusions and future directions.

CPN BASED MODELING FOR THE SHER MOBILITY MODEL

Environment Scenario

The SHER mobility model is developed using Petri net based formalism while basic concepts and terminology about Petri nets, its formal definitions, and CPN can be found in [37]. Moreover, it is a cumbersome task to create intricate models; however, similar to the other modular programming languages, CPN supports a hierarchical module concept in which large nets can be broken into smaller components.

The basic theme of the SHER synthetic random mobility model is based on the theory of the well-known RWP mobility model [8], which has already been implemented in many simulators such as NS-2 [38]. The CPN model of the SHER mobility model is organized as a set of eight modules. Because the system components are often used repeatedly, it is inefficient to draw these components from scratch every time. Fig 1 shows the graphical representation of the module *hierarchy* for the SHER model. The modules names are written inside the nodes. The arcs annotate the name of the corresponding substituting transitions.

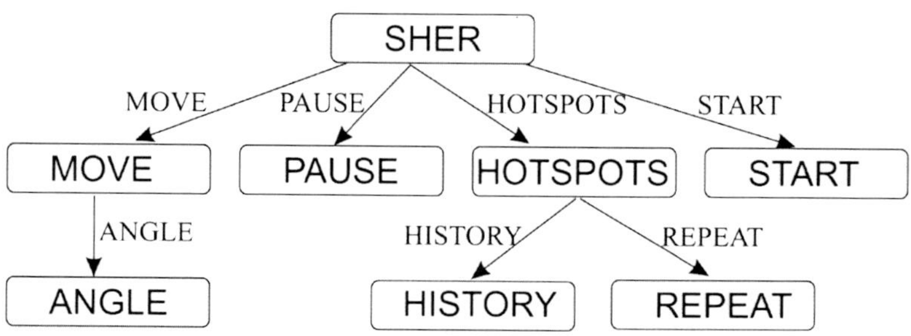

Figure 1: Instance hierarchy for the SHER mobility model.

The SHER module has no incoming arc; hence, it is the root of the hierarchy and is called the prime module. The SHER model consists of four main parts. Page MOVE with one sub-page ANGLE models the movement scenarios of an MH. Page HOTSPOTS is further decomposed into two subpages, HISTORY and REPEAT, and is responsible to keep track of every epoch of an MH and models the next itinerary based on the previous movement.

In addition, the PAUSE page models the pause time dependency based on the attraction point's category of the MH and finally the START module randomly selects the first trajectory movement coordinates and other parameters of an MH. The model has a dynamic nature; hence, an MH can be placed in $100 \times 100\ m^2$ communication area using a uniform random distribution. The model contains a finite set of places P, a finite set of transitions T, a set of directed arcs A, a finite set of non-empty color sets Σ, a finite set of typed variables V, a color set function C that assigns a color set to each place, a guard function G, an arc expression function E that assigns an arc expression to each place, and an initialization function I. Fig 2depicts the abstract SHER module that has four *substituting transitions* MOVE, START, PAUSE, and HOTSPOTS as indicated by the associated HS-tag and nine places, which are ND, STA_HOM1, PRIORITY CHK, EVERY MOVE, NEW DEST, PRIORITY4, MAX PR, PAUSE DEPND, and MONITOR.

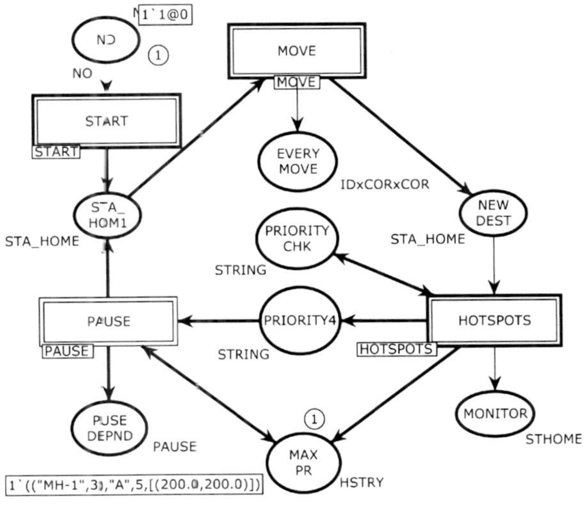

Figure 2: The SHER page–Architecture of the CPN model with initial marking M_0.

The declarations of the color sets used in the SHER module (see Fig 2) are listed in Table 1. The color sets are defined using the basic Standard ML types. A constant tn, which represents the total nodes, is *globally* declared as one and it has a type Val. The color set NO is used for identity (ID) number of an MH with the form MH-(i) where $1 \leq i \leq tn$. The color set RCOOR (Real Coordinates) is defined as a *product color set* of the simple color set RCOR and LCOOR. In addition, the color set RCOOR is of a type *list*.

Table 1: Declaration of the color sets for the SHER page

Line No.	Color Name	Color Type
1.	colset NO	int with 1..tn timed;
2.	colset INT	int;
3.	colset ART	int;
4.	colset REAL	real;
5.	colset STRING	string;
6.	colset ID	string;
7.	colset RCOR	REAL;
8.	colset RCOOR	product RCOR*RCOR;
9.	colset LCOOR	list RCOOR;
10.	colset NODE	product ID*ART timed;
11.	colset STA_HOME	product NODE*LCOOR*LCOOR timed;
12.	colset PAUSE	product INT*NODE*STRING*LCOOR timed;
13.	colset STHOME	product INT*NODE*LCOOR*STRING*LCOOR timed
14.	colset IDxCORxCOR	product INT*NODE*LCOOR*LCOOR;
15.	colset HSTRY	product NODE*STRING*INT*LCOOR;

doi:10.1371/journal.pone.0133634.t001

The color set NODE denotes the MH ID number with its arrival time. The color set STA_HOME is used to model the node ID with home and destination coordinates for the next epoch. The place MONITOR has a color set STHOME whose elements are 5-tuples consisting of sequence number, node, home coordinates, hotspot, and destination. The color set PAUSE is used to model the pause time after completing every epoch based on the attraction point category. The place EVERYMOVE with color set IDxCORxCOR is used to keep track of the every move of an MH. The places PRIORITYCHK and PRIORITY4 with color set STRING are used in modeling the attraction point category. The place MAX PR has color set HSTRY whose elements are 4-tuples and shows top attraction points of n MH.

Hierarchical Pages of the CPN Model

The Hierarchical START page is depicted in Fig 3 and is the sub-module of the *substituting*transition START in Fig 2. The functionality of this page is to produce an MH for simulation. This module contains four *places* and two ordinary *transitions*. The transition TimeofArival models the mobile node identity and its arrival time. The variable n is of type NO, and the variable id is of type NODE (see Table 1). In initial marking *M0*, this transition is enabled and after one token is fired, it moves to the place MH2 of color set NODE. The place VLCTYDEPND is a *fusion* place and is a member of *fusion* set VLDPNDY. A *fusion* set allows different places from multiple pages to be glued together and all member places always share the same tokens.

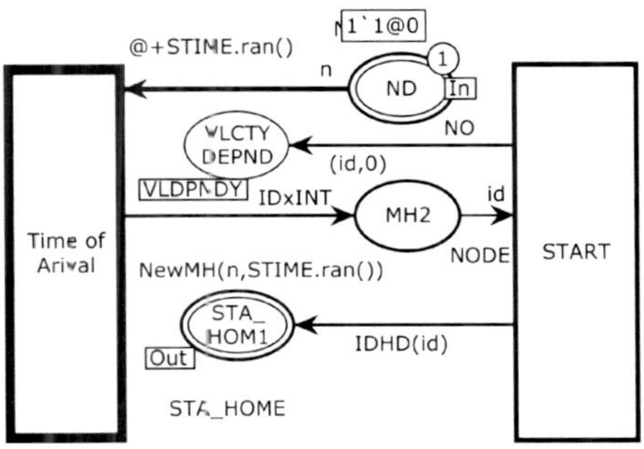

Figure 3: The START module with initial marking M_0.

The place ND in this module is called port place and represents the total number of MHs. Place ND is an *input socket port* port $P^{in}_{sock}(t)$ while place STA_HOM1 is an *output socket port* $P^{out}_{sock}(t)$.

$$P^{in}_{sock}(START) = \{\text{ND}\}$$

$$P^{out}_{sock}(START) = \{\text{STA\_HOM1}\}$$

$$VLDPNDY = \text{VLCTY DEPND}^{START}, VLCTY\ DEPND1^{ANGLE}\}$$

$$P = \{\text{MH2}\}$$

$$T = \{\text{START, Time of Arival}\}$$

After firing transition TimeofArival, the following two-tuple token are moved to the place MH2, which has NODE color set. The function *New MH* takes two inputs of the host ID and arrival time and produces the following token of type NODE:

$$\text{MH} \rightarrow 1`(\text{"MH} - 1\text{"}, 3)@3$$

Fig 4 illustrates page MOVE, which is the sub module of the *substituting* transition MOVE in Fig 2 and is responsible for mobility management of an MH. This page has two ordinary places, two *output socket* places $P^{out}_{sock}(t)$, one *input socket* place $P^{out}_{sock}(t)$ and two *transitions*, one ordinary and one substituting as noted below:

$$P^{out}_{sock}(MOVE) = \{\text{NEW DEST, EVERY MOVE}\}$$

$$P^{in}_{sock}(MOVE) = \{\text{STA\_HOM1}\}$$

$$T_{sub} = \text{ANGLE}^{MOVE}$$

$$P = \{\text{TSP, CNTR}\}$$

$$T = \{\text{RUN}\}$$

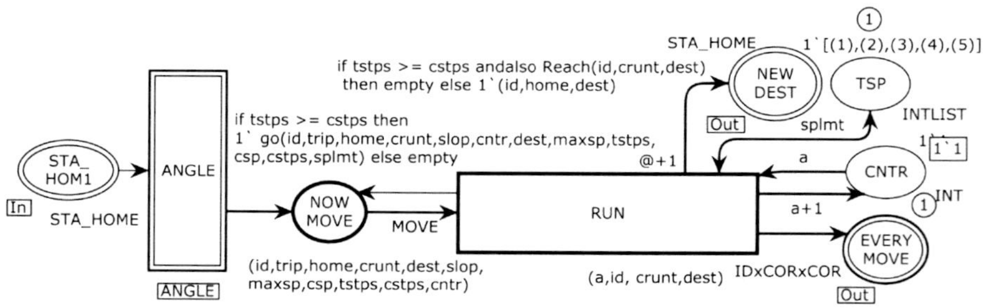

Figure 4: The MOVE module models the mobility management.

fun Reach (id:NODE,x1:LCOOR,x2:LCOOR)

This function is used to monitor whether MH has reached the destination or not. The Reach function takes a three-tuple as domain and returns a type boolean.

fun slow(csp:INT,maxsp:INT,tstps:INT,cstps:INT,splmt:INTLIST)

This function is used to model the removal of sudden stops problem. To exhibit realism, MH starts with low speed and gradually increases up to the maximum speed limit, and gradually decreases when it reaches the destination.

fun xaxis (x:LCOOR, a:REAL, c:REAL)

This function generates the next x-axis according to the parametric equation formula. $x = r\ cos(t)$

fun yaxis (x:LCOOR, a:REAL, c:REAL)

This function generates the next y-axis according to the parametric equation formula. $y = r\,sin(t)$

fun go(id:NODE,trip:INT,home:LCOOR,crunt:LCOOR,slop:RCOR,

cntr:REAL,dest:LCOOR,maxsp:INT,tstps:INT,csp:INT, cstps:INT,

splmt:INTLIST)

The go function is used to restrict the MH to move to the next coordinate after satisfying all imposed conditions.

The sub module ANGLE computes the desired angle and other information to reach its destination and transmits eleven-tuple token to the NOWMOVE place. The RUN transition in Fig 4 is the most important one in the model, and has three *input* arcs and five *output* arcs. It models the actual movement of an MH according to a specified criteria. We define two functions Reach and go for the use in arc expression from transition RUN to NOWMOVE place. The go function calls three functions: slow, xaxis, and yaxis. These functions are described as follows:

When RUN transition occurs, it fetches one token from the NOW MOVE input place with input arc expression (id,trip,home,crunt,dest,sl op,maxsp,csp,tstps,cstps,cntr), one token from the CNTR place, and one token from the TSP place. The variables of the incoming arc expressions are declared as:

var slop: RCOR; (* *The itinerary angle of movement*)

var trip,maxsp,csp,cstps,: INT; *(* The integers are used to describe trip number, maximum*

tstps,cntr,a *speed limit, current speed, current step number, total steps of epoch, increasing counter *)*

var home,crunt,dest: LCOOR; (* *The home, current and destination coordinates of MH*)*

var id: NODE; (* *The Identity Number of MH, with time*)*

var splmt: INTLIST; (* *The current status of MH*)*

The following arc expression is implemented on an outgoing arc from the transition RUN to the NOW MOVE place.

if tstps > = cstps andalso Reach(id,crunt,dest) then 1`go(id,trip,home ,crunt,slop,cntr,dest,maxsp,tstps,csp,cstps,splmt) else empty

If the above condition is satisfied, then eleven-tuple token will be moved back to the NOW MOVE place after increasing one step to the next co-ordinates.

The substituting transition ANGLE in Fig 3 corresponds to the modeling of moving parameters and changes for every epoch. Fig 5 shows the ANGLE module, which enables the CPN to model the velocity dependency, angle to move, and total number of steps to reach the destination. This page has seven ordinary places, one *input socket* place, i.e., $P^{in}_{sock}(t)$, one *output socket* place, i.e. $P^{out}_{sock}(t)$, and two ordinary transitions as presented below:

$$P^{in}_{sock}(ANGLE) = \{STA\_HOME\}$$

$$P^{out}_{sock}(ANGLE) = \{NOWMOVE\}$$

$$P = \{SLOPE, QURDNT, CONTER, QURDNT\ SLOPE, TOTAL\ STPS, OK, VLCTY\ DEPND1, MAX\ SPEED\}$$

$$T = \{OUT, READY\}$$

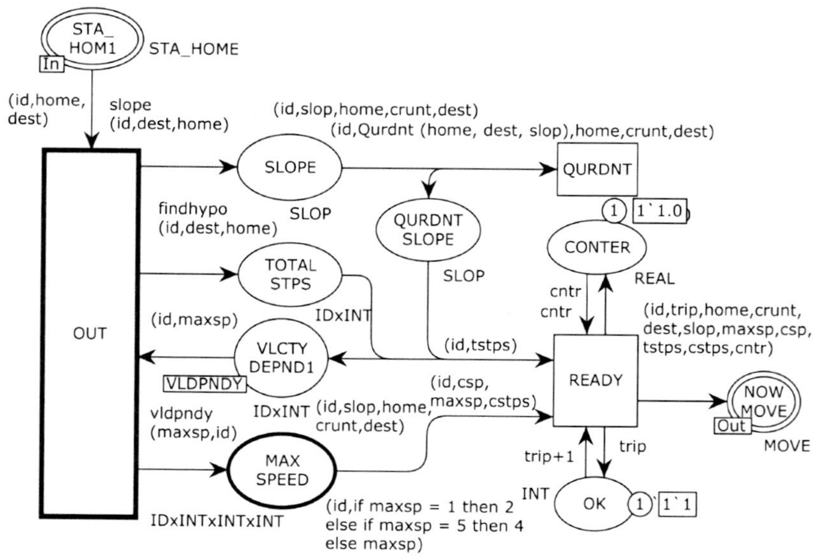

Figure 5: The ANGLE module which is responsible to demonstrate the moving paramaters.

The output arc from the OUT transition applies three functions, i.e., slope with product (id,dest,home), findhype with product (id,dest,home), and vidpndy with product (maxsp,id). When the OUT transition occurs with a given binding, it fetches one token from the STA_HOME1 and VLCTYDEPND1 places to evaluate the arc expressions of the output arcs to the SLOP, TOTALSTPS, and MAXSPEED places. The slope function takes the expression (id,dest,home) as its arguments and returns the angle to move towards the destination based on the current coordinates using the CPN tools built-in *Math.atan()* function. The findhype function with the expression (id,dest,home) as its argument is used on the arc from the OUT transition to the TOTAL STPS place to calculate the total steps from home to destination by implementing the *Math.sqrt ()* and *Math.pow()* functions. The vidpndy function with the arguments (maxsp.id) is used to derive the mobility characteristic, which is the *temporal dependency of velocity* to represent a more realistic behavior by incorporating the velocity dependency of an MH. This function calls the *VLCTY.ran()* function to decide the next epoch speed depending on the previous speed to avid the sudden increase or decrees in speed. Now we consider the QURDNT transition, which implements Qurdnt function on outgoing arc towards the QURDNT SLOPE place to find quadrants of the destination to finalize the moving angle. An MH can be in any one of four quadrants, i.e., Quadrant-I (0° - 90°), Quadrant-II (90° - 180°), Quadrant-III (180° - 270°), and Quadrant-IV (270° - 0°). Then, the READY transition with eleven-tuple arc expression to the port NOW MOVE place produces final input to the MOVE module (see Fig 4) for traveling the MH to the destination. The READY transition fetches five tokens from the input places of CONTER, OK, QURDNT SLOPE, TOTAL STPS, and MAX SPEED and produces four tokens to the output places of CONTER, OK, and VLCTY DEPND1. The CNTR (counter) and OK places are used to model the incremental counters to keep track of every epoch sequence.

Fig 6 depicts the abstract HOTSPOTS page, which renders the *temporal dependency* behavior to overcome the memory-less nature problem of the RWP and its other variants. The HOTSPOTS module corresponds to the *substituting* transition HOTSPOTS in Fig 2, and it is used to tie the REPEAT and HISTORY sub-modules. This page has one ordinary place, three *output socket* places $P^{out}_{sock}(t)$, one *input/output socket* place $P^{i/o}_{sock}(t)$ one *input socket* place $P^{in}_{sock}(t)$, and two substituting transitions as presented below:

$$P^{in}_{sock}(HOTSPOTS) = \{\text{NEW DEST}\}$$

$$P^{out}_{sock}(HOTSPOTS) = \{\text{MAX PR, PRIORITY4, MONITOR}\}T_{sub} = \text{HISTORY}^{HOTSPOTS}, \text{REPEAT}^{HOTSPOTS}$$

$$P^{I/O}_{sock}(HOTSPOTS) = \{\text{PRIORITY CHK}\}$$

$$P = \{\text{RCORD4}\}$$

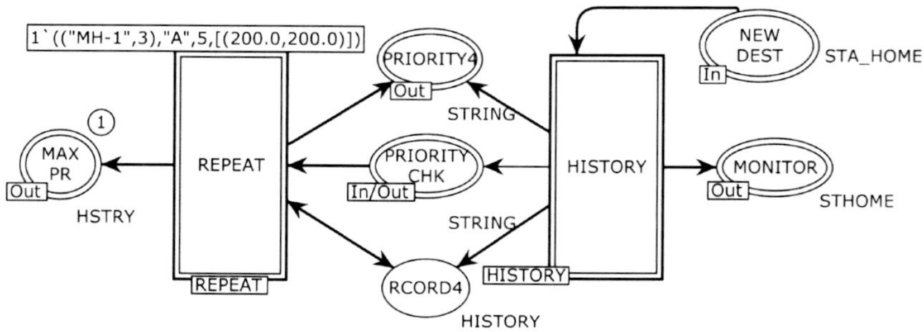

Figure 6: The HOTSPOTS module to resolve the memory-less issue.

The five input, output, and input/output places constitute an interface through which the HOTSPOTS module exchanges tokens with other pages. The declarations of the color sets used in the HOTSHOTS module and its two sub modules (see Fig 6) are listed in Table 2. The process to find attraction points (hotspots) is modeled using the HISTORY and REPEAT substituting transitions.

Table 2: Declaration of Color set for HOTSPOTS and its substitution transitions

Line No.	Color Name	Color Type
1.	colset STHOME	product INT*NODE*LCOOR*STRING*LCOOR timed;
2.	colset HISTORY	list HSTRY;
3.	colset IDxSTxCOR	product NODE*STRING*LCOOR;
4.	colset HSTCNTR	product NODE*INT*INT*INT*STRING*LCOOR;
5.	colset IDxINTxINTxINT	product NODE*INT*INT*INT;
6.	colset TPLACE	list IDxSTxCOR;

doi:10.1371/journal.pone.0133634.t002

The HISTORY substituting transition in Fig 6 corresponds to the modeling of the HISTORY module, which is used to keep the track record of attraction points of the MH as shown in Fig 7. The HCNTR, PRITY PLACES, and PHIST places are *fusion* places. There are nine ordinary places, one *input socket* place $P^{in}_{sock}(t)$, four *output socket* places $P^{out}_{sock}(t)$, and five ordinary transitions as listed below:

$$P^{in}_{sock}(HISTORY) = \{\text{NEW DEST}\}$$

$$P^{out}_{sock}(HISTORY) = \{\text{MONITOR, PRIORITY CHK, PRIORITY4, RCORD4}\}$$

$$HCnters = \{\text{HCNTR}^{HISTORY}, \text{HCNTR3}^{PAUSE}\}$$

$$TPRITY = \text{PRITY PLACES}^{HISTORY}, \text{PRITY PLACES2}^{PAUSE}\}$$

$$PrityChk = \text{PHIST}^{HISTORY}, \text{PHIST2}^{PAUSE}\}$$

$$P = \{\text{PHIST5, PRIORTY2, HCNTR4, PHIST9, PHIST8, PRIORITY, HSTY3, RCORD3, HCNTR2}\}$$

$$T = \{\text{PRITY, H3ND, H2ND, UPHSTRY, CHKHIST}\}$$

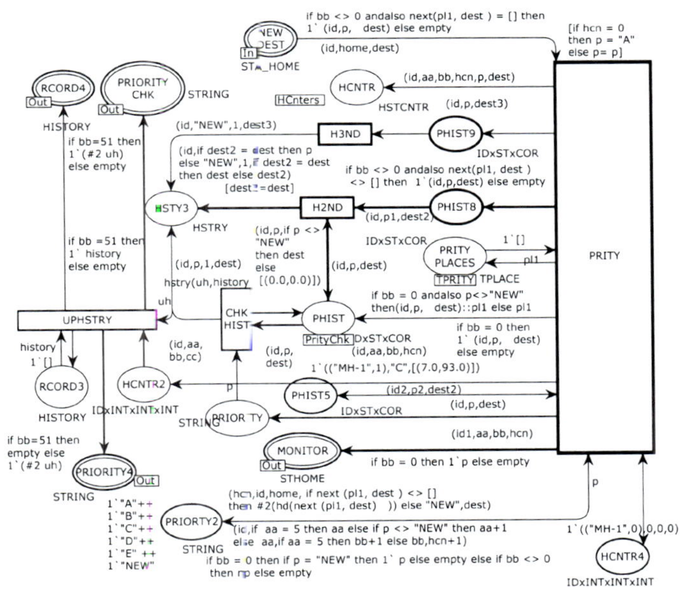

Figure 7: The HISTORY module which models the attraction points of MH.

The PRITY transition fetches five tokens from the input places of NEW DEST, PHIST5, PRIORITY2, PRITY PLACES, and HCNTR4 and produces tokens to the output places of HCNTR, PHIST5, PRIORITY2, HCNTR4, MONITOR, PRITY PLACES, PHIST, PHIST8, PHIST9, HCNTR2, and PRIORITY.

We define a polymorphic function next to use as an arc expressions from the PRITY transition to the MONITOR and PHIST8 places with a product argument (pl1, dest). When the PRITY transition occurs with a given binding, it yields one token to the HCNTR4 place to keep track of three counters, one token to the output PRITY PLACES place to maintain the history of attraction points of the mobile user, and one five-tuple token to the MONITOR place for monitoring and statistical analysis requirements. The places HCNTR, PRIORITY, PHIST9, HSTY3, PHIST, and PHIST8 assist places used in developing the CPN model to extract the history based information. The CHKHIST transition models a four-tuple arc expression ((“MH-1”,0),”A”,1,[(40.0,97.0)]) for the HISTY3 place where the first tuple reflects an MH ID, the second element represents the attraction point, the third one is a counter, and the fourth represents the coordinates. Then, we implement three arc expressions on the input and four on the output arcs of the UPHSTRY transition. The recursive function hstry takes expression (uh,history) as arguments and updates the list of attraction points. It obtains an attraction point p from the variable uh to be added and a list history, as parameters. Initially, the list is empty, and we add attraction point p to the list. In the inductive step, we first check whether the head of the list and attraction point p have the same attraction point attribute. If this is the case, then we increment the third tuple priority counter by one to show the total number of trips to the specific destination. If the attraction points are different, then we add the attraction point p with its coordinates to the next element on the history list. This is done using the hstry function to the variable uh and tail of the history list.

The instance reflected in Fig 8 corresponds to the REPEAT substituting transition in Fig 6, which is used to model the final sorted list of attraction points based on the maximum number of trips of the MH. There are seven ordinary places, one *input socket* place $P^{in}_{sock}(t)$, one *input/output socket* place $P^{i}_{o\,sock}(t)$ two *output socket* places $P^{out}_{sock}(t)$ and four ordinary transitions as follows.

$$P^{in}_{sock}(REPEAT) = \{\text{PRIORITY}\}$$

$$P^{out}_{sock}(REPEAT) = \{\text{MAX PR, PRIORITY4}\}$$

$$P^{i/o}_{sock}(REPEAT) = \{\text{PRIORITY CHK}\}$$

$$P = \{\text{SRTCNTR, BCNTR, MAXP, SORTED, PR\_INT, RCORD, BCNTR2}\}$$

$$T = \{\text{MAX PRITY, SORT, FMAX, PRIORITY CNTR}\}$$

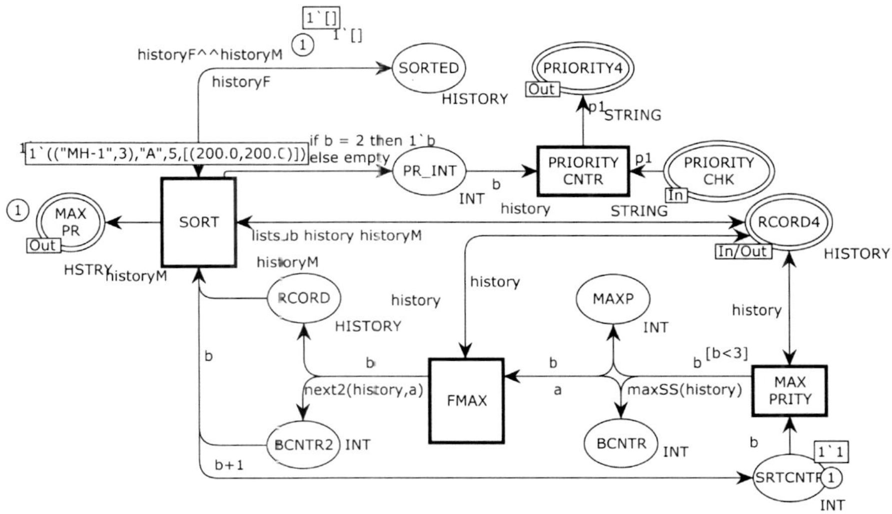

Figure 8: The REPEAT module which represents final five attraction points based on frequency of visits.

The REPEAT module of the SHER mobility model enables only once when the integer counter, i.e., <bb = 51> is evaluated by the UPHSTRY transition via an arc expression to the output RCORD4 place (see Fig 7). We specified five types of attraction points as *"A", "B", "C", "D", and "E"*. Other type of an attraction point is *"NEW"* and specifies that the MH traveled to a new destination other than the five declared attraction points. The REPEAT module finds two *hotspots* from the five attraction points and identifies these as the *home* and *work place* of an MH, where it repeatedly travels. The maximum frequency of trips (the third attribute of the history variable) is declared as hotspot *"A"* and the second highest is *"B"*. The MAX PRITY transition takes a list of attraction points with their visiting frequency as an input from the port RECORD4 place and generates the first hotspot based on the maximum number of visits using the maxSS (history) function to the output MAXP place. The SRTCNTR place with INT color set maintains a counter to the MAX PRITY bound transition to produce two hotspots. The maxSS() recursive function takes the expression (history) as an argument and produces an integer showing the maximum number of visits. This integer is further used by the FMAX transition as an input to determine the first hotspot. The FMAX transition fetches three tokens from the MAXP, BCNTR, and RCORD4 places and its objective is to produce the first hotspot using the next2(history,a) function to the output RECORD place. The next2() function initially takes an empty list, then we add the maximum visits using the variable a from the MAXP place. Its other input is from the RECORD4 place, which contains a complete record of attraction points. In the next step, we check whether the head (3rd attribute) of the list and variable a are equal. If this is the case, then the next2() function produces a *head* to the RECORD place; otherwise, this function is implemented to the *tail* of the history list. Now we consider the transition SORT, which delivers the first hotspot to the MAX PR and SORTED places. This transition has four input and five output places with expressions. After finding the first hotspot the same process is repeated for the second hotspot, and the expression <b + 1> to the output arc of the SRTCNTR place enables the MAX PRITY transition to produce the next hotspot. An occurrence of the PRIORITY CNTR transition models the control transfer to the PAUSE module and is enabled once during the simulation with bindings <b = 2> and <bb = 51>.

Fig 9 shows the PAUSE module. The PAUSE substituting transition in Fig 2 corresponds to this module and is used to decide the next destination based on the previous history. This sub-process also models the pause time dependency based on the hotspot's category. In a real time scenario, a user spends more time in home or office; therefore, this realistic behavior is represented by this PAUSE module. Three places of PRITY PLACES2, HCNTR3, and PHIST2 are *fusion* places. There are eight ordinary places, one *input socket* place $P^{in}_{sock}(t)$, one *input/output socket* place $P^{i/o}_{sock}(t)$ two *output socket* places $P^{out}_{sock}(t)$, and four ordinary transitions as follows.

$$P^{in}_{sock}(PAUSE) = \{\text{PRIORITY4}\}$$

$$P^{out}_{sock}(PAUSE) = \{\text{STA\_HOM1, PAUSE DEPND}\}$$

$$HCnters = \text{HCNTR}^{HISTORY}, \text{HCNTR3}^{PAUSE}\}$$

$$TPRITY = \{\text{PRITY PLACES}^{HISTORY}, \text{PRITY PLACES2}^{PAUSE}\}$$

$$PrityChk = \text{PHIST}^{HISTORY}, \text{PHIST2}^{PAUSE}\}$$

$$P_{sock}^{i}(PAUSE) = \{\text{MAX PR}\}$$

$$P = \{\text{PRIORTY3, MAX PR2, PS CNTR, NEW DEST\_PAUSE, NEW DEST, PS CNTR2, PAUSE MOINTOR}\}$$

$$T = \{\text{HIST2, OUT PAUSE, OUT5, PRE OUTPAUSE}\}$$

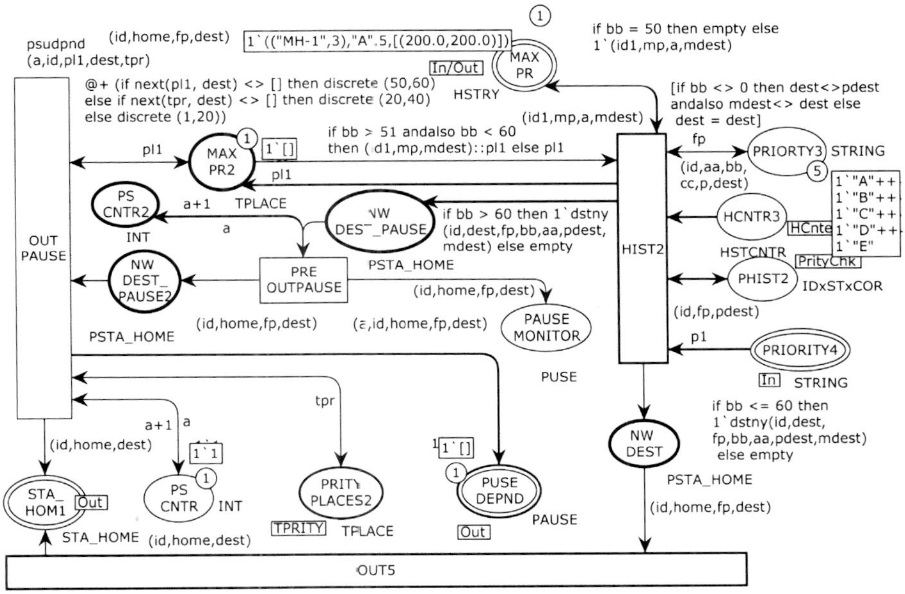

Figure 9: The PAUSE module to show the next destination based on previous history.

The HIST2 transition fetches six tokens from the input places PRIORTY3, MAX PR2, PRIORTY4, MAX PR, HCNTR3, and PHIST2 and produces tokens to the output places PRIORTY3, PHIST2, MAX PR2, NEW DEST_PAUSE, MAX PR, and NEW DEST. We define four functions of prity(), prity2(), prityF(), and dstny to model the next destination after completing one epoch of the previous history.

Table 3 shows the declaration of polymorphic function dstny, which is used in the arcs expressions from the HIST2 transition to the NW DEST_PAUSE and NEW DEST output places.

Table 3: Declaration of functions used in an arc expression to model the next destination in Fig 8

Line No.	Function
1.	val pr = 0.95;
2.	valpr2 = 0.70;
3.	val prF = 0.50;
4.	fun prity () = uniform (0.0,1.0) < = pr;
5.	fun prity2 () = uniform (0.0,1.0) < = pr2;
6.	fun prityF () = uniform (0.0,1.0) < = prF;
7.	fun dstny(id:NODE,dest:LCOOR fp:STRING,bb:INT,aa:INT, pdest:LCOOR, mdest:LCOOR) =
8.	(id,dest, fp, if aa+1 = 6 andalso bb = 0 then pdest else if aa+1 = 6 andalso bb > 0 andalso bb < 51
9.	then if prity () then pdest else [(real(discrete(0,99)), real(discrete(0,99)))]
10.	else if aa+1 = 6 andalso bb > = 51 then if prity2 () then if prityF () then mdest else pdest
11.	else [(real(discrete(0,99)), real(discrete(0,99)))]
12.	else [(real(discrete(0,99)), real(discrete(0,99)))]);

doi:10.1371/journal.pone.0133634.t003

In order to model the history based destination, we first define the prity() function in line 4 of Table 3. When this function is called, it returns either *true* or *false* by evaluating the uniform (0.0,1.0) expression and produces a real number from the interval [0.0,1.0] where all numbers have the same selection probability. We define a constant <pr = 0.95> (line 1). If the number returned by the *uniform* function is less than or equal to the constant pr, then the prity() function is considered as *true;* otherwise, it is *false*. In other words, there is 95% chance of the occurrence of *true* and 5% chance of *false*: however, these parameters can be modified. The same logic can be applied to the prity2() and prityF() functions in the lines 5 and 6 of Table 3. To demonstrate a more realistic approach to find the destination, we selected the first fifty destinations to find five attraction points, out of which the first two attraction points are declared as hotspots (home and office). The destny polymorphic function has the objective to model the history based selection of the next destination of the MH. This procedure is defined in Algorithm-I. The destny function takes seven parameters as (id,dest,fp,bb,aa,pdest,mdest) and produces a four-tuple token, i.e., (id,home,fp,dest). The PAUSE MONITOR place is a monitoring place and holds the pause time intervals for future statistical analysis.

To define the pause time dependency, counter bb is modeled and shows the completed trips. To obtain realistic stable results, we implemented a built-in *discrete uniform distribution*function, and per policy, hotspots are given the pause time of (50–60), other attraction points of (20–40), and remaining new destination of (1–20). A user can modify these parameters. In our implementation, we applied the pause dependency policy after 60 completed trips. The OUT5 transition has one input and one output. This transition occurs when (bb < 60). The pause dependency is applied on its guard. In fact, the OUT PAUSE transition implements the pause dependency on its guard, and the next () recursive function is called to generate the pause time dependency. The PUSE DEPND port place is a monitoring place where the psudpnd() function with arguments (a,id,pl1,dest,tpr) has been implemented and returns the pause time delay based on the attraction point's category.

Algorithm-I: History based destination

Input: $B_{bb,}$ Counter used to find attraction points

A_{aa}, Counter for initial setup

A_{pdest}, Attraction point coordinates

H_{mdest}, Hotspot coordinates

F_{prity}. Probability function (95% chance to true)

F_{prity2}, Probability function (70% chance to true)

F_{prityF}, Probability function (50% chance to true)

Output D_{Dest}, New destination based on previous movement history

1 ((aa+1 = = 6) and (aa+1 = = 6)-> pdest))

2 &

3 ((aa+1 = = 6) and (51<bb>0))

a. (prity = = true-> pdest)

b. else

c. [(real(discrete(0,99)), real(discrete(0,99))]

4 &

5 ((aa+1 = = 6) and (bb > = 51))

a. (prity2 = = true)

i. (prityF = = true-> mdest)

ii. else

iii. (pdest)

b. else

c. [(real(discrete(0,99)), real(discrete(0,99))]

6 else

7 [(real(discrete(0,99)), real(discrete(0,99))].

Overview of the Occurrence Sequence

When the simulation starts, the only enabled transition for the proposed SHER CPN model is TimeofArival at page START. The model contains four parts: START, MOVE, HOTSPOTS, and PAUSE (see Fig 2). The MH identity with its availability time is positioned at the ND place and is represented by a token as *<1`1@0>*. This single tuple token specifies that an ID 1 is available at time 0. The TimeofArival transition generates two-tuple token representing MH-ID with arrival time, i.e., *<1`("MH-1",6)@6>*. The MH2 place receives the token from the TimeofArival transition and enables the START transition, which is responsible to produce three-tuple token to represent MH-ID, home-grid-coordinates, and destination-grid-coordinates, i.e., *<1`(("MH-1",6),[(49.0,34.0)],[(25.0,10.0)])@6>*. This token specifies that MH-1 wants to go from coordinates (49.0, 34.0) to coordinates (25.0, 10.0). The STA_HOM1 place that is the *port-socket* place between the START and SHER pages captures the token from the START transition and enables OUT transition on the ANGLE page. When the OUT transition occurs, it produces three tokens to the SLOP, TOTAL STPS, and MAX SPEED places. The five-tuple token, i.e., <1`(("MH-1",6),45.0,[(49.0,34.0)],[(49.0,34.0)],[(25.0,10.0)])> at the SLOPE place represents (MH, angle-to-move, Home-coordinates, Current-coordinates and Destination-coordinates). The TOTAL STPS place receives the two-tuple token <1`(("MH-1",6),34)> that contains the MH and total steps to reach the destination. The third output at the MAX SPEED place reflects four tuples as <1`(("MH-1",6),1,4,1)>. This token contains the MH, current speed, maximum speed, and current step number information. From these three outputs, we can conclude that OUT transition produces MH-1 from home coordinates (49.0, 34.0) to the destination coordinates (25.0, 10.0) with the moving angle of 45° and it will take 34 single steps, and the selected speed for this epoch is four. The

QURDNT transition delivers final angle with respect to four quadrants, and in this case the destination falls in the fourth quadrant. Therefore, the final angle is 225° when the token is at the QURDNT SLOP place, i.e., <1`((“MH-1”,6),225.0,[(49.0,34.0)],[(49.0,34.0)],[(25.0,10.0)])>. The READY transition takes all basic information from the five input places and produces the following eleven-tuple token at the NOW MOVE output place:<1`((“MH-1”,6),1,[(49.0,34.0)], [(49.0,34.0)],[(25.0,10.0)] ,225.0,4,1,34,1,1.0)>.

The contents of this token are MH, trip number, home coordinates, current coordinates, destination coordinates, angle to move, maximum speed, current speed, total steps, current step number, and tracking counter. Now, the RUN transition at the MOVE page becomes enabled by the NOW MOVE input place. It takes three inputs and produces an eleven-tuple token to the NOW MOVE place after incrementing one step in the given binding. The go function implemented on the arc from the RUN transition to the NOW MOVE place elegantly takes steps towards the destination by calling the slow function to gradually increase or decrees the speed. The EVERY MOVE place is a monitoring place, which keeps the record of every step, and in current epoch, the MH has reached its destination in twelve steps <1`(12,(“MH-1”,6),[(25.95,10.95)],[(25.0,10.0)])>. After successful completion of the first trip, the RUN transition sends a token to the NEW DEST output place, which enables the PRITY transition at the HISTORY page. The PRITY transition produces a token at the PHIST place after mentioning the first attraction point “A” with coordinates. Now the token can be seen as <1`((“MH-1”,6),”A”,[(25.0,10.0)])>. The CHKHIST transition fetches the token from the PHIST place and forwards it to the HSTY3 place after keeping the record back at the PHIST place. The UPHSTRY transition enables after the token is at the HSTY3 place, and when it occurs, it leads the posting of the history based token at the RCORD3 place and one token at the PRIORITY4 output place reflecting the attraction point “A”. Now control moves to the PAUSE page by having a token at the PRIORITY4 input place. The objective of the HIST2 transition is to select a new destination; hence, when it occurs, it produces the token <1`((“MH-1”,6),[(25.0,10.0)],”A”,[(54.0,8.0)])@18 > at the NW DEST place. Here, we can see that the previous destination is now converted to home and a new destination is presented as [(54.0, 8.0)]). The OUT5 transition fetches a token from the NW DEST place (see Fig 9) and sends it to the STA_HOM1 place at the SHER page (see Fig 2). Thus, the SHER model represents acyclic non-terminating behavior. In order to obtain a complete list of five attraction points, Fig 10demonstrates anther execution of the SHER model, where we repeated the cyclic firing sequence of the transitions 50 times. The marking of the HOTSPOT module after 2300 steps represents two hotspots and three attraction points. It can be seen that the MAX PR place indicates two hotspots: <1`((“MH-1”,9),”A”,13,[(20.0,80.0)])> and <1`((“MH-1”,9),”E”,12,[(42.0,22.0)]) >. These two attraction points are declared as hotspots on the basis of maximum number of visits and in the given case, 13 visits are at point “A” and 12 visits are at point “E”. The RCORD4 place indicates three attraction points with visit frequencies of 10, 9, and 7 as <1`((“MH-1”,9),”C”,10,[(0.0,90.0)])>, <1`((“MH-1”,9),”B”,9,[(13.0,54.0)])>, and <1`((“MH-1”,9), “D”,7,[(82.0,42.0)])>. In addition, five visits are towards any other ordinary places.

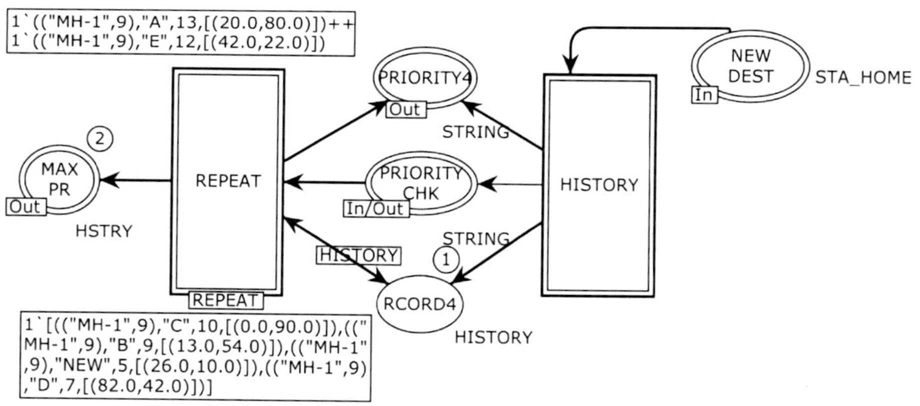

Figure 10: The HOTSPOT module after 2300 steps which reflects two hotspots “A” and “E.”

SIMULATION ANALYSIS AND DISCUSSION

In order to simulate and verify the SHER mobility model, we used the CPN state space tool and implemented a state space construction algorithm. The state space analysis allowed us to analyze all the standard behavioral properties of the model such as *boundedness*, *reachability*, *liveness*, *home* and *fairness*. For simplify the analysis and monitor the behavior of the proposed model and its movement patterns, the state space tool's options were fixed in order to partially generate a simulation up to 1000 sec. Table 4 shows the initial part of the standard state space report for the movement of one MH and its statistics. It specifies that the O-graph (occurrence graph) has 42244 nodes and 57145 arcs, and the Strongly Connected Graphs (SSG) immediately reveals that cycles exist, and the model has an infinite occurrences sequences and does not terminate. It took four seconds to calculate the SSG. The MH moved in communication range without any restriction. Fig 11 depicts the partial state space that represents the O-graph.

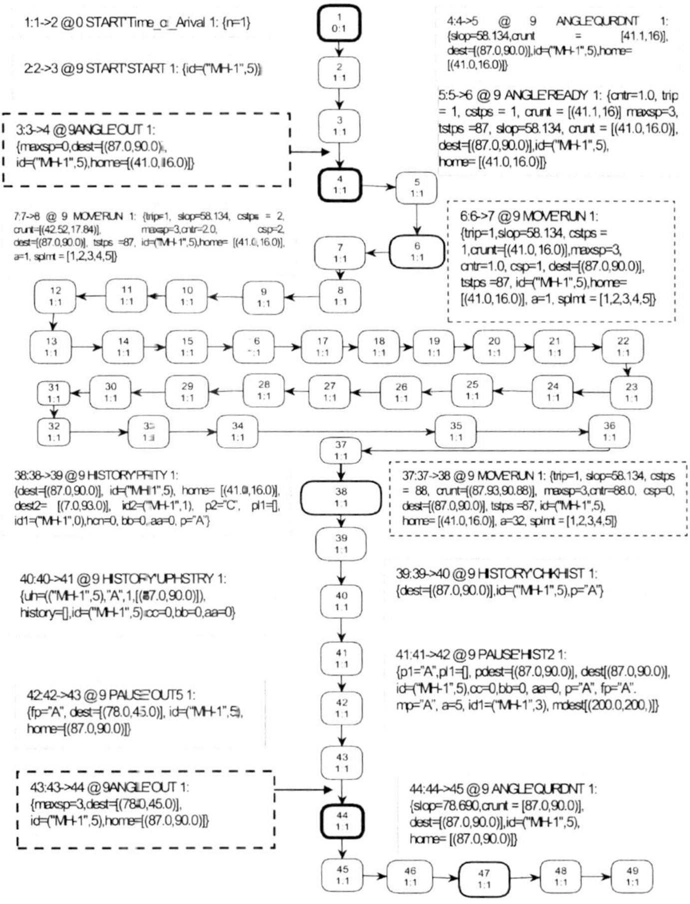

Figure 11: Partial state space representing the occurrence graph of the SHER mobility model.

Table 4: State space report–statistics

Line No.	State Space	Scg Graph
1.	Nodes:42244	Nodes:42244
2.	Arcs: 57145	Arcs: 57145
3.	Secs: 1000	Secs: 4
4.	Status: Partial	

doi:10.1371/journal.pone.0133634.t004

Reachability Graph

Reachability analysis techniques are widely used in formal verification of the concurrent systems and protocols [39][40]. As shown in Fig 11, the initial fragment of the O-graph has 49 nodes and 48 arcs, and it can be seen that each node (marking) is inscribed with three integers where the topmost integer in the node of the O-graph indicates the node number and the other two separated by colon (:) represent the total number of successor and predecessors. The state space in Fig 11 is represented by the directed graph where each node shows reachable marking and an arc illustrates the occurrence binding element. There is a single one to one (1:1) sequence of the occurrence without overtaking. The rectangular box positioned next to the node reflects the binding information. The arc binding (thick dashed border) of node 4 is <3:3->4 @ 9 ANGLE›OUT 1: {maxsp = 0,dest = [(87.0,90.0)], id = ("MH-1",5),home = [(41.0,16.0)]}> and the binding for node 44 is <43:43->44 @ 9 ANGLE›OUT 1: {maxsp = 3,dest = [(78.0,45.0)],id = ("MH-1",5),home = [(87.0,90.0)]}>. These bindings provides the evidence of a cyclic non-terminating behavior of the SHER model. The structure of node 4 and 44 is the same; however, there are variable parameters according to the destination coordinates of the MH. The first two nodes (1 and 2) represent the occurrence of transitions that takes place from the START module, then control is transferred to the ANGLE module (node 3, 4, and 5). Next, the MH travels to the destination coordinates via the MOVE sub-page, and 32 nodes (from 6 to 37) represent the traveling pattern of the MH from home to destination. In each epoch, these nodes are changed according to the destination distance from home. When MH finishes the first trip, the HISTORY submodule is enabled. Moreover, three nodes (38 to 40) in the O-graph represents the behavior of this sub-page. We can proceed analogously in the PAUSE module where three nodes (i.e., 41, 42, and 43) define the pause time structure after completion of the first epoch.

Next, the SHER model repeats the process for the next destination from the ANGLE module. Node 44 represents the start point of the repeating process (the OUT transition of the ANGLE module).

Boundedness Properties

Upper and lower bounds property specifies the maximum and minimum number of tokens that can reside on a specific place in any reachable marking. It is important to determine whether the proposed model prevents an overflow. A net is said to be *k-bounded*, if any place contains less than or equal to *k* tokens where *k* is any non-negative integer. If the bound for the number of tokens is equal to one (1-bounded), then this net is *safe*. Table 5 shows part of the state space report for the *boundedness* properties. The CPN model has 52 places. Among these, 34 places have one *best upper integer bound* (1-bounded), and this means that the proposed model is *safe*. The PAUSE'PAUSE_MONITOR, SHER'MONITOR, SHER'PUSE_DEPND, and SHER'EVERY_MOVE places are *unbounded*, and have *best upper integer bound* as 7, 5, 25, and 65 respectively. In fact, these places are monitoring places with the purpose to keep track of every step and their fetched results are used in statistical analysis. If these places are removed, there will be no effect on the model's execution and performance. The PAUSE'PRIORTY3 place has the *best upper* and *lower* bound that are equal to five. This implies that this place always contains equal number of tokens in any reachable marking. The PRIORTY3 place is used to model five attraction points.

Table 5: State space report—Boundedness properties and integer bounds

Best Integer Bounds	Upper	Lower	Best Integer Bounds	Upper	Lower
ANGLE'CONTER	1	1	PAUSE'NW_DEST	1	0
ANGLE'MAX_SPEED	1	0	PAUSE'NW_DEST_PAUSE	1	0
ANGLE'OK	1	1	PAUSE'NW_DEST__PAUSE2	1	0
ANGLE'QURDNT_SLOPE	1	0	PAUSE'PAUSE_MONITOR	7	0
ANGLE'SLOPE	1	0	PAUSE'PHIST2	5	0
ANGLE'TOTAL_STPS	1	0	PAUSE'PRIORTY3	5	5
ANGLE'VLCTY_DEPND1	1	0	PAUSE'PRITY_PLACES2	1	1
HISTORY'HCNTR	2	0	PAUSE'PS_CNTR	1	1
HISTORY'HCNTR2	2	0	PAUSE'PS_CNTR2	1	0
HISTORY'HCNTR4	1	1	REPEAT'BCNTR	1	0
HISTORY'HSTY3	2	0	REPEAT'BCNTR2	1	0
HISTORY'PHIST	5	0	REPEAT'MAXP	1	0
HISTORY'PHIST5	1	1	REPEAT'PR_INT	1	0
HISTORY'PHIST8	1	0	REPEAT'RCORD	1	0
HISTORY'PHIST9	1	0	REPEAT'SORTED	1	1
HISTORY'PRIORITY	2	0	REPEAT'SRTCNTR	1	1
HISTORY'PRIORTY2	6	1	SHER'MAX_PR	2	1
HISTORY'PRITY_PLACES	1	1	SHER'MONITOR	5	0
HISTORY'RCORD3	1	1	SHER'ND	1	0
HOTSPOTS'RCORD4	1	0	SHER'NEW_DEST	2	0
MOVE'CNTR	1	1	SHER'PRIORITY4	2	0
MOVE'NOW_MOVE	2	0	SHER'PRIORITY_CHK	1	0
MOVE'TSP	1	1	SHER'STA__HOM1	1	0
PAUSE'HCNTR3	2	0	START'MH2	1	0
PAUSE'MAX_PR2	1	1	SHER'PUSE_DEPND	25	0
START'VLCTY_DEPNE	1	0	SHER'EVERY_MOVE	65	0

doi:10.1371/journal.pone.0134634.t005

Moreover, we considered only the maximum and minimum number of tokens that can reside in a specific place ignoring the token types. Fig 12 illustrates the best upper and lower multi-set bounds for both quantity and the color of residing tokens. To save the space, we mentioned the multi-set bounds and number of tokens of some places. As expected, these multi-sets are an example that the MAX_SPEED place at the ANGLE page specifies three 4-tuple tokens and in the third tuple the speed of the MH gradually increases. The OK place at the ANGLE page shows the counter for the number of trips, which increases in every turn. The PRIORITY place on the HISTORY page specifies string type tokens that represent five attraction points. The PRITY_PLACES place at the HISTORY page shows one token as empty list, then this list increases by adding attraction points and their coordinates. The TSP place at the MOVE page contains a single token in both *upper* and *lower* bound cases and it remains unchanged during simulation.

Best Upper Multi-set Bounds(partial)

ANGLE'CONTER	1`1.0	HISTORY'HCNTR2 ,	1`(("MH-1",5),0,0,0)++
ANGLE'MAX_SPEED	1`(("MH-1",5),1,1,1)++	HISTORY'HCNTR4	1`(("MH-1",5),1,0,1)++
	1`(("MH-1",5),1,2,1)++		1`(("MH-1",5),1,0,2)++
	1`(("MH-1",5),1,3,1)++	HISTORY'HSTY3 ,	1`(("MH-1",5),"A",1,[(87.0,90.0)])++
ANGLE'OK	1`1++	HISTORY'PHIST ,	1`(("MH-1",5),"B",1,[(0.0,32.0)])++
	1`2++	HISTORY'PHIST5	1`(("MH-1",5),"C",1,[(10.0,79.0)])++
	1`3++	HISTORY'PRIORITY ,	1`"A"++
ANGLE'QURDNT_SLOPE	1`(("MH-1",5),~0.0,[(20.0,22.0)],[(20.0,22.0)],[(37.0,22.0)])++	HISTORY'PRIORTY2	1`"B"++
	1`(("MH-1",5),1.70,[(20.0,22.0)],[(20.0,22.0)],[(87.0,24.0)])++		1`"C"++
	1`(("MH-1",5),1.76,[(30.0,10.0)],[(30.0,10.0)],[(95.0,12.0)])++		1`"D"++
	1`(("MH-1",5),5.19,[(20.0,22.0)],[(20.0,22.0)],[(64.0,26.0)])++		1`"E"++
ANGLE'SLOPE	1`(("MH-1",5),~90.0,[(20.0,22.0)],[(20.0,22.0)],[(20.0,53.0)])++		2`"NEW'
	1`(("MH-1",5),~90.0,[(30.0,10.0)],[(30.0,10.0)],[(30.0,93.0)])++	HISTORY'PRITY_PLACES	1`[]++
	1`(("MH-1",5),~89.34,[(38.0,1.0)],[(38.0,1.0)],[(37.0,89.0)])++		1`[(("MH-1",5),"A",[(87.0,90.0)])]++
ANGLE'TOTAL_STPS ,	1`(("MH-1",5),4)++		1`[(("MH-1",5),"B",[(0.0,32.0)]),(("MH-1",5),"C",[(78.0,45.0)]),(("MH-1",5),"A",[(87.0,90.0)])]++
ANGLE'VLCTY_DEPND1	1`(("MH-1",5),5)++	MOVE'NOW_MOVE	1`(("MH-1",5),1,[(41.0,16.0)],[(41.0,16.0)],[(87.0,90.0)],58.134,3,1,87,1,1.0)++
	1`(("MH-1",5),8)++		1`(("MH-1",5),1,[(41.0,16.0)],[(42.52,17.84)],[(87.0,90.0)],58.13,3,2,87,2,2.0)++
	1`(("MH-1",5),9)++		1`(("MH-1",5),1,[(41.0,16.0)],[(43.05,18.69)],[(87.0,90.0)],58.13,3,3,87,4,4.0)++
HISTORY'HCNTR	1`(("MH-1",5),0,0,0,"A",[(87.0,90.0)])++	PAUSE'HCNTR3	1`(("MH-1",5),0,0,0,"A",[(87.0,90.0)])++
	1`(("MH-1",5),1,0,1,"B",[(78.0,45.0)])++		1`(("MH-1",5),1,0,1,"B",[(78.0,45.0)])++
	1`(("MH-1",5),1,0,2,"NEW",[(10.0,79.0)])++	MOVE'TSP	1`[1,2,3,4,5]

Best Lower Multi-set Bounds (partial)

ANGLE'MAX_SPEED	empty	MOVE'TSP	1`[1,2,3,4,5]
ANGLE'OK	empty	PAUSE'MAX_PR2	1`[]
HISTORY'HCNTR	empty	PAUSE'PS_CNTR	1`1
MOVE'NOW_MOVE	empty	REPEAT'SORTED	1`[]

Figure 12: State space report-multi-set bounds.

Deadlock freedom

To determine the failure cause of the model, Holzmann [41][42] presented three prominent properties: *deadlocks* are the cause when the protocols are in waiting state for occurrence of conditions that can never be fulfilled and leads to deadlock of the model; *livelocks* represent the situation when every process constantly changes with regard to one another without making any effective progress. Finally, *improper termination* is the situation when the protocol accomplishes without satisfying the termination conditions. Our proposed model is deadlock free and the state space report in Table 6 specifies that there are 15671 dead markings including [42244,42243,42242,42241,42240,…]. There are 42244 dead marking because we fixed the state space tool to generate state space report up to 1000 sec for the purpose of simplicity; hence, the total generated nodes are 42244 (see Table 4). Our proposed SHER model satisfies all the termination specifications and Figs 13 to 16 illustrate these conditions.

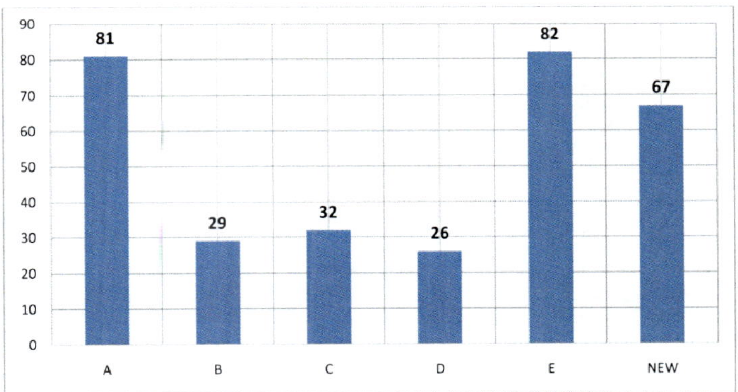

Figure 13: Hotspots, attraction points vs number of trips.

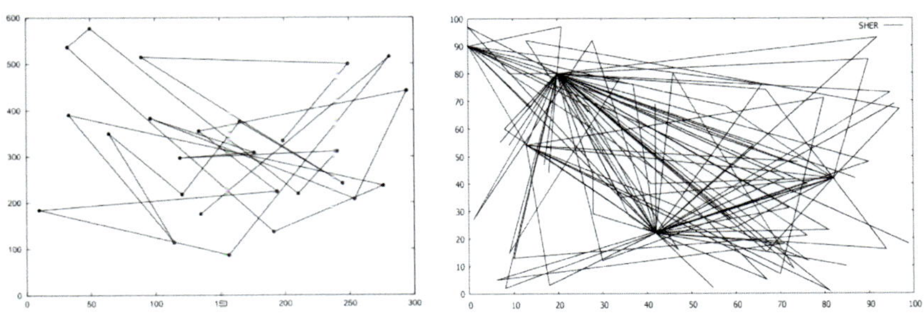

Figure 14: Traveling pattern of a mobile node (MN) using the RWP mobility model [12], Cyclic history based behaviour of the SHER mobility model.

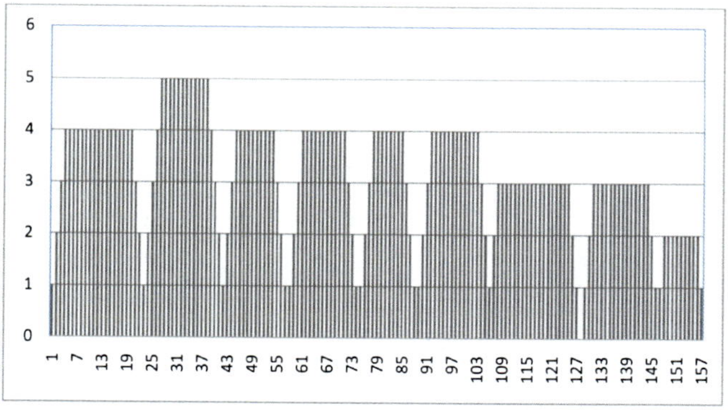

Figure 15: Slow start, stop, and velocity dependency.

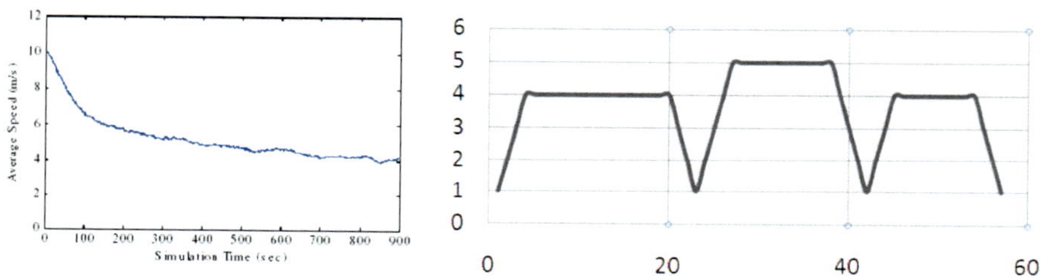

Figure 16: Average speed decay (speed = (0, 20) m/s, pause = 0 sec)[17], Cyclic history based behaviour of the SHER mobility model.

Table 6: State space report-home and liveness properties

Sr. No.	Properties	Sub-Properties	Description
1.	Home Properties	Home Markings	Initial Marking is not a home marking
2.	Liveness Properties	Dead Markings	15671 [42244,42243,42242,42241, 42240,...]
		Dead Transition Instances	HISTORY'H2ND 1
			HISTORY'H3ND 1
			PAUSE'OUT_PAUSE 1
			PAUSE'PRE_OUTPAUSE 1
			REPEAT'FMAX 1
			REPEAT'MAX_PRITY 1
			REPEAT'PRIORITY_CNTR 1
			REPEAT'SORT 1
		Live Transition Instances	None
3.	Fairness Properties	Fairness	No infinite occurrence sequences.

doi:10.1371/journal.pone.0133634.t006

The home properties in Table 6 specifies that initial marking is not home marking. However, Fig 11 illustrates that we can repeat the process (see the bold node 4 and 44 of Fig 11). In markings 4 and 44, the tuples, color sets, and variables can never be changed; however, values of variables can be changed according to the current scenario. The *liveness* property ensures that a transition *t* can be fired again and is stronger than the absence of dead transition. Similarly, the home property specifies that a marking *m* can always be reached again during the model execution. The proposed SHER mobility model has *partial home-marking* and *partial liveness* as presented in Fig 11.

Livelock Deadlock

As stated above *livelocks* are special cases for resource starvation when a specific module or process does not progress. Our implementation of the SHER model is without any *livelock.* Fig 11 provides the relevant supporting evidence for the node's one to one (1:1) relation.

Termination

Improper termination is another prominent property used for verification and specifies whether a proposed model is *terminating* or *not.* A termination state reflects a marking when no further transition is enabled or the model has finite runs. The proposed SHER mobility model has infinite runs; therefore, it is *not terminating* because the model has a cyclic structural behavior. Fig 11 illustrates the O-graph generated from the CPN model where bold *nodes* (see 4 and 44) *verifies* acyclic *non terminating* property of CPN model.

Dead Transition

A transition *t* is called a dead transition in the marking *m* if it can never become enabled in any reachable marking from m_0 during execution. This means that every transition should be occurred at least once on every run. Our proposed model does not have any dead transition (see Fig 11). This can also be verified by implementing the following query that shows an empty list.

ListDeadTIs () → val it[]=:TI.TransInst list

History Based Movement Patterns without Border Effect Problem

After successful termination of 1000 sec simulation, the data shows 317 completed trips for the statistical analysis. We obtained two hotspots ["A", (20,80)] and["E",(42,22)] with the frequency of visits equal to 81 and

82, three attraction points ["B",(13,54)], ["C",(0,90)], and ["D",(82,42)] with 29, 32, and 26 number of visits respectively. There are also 67 trips to a "NEW" (anonymous) locations. Fig 13 yields the frequency of visits while the graphical representation of these trips is illustrated in Fig 14.

The broad criticism about the RWP mobility model is that it generates memory-less mobility patterns, because it retains no knowledge to its past locations. This behavior is depicted in the left part of Fig 14 [12]. In addition, the researchers investigated that the RWP mobility model suffers from the border effect phenomena. The proposed SHER mobility model precisely avoids such problems that are discussed in the literature. The traveling pattern generated by the SHER, which is depicted in the right part of Fig 14, exhibits its improved behaviors.

Slow Start, Stop, and Velocity Dependency

Fig 15 shows more a realistic mobility pattern through slow start, stop, and velocity dependency algorithms that are implemented in the SHER mobility model. It can be seen that there were nine completed epochs, where the first trip had a maximum speed equal to four and in the second trip, the speed was increased by one and the MH completed the trip with the speed of five. Thereafter, speed was gradually decreased by one in the third trip and resulted in a maximum speed of four. In the 4th, 5th, and 6th trip, speed remained stable at four. Later on, in the 7th trip, speed decreased again and was three. In the 8th trip, it remained constant. Finally, in the last trip, the speed decreased by one and became two.

The slow start and stop procedure was intelligently adopted by the SHER model and is depicted in Fig 15. It is evident that the MH started each epoch with speed of one and gradually increased up to the maximum speed. After achieving its maximum limit, the MH traveled towards the destination with this speed and gradually decreased speed up to one before its stop. The same process was repeated until simulation stopped.

No Speed Decay Problem

Another problem mentioned in the literature about the random models is the *"speed decay"*issue[17] when instantaneous average speed of the MH is consistently decreasing (see left part of Fig 16). The proposed SHER mobility model exhibited an MH speed without *speed decay*problem. The right part of Fig 16 demonstrates this behavior. It is pertinent to mention that after taking the first step with slow start, MH gradually achieved steady speed, then remained constant, and gradually decreased near destination. To elaborate further, Fig 16 presents comparison between the SHER and RWP mobility models.

Pause Time Dependency

Fig 17 demonstrates the pause time dependency generated by the SHER mobility model. As narrated in Section 3.3, the pause time dependency is based on the destination type. We modeled the pause time, i.e., (50–60) for hotspots, (20–40) for attraction points, and (1–20) for "NEW" destinations. The pause time dependent algorithm randomly selected the pause time of an MH based on the explained criteria. There are 15 slots for the pause time shown in Fig 17, and we can recognize six hotspots, three attraction points, and six "NEW" (anonymous) destinations.

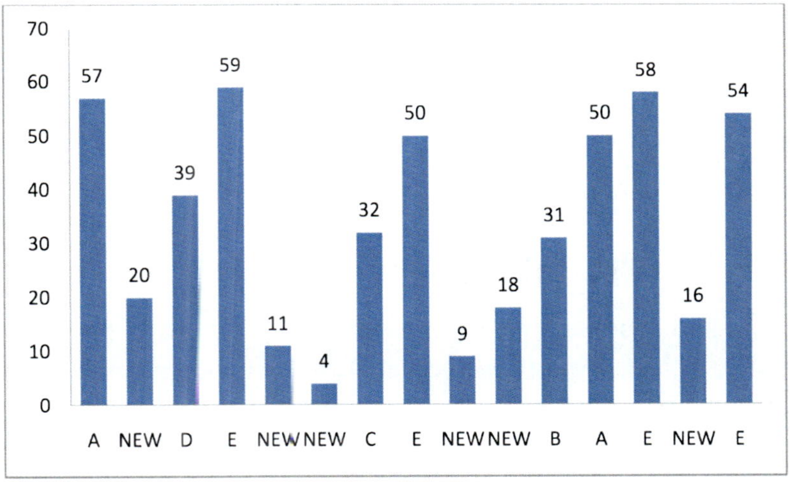

Figure 17: Pause time intervals of 15 epochs.

CONCLUSION

The world of wireless network communication is rapidly changing with recent innovations like WMNs. To the best of our knowledge, we are the first research group to present the SHER mobility model as explained in the introduction in order to remove the six key issues, i.e., *sudden stops, memory less movements, border effect, temporal dependency of velocity, pause time dependency, and speed decay* from the existing random mobility models. In this study, a timed-hierarchical CPN based formal model was developed that was created based on the social aspects of human mobility to produce realistic history based movement patterns. Most of the existing researches are based on simulators such as NS-2, OPNET, and QualNet, while our work opens a new formal modeling based paradigm of research. Extensive simulation experiments were conducted in order to verify the validity of the proposed model. Our results confirmed that the proposed SHER mobility model exhibited a reliable approximation of realism. The proposed model was suitable to develop different topologies and produced diverse trajectories. These patterns was further implemented to remove the mobility management performance issues. The model was easily altered and broadened to capture complex scenarios. In addition, the model was suitable for newcomers to the research community due to its simplicity. As part of our future work, we propose a dynamic mobility model where a token represents obstacles. At this stage, the SHER mobility model produces mobility patterns of a single user while in the next version, we will enhance the capabilities of the SHER to exhibit group based movement patterns. Further research may be devoted to develop realistic mobility models.

AUTHOR CONTRIBUTIONS

Conceived and designed the experiments: NAK FA SAK. Performed the experiments: NAK. Analyzed the data: FA SAK. Contributed reagents/materials/analysis tools: NAK FA SAK. Wrote the paper: NAK FA.

REFERENCES

1. Akyildiz IF, Wang X, Wang W. Wireless mesh networks: a survey, Tech. rep., Georgia Institute of Technology, Computer Networks, March 2005,47(4): 445–487.
2. Aschenbruck N, Munjal A, Camp T. Trace-based mobility modeling for multi-hop wireless networks", Computer Communications, 2011;34: 704–714.
3. Zheng Q, Hong X, Ray S. "Recent advances in mobility modeling

for mobile ad hoc network", In Proc. of the ACM-SE 42nd annual Southeast regional conference,2004: 70–75.

4. Xia C, Sun S, Rao F, Sun J, Wang J, Chen Z. SIS model of epidemic spreading on dynamical networks with community. Frontiers of Computer Science in China, 2009, 3(3): 361–365.
5. Xia CY, Meloni S, Moreno Y. Effects of environment knowledge on agglomeration and cooperation in spatial public goods games. Advances in Complex Systems, 15(supp01), 2012, 1250056.
6. Roy RR. Handbook of Mobile Ad Hoc Networks for Mobility Models, Springer Science+Business Media, LLC, 2011.
7. Sanchez M, Manzoni P. Anejos: A java based simulator for ad-hoc networks", Future Generation Computer Systems, 2001, 17(5):573–583.
8. Johnson D, Maltz D. Dynamic source routing in ad hoc wireless networks, In Imelinsky T. and Korth H.,editors, Mobile Computing,Kluwer Academic Publishers, 1996: 153–181.
9. Royer EM, Melliar-Smith PM, Moser LE. An analysis of the optimum node density for ad hoc mobile networks," IEEE International Conference on Communications, 2001;3: 857–861.
10. Kurkowski S, Camp T, Colagrosso M. MANET simulation studies: The incredible, ACM SIGMOBILE Mobile Computing and Communications Review, 2005,vol.9: 50–61.
11. Pazand B, McDonald C. A critique of mobility models for wireless network simulation, in: Proceedings of the 6th IEEE/ACIS International Conference on Computer and Information Science, 2007: 141–146.
12. Camp T, Bolengand J, Davies V. "A Survey of Mobility Models for Ad Hoc Network Research", Wireless Communications & Mobile Computing (WCMC), Special issue on Mobile Ad Hoc Networking: Research, Trends and Applications, Vol. 2, No. 5, pp. 483–502, 2002.
13. Resta G, Santi P. An analysis of the node spatial distribution of the random waypoint mobility model for ad hoc networks. In Proc. on the Second ACM International Workshop on Principles of Mobile Computing, 2000,pages 44–50.

14. Kim D, Hwang SK. "Swarm Group Mobility Model for Ad Hoc Wireless Networks", TR ECE-07-01, Nov. 2007, 1(1): 53–59.
15. Abdullah SJ, Alam S, Minhas AA. Location Prediction for Improvement of Communication Protocols in Wireless Communications: Considerations and Future Directions, Proceedings of The World Congress on Engineering and Computer Science,2011, 2: 19–21.
16. Gyarmati M, Schilcher U, Brandner G, Bettstetter C, Chung YW, Kim YH. "Impact of random mobility on the inhomogeneity of spatial distributions," in Proc. IEEE Global Telecommunications Conference (GLOBECOM),2008: 404–408.
17. Yoon J, Liuet M, Nobel B. Random waypoint considered harmful", Infocom, San Francisco,2003, Vol. 2: 1312–1321.
18. Macintosh A, Ghavami M, Siyau MF. "Investigating the Impact of Speed on the Performance of Position Based Routing Protocols in Mobile Ad hoc Networks," International Journal of Research in Wireless Systems (IJRWS), April. 2014,Vol. 3, Issue No. 1: 9–22.
19. Meghanathan N. Graph Theory Algorithms for Mobile Ad Hoc Networks, Informatica,2012; 36: 185–200.
20. Clarke EM, Wing JM. Formal Methods: State of the Art and Future Directions. ACM Computing Surveys, December 1996, 28(4):626–643.
21. Kraus V, Dehmer M, Schutte M. On sphere-regular graphs and the extremality of information-theoretic network measures, MATCH Commun. Math. Comput. Chem.70 2013: 885–900.
22. Cao S, Dehmer M, Shi Y. Extremality of degree-based graph entropies, Inform. Sci. 278(2014), 22–33.
23. Dehmer M, Grabner M. The discrimination power of molecular identification numbers revisited, MATCH Commun. Math. Comput. Chem.2013, 69: 785–794.
24. Li X, Li Y, Shi Y, Gutman I. Note on the HOMO-LUMO index of graphs, MATCH Commun. Math. Comput. Chem. 2013;70: 85–96.
25. Jensen K. Coloured Petri Nets. Basic Concepts, Analysis Methods and Practical Use. vol 1–3. Monographs in Theoretical Computer Science. Springer-Verlag, 1997.

26. Kristensen LM, Christensen S, Jensen K. The Practitioner's Guide to Coloured Petri Nets, International Journal on Software Tools for Technology Transfer, 1998, 2(2):98–132.
27. Desel J, Reisig W. Place/transition Petri nets. In Lectures on Petri Nets I: Basic Models, Springer, Berlin Heidelberg, 1998: 122–173.
28. Ullman JD. Elements of ML Programming. Prentice-Hall, 1998.
29. CPN Tools. Available: www.daimi.au.dk/CPN tools.
30. Kristensen LM, Jørgensen JB, Jensen K. Application of Coloured Petri Nets in System Development", Lectures on Concurrency and Petri Nets, 2003: 626–685.
31. Xiong C, Murata T, Tsai J. Modeling and Simulation of Routing Protocols for Mobile Ad Hoc Networks Using Colored Petri Nets, Conferences in Research and Practice in Information Technology, 2002; 12:145–153.
32. Khan NA, Ahmad F, Baig WA. Formal Model of Random Walk Mobility Model for WMN using Coloured Petri Nets, In Proc. IEEE 11th International Bhurban Conference on Applied Sciences & Technology (IBCAST), 2014: 436–444.
33. Agrahari S, Chinara S. Simulation of Random Waypoint Mobility Model Using Colored Petri Nets". In Proc. on the Second International Conference on Computer Science, Engineering and Applications (CCSEA-2012), 2012: 65–75.
34. Khan NA, Ahmad F, Khan SA. "Formal and Executable Specification of Random Waypoint Mobility Model Using Timed Coloured Petri Nets for WMN", In Abstract and Applied Analysis, vol. (2014), 2014, 9 pages,
35. Denizhan N, Khosrow S. "A Generalized Random Mobility Model for Wireless Ad Hoc Networks and Its Analysis: One-Dimensional Case," IEEE/ACM transactions on Networking, June,200715(3): 602–615.
36. Khan NA, Ahmad F, Khan SA. Coloured Petri Net Modeling and Analysis for Community based Wireless Mesh Networks.In Proceedings of the IEEE International Conference on Systems, Man and Cybernetics (SMC2014), San Diego, USA, 2014: 139–144.
37. Jensen K, Kristensen L. Coloured Petri Nets Modeling and Validation of Concurrent Systems,Springer, 2009.

38. The Network Simulator ns-2. Available: http://www.isi.edu/nsnam/ns/.
39. Holzmann GJ. An improved protocol reachability analysis technique," Software: Practice and Experience, 1988,18(2): 137–161.
40. Qadir J, Hasan O. Applying Formal Methods to Networking: Theory, Techniques and Applications, CoRR abs/1311.4303, 2013, 17(1), 256–291.
41. Holzmann GJ. Design and validation of protocols: a tutorial," Computer Networks and ISDN Systems, 1993, 25(9): 981–1017.
42. Holzmann GJ. Design and Validation of Computer Protocols. Prentice Hall, 1991.

CITATIONS

CHAPTER 2

Mangla K, Dill DL, Horowitz MA (2010) Timing Robustness in the Budding and Fission Yeast Cell Cycles. PLoS ONE 5(2): e8906. https://doi.org/10.1371/journal.pone.0008906.

CHAPTER 3

Pârvu O, Gilbert D (2016) A Novel Method to Verify Multilevel Computational Models of Biological Systems Using Multiscale Spatio-Temporal Meta Model Checking. PLoS ONE 11(5): e0154847. https://doi.org/10.1371/journal.pone.0154847.

CHAPTER 4

Xu H, Wang P (2016) Real-Time Reliability Verification for UAV Flight Control System Supporting Airworthiness Certification. PLoS ONE 11(12): e0167168. https://doi.org/10.1371/journal.pone.0167168.

CHAPTER 5

Bartocci E, Lió P (2016) Computational Modeling, Formal Analysis, and Tools for Systems Biology. PLoS Comput Biol 12(1): e1004591. https://doi.org/10.1371/journal.pcbi.1004591.Chapter 6

CHAPTER 6

Razzaq M, Ahmad J (2015) Petri Net and Probabilistic Model Checking Based Approach for the Modelling, Simulation and Verification of Internet Worm Propagation. PLoS ONE 10(12): e0145690. https://doi.org/10.1371/journal.pone.0145690.

CHAPTER 7

Minervini G, Panizzoni E, Giollo M, Masiero A, Ferrari C, Tosatto SCE (2014) Design and Analysis of a Petri Net Model of the Von Hippel-Lindau (VHL) Tumor Suppressor Interaction Network. PLoS ONE 9(6): e96986. https://doi.org/10.1371/journal.pone.0096986.

CHAPTER 8

Jacobsen A, Heijmans N, Verkaar F, Smit MJ, Heringa J, van Amerongen R, et al. (2016) Construction and Experimental Validation of a Petri Net Model of Wnt/β-Catenin Signaling. PLoS ONE 11(5): e0155743. https://doi.org/10.1371/journal.pone.0155743.

CHAPTER 9

Albergante L, Timmis J, Beattie L, Kaye PM (2013) A Petri Net Model of Granulomatous Inflammation: Implications for IL-10 Mediated Control of *Leishmania donovani* Infection. PLoS Comput Biol 9(11): e1003334. https://doi.org/10.1371/journal.pcbi.1003334.

CHAPTER 10

Khan NA, Ahmad F, Khan SA (2015) SHER: A Colored Petri Net Based Random Mobility Model for Wireless Communications. PLoS ONE 10(8): e0133634. https://doi.org/10.1371/journal.pone.0133634.

INDEX